Comparative Constitutional History

History of European Political and Constitutional Thought

VOLUME 10

The titles published in this series are listed at *brill.com/hepct*

Comparative Constitutional History

Volume Two: Uses of History in Constitutional Adjudication

Edited by

Francesco Biagi
Justin O. Frosini
Jason Mazzone

BRILL

LEIDEN | BOSTON

Cover illustration: Old Courthouse in Towson, MD, USA. Photo by Colin Lloyd on Unsplash.

Library of Congress Cataloging-in-Publication Data

Names: Biagi, Francesco, editor. | Frosini, Justin Orlando, editor. |
Mazzone, Jason, 1970- editor.
Title: Comparative constitutional history / edited by Francesco Biagi,
Justin O. Frosini, and Jason Mazzone.
Description: Leiden ; Boston: Brill, 2020- |Series: History of European
political and constitutional thought, 2589-5966; volume 3 |
Includes bibliographical references and index.
Identifiers: LCCN 2020022169 (print) | LCCN 2020022170 (ebook) |
ISBN 9789004393113 (hardback) | ISBN 9789004435315 (ebook)
Subjects: LCSH: Constitutional law. | Constitutional history. | Separation
of powers. | Constitutional courts. | Federal government.
Classification: LCC K3161. C6625 2020 (print) | LCC K3161 (ebook) |
DDC 342.02/9–dc23
LC record available at https://lccn.loc.gov/2020022169
LC ebook record available at https://lccn.loc.gov/2020022170

Typeface for the Latin, Greek, and Cyrillic scripts: "Brill". See and download: brill.com/brill-typeface.

ISSN 2589-5966
ISBN 978-90-04-43705-0 (hardback)
ISBN 978-90-04-52373-9 (e-book)

This book is printed on acid-free paper and produced in a sustainable manner.

Contents

PART 3
A Matter of Narratives

PART 4
New Democracies and Illiberal Regimes

Acknowledgments

In producing this volume, we have incurred many debts. We thank first of all our contributing authors. They first presented the papers that would ultimately become the chapters to this volume at the *Constitutional History: Comparative Perspectives* conference in Chicago in the spring of 2019. Since then, they have worked with great diligence and with good humour to finalize their chapters and to respond to our multiple requests for revisions. Many of our contributors experienced suffering and loss as a result of the Covid-19 pandemic. We are especially grateful for their perseverance in such challenging times.

We thank the University of Illinois Program in Constitutional Theory, History and Law for proving generous funding for our conference. Grant Huscroft, our conference keynote speaker, deserves special recognition for framing the conference discussions and for the feedback he gave to our individual authors. We thank Mary Parsons, Carrie May-Borich and Laura Lotzgesell for their help. We thank again Mark Somos for finding us a publishing home with Brill and for his unwavering enthusiasm for the project. We also thank Alessandra Giliberto at Brill for her hard work. A special thanks goes to Katherine Schauer for her excellent research assistance.

Most of all, we thank our families for their love, patience, and support.

FB-JOF-JM
Champaign-Bologna, April 2022

Tables

Notes on Contributors

Diego Werneck Arguelhes
(LL.M., J.S.D., Yale Law School) is Associate Professor of Law at the Insper Institute for Education and Research (São Paulo, Brazil).

Jean-Christophe Bédard-Rubin
is Assistant Professor of the Faculty of Law of the University of Toronto.

Francesco Biagi
is Senior Assistant Professor of Comparative Public Law at the University of Bologna, Department of Legal Studies, Research Fellow at the Center for Constitutional Studies and Democratic Development (Johns Hopkins University SAIS Europe – University of Bologna), and Legal Consultant at the Max Planck Foundation for International Peace and the Rule of Law (Heidelberg). His latest book is *European Constitutional Courts and Transitions to Democracy* (Cambridge University Press, 2020).

Justin Collings
is Associate Academic Vice President for Faculty Development and Professor of Law at Brigham Young University. His most recent book is *Scales of Memory: Constitutional Justice and Historical Evil* (Oxford University Press, 2021).

Jorge M. Farinacci-Fernós
is Associate Professor at the Interamerican University of Puerto Rico Law School. He has a B.A. and M.A. (both in History) from the University of Puerto Rico at Rio Piedras, a J.D. from the UPR School of Law, an LL.M. from Harvard Law School, and an S.J.D. from Georgetown University Law Center. His books include *Hermenéutica Puertorriqueña* (InterJuris, 2019) and *La Carta de Derechos* (Editorial Universidad Interamericana, 2021).

Justin O. Frosini
is Associate Professor at Bocconi University, Milan and Adjunct Professor at the Johns Hopkins University SAIS Europe, Bologna and Director of the Center for Constitutional Studies and Democratic Development in Bologna (Italy). He has published extensively in the field of comparative public law and is the author of a groundbreaking book on *Constitutional Preambles. At a Crossroads Between Politics and Law* (Maggioli Editore, 2012). His latest monograph, in Italian, is devoted to Brexit: *From Sovereignty of Parliament to Sovereignty of*

the People. The Constitutional Revolution Ignited by Brexit (*Dalla Sovranità del Parlamento alla Sovranità del Popolo. La rivoluzione costituzionale della Brexit*) (Wolters Kluwer – Cedam, 2020).

Ángel Aday Jiménez Alemán
is García Pelayo Research Fellow at the Center for Political and Constitutional Studies and Senior Lecturer of Constitutional law at the University of Vigo (on leave). He is the Co-secretary of Spain's ICON-S Chapter and Editor of IberIconnect. He has published articles and book chapters in distinguished journals and publishers, such as *Revista Española de Derecho Constitucional*, *Teoría y Realidad Constitucional* or the *Max Planck Encyclopedia of Comparative Constitutional Law*, among others.

Jason Mazzone
is the Albert E. Jenner, Jr. Professor of Law at the University of Illinois Urbana-Champaign and Director of the Illinois Program in Constitutional Theory, History and Law.

Keigo Obayashi
is Professor of Law at the Keio University in Japan where he teaches constitutional law. He is editor of *The Constitution Under the COVID-19 Crisis* (Kobundo, 2021).

Ana Beatriz Robalinho
is a J.S.D. candidate at Yale Law School.

Mark D. Rosen
is University Distinguished Professor of Law at the Chicago-Kent College of Law.

Zoltán Szente
is a Research Professor at the Institute for Legal Studies, Centre for Social Sciences, and a Professor of Law at the Department of Constitutional Law and Comparative Public Law of the National University of Public Service, Budapest. His latest books are *Constitutional Law in Hungary* (Kluwer, 2021) and *Populist Challenges to Constitutional Interpretation in Europe and Beyond* (co-edited with Fruzsina Gárdos-Orosz, Routledge, 2021).

Cem Tecimer
is a doctoral candidate in law (S.J.D.) at Harvard Law School, where his research focuses on American and comparative constitutional law. He obtained his Master of Laws (LL.M.) from Harvard Law School as a Fulbright scholar. Cem's publications either appeared or are forthcoming in various publications, including the *Yale Law Journal* and the *International Journal of Constitutional Law*. He is a regular blogger at *Verfassungsblog*, where he comments on the recent developments in Turkish constitutional law and politics. Cem is a dual-qualified lawyer, admitted to practice law in New York and Turkey.

Shih-An Wang
is a J.S.D. candidate at the University of Chicago Law School.

Introduction

Francesco Biagi, Justin O. Frosini and Jason Mazzone

Constitutions are a product of history but what is the role of history in interpreting and applying a constitution's provisions? This volume addresses that question from a comparative perspective. It brings together experts from different countries to examine, assess, and reflect upon uses of history by courts in various countries in determining constitutional meaning.

The volume itself has a history. Beginning in 2014, researchers at the University of Illinois College of Law, the University of Bologna Department of Legal Studies, and the Center for Constitutional Studies and Democratic Development (CCSDD) have sought to energize the comparative study and analysis of constitutional history by organizing a regular series of academic conferences on the topic. These conferences, which bring together scholars from around the globe, rotate between Bologna and Chicago. Starting with the third conference—held in Bologna on November 13 and 14, 2017—the essays presented at these meetings have been published in the Brill series *History of European Political and Constitutional Thought*. The first volume was published in 2020, with the title *Comparative Constitutional History. Volume One: Principles, Developments, Challenges*.[1] The present (second) volume of the series contains a set of essays that were first prepared for and presented at the fourth conference on 'Constitutional History: Comparative Perspectives,' held in Chicago on April 29 and 30, 2019. The theme of that conference was 'Uses of History in Constitutional Adjudication.'

In a basic sense, constitutional adjudication always involves historical analysis. After all, in almost every case, courts are considering the compatibility with the constitution of a law enacted in the past or assessing the constitutionality of governmental action that has occurred or been threatened. The analysis necessarily requires attention to historical events, even if only in understanding the scope and meaning of an enacted law, making sense of what a government agent or entity did, sorting out factual disputes, discerning the motivations for governmental conduct, or deciding the extent of injury a party has suffered. In these respects, history matters to constitutional adjudication and courts routinely play the role of historian.

1 The essays presented at the second Illinois-Bologna conference, held in Chicago on April 12 and 13, 2016, were published in the *University of Illinois Law Review*, vol. 2017, no. 2.

 | DOI:10.1163/9789004523739_002

As the chapters in the volume demonstrate, however, there is considerable debate around uses by courts in constitutional cases of other sorts of history. Should, for example, the words of a constitution be understood to mean today what they meant at the time the constitution was adopted? Should constitutional meaning be informed by what the drafters of the constitution stated as their understanding of the document or the way in which they expected it to operate? Are historical public debates over the adoption of a constitution relevant to reading its provisions today? How does a country's history before the adoption of the constitution bear on constitutional meaning? If a constitution represents a break from a prior repressive or otherwise unjust regime should courts construe the constitution's provisions in light of that background? Are historical origins more—or less—relevant in a country where there has been a revolution or other dramatic development than in nations that have adopted a new constitution but without a fundamental shift in the political system? Are former constitutions relevant to interpreting a new constitution—by, for example, demonstrating points of continuity or change—or should past constitutions just be set aside? To what extent does history reduce indeterminacy in constitutional interpretation?

In the United States, the use of history as an interpretative resource in construing and applying the provisions of the U.S. Constitution is a topic that has received enormous attention from scholars. Today, much of that attention centers around theories of constitutional originalism. Comparative studies of uses of history in constitutional adjudication are, by contrast, relatively rare. While some scholars—notably Renáta Uitz,[2] Daphne Barak-Erez,[3] Ozan O. Varol,[4] and Jamal Greene and Yvonne Tew[5]—have explored how different national courts engage with historical arguments, there remains considerable work to be done in the area. This volume seeks to help fill the scholarly gap.

As the chapters in this volume vividly illustrate, courts in different jurisdictions have taken quite different approaches to uses of history in constitutional adjudication. The volume's authors themselves also have different perspectives as to when history should matter and when courts should (and should

2 Renáta Uitz, *Constitutions, Courts And History. Historical Narratives in Constitutional Adjudication* (Central European University Press 2006).

3 Daphne Barak-Erez, "History and Memory in Constitutional Adjudication", 45 *Federal Law Review* 1 (2017), pp. 1 ff.

4 Ozan O. Varol, "The Origins and Limits of Originalism: A Comparative Study", 44 *Vanderbilt Journal of Transnational Law* (2011), pp. 1239 ff.

5 Jamal Greene & Yvonne Tew, "Comparative Approaches to Constitutional History" in Erin F. Delaney & Rosalind Dixon (eds.), *Comparative Judicial Review* (Edward Elgar 2018), pp. 379 ff.

not) make use of history in constitutional cases. The enormous attention in the United States to the role of history in constitutional interpretation is explained in good part by the fact that the U.S. Supreme Court is itself a 'champion' in using history, such that one 'can identify Supreme Court decisions that rely heavily on historical argument throughout the Court's history.'[6] Many other courts in the world have adopted quite different approaches. The Supreme Court of Canada, for example, far from relying on originalism, has embraced the well-known notion of the constitution as a 'living tree,'[7] the idea that the constitution has to be interpreted in a progressive manner so as to adapt to the changing times. European courts have adopted mixed approaches, under which constitutional history is typically just one consideration and often not the most important. An analysis of the case law of the Italian Constitutional Court shows that 'original intent can be important, but historical analysis alone has never been used as a conclusive argument to resolve a constitutional issue.'[8] In Germany, the Federal Constitutional Court has made reference, in some very important judgments, to the country's authoritarian past.[9] In general terms, however, in the case law of the Court, 'Neither original history nor the ideas and intentions of the framers are of decisive importance in interpreting particular provisions of the Basic Law.'[10] At the same time, some European courts, such as the Constitutional Court of Spain,[11] rely on history much more frequently.

As several chapters of this volume demonstrate, historical arguments are often deployed by courts in transitional contexts, especially when judges seek to mark a clean break with the previous autocratic regime. But even this is not inevitable. In Italy, for example, the key judgments dealing with the country's authoritarian past have been based on purely *legal* reasoning, technical considerations with little scope for historical or political considerations. The example *par excellence* is the judgment of the Italian Court of Cassation of February 7, 1948, relating to transitional justice. In that case, in upholding prosecution of Fascist crimes notwithstanding the Article 25 ban on retroactivity, the Court introduced for the first time a distinction between 'programmatic

6 Greene & Tew, *supra* note 5, at 384.

7 See Jean-Christophe Bédard-Rubin's chapter in this volume.

8 Vittoria Barsotti et al., *Italian Constitutional Justice in Global Context* (Oxford University Press 2016), p. 67.

9 See Justin Collings's chapter in this volume.

10 Donald P. Kommers & Russell A. Miller, *The Constitutional Jurisprudence of the Federal Republic of Germany* (Duke University Press 2012), p. 365.

11 See Ángel Aday Jiménez Alemán's chapter in this volume.

constitutional provisions' (i.e. provisions that exist only as 'programs' for the legislator, and thus could not be immediately enforced) and 'preceptive constitutional provisions' (i.e. provisions that could be immediately enforced) and deemed Article 25 to be programmatic. Historical references to the previous Fascist regime were entirely lacking.[12]

The case of Hungary shows that courts might rely on history not only during transitions to democracy but also during periods characterized by democratic backsliding. The 2011 Hungarian Fundamental Law states that its provisions must be interpreted in light of the preamble and the achievements of the unwritten 'historical constitution.' So far, the Constitutional Court has relied on this vague concept only incidentally. Full implementation of the mandated historical method poses some serious risks because key components of the historical constitution—such as the rejection of the idea of popular sovereignty, state sponsored religion, and the territorial integrity of the historical Kingdom of Hungary—stand in stark contrast with modern principles of constitutionalism.[13]

History can be an important source of interpretation not only for domestic courts, but also for *supranational* courts. The European Court of Human Rights, for example, has made extensive use of historical arguments, particularly in cases involving electoral legislation, transitional justice, and religious freedom. In these cases, 'far from representing a mere cultural framework to be used to 'embellish' the judgment or make it more persuasive, the historical argument often ends up determining the ... decision.'[14] This Court's reliance on history is not entirely surprising given that in applying the provisions of the European Convention on Human Rights, the Court confronts complex—and often contested—national traditions.[15]

In addition to issues of when and how history is relevant to constitutional adjudication, there are also basic questions about the reliability of historical evidence. Historical evidence is often mixed: there can be multiple accounts of what happened and why. Historical records might be lost, incomplete, or inaccurate. Incidents of deep significance might have occurred in secret. Those who took the time to leave behind evidence might have exaggerated their own roles or a particular perspective. Courts do not necessarily have the resources

---

12 See Francesco Biagi, *European Constitutional Courts and Transitions to Democracy* (Cambridge University Press 2020) p. 176.

13 See Zoltán Szente's chapter in this volume.

14 Andrea Buratti, "L'uso della storia nella giurisprudenza della Corte Europea dei Diritti dell'Uomo", 2 *Rivista dell'Associazione italiana dei costituzionalisti* (2012), p. 13.

15 Buratti, *supra* note 14, at 18.

or time to generate historical accuracy and likely cannot depend upon lawyers to do so when they represent one side in a dispute. Courts that rely on history run the risk that they are deploying it in service of outcomes they reached on other grounds. Finally, constitutional adjudication, in which one side wins and the other loses, might often demand a degree of definitiveness that history does not supply.

Given that this volume is part of a larger project in comparative constitutional history, it bears noting that debates about uses of historical materials in constitutional interpretation track, in some respects, debates about uses of foreign and comparative law in determining the meaning of a domestic constitution. In a famous conversation with Justice Breyer, Justice Scalia criticized uses of foreign sources as 'cherry-picking.'[16] A similar concern might be raised with respect to uses of historical evidence: why is the judge placing special emphasis on certain past events and less emphasis on others? So, too, looking abroad carries a risk of undue idealization: courts, especially those operating in young democracies, do not always view foreign precedents with a sufficiently critical eye. The past might likewise be romanticized.

1 The Plan of the Book

Three chapters (*Part 1—Framing the Problem*) set the stage with close consideration of the roles and limits of history in constitutional adjudication. Drawing particularly on the practices of courts in the United States, Mark Rosen observes that when judges deploy history to answer constitutional questions, they tend to do so in a way that denies them agency. That is, historical analysis is presented as generating answers determined by historical fact, in a way that minimizes the input of the judge. Rosen argues, however, that history can serve to license rather than to limit judicial agency. He presents an account of constitutionalism as a social practice involving the exercise of shared agency by multiple participants themselves constrained by interpretive norms. History, then, limits agency with respect to a constitution's definitive settlements. But history licenses agency with respect to a constitution's partial settlements and open-ended commitments, even as the license is limited and does not involve judges merely legislating from the bench.

16 "A Conversation Between U.S. Supreme Court Justices", 3 *International Journal of Constitutional Law* 4 (2005), p. 521.

Jorge Farinacci-Fernós offers a general model for when history should be used in constitutional adjudication. His model is based on the insight that history itself can determine the appropriate uses of history in deciding constitutional questions. On this account, the history of the creation of a constitution should guide the choice of interpretive method, including as to the relevance and power of historical sources. Farinacci-Fernós contends that the more democratic, public, participatory, popular and socially transcendental the process of creation, the stronger the justification for history as an authoritative source of constitutional meaning. Accordingly, he explains, constitutions that were the result of undemocratic, secret, exclusionary, elite or socially inconsequential processes of creation present a weak case for using history, and particularly adoption history, in interpreting constitutional provisions and adjudicating constitutional disputes. Farinacci-Fernós's approach means that the legitimacy of using history in constitutional adjudication cannot be assessed in the abstract but instead requires close attention to a nation's individual past.

Justin Collings explores the significance to constitutional adjudication of a particular kind of history: memory of a nation's own evil past. Collings is interested in how courts wrap themselves in what he calls the mantle of memory in order to secure their own authority. He draws on the examples of the Constitutional Court of South Africa and the German Federal Constitutional Court to show that past evils provide a reference point for constitutional interpretation but also, and perhaps more significantly, as a basis for judicial power. Collings explores how both of these courts have presented themselves as playing important roles in responding to and overcoming historical evils. But, Collings shows, the two courts invoke memory in different ways. While the South African Court has regularly drawn linkages to colonialism and apartheid, the German Court has been far more sparing in its references to Nazism. In addition, in both systems, memory has at times meant judicial deference rather than a heightened role for courts. Nonetheless, memory as mantle has allowed both courts to secure a role as democratic guardian. Collings concludes his chapter with some intriguing suggestions about the possible antidemocratic purposes memory as mantle might play in other contexts.

The next two chapters (*Part 2—Historical Precedents and Inter-Constitutional Interpretation*) offer a close analysis of courts engaging with legally authoritative sources from the past. Jean-Christophe Bédard-Rubin focuses on precedent as a vehicle for exploring some striking differences in the influence of history in constitutional adjudication in the United States and in Canada. Bédard-Rubin shows that while adherence to precedent is an important aspect of constitutional adjudication in the United States, precedent has much less significance to courts in Canada. As he explains, for the US Supreme Court to overrule a past decision under the Constitution requires special justification and generates significant public attention. On the other hand, Bédard-Rubin demonstrates, the Supreme Court of Canada revisits its own rulings under the Charter with little fanfare. Bédard-Rubin incisively explains why the role of precedent is so different in these two neighboring countries. Among other factors, he points to a constitutional culture in the United States in which there is a dominant historical narrative about the origins and trajectory of the constitutional system and the rights it protects. That culture, Bédard-Rubin contends, supports a strong commitment to precedent in American jurisprudence—and has no counterpoint in Canada.

Cem Tecimer explores the phenomenon of inter-constitutional interpretation: uses of a nation's own past constitution (or constitutions) in interpreting its existing constitution. Tecimer shows that inter-constitutional interpretation must be understood as a distinct, and distinctively historical, mode of constitutional analysis that deserves greater attention than it has so far received. He explores the ways in which inter-constitutional interpretation operates and its significance with a case study of the US Supreme Court's invocations of the 1781 Articles of Confederation—the charter that preceded (and was replaced by) the 1789 US Constitution. Tecimer collects and analyzes the cases in which the Supreme Court invokes the Articles of Confederation, including for discerning the textual meaning of constitutional provisions, to show continuity between the Constitution and the Articles, and to identify ways in which the Constitution departed from the system of government the Articles created. Tecimer's chapter provides an unexpected lesson about history: abrogated constitutions often exercise continued influence in constitutional adjudication, in a way that makes escaping the past difficult.

Three chapters (*Part 3—A Matter of Narratives*) explore uses of historical materials and narratives by courts in individual countries. Ángel Aday Jiménez Alemán takes up the case of Spain. His detailed analysis demonstrates that the Spanish Constitutional Court regularly makes use of history to explain its interpretations and applications of the Constitution. In particular, the Court often deploys phylogenetic history, the history of the origin and evolution of Spanish legal institutions, as a basis for its understanding of provisions of the current constitution. Alemán also finds some tensions in the Court's reliance on history, in particular in the Court's struggle to appear entirely neutral when presenting and analyzing historical events in a country with a long, complex, and contested past.

In a chapter assessing the Brazilian Supreme Court's engagement with history in its constitutional ruling, Ana Beatriz Robalinho concludes that the Court has come up short. Robalinho finds that the Court has undermined the development in Brazil of a national constitutional identity grounded in a coherent understanding of the nation's constitutional origins. In particular, Robalinho views the Court's own embrace of weak and shifting historical arguments as further fuelling a national divide between those who understand the 1988 Brazilian Constitution as involving a revolutionary break with Brazil's colonial, and later dictatorial, past, and those who instead view the constitution as a negotiated transaction among political elites preserving key aspects of the prior legal order. Robalinho urges the Court, in its consideration of history in constitutional cases, to work to overcome the division in a way that can secure a reliable account of Brazil's constitutional origins and developments.

Keigo Obayashi examines the role of history in the decisions of the Japanese Supreme Court. He demonstrates that attention to constitutional history is not necessarily limited to the constitution's origins but can include also consideration of subsequent developments. Obayashi shows that Japan's Supreme Court invokes history as an element of its 'dynamic' approach to interpreting that country's constitution. The Court, Obayashi explains, assesses the meaning and constitutionality of laws in light of developments over time in the social and political life of the country. That approach to history, one that resembles certain theories of living constitutionalism, invites criticism of the Court as engaging in judicial activism. Obayashi concludes, however, that the Court's approach instead ensures consistency between laws and the views of the public and reflects also a healthy balance in a nation that has experienced long periods of control by a single political party.

The final two chapters (*Part 4—New Democracies and Illiberal Regimes*) in the volume concern the role of history in constitutional adjudication in new democracies and illiberal political regimes. Zoltán Szente takes up the question of *which* history should count. Szente's focus is Hungary, a country that in recent years has experienced democratic backsliding. Szente explores the efforts in Hungary to tie the nation's illiberal 2011 Constitution (known as the Fundamental Law) to a thousand-year-old unwritten constitution in place in Hungary before World War II. These efforts culminated in a preamble to the 2011 Constitution asserting continuity with the earlier constitutional tradition and a provision requiring that the 2011 Constitution be interpreted in accordance with the achievements of the historical unwritten constitution. To some extent, this recalls the notion of inter-constitutional interpretation discussed above in Cem Tecimer's chapter. Szente explores some theoretical and practical problems this resurrection of the ancient constitution has generated and he examines how the Constitutional Court, for many years a fierce defender of liberal values, has sought to navigate the difficulties.

Shih-An Wang examines how the Taiwan Constitutional Court has engaged with Taiwan's authoritarian past. The Court began in 1948 under the Constitution of the Republic of China, but with Taiwan under the authoritarian rule of the Kuomintang until 1991 the Court's role in reviewing governmental action remained limited for a long period. In the post-authoritarian period, however, the Court has been far more active and in a series of well-known decisions has confronted the nation's authoritarian past. Wang shows that until very recently, the Court depicted the modern constitutional regime as representing a break from the past. That perspective, Wang reports, prevented a true recognition of and grappling with historical injustice. Beginning in 2020, however, the Court has confronted past injustices more squarely, and as requiring redress. Wang concludes that the Taiwan example shows how courts in new democracies, attuned to the past but with an eye on the future, can play a valuable role in guiding a successful transition to constitutional reform.

In his conclusion to the volume, Diego Werneck Arguelhes assesses the contributions the volume's authors have made. He also draws out and builds on some overall themes, brings them to bear on the fascinating case of the Brazilian Supreme Court, and suggests some fruitful paths for further study. That is a fitting end to a volume in which all of the authors provide the tools and inspiration for future efforts that build on the work they have now done.

PART 1

Framing the Problem

CHAPTER 1

History

Limit or License in Constitutional Adjudication?

Mark D. Rosen

When American courts invoke history to address constitutional questions, their answers typically seem determined by historical facts rather than the judge's will or choice.[*,1] In other words, history usually is deployed in a way that seems to deny judges agency in answering constitutional questions.[2] Such agency-restricting use of history is perhaps most evident in originalist analysis, which understands constitutional meaning to have been fixed at ratification.[3] Because history alone is thought to determine ratification-era meaning, history alone may appear to answer the constitutional question.[4] Consider as well

* I would like to thank Tyler Dallas, Steve Heyman, Jason Mazzone, Ioan-Radu Motoarca, Chris Schmidt, and participants at the conference 'Constitutional History: Comparative Perspectives' for enormously helpful comments.

1 See generally Richard H. Fallon, Jr., 'The Many and Varied Roles of History in Constitutional Adjudication' (2015) 90 Notre Dame L. Rev. 1753, 1763–84. Fallon astutely observes that historical facts sometimes indicate that history cannot answer the constitutional question, see ibid 1792, 1796, though his article primarily explores the numerous ways judges rely on history to answer constitutional questions.

2 I do not use 'agency' in the legal doctrinal sense concerning agents and principals, but in the philosophical sense. As to that, agency for human beings refers to making choices, and acting pursuant to those choices in circumstances where such acts can make an anticipatable difference in the world. See generally Christine M. Korsgaard, *Self-Constitution: Agency, Identity, and Integrity* (Oxford University Press 2019) 84–9. From this it follows that exercises of agency entail taking responsibility for one's choices and actions, as opposed to seeing oneself as a passive actor. Human agency does not presuppose that the agent is the sole cause of an outcome, nor that her acts will be successful. But human agency does presuppose autonomy and potential efficacy. See ibid. This is not to suggest that non-human animals, which on most accounts lack humans' capacities for intention and choice, do not exercise agency. They do. But the nature of each species' agency differs on account of each's distinctive capacities. See ibid.

3 Different schools of originalism identify differing relevant populations whose understandings matter. The three main contenders are the drafters, ratifiers, and the public.

4 See, e.g., *Obergefell v. Hodges*, 135 S Ct 2584 (2015) (Scalia, J., dissenting) ('When the Fourteenth Amendment was ratified in 1868, every State limited marriage to one man and one woman, and no one doubted the constitutionality of doing so. That resolves these cases.'). For originalists who distinguish between meaning and application, agency persists when determining the contemporary application of the (historically fixed) meaning,

 DOI:10.1163/9789004523739_003

Chief Justice Roberts' assertion that '[t]he purpose of insisting that implied fundamental rights have roots in the history and tradition of our people is to ensure that when unelected judges strike down democratically enacted laws, they do so based on something more than their own beliefs.'[5] The Chief Justice's effort to restrict judicial agency recalls his confirmation hearing testimony that likened judges to umpires.[6]

History functions in a similar agency-limiting modality on Justice Frankfurter's more evolutionary jurisprudence. Frankfurter thought it 'an inadmissibly narrow conception of American constitutional law to … disregard the gloss which life has written upon constitutional text.'[7] But because the political branches' past practices alone determine the gloss – Frankfurter demanded 'a systematic, unbroken, executive practice, long pursued to the knowledge of the Congress and never before questioned'[8] – there does not appear to be room for judicial agency when Frankfurterian constitutional law ventures beyond constitutional text.

Might history, though, sometimes operate as a *license for,* rather than a *limit to,* the exercise of judicial agency? This chapter argues in the affirmative, and explores the implications of that claim.

1 Six Origin-Accounts

Imagine that historical research revealed any or all of the following:

1. that a constitution's drafters created novel institutions without having fully worked out their properties, roles, and relations to other institutions;[9] or

though not all originalists acknowledge this. See, e.g., Mark D. Greenberg & Harry Litman, 'The Meaning of Original Meaning' (1998) 86 Geo. L.J. 569; Christopher R. Green, 'Originalism and the Sense-Reference Distinction' (2006) 50 St. Louis U. L.J. 555. Agency also persists for originalists who accept the distinction between interpretation and construction. See, e.g., Lawrence B. Solum, 'Originalism and Constitutional Construction' (2013) 82 Fordham L. Rev. 453, 468.

5 *Obergefell* (n 4) 2623.

6 See Neil S. Siegel, 'Umpires at Bat: On Integration and Legitimation' (2007) 24 Const. Comment. 701.

7 *Youngstown Sheet & Tube Co. v. Sawyer*, 343 US 579 (1952) (Frankfurter, J., concurring); see generally Curtis A. Bradley & Trevor W. Morrison, 'Historical Gloss and the Separation of Powers' (2012) 126 Harv. L. Rev. 411.

8 Ibid.

9 John Jay described the United States' new national government as an 'experiment,' and hoped that the 'good [s]ense of the [p]eople will be enabled by [e]xperience to discover and correct its imperfections.' William R. Casto, 'The Early Supreme Court Justices' Most

2. that drafters adopted open-ended constitutional language so that conventioneers and ratifiers could come to agreement;[10] or
3. that the absence of constitutional language reflected the drafters' decision to facilitate ratification by leaving unspecified those matters they thought would be sharply divisive;[11] or
4. that a constitution incorporated compromises among divergent positions that were deeply in tension, if not conceptually inconsistent, with one another;[12] or

Significant Opinion' (2003) 29 Ohio N.U. L. Rev. 173, 186 & n 113 (quoting John Jay's Charge to the Grand Jury of the Circuit Court for the District of New York of April 12, 1790). There is much to support Jay's descriptive claim. See generally Michael J. Klarman, *The Framers' Coup: The Making of the Constitution* (Oxford University Press 2016). For example, never before the U.S. Constitution had there been a republican government headed by a president, and delegates to the constitutional convention wanted to create a novel non-monarchical executive that had far more powers than had been enjoyed by the states' chief executives. See ibid 214; see also ibid 230–31 (describing creation of the electoral college). During the month-long post-ratification debate in Congress as to whether the removal of executive officers was inherent in the president's constitutional powers – a topic unaddressed by constitutional text – both Madison and Hamilton changed their minds. See Saikrishna B. Prakash, 'New Light on the Decision of 1789' (2006) 91 Cornell L. Rev. 1021, 1034, 1038. Whereas the third Article of the U.S. Constitution created an independent federal judiciary, Montesquieu had thought the judiciary was an aspect of executive power. See Montesquieu, *Spirit of the Laws, Book XI* (1748). Finally, Madison and Hamilton had divergent views concerning a basic question of constitutional architecture: whether the powers of the several institutions created by the Constitution might overlap. See Mark D. Rosen, 'From Exclusivity to Concurrence' (2010) 94 Minn. L. Rev. 1051, 1073–76 (contrasting Hamilton's view that multiple institutions might have concurrent powers with Madison's generally exclusivist understanding).

10 See, e.g., Klarman (n 9) 322 & footnote* (quoting Madison's observation that the Constitution's explicit avowal of *McCulloch v. Maryland*'s 'pliant' understanding of the Sweeping Clause would 'have prevented its ratification').

11 See Klarman (n 9) 611 (discussing the constitutional convention's decision to not address whether congress would have the power to incorporate a bank); David S. Schwartz, 'Coin, Currency and Constitution: Reconsidering the National Bank Precedent' (2020) 117 Mich. L. Rev. 1005 (quoting Madison's explanation to the House Ways and Means Committee for his support of a national bank: the '1814–1816 currency crisis' that led Madison to ultimately support the bank 'was not foreseen' at the time of the Constitution's drafting and even 'if it had been apprehended, it is questionable whether the Constitution of the United States, which had so many obstacles to encounter, would have ventured to guard against it by an additional provision').

12 The draft constitution was susceptible to being characterized as both pro- and anti-slavery, and indeed was characterized as both (in different states) during the state ratifying conventions. See Klarman (n 9) 6, 153, 291–96, 541; Avishai Margalit, *On Compromise and Rotten Compromises* (Princeton University Press 2013). And compromise was not confined to the issue of slavery, of course. See Max Farrand, *The Framing of the Constitution of*

5. that constitutional language, or the absence thereof, was attributable to the drafters' having overlooked something,[13] whether due to the press of time or to human fallibility;[14] or
6. that drafters thought imprecise constitutional language would be made determinate (or, in Madison's language, "liquidated") by post-ratification practice.[15]

Notice that the six *origin-accounts* described above are not mutually exclusive; a constitutional provision's origins might be accurately described by more than one account. Nor are the six accounts exhaustive; the origins of some constitutional provisions may be otherwise describable. For example, some provisions might memorialize definitive settlements.

But I *do* claim that each of the six origin-accounts is conceptually plausible. There is nothing internally inconsistent, self-undermining, or oxymoronic about any of them.[16] Indeed, as the footnotes attached to each account show, there is strong historical evidence that every one of the origin-accounts has

the United States (Yale University Press 1913) 201 (describing the Constitution as a 'bundle of compromises').

13 For example, the United States Constitution specifies how legislation and treaties are created, and how officers of the United States are to be appointed, but is silent as to how each is undone: the Constitution doesn't specify how statutes are repealed, treaties abrogated, or (apart from impeachment) how executive officers are removed. Representative Laurance not unreasonably referred to the Constitution's silence regarding the removal of executive officers as 'a deficiency in the Constitution.' See Prakash (n 9) 1038 & n. 123. James Wilson, among the most influential delegates at the constitutional convention and a future Supreme Court Justice, recalled that the idea of a bill of rights 'never entered the mind of many' of the delegates, and that the subject was not raised until just a few days before the convention's end. See Klarman (n 9) 549. Perhaps most significantly, the Framers failed to foresee the rise of political parties, which had monumental effects on both the feasibility of Article V's amendment process and the relations among the different branches of the federal government. See Klarman (n 9) 316–17, 629; Daryl J. Levinson and Richard H. Pildes, 'Separation of Parties, Not Powers' (2006) 119 Harv. L. Rev. 2311.

14 The conventioneers created numerous novel institutions and institutional arrangements in a short period of time (about the length of a single semester), with virtually no advance planning (since all but four conventioneers had come to amend the Articles of Confederation, not to create a new constitution) and without having had models from other countries upon which they could draw (because there were none). See Klarman (n 9) 6, 426, 605–06; Robert Dahl, *How Democratic Is the Constitution?* (Yale University Press 2002) 8–9.

15 See William Baude, 'Constitutional Liquidation' (2019) 71 Stan. L. Rev. 1; Jack N. Rakove, Original Meanings: Politics and Ideas in the Making of the Constitution (Vintage 1997); Ilan Wurman, A Debt Against the Living: An Introduction to Originalism (Cambridge University Press 2017) 94–96 (discussing Madison's concept of liquidation).

16 For a more theorized defense of this position, see text accompanying notes 98–116.

application to some of the constituent parts of what is ordinarily understood to be American constitutional law.

To put the point more abstractly, each of the six origin-accounts describes parts of constitutional law because written constitutions memorialize three different types of things: definitive settlements, partial settlements, and open-ended commitments.[17] The six origin-accounts describe circumstances that populate the latter two categories of partial settlements and open-ended commitments.[18]

Each of the six origin-accounts undermines the logic of an agency-limiting use of history to answer constitutional questions that fall under any of the accounts. Historical facts alone cannot answer constitutional questions when history itself – as exemplified by the six origin accounts – admits of no answer.

The rest of this chapter explores what is to be done when a political community confronts questions that its constitution does not answer. If the political community elects to generate an answer that is to belong to the constitutional domain (Part 2), then agency necessarily will have to be exercised in so doing (Parts 3–4). This is not tantamount to licensing judges to 'legislate from the bench' (Part 5) because such questions should be answered through exercises of *shared agency* by multiple institutions whose participants are disciplined by shared agency's constitutive norms (Parts 6–8). The chapter then identifies and responds to a series of objections that might be posed to its 'shared agency' account of constitutionalism (Parts 9–12).

2 The Status of Answers to Questions Belonging to the Six Origin-Accounts

One possible response to the six origin-accounts would be to conclude that issues describable by any of them do not belong to the domain of constitutional law. They instead belong to the non-constitutional domain[19] for the very reason that such issues were not decided, or were left unspecified, by the constitution's drafters and ratifiers.

But relegating such matters to the non-constitutional domain may not always be possible. This is because on some accounts of what a constitution is,

17 See text accompanying notes 33–35.

18 There may be additional origin-accounts that explain why particular constitutional questions are either partial settlements or open-ended commitments.

19 By non-constitutional I simply mean not having the status of constitutional law. Non-constitutional does not mean the same thing as unconstitutional.

certain subjects belong to the constitutional domain by virtue of the subject's nature.[20] On these accounts, a matter can have the status of constitutional law even if it has not been memorialized in a formally adopted constitution, and even if the political community does not regard it as being of constitutional stature.

In any event, American constitutional practice typically does not relegate questions belonging to the six origin-accounts to the non-constitutional domain. For example, although the U.S. Constitution is silent as to how a treaty is abrogated, the abrogation mechanism is widely assumed to be of constitutional dimension.[21] The same is true, *mutatis mutandis*, of the mechanisms for repealing statutes and removing executive officers. As to the latter, although a minority of Representatives during the so-called Decision of 1789 thought that the removal of officers belonged to the non-constitutional domain, this view has never prevailed.[22] So even though many substantive issues regarding removal remain unresolved and disputed today, it is common ground that questions concerning the scope of the President's removal authority – for instance to what extent it may be restricted, and whether it may be jointly exercised with Congress[23] – have answers that belong to the domain of constitutional law.[24]

3 The License Thesis

So now we arrive at one of this chapter's primary claims. If constitutional answers are necessary, or nonetheless are to be provided, to questions that historical evidence places in any of the six origin-accounts, that historical evidence should be recognized as licensing, rather than limiting, the agency of those who answer the question. Call this the *License Thesis*.

---

20 See, e.g., John Gardner, 'Can There be a Written Constitution?' in Leslie Green and Brian Leiter (eds), *Oxford Studies in Philosophy of Law: Volume 1* (Oxford University Press 2011); Ernest A. Young, 'The Constitution Outside the Constitution' (2007) 117 Yale L. J. 407.

21 See *Goldwater v. Carter*, 444 US 996 (1979).

22 See Prakash (n 9) 1039–40 (noting that the 'congressional-delegation theory' of presidential removal power, which was supported by sixteen members of the House of Representatives, was ultimately rejected).

23 The Supreme Court has definitively resolved this latter question. See *Bowsher v. Synar*, 478 US 714 (1986). Though the Justices divided on the substantive answer, all agreed that the answer had the status of constitutional law.

24 See *Myers v. United States*, 272 US 52, 163–64 (1926).

The License Thesis is constituted by two interlocking claims. First, *contemporary agency* must be exercised when it is time to provide constitutional answers to questions that fall under any of the six origin-accounts. To be clear, 'contemporary' does not necessarily mean 'today,' for the License Thesis leaves room for constitutional questions to be answered and settled after drafting and ratification.[25] 'Contemporary' simply indicates that agency must be exercised *whenever it is* that a constitutional question describable by any of the six origin-accounts is answered. The inescapability of contemporary agency is literally axiomatic in relation to constitutional questions that drafters wholly overlooked, and to matters deliberately unanswered or left to be 'liquidated' by post-ratification practice. And as to constitutional language incorporating conflicting or mutually inconsistent perspectives, contemporary agency is likewise unavoidable if and when a definitive resolution is needed.

Second, where contemporary agency is inescapable, such agency should be acknowledged by scholars, the decisionmakers who exercise agency in generating constitutional answers, and the designers of constitutions. As well, the understanding that agency must be exercised when answering constitutional questions belonging to the six origin-accounts should not be kept from citizens. Though agency-hiding is a conceivable strategy in some contexts,[26] it is deeply in tension with, and may be flatly incompatible with, constitutional democracy.[27]

---

25 For a fuller explanation and defense, see Part 8.

26 Religious contexts come to mind. See, e.g., *Commentary of Nachmanides on Numbers 30:2* (Mossad Harav Kook 1986) (explaining that the general population should be kept ignorant about loopholes that allow judges to annul vows because otherwise 'they would take the obligations regarding vows lightly') (translation by author).

27 The discussion above in text may be informed by the literature that explores the surprisingly thorny questions concerning judicial candor. Compare Scott C. Idelman, 'A Prudential Theory of Judicial Candor' (1995) 73 Tex. L. Rev. 1307 with Micah Schwartzmann, 'Judicial Sincerity' (2008) 94 Va. L. Rev. 987. This chapter is not the place to fully explore whether partial transparency in relation to government actors' constitutional decision-making may sometimes be acceptable in a constitutional democracy. In any event, the proposition that governmental actors should be conscious of agency they exercise is far more tractable than the question of what degree of candor is owed to the public. If contemporary agency in relation to questions falling under the six origin-accounts is inevitable, then agency-acknowledgment should be rejected only if false-consciousness on the part of agency-exercisers reduces decisional error-costs. This seems unlikely, though I shall not further explore this matter here. I thank Chris Schmidt for pressing me on this family of issues.

4 Constitutionalism's Recursive Character

Even if it is agreed that contemporary agency is necessary to decide constitutional questions that fall under any of the six origin-accounts, and that such agency should be acknowledged, there remains the important question of *how* such agency should be exercised. Many of the six origin-accounts raise challenging questions in this regard.[28] For instance, what if history showed that constitutional language reflected the most that a fledgling political community, composed of mutually suspicious subgroups with divergent interests and aspirations, had been able to agree upon when the constitution was ratified?[29] If political relations deepen over time, what appropriately guides answers to constitutional questions only touched upon by open-ended or compromise constitutional language, or that the written constitution left unaddressed? The past – that is to say, the sensibilities that pertained when the constitution was drafted and ratified? Or the present?

The answer is the present: the deeper political affiliations fostered by a political community's having governed itself under the constitution over time are the appropriate inputs for answering constitutional questions that could not have been fully resolved, or even addressed at all, at the polity's infancy.[30] While later sections of this chapter provide a tightly argued theoretical justification for this claim,[31] the conclusion seems attractive as a *prima facie* matter. Historical evidence shows that when the U.S. Constitution was drafted and ratified, citizens' political identity was linked more to state than country; the 'United' in United States operated as a true adjective that reflected the centrality of state identity.[32] National identity has grown in importance in the ensuing

28 Liquidation is the least normatively complex in this respect because it explicitly calls for future specification of what was unspecified at the time of drafting and ratification on account of epistemic limits.

29 This fairly characterizes Klarman's account of the United States Constitution's drafting and ratification history.

30 While those deepened political affiliations facilitate the answering of many constitutional questions, they may complicate others. For example, heightened national sensibilities coupled with an exponential increase in the number and diversity of its citizens give rise to difficult questions as to whether the application of constitutional rights might vary across the country's various sub-federal political units. See generally Mark D. Rosen, 'The Surprisingly Strong Case for Tailoring Constitutional Principles' (2005) 153 U. Pa. L. Rev. 1513, 1601–27.

31 See Parts 6–10.

32 See Sean Wilentz, The Paradox of the American Revolution, *New York Review of Books* 26, 28 (January 13, 2022) (noting that until 1850 "Americans remained firmly, even passionately tied to their state and local allegiances" such that "the United States was less a nation and more like a league of autonomous states").

200-plus years, eclipsing the significance of state and regional identities for almost everybody. Today's New Yorkers and Virginians share a deeper political affiliation than did their nineteenth century counterparts, owing to the deep and meaningful national political identity they hold in common. It seems appropriate that today's sensibilities concerning national identity, rather than those of the past, should be the inputs for answering a contemporary constitutional question whose resolution is properly informed by national identity considerations.

More generally, at least as regards constitutional issues that fall under any of the six origin-accounts,[33] democratic constitutionalism should be understood as being *recursive*, rather than unidirectional. Here is what I mean. A successful constitution memorializes the settlements and commitments that establish the ongoing social practices through which a community works out, over time, its political relations. Those post-ratification workings-out primarily consist of non-constitutional settlements that are codified in statutes and regulations.[34] But the political community's constitutionally-established social practices also can generate refinements and additions that themselves can achieve constitutional status if they become sufficiently constitutive of the political community.[35]

Thus, democratic constitutionalism is a recursive process because constitutionalism's outputs and effects – for example, a deepening and broadening of the political community's bonds[36] – may themselves become part of the constitutional domain.[37] When this occurs, it is fair to say that the immediately

---

33 This is an important caveat. See note 37.

34 As well as extra-legal norms.

35 See Part 8 (justifying this claim). A book-in-progress that explores in detail what might be called a political community's *constitutional rule-of-recognition* provides additional justification for the claim above in text. See Mark D. Rosen, 'Shared Agency and the Uncompleted Constitution' (manuscript on file with editors).

36 During the past several centuries, this 'working out' generally has pushed in the direction of increasingly intertwined political relations among populations that at first shared little in common. But the vector of affiliation can point otherwise. Such open-endedness is unavoidable because a truly *democratic* constitutionalism necessarily holds out the possibilities of both extension and retrenchment of the relevant political community, depending on the contemporary political community's preferences.

37 An important question this chapter only briefly addresses is whether the recursive process operates as a one-way or two-way ratchet: does it run only in the direction of extending the constitutional domain, or does it also allow for contraction (such that a constitutional provision in effect can be demoted or even obliterated)? This chapter largely sidesteps this question, for it mainly addresses constitutional recursion in relation to questions that fall under the six origin-accounts, i.e., matters that a constitution has not decided. See text accompanying note 33. Part 10 preliminarily considers if and how recursion might

prior constitutional domain has been modified. The modified domain then becomes the environment within which subsequent workings-out are fashioned. And things do not stop there. Like its predecessor, the new environment may be subject to modification by subsequent workings-out that become sufficiently constitutive of the political community. This iterative process means that democratic constitutionalism is not only a recursive social practice, but an endlessly recursive one.[38]

The thought that democratic constitutionalism is a permanently iterative process may be invigorating to many. But it should also be sobering, for there is no iron-clad guarantee that any given modification will be an improvement. History suggests that, in the short run at least, both progression and retrogression are possible. This is the promise and peril of *democratic* constitutionalism: it is a form of constitutionalism that is ultimately responsive to the people.

5 Does the License Thesis Authorize Judges to Legislate from the Bench?

The idea that history sometimes licenses agency can provoke a serious anxiety: that judges will overstep appropriate judicial bounds and 'legislate from the bench.' In fact, the apprehension is even deeper: that judges will not just legislate, but 'constitutionate,' from the bench. Concerns of judicial overstepping have led to claims that judges do not, or at least should not, exercise agency[39] – a position that the six origin-accounts suggests is untenable.

Fortunately, there is a conceptually defensible middle ground between the extremes of agency-denial, on the one hand, and legislating-from-the-bench, on the other.[40] It is this: the agency invariably present in answering

---

operate in relation to a constitution's definitive settlements. That discussion suggests that recursion might be a two-way ratchet.

38 So understood, democratic constitutionalism is, in Hegelian terms, an 'infinite end.' See Terry Pinkard, *Does History Make Sense? Hegel on the Historical Shapes of Justice* (Harvard University Press 2017) 41–42 (contrasting a 'finite end,' which is 'something that can be achieved by doing something specific,' with 'infinite ends,' which 'can only be manifested by various actions').

39 See Part 1.

40 Other scholars also have tried to identify a middle path between agency-denial and unconstrained agency. For example, David Strauss' common-law constitutionalism proposes that judges are constrained by the characteristics of the common law process, which includes respect for precedent and the demand for reasoned justification for change. See David Strauss, *The Living Constitution* (Oxford University Press 2010).

constitutional questions that fall under any of the six origin-accounts should, in a constitutional democracy, be jointly exercised by multiple societal institutions, not just courts. Answers to those constitutional questions should result from an exercise of *shared agency* by judges, legislators, executives, and (likely) citizens.[41]

The understanding that constitutionalism is a joint project that requires the exercise of many participants' shared agency can tame anxiety about judicial overstepping.[42] To see why, it first is necessary to have a basic understanding of what shared agency is.

6 Shared Agency: An Introduction

Agency refers to making choices, and then acting pursuant to those choices, in circumstances that can make a predictable difference in the world.[43] Shared agency is agency that is exercised by more than just an individual. Shared agency is a widespread human practice that permits intertemporal (especially intergenerational) projects to be worked on by large numbers of people. Prominent examples include science and art.[44]

---

41 My argument extends the analysis of the philosopher Michael Bratman, who has developed a sophisticated account of the 'shared agency' that is exercised by small groups of people who engage in joint projects. See Michael E. Bratman, *Shared Agency: A Planning Theory of Acting Together* (Oxford University Press 2014) 7 (noting that his 'focus will be primarily on the shared intentional activities of small, adult groups in the absence of asymmetric authority relations within those groups, and in which the individuals who are participants remain constant over time.'). For a preliminary discussion of how Bratman's approach can be applied to larger social contexts, see Part 10. For concerns as to whether citizens are among the agents who properly exercise shared agency in democratic constitutionalism, see text accompanying note 128.

42 For some other important implications of a shared agency approach to constitutionalism, see Parts 8 & 10. A book length work-in-progress of mine fully defends the thesis that constitutionalism is an uncompleted project well suited to shared agency, and cashes out its many important implications.

43 See note 2.

44 Bratman is best understood as elaborating the norms found in paradigmatic instances of shared agency, rather than specifying norms that must be present in all shared agency projects. While all shared agency projects can be expected to share a "family resemblance," a shared agency project need not share all elements found in those paradigmatic instances, or even any single element. Cf. Ludwig Wittgenstein, *Philosophical Investigations* §§ 65–66. For a fascinating account of the rise of modern science in terms that are largely consistent with shared agency, see Michael Strevens, *The Knowledge Machine* (Liveright Publishing Corporation 2020).

Shared agency is a form of collective activity, and is probably unique to human beings. Though many animals engage in collective activities – think of a swarm of bees[45] – shared agency involves overlapping intentions among participants that make their activities not merely collective, but meaningfully *shared*. In the words of philosopher Michael Bratman, '[a] swarm of bees … may act as a unit that tracks a goal, yet ideas of intention – individual or shared – are unlikely to get at the relevant explanatory mechanisms.'[46] The sharedness of 'shared agency' depends upon participants' intentions.

Intentionality's centrality to shared agency makes it necessary to clarify the concept of intention. An intention is a mental state that represents a commitment to carry out an action in the future. Bratman further proposes that an individual's intentions are 'elements of larger and typically partial plans,'[47] and for that reason are 'central to our internally organized temporally extended agency and to our associated abilities to achieve complex goals across time … '[48] So understood, intentions are different from desires, beliefs and evaluations. Intentions play characteristic roles in the agency that humans effectuate through their plans. Especially important, intentions give rise to norms that govern people's reasoning and actions in relation to their plans.[49]

What is true of an individual's intentions in relation to her personal plans largely carries over to a group's shared intentions.[50] Shared intentions allow for

---

45 See Bratman (n 41) 10. Bratman claims that while non-human animals can be 'purposive agents,' only humans can be 'planning agents.' See ibid 23. What distinguishes purposive-agency from planning-agency is time: planning is 'cross-temporal organization' that permits 'temporally extended agency.' See ibid. The human ability to make and execute plans depends upon a capacity for intentionality that appears to be uniquely human. See ibid. Intentionality allows for an elasticity of complex social organization that seems unique to humanity in degree if not kind. See ibid 24.

46 See Bratman (n 41) 10. Bratman persuasively distinguishes shared agency from the strategic equilibria that are modeled by game theory. See ibid 6. This means that game theory illuminates some, but not all, human interactions. To think that game theory describes all human interactions would be an instance of the fallacy of composition. See generally Hans Hansen, 'Fallacies' in Edward N. Zalta (ed), *Stanford Encyclopedia of Philosophy* (Stanford University 2018), https://plato.stanford.edu/entries/fallacies [https://perma.cc/3RXN-W234] (noting that the fallacy of composition occurs when the 'properties of parts … are mistakenly thought to be transferable' to the composite).

47 Michael E. Bratman, *Planning, Time, and Self-Governance: Essays in Practical Rationality* (Oxford Univ. Press 2018) 18.

48 Bratman (n 41) 15.

49 See Bratman (n 41) 19.

50 See Bratman (n 41) 8–9, 35–37. Not all philosophers agree. John Searle and Margaret Gilbert each argue that group agency requires the introduction of some entirely new element that is not present in individual agency. See ibid 9. I am persuaded by Bratman's

the exercise of agency by many people – for *shared agency*. Shared intentions are those intentions of individuals that are elements in the plans that are held by many people.[51] Shared intentions play a set of crucial roles for the group that is analogous to the role that intentions play for the individual: shared intentions coordinate, structure, organize, guide, and help to settle matters. Shared intentions thereby 'help to constitute and to support basic forms of social organization.'[52]

Intentionality sets shared agency apart from other forms of collective activity.[53] Intentionality enables otherwise unattainable flexibility in both project-selection and cooperative project-execution. It is largely owing to humans' capacities for intentionality that our species is not limited to the behaviors that have been genetically programmed in us.[54] Intentionality accounts for the unique flexibility of undertakings, in both responding to the world's challenges and in discretionarily taking on life-enhancing projects, that may be unique to our species.[55] Shared intentions enable humans to engage in massive feats of coordination over time and space in the pursuit of plans that they have selected.

The capacity to engage in cooperative endeavors across time and space has been a *sine qua non* of many of our species' greatest achievements. Constructing

approach, though this chapter is not the place to explain why. For further discussion of shared intentions, see Section 12.

51 See Bratman (n 41) 26.

52 See Bratman (n 41) 27.

53 Humans also engage in collective activities that do not rely on participants' intentions, and for that reason are not examples of shared agency. For an informative discussion of circumstances where there can be complex design without designers or intention, see Daniel C. Dennett, *From Bacteria to Bach and Back: The Evolution of Minds* (W.W. Norton & Company 2017).

54 To be sure, there are mechanisms independent of intentionality through which non-human animals' responses to their environment can go beyond what is genetically programmed. The claim here is that the intention-based mechanism upon which humans so heavily rely is particularly, probably uniquely, capable in generating rapid and high-quality responses. More than this, intentionality opens the door to proactive choice, not just to responsiveness to the environment. In so doing, intentionality gives rise to many apparently uniquely (in degree if not kind) human activities, such as the production of art. See generally Michael Tomasello, *Why We Cooperate* (The MIT Press 2009) (arguing that although the great apes have the capacity to make plans, they do not have a capacity for shared intentional activity). 'Shared intentionality is a small psychological difference' vis-à-vis non-humans 'that made a huge difference in human evolution.' Michael Tomasello and Malinda Carpenter, 'Shared Intentionality' (2007) 10 Developmental Science 121, 124.

55 See note 54.

skyscrapers, building bridges, sending people to the moon, conducting scientific research, and generating technological advances are all projects that have been undertaken through many participants' exercises of shared agency. The same is true of music, art, and culture. This chapter's central claim is that democratic constitutionalism is yet another project that calls for shared agency, and in this sense is akin to all these other human endeavors.

Human beings' practice of engaging in sustained cooperative activities of our own choosing, which is dependent upon people's capacities for exercising shared agency, may account for our species' dominant position on the planet. As Yuval Harari has powerfully reminded us, for much of homo sapiens' existence we did not occupy the perch of master species, but were just one among many animals that lived on the savanna.[56] It may be that humans did not become the planet's dominant species until we developed an array of tools that enabled large-scale cooperation. The capacity for shared intentions, which allows for exercises of shared agency, appears to be one of those tools.[57]

7 That Shared Agency Licenses Only a Bounded Agency

Because democratic constitutionalism should be a domain of shared agency, shared agency's generic properties can shed light on constitutionalism. To begin, shared agency relies upon a division of labor among agents.[58] A shared agency account of democratic constitutionalism thus understands that courts do, and should, exercise agency. But this is not tantamount to licensing judges to 'legislate from the bench.' A shared agency account of democratic constitutionalism understands that judicial agency is appropriately bounded on account of three sets of considerations.[59]

First. Because courts are not the only agents, constitutional decisions are not theirs alone to make. Constitutional decisions instead should be the result

56 See generally Yuval Harari, *Sapiens: A Brief History of Humankind* (Harper 2015).

57 Other tools were necessary for the exercise of shared agency, including the moral reflection and emotions that facilitate cooperation by enabling individuals to reliably forgo what is in their short-term self-interest. And yet other important tools, like money, have facilitated cooperation that is not best described under the rubric of shared agency, but is more unilateralist or game theoretic in nature.

58 See n. 42.

59 What follows in this Part 7 is an ideal account of how shared agency should operate in a constitutional democracy more than a description of what presently occurs. For an explanation as to why deviations between practice and ideal do not undermine this chapter's thesis, see Part 12.

of a shared activity in which other agents also participate and exercise agency. These other agents include Congress, the executive branch, states, and (probably) citizens, in both their individual and collective capacities.[60]

Second. All agents – courts included – are subject to a set of norms when they participate in the joint project of democratic constitutionalism. Participating in a project that calls for shared agency subjects participants to norms because norms are constitutive of shared agency. To put it another way, by engaging in a shared agency-project, a person takes certain demands upon herself. Failing to comply with those demands appropriately subjects a participant to criticism, which is what qualifies those demands as norms. For example, if you and I are engaged in the shared activity of walking together to Times Square, my abruptly turning and leaving you without explanation would be appropriately subject to censure.[61] My departure would have breached a norm that was constitutive of our shared activity.[62]

There are two steps to unpacking how shared agency's constitutive norms should shape the behavior of courts and other participants in the project of democratic constitutionalism. The first step is elucidating the norms that are generically operative in projects that call for shared agency.[63] The second is cashing out how those norms apply to the specific project of democratic constitutionalism.

Let's start with the first step, shared agency's generic norms. Shared agency coordinates people as they navigate projects that are incomplete on account of human beings' limited mental resources.[64] Because projects are partial, they 'must be filled in as time goes by.'[65] Shared agency's norms guide this filling-in process by disciplining participants' reasoning, bargaining, and other activities that are connected to the project.[66]

Shared agency's generic norms constrain participants in two principal ways. Some norms require that participants take account of people and considerations that are external to themselves, and for that reason might be called

---

60 In other words, corporations and non-corporate associations have roles to play in the shared project of democratic constitutionalism. But see text and note accompanying ibid note 128.

61 See Bratman (n. 41) 16.

62 An action that breaches a norm constitutive of a shared agency-project is subject to criticism even the norm-breaching action does not rise to the level of immorality or illegality.

63 The shared agency project of democratic constitutionalism shares most elements with Bratman's paradigmatic cases. See notes 44 & 68.

64 See Bratman (n. 41)19; see also ibid 15.

65 See Bratman (n 41) 19.

66 See Bratman (n 41) 27.

'external' norms. Other norms impose consistency obligations on the positions that each participant can take in connection with the shared project, which for that reason might be called 'internal' norms. Shared agency's external and internal norms together disallow each agent from simply pursuing her own agenda in the way she sees fit. While all participants exercise agency in the shared project, their agency is *bounded* on account of the external and internal norms that are constitutive of shared agency.

One of shared agency's most important external norms is that there be *shared deliberation* among participants when filling in the plan's details.[67] Shared deliberation is very different from unilateral decisionmaking, a form of behavior that is unobjectionable in many other social contexts. Shared deliberation also differs from ordinary bargaining. In ordinary bargaining, 'we each bring to bear considerations that matter to each of us without assuming that the very same considerations directly matter to the others.'[68] By contrast, in shared deliberation 'we reason together in a way that involves a *common ground* of *shared* commitments to treating certain considerations as mattering in our shared deliberation.'[69]

Reasoning together on the basis of shared commitments gives rise to well-known patterns. While commitments typically are not wholly indefeasible, they have a weightiness that is not readily displaced by countervailing

---

67 See Bratman (n 41) 132–34. An earlier project of mine cashed these norms out in detail, but without relying on the conceptual framework of shared agency. See Mark D. Rosen, 'The Special Norms Thesis' (2019) 40 Cardozo L. Rev. 2769. Shared agency enriches and fortifies that earlier project's argument. At the same time, shared deliberation is both underspecified and perhaps unnecessarily demanding. As to the former, for example: Can deliberation among a subset of participants still qualify as shared agency? And temporally, might shared deliberation sometimes occur after preliminary actions have been undertaken? As to the latter, need shared deliberation always include reasoned communication? Or might it include responsive actions so long as participants understand themselves to be engaged in a common project? (The answer to the last question would have to be 'yes' if art and music are understood as shared agency-projects, as I think they should be. See supra n 44). These questions have important implications for constitutionalism, particularly for determining the roles of legislators and executives. I do not pursue these questions here because this chapter focuses on courts, whose deeply entrenched practice of reason-giving in the form of opinions easily fits a straightforward understanding of 'shared deliberation.'

68 See Bratman (n 41) 132 (emphasis in original).

69 See Bratman (n 41) 132. Bratman makes the important point that shared commitments can play this role even if there is not a 'public convergence of value judgment' or belief. Ibid 137. Section 11 addresses the important objection that constitutionalism is not so much a shared project as an extension of unilateralist behavior of the sort found in ordinary bargaining or participating in a market.

considerations.[70] For this reason, shared deliberation can lead to consensus that the commitment trumps competing considerations. And even when shared deliberation does not lead to a single consensus position, shared deliberation can meaningfully constrain by channeling decisional outcomes into a narrower range than otherwise would have obtained in the absence of shared commitments.

Shared deliberation is mostly a matter of process. Other norms of shared agency make substantive demands on the positions each participant can take during shared deliberation, and on participants' non-deliberative actions in connection with the shared project.

Let us begin by considering shared agency's substantive external norms. First, each participant's intentions (including her plans and sub-plans) must be minimally consistent with the intentions of other participants: in addition to sharing the plan,[71] each participant's sub-plans must 'mesh' with others' sub-plans.[72] Meshing does not demand identicality, *i.e.* that one participant's sub-plans perfectly 'match' others' sub-plans.[73] But meshing does require that each's sub-plans be 'co-realizable,' meaning that there should be a 'compatibility across the relevant sub-plans of each ... '[74] Second, participants are expected to track and respond to other participants' intentions.[75] In other words, my co-participants' interests may filter out intentions that I otherwise may have held were I not a participant in a shared project. Third, shared agency entails a

70 For example, the shared commitment might operate as a Razian exclusionary reason, or establish difficult to displace defaults. See Bratman (n 41) 19–20, 132–41; see also Mark D. Rosen, 'When are Constitutional Rights Non-Absolute? McCutcheon, Conflicts, and the Sufficiency Question' (2015) 56 Wm. & Mary L. Rev. 1535, 1573–88.

71 For clarification as to what sharing intentions means, see Part 11.

72 See Bratman (n 41) 53.

73 See Bratman (n 41) 53; see also ibid 28–9 (noting that shared agency 'does not require interpersonal consistency of judgment about the values at stake in the shared activity'; shared agency requires 'interpersonal consistency and coherence *in plan* – not in evaluative judgment ... ').

74 See Bratman (n 41) 53–54. Participating in a project that calls for shared agency entails a commitment to achieving a mesh of sub-plans through negotiation or bargaining. See ibid.

75 See Bratman (n 41) 93 (arguing that shared agency carries with it a disposition to 'track and support and not to thwart the other's role in the joint activity' and 'to help the other if need be.'); see also ibid 56. These duties derive from the rationality requirement of ends-norm coherence. See ibid 27–28 (referring to this as the norm of 'social consistency'). These requirements help account for the 'coordinating role' that shared intention plays. See ibid 53.

disposition to help others in their sub-plans, so as to assist them in performing their roles in the joint activity.[76]

Shared deliberation and the three above-mentioned substantive norms are constitutive of shared agency because shared agency requires a meaningful overlap of intention among participants. Without such overlap there is no shared intention, and hence no shared agency in carrying out the collective activity. To see why, consider two cases. In the first, you and I decide to take a trip to New York City in which we each take a turn driving the car. In the second, I kidnap you, forcing you by gunpoint to drive half way to New York City. Though both are instances of collective activity, only the first is a circumstance of shared agency. The second case is not because the kidnapper is unconcerned with her victim's intentions.[77] These two examples illustrate that shared agency requires that each agent intend to accomplish a given project '*in part by way of the intention of the other*.'[78] Intentions must be 'interlocking' in the sense that 'each treats the other as an intentional co-participant ... '[79] Because the procedural norm of shared deliberation and the three substantive norms discussed above aim to operationalize the interlocking intentions that shared agency requires, I shall refer to all four collectively as shared agency's *Interlock Norms*.

Shared agency also is constituted by substantive internal norms that impose several consistency requirements on participants.[80] What Bratman calls the norm of agglomeration requires that a participant's own various intentions in relation to the project be mutually compatible in the sense that all can be pursued together.[81] So when a participant formulates her position, she must think globally (that is to say, about all positions she has taken, is taking, and plans to take across the project's entire domain) rather than locally (about only the thing she presently is focusing on).[82] Another norm requires coherence between an intention's end and the means that a participant uses to achieve

---

76 See note 76.

77 See Bratman (n 41) 6; see also ibid 49 (distinguishing shared agency from responding to a mafiosa's threat).

78 Bratman (n 41) 49 (emphasis supplied).

79 See Bratman (n 41) 51–2. For a preliminary consideration of challenges that attend the concept of shared intentions, see Part II.

80 These limitations apply to participants only insofar as they are operating in the project.

81 See Bratman (n 41) 15–16, 22–23. Elsewhere I have called this a requirement of 'holism.' See Rosen (n 68) 2824–26.

82 See Mark D. Rosen, 'Marijuana, State Extraterritoriality, and Congress' (2017) 58 B.C. L. Rev. 1013, 1045. As it true of all norms, the requirements of shared agency's norms are not absolute. See ibid note 71. For this reason, the norm of agglomeration doesn't categorically preclude a participant from changing her mind in the future. But non-absoluteness is not tantamount to toothlessness. Republican senators' flip-flop in respect of the Supreme

it.[83] Finally, because plans must remain relatively stable for shared agency to be effectively exercised, shared agency includes a norm of diachronic consistency.[84] I shall refer to these norms of agglomeration, ends-means coherence, and diachronic stability as shared agency's *Consistency Norms*.

Shared agency's constitutive norms impose a final substantive external constraint: each agent's intentions must be compatible with the shared project. What is concretely required by what I shall call shared agency's *Compatibility Norm* depends on the nature of each particular project of shared agency. In democratic constitutionalism, the Compatibility Norm requires that participants aim to reach consensual decisions where possible.[85] Where consensus is not possible, the Compatibility Norm demands that participants take positions that can plausibly be endorsed by the other agents.[86]

These requirements of consensus-seeking and endorsability reflect constitutional democracy's foundational commitment to equal citizenship, which in turn entails an ethic of mutual respect and reciprocity among citizens when setting the foundational rules through which the community's political relations are to be settled. This means that whereas purely self-regarding behavior may be acceptable in the domain of ordinary politics,[87] shared agency in the constitutional domain calls for reasoning, bargaining, and action that is guided by something more. As I've described it elsewhere, even if the hardest of 'hardball politics' is permissible in the domain of ordinary politics, constitutional decisionmaking should proceed by a *tempered politics* that reflects equal citizenship's constitutive demands of mutual respect and reciprocity.[88]

Court nominations of Merrick Garland and Amy Coney Barrett is an egregious example of agglomeration's violation.

83 See Bratman (n 41) 15.

84 See Bratman (n 41) 1515, 21–22; see also ibid n. 83.

85 By contrast, in music and science, two other domains of shared agency, the Compatibility Norm does not require that participants aim to achieve consensus (although consensus tends to emerge over time in science, see Strevens (n 44) 110–12). For a comprehensive justification of the claim that democratic constitutionalism calls for consensual decisionmaking in the constitutional domain, see Rosen (n 68) 2771–2812 & 2835–59. More precisely, participants in the shared project of democratic constitutionalism should seek what Avishai Margolit has called 'sanguine compromises,' as opposed to 'anemic compromises.' Avishai Margolit, *On Compromise and Rotten Compromises* (Princeton University Press 2009) 41. For another important implication of this external norm, see Part 9.

86 Endorsability should be determined in relation to how the other agents presently are, not as one might wish other participants were. See Rosen (n 68).

87 Though not required, and certainly not ideal.

88 See Rosen (n 68) 2820–35. It might be thought that equal citizenship's ethic of mutual respect and reciprocity likewise should constrain non-constitutional lawmaking. For an explanation why it does not, see Rosen (n 68) 2800–2810.

Detailing the requirements of shared agency's norms of Interlock, Consistency, and Compatibility is challenging. But this is to be expected; nebulousness is unavoidable on account of shared agency's being a general account of a wide-ranging domain of human activity. Even so, shared agency's constitutive norms are sufficiently specific to provide meaningful guidance, for they identify an array of affirmative obligations as they also mark off as unacceptable a wide swath of behavior that is unobjectionable in social practices that are not instances of shared agency.[89] The norms' concrete requirements in each domain of shared agency can be expected to become clarified over time as participants self-consciously exercise shared agency.[90] In democratic constitutionalism, shared agency's norms can cabin judges' agency, as well as the agency of constitutional democracy's other participants, as the norms' concrete demands become better understood over time.

Third. Each agent is appropriately constrained by her role in the project. In democratic constitutionalism, each agent's role is determined by the institution she inhabits. Courts, legislatures, executives, and the states are distinctive institutions that each have distinctive roles. So do non-governmental actors, which may include citizens, non-governmental organizations, corporations, and non-corporate entities.[91] Distinctive roles are an artifact of shared agency's division of labor among agents, which is among the properties of shared agency that make it so excellent a tool for coordinated cooperation. Elaborating each actor's appropriate role in a constitutional democracy is a challenging task that itself probably belongs to the domain of constitutional decisionmaking. The difficulty of specifying each's roles owes partly to the fact that they depend in part on the kind of constitutional question that is to be answered.[92]

The upshot of the three sets of considerations discussed above is that shared agency acknowledges judicial agency in answering constitutional questions

89 Unilateralism and ordinary bargaining are each perfectly acceptable behaviors in other social contexts.

90 See Rosen (n 68) 2789–93 (explaining how norms' requirements can be clarified over time).

91 See ibid text and note accompanying note 127.

92 Some constitutional decisions might appropriately depend in substantial part on the views of citizens and corporations. See, e.g., *Grutter v. Bollinger*, 539 U.S 306 (2003). Others might rely heavily on the input of Congress and the President. Compare *Goldwater v. Carter*, 444 U.S. 996 (1979). And yet others might primarily depend upon the views of judges. Determining the nature of each actor's role likely belongs to the constitutional domain, and can be expected to be made increasingly determinate over time in accordance with democratic constitutionalism's recursive character. See Part 8.

without licensing judges to legislate-from-the-bench. As one of many participants in the project of democratic constitutionalism, judges must comply with shared agency's norms of Interlock, Consistency, and Compatibility. These norms create a middle ground between the extremes of agency-denial and legislating-from-the-bench.

So while judges necessarily exercise agency when they confront unanswered constitutional questions, shared agency's constitutive norms circumscribe judicial agency. In place of agency-denial or legislating-from-the-bench, shared agency recognizes that judges – as well as constitutional democracy's other participants – properly exercise *bounded agency*.

8 Plan Partiality and Constitutionalism's Recursive Character

A shared agency account of constitutionalism does more than illuminate the middle ground between agency-denial and legislating-from-the-bench. Shared agency also justifies two substantive claims this chapter advanced in Part 4. The first was that answers to constitutional questions belonging to any of the six origin-accounts should be informed by the deepened and broadened communal bonds that more than two centuries' constitutional practice has given rise to.[93] The second claim is a generalization of the first: that democratic constitutionalism is a recursive process whose outputs and effects can become part of the constitutional domain.[94]

Shared agency sustains these two claims because it understands that the coordinating plans that are the objects of shared agency are 'normally partial.'[95] Plans have their 'characteristic partiality' on account of epistemic reasons, most importantly humans' limited mental resources.[96] And partiality may be endemic to some projects for yet other reasons. For example, partiality might be characteristic of creative domains.

Each of the six origin-accounts in effect explains the partiality of (at least some of) a constitution's components. The first account suggests that a constitution may be understandably incomplete in relation to novel governmental institutions it created, whereas the fifth account identifies the possibility that drafters might overlook some things due to the press of time, a lack of

93 See text accompanying notes 29–33.
94 See text accompanying notes 33–38.
95 See Bratman (n 41) 19.
96 See Bratman (n 41) 19.

imagination, or simple oversight. The second, third, and fourth accounts identify drafters' decision to leave some matters unanswered or ambiguous to facilitate a consensus so the political community can be constituted and launched.

Shared agency provides resources for understanding that a plan's partiality does not undermine the point of having a plan.[97] To the contrary, partiality can be a virtue rather than a vice for two reasons. First, plan-partiality is superior where comprehensive settlement would be premature on epistemic grounds, because plan-partiality allows specification to occur at a later, more epistemically opportune time. Second, in leaving some matters undecided for now, partiality might be the only way that some shared projects can even begin.

Both these justifications for partiality seem applicable to the United States' project of democratic constitutionalism. The Constitution's drafters were not in an epistemic position to fully specify the details of the many novel institutions they had just created over just a few months.[98] Further, full specification of the new political community's approach to many issues – including, for instance, slavery – may would have precluded the Constitution's ratification.[99] Partiality allowed a new political community to be launched, delaying reconciliation of the Constitution's internal inconsistencies until a later time when the community's ties had substantially strengthened.[100]

Shared agency allows a partial plan to be 'filled in as time goes by'[101] by the multiple agents who work together. Each agent can play the role that reflects her institution's distinctive competencies and perspectives. Insofar as the partial plan facilitates the cooperation and coordination that fills in its own blanks, shared agency describes a recursive process: the partial plan guides its own fleshing-out, over time, as participants exercise shared agency. Refusing to allow a plan to be filled in – for example, by insisting that a constitution's drafters produced a complete plan[102] – would subvert one of shared agency's most valuable functions.

---

97 For a contrasting account that treats constitutionalism mainly as a settlement mechanism, see Larry Alexander & Frederick Schauer, 'On Extrajudicial Constitutional Interpretation' (1997) 110 Harv. L. Rev. 1359, 1371–77.

98 See note 9.

99 See Sean Wilentz, *No Property in Man: Slavery and Antislavery at the Nation's Founding* (Harvard University Press 2018) 58-114. In saying this, I do not intent to take a position on the difficult question of whether the Great Compromise in relation to slavery was normatively justifiable. For a powerful argument that it was not, see Margolit (n 86) 54–61.

100 Of course slavery remained so divisive even after seventy years of union that many States preferred to dissolve the national polity rather than submit to a single nationwide solution. See also note 100.

101 See Bratman (n 41) 19.

102 Some forms of originalism appear to come close to this. For a full discussion of the concept of a 'complete constitution,' see Rosen (n 35).

9 First Objection: Is Shared Agency Too Destabilizing?

Some readers might be alarmed that the License Thesis threatens to destabilize longstanding settlements that were not explicitly stated in constitutional text. But a shared agency account of constitutionalism fully addresses this concern. In determining what belongs to the constitutional domain, shared agency does not only look to the point in time when a constitution was drafted and ratified. Shared agency anticipates only a partial plan at that time, which will be filled in over time through participants' exercises of shared agency. Insofar as these fill-ins become part of the plan, shared agency understands democratic constitutionalism to be a recursive process whose outputs and effects can become part of the constitutional domain. Such recursiveness is why the License Thesis is less destabilizing than might first appear. Shared agency does not limit the constitutional domain to what was settled on by a constitution's drafters and ratifiers.[103]

To return to an earlier example, though the United States Constitution does not specify the mechanism for repealing statutes, this does not mean that the constitutional question of how statutes are repealed remains unanswered today. To be sure, determining when shared agency's outcomes attain the status of a settled fill-in requires a rule-of-recognition for determining what belongs to the constitutional domain.[104] While this chapter is not the place to provide a full-blown rule-of-recognition, the practice of effectuating repeal by means of a subsequent statute is sufficiently entrenched and accepted so as to unquestionably fall within it.[105]

10 Shared Agency and Definitive Settlements

Up to this point, this chapter has addressed how shared agency operates in relation to the partial settlements and open-ended commitments described by the six origin-accounts. As to those, shared agency licenses a bounded agency for

---

103 The degree of entrenchment that such fill-ins have turns on what shared agency's norm of diachronic consistency requires for the particular project of democratic constitutionalism. Cf. Richard Primus, 'Unbundling Constitutionality' (2013) 80 U. Chi. L. Rev. 1079, 1110.

104 See note 35.

105 This chapter's argument is directed against *fictive settlements* – claims that an unanswered constitutional question describable by one or more of the six origin accounts was answered the the constitution's drafters — not settlements that occur over time on account of democratic constitutionalism's recursive character.

all participants. But a shared agency account of constitutionalism carries a final important lesson: contemporary participants' agency is more limited in relation to a constitution's definitive settlements, such as the conventioneers' adoption of a fixed term for the president in lieu of Hamilton's suggestion that the president serve for life.

Definitive settlements limit participants' going-forward agency on account of shared agency's Compatibility Norm.[106] A democratic constitution lays down the settlements and commitments that establish the ongoing social practices through which a community continues to work out, over time, the nature and character of its political relations. Insofar as definitive settlements can serve as the grounding that launches a political community only if they are treated as firmly and finally settled, the project of democratic constitutionalism demands that definitive settlements be so treated. Inasmuch as this is true, democratic constitutionalism's Compatibility Norm demands that definitive settlements be treated as firmly and finally settled. For these reasons, definitive settlements are exempt from the general rule that democratic constitutionalism is a recursive process whose components are subject to iterative development.[107]

Even so, not all contemporary agency is eliminated vis-à-vis constitutional questions that belong to the domain of definitive settlements. This is so for two reasons, and perhaps a third.

First, the source of the obligation to respect definitive settlements comes from participants' participation in the project. Obligations are not imposed by actions of those who lived in the past,[108] but result from participants' present participation. Insofar as participation reflects a choice, there is contemporary agency even vis-à-vis definitive settlements.[109]

Second, definitive settlements still leave important room for contemporary agency insofar as norms typically are not categorically indefeasible. Agency remains because it must be decided if and when the Compatibility Norm's obligation to treat a constitution's definitive settlements as firmly and finally settled might be overridden by countervailing considerations. That a norm might

106 See text accompanying notes 85–89.

107 See note 36.

108 Shared agency thus provides a retort to Thomas Jefferson's dead-hand of the past argument, and to Ilan Wurman's argument that today's generation is indebted by decisions made by the Framers. See Wurman (n 16) 3; Letter from Thomas Jefferson to James Madison (Sept. 6, 1789) in *The Essential Jefferson* 176, 179 (Jean M. Yarbrough ed., 2006).

109 This has many important implications. It suggests, for example, that a constitution is not binding on those who do not participate in the project, such as dissenters who fully opt out of the dominant political community's laws and institutions. Fully elaborating this is beyond this chapter's scope.

be defeasible is not a logical contradiction because defeasibility does not render a norm meaningless as a theoretical or practical matter.[110] Norms can exercise real constraining force without being categorically decisive. The necessity of determining the defeasibility conditions of a constitutional democracy's definitive settlements, and what circumstances satisfy those conditions, leaves room for contemporary agency.[111] Even hard-to-satisfy defeasibility conditions leave room for present-day agency.

Third and finally, democratic constitutionalism may not be flatly incompatible with revisiting the past's definitive settlements after all. This part's efforts to cash out the Compatibility Norm's implications for democratic constitutionalism has deliberately relied on the contingent language of *insofar*: it repeatedly has stated that the need to respect definitive settlements as forever set is constitutive of democratic constitutionalism *insofar as* democratic constitutionalism depends upon definitive settlements being so treated. But perhaps democratic constitutionalism only requires that definitive settlements be treated as settled for a 'significant,' though not infinite, period of time. If so, forever-settledness would not be constitutive of democratic constitutionalism, and shared agency's Compatibility Norm would not demand that definitive settlements be treated as settled beyond that 'significant' period of time.

In the end, the Compatibility Norm's concrete requirements for democratic constitutionalism cannot be determined by abstract conceptual analysis that seeks to ponder democratic constitutionalism's essential nature and necessary properties. This is so because democratic constitutionalism is not a natural object in the world, like seashells, that is unchanged by the investigation to which humans subject it.[112] Instead, democratic constitutionalism is a system of understandings and practices that accords with, and channels, human interests and motivations. Because democratic constitutionalism is embedded in humanity, it is dependent upon human beings. If humans' sensibilities in relation to political relations can change over time,[113] it follows that democratic constitutionalism's properties likewise are malleable – on the margins at least,

110 See Rosen (n 71) 1587–1604.

111 Insofar as a norm's force is constraining but not paralyzing, agency is bounded but not paralytic.

112 Though some features of the physical world (namely those at the quantum level) also may be altered by human observation. See Strevens (n 86) 148–9.

113 There is powerful evidence that it does. See, e.g., Edmund S. Morgan, Inventing the People: The Rise of Popular Sovereignty in England and America (W.W. Norton & Company 1989); Terry Pinkard, Does History Make Sense?: Hegel on the Historical Shapes of Justice (Harvard University Press 2017).

and likely even more so over the long run.[114] For these reasons, people's deep investigations and interrogations of democratic constitutionalism might not only clarify its nature and properties, but refashion them.

11 Second Objection: Can Shared Agency Be Scaled-Up to a Political Community?

Intentionality's centrality to shared agency presents challenges to any attempt at scaling-up shared agency from the small groups that are the focus of Bratman's work[115] to larger groups like a political community. Simply stated, can a political community share the intentionality that shared agency presupposes?

Although Bratman concentrates on small groups, he anticipates the extension of his framework to larger groups.[116] Indeed, because shared intentions among even small groups poses substantial analytical challenges, many of Bratman's insights that elucidate the phenomenon of shared intentions in small groups are readily adaptable to make sense of shared intentions among large groups. For example, Bratman persuasively argues that the explicitness of intention requisite for shared agency,[117] as well as the substance of what must be shared among participants, are much less than what might initially be thought. Although shared agency requires a shared plan, there need not be shared evaluative judgments concerning the plan. A plan can be shared notwithstanding 'conflict[ing] judgments about the right and the good, or even certain conflicts of goals.'[118] Furthermore, Bratman relies on something he calls 'action concepts' that, as he puts it, are 'intentionally loaded' by the 'complex culture' in which a person lives.[119] If a person engages in such an action, then

114 This is another example of the Compatibility Norm's dependence upon the particularities of each project of shared agency. The norm's demands in relation to the shared project of science, for example, would not seem to be a function of human sensibilities.

115 See Bratman (n 41) 7.

116 See Bratman (n 41) 9–10.

117 Among the book's most analytically subtle arguments is its claims as to what needs to be shared for there to be a shared intention. Bratman argues that there can be shared intentions for purposes of shared agency even if people do not explicitly understand that their intentions are shared by others. In Bratman's words, 'in at least many cases we have available a concept of *our* activity that, while it draws on ideas of individual intentional action, is neutral with respect to *shared* intentionality.' Bratman (n 41) 46–47 (emphasis in original). Instead, intentions can be shared so long as certain conditions pertain as to each individual's intention. See text accompanying note 122.

118 See Bratman (n 41) 28–29.

119 See Bratman (n 41) 46.

the intention that is culturally loaded into it can be imputed to her.[120] These Bratmanian arguments for fending off challenges to the possibility of shared agency in small groups can be readily adapted to explain shared agency among large groups of people.

Moreover, Bratman builds flexibility into the definition of shared intention, understanding it as 'consisting of relevant plan-embedded intentions of each of the individual participants, *in a suitable context* and *suitably interconnected*.'[121] In other words, the nature of the particular plan determines what specifically is required for there to be shared intentions. This seems sensible. Context counts, with the result that interconnections that are insufficient to constitute shared intentions for one sort of project might be sufficient for another. Thus interlockingness insufficient to generate shared intentions for a small group might be adequate for a large group.[122]

Another possible objection that might be leveled at this chapter's thesis is that shared agency is inapposite to the practice of constitutionalism because there is no group subject that can serve as the agent of the shared intention. The present population of the United States is about 330 million, and the country's aggregate population since 1789 is a far larger number. According to this objection, even if imagination can sustain the fiction that this collection of people over time constitutes a single group, the fiction cannot support the shared intentionality that shared agency requires.

Bratman's framework has resources for responding to this objection as well. Bratman argues there can be a 'causal agent of a shared intentional activity' without there being 'a subject of a shared intention.'[123] All that is necessary is

120 See Bratman (n 41) 46.

121 See Bratman (n 41) 11 (emphasis supplied).

122 To elaborate, democratic constitutionalism is a different sort of shared plan than is putting on a play. Both contexts can be loci of shared agency even though the nature of the interconnections between participants' intentions may vary substantially across each. Bratman's fine grained definition of shared intention invites a context-sensitive inquiry into the type of interconnectedness of intentions that would qualify democratic constitutionalism as a locus of shared agency. At least one prominent scholar already has made substantial work extending Bratman's approach beyond small groups. Scott Shapiro identifies 'massively shared agency' in corporations, universities, and legal systems. See Scott J. Shapiro, *Legality* (Harvard University Press 2013) 148–50. More remains to be done. I suspect that a fully adequate extension of Bratman's framework may have to draw upon what philosophers call 'common knowledge.' See generally Peter Vanderschraaf and Giacomo Sillari, 'Common Knowledge' in *The Stanford Encyclopedia of Philosophy* (Metaphysics Research Lab, Stanford University 2013) http://plato.stanford.edu/entries/common-knowledge; Bratman (n 41) 57.

123 See Bratman (n 41) 127.

that there be an 'internally organized group.'[124] Such a 'structured collection of individuals' can serve as the 'causal agent of [the] shared intention activity' so long as those individuals' intentions are sufficiently related that they qualify as shared intentions,[125] and participants' awareness that they are part of a structured institution may be sufficient for this.[126] The federal institutions that were created by the Constitution, and the state institutions that the Constitution recognized, conceivably can satisfy these conditions, though a thorough development of this argument must await another day.[127]

12 Third Objection: Is Constitutionalism More Akin to Ordinary Politics or the Market than to Shared Agency?

A final possible objection is that shared agency does not accurately model democratic constitutionalism. Instead, the objection continues, democratic constitutionalism looks more like one of two alternatives.[128] First, democratic constitutionalism may just be a process of ordinary bargaining where each group, with its own ideology and preferences, tries to advance its own interests. On this account, what occurs when constitutional decisions are made is no different from ordinary politics. And this should not be surprising, the objection continues, because citizens are bound to have deeply conflicting values that bear on how constitutional questions are answered. Shared agency is inapposite to constitutionalism, continues the objection, because constitutionalism is a domain of deep value conflict.

Second, democratic constitutionalism perhaps is best modeled like a market in the sense that constitutional outcomes are not so much end products of thoughtful decisionmaking as they are the resultants of a multitude of colliding forces that include economic events, political phenomena, and social pressures that originate in the media and the arts. On this second alternative to shared

124 See Bratman (n 41) 127.

125 See Bratman (n 41) 127.

126 See Bratman (n 41) 122–24.

127 It is more difficult to see how this objection can be answered vis-à-vis citizens and other non-public groups, though perhaps their interactions with federal and state institutions might suffice. In the end, the challenge of adequately answering this objection may be a reason to conclude that private persons and institutions are not participants in the shared agency project of democratic constitutionalism. This issue requires additional consideration, for such a conclusion seems troubling.

128 I am indebted to Ioan-Radu Motoarca for pressing this line of criticism.

agency, democratic constitutionalism proceeds by some mix of rational behavior, irrational behavior, and pure chance.

We might put it this way: in contrast to shared agency's understanding that democratic constitutionalism's participants engage in a shared activity, the objection's two alternatives conceptualize democratic constitutionalism as a domain of self-oriented activity that generates outcomes that are highly contingent on happenstance. We might call each of these two alternative accounts of constitutionalism the Unilateralist Objection to shared agency.

It must be conceded that democratic constitutionalism sometimes more closely resembles unilateralist than shared activity, and that luck and chance contribute to constitutional outcomes. But empirics cannot undermine this chapter's thesis. Because democratic constitutionalism is a social practice, not a natural object in the world, it is always subject to being refashioned. As such, it is crucial not to mistake what is for what must be. Regardless of how things may be, the question is whether we would be better served were our social practice of democratic constitutionalism conceptualized as a domain of unilateralism or shared agency.

As to that question, this chapter joins a family of articles that together constitute a project whose foundational claim is that democratic constitutionalism is a social practice that presupposes certain norms.[129] The project seeks to articulate what 'holds [the] practice[]' of democratic constitutionalism together, in effect identifying what is immanent in democratic constitutionalism.[130] The project's underlying methodology is an admixture of empirical and normative. It is empirical insofar as it relies upon an actual social practice. And it is normative because the norms that exist within that social practice 'can never be fully realized,' though they can 'serve as a critical standard'[131] for refining our understanding of, and ultimately our way of undertaking, the practice. This is why empirics alone cannot undermine the project.

---

129 The other major theoretical component is Rosen, 'Special Norms Thesis' (n 68). Application pieces include Mark D. Rosen, 'Legislatures and Constitutions in Times of Severe Financial Crisis' in Tom Ginsburg, Mark D. Rosen and Georg Vanberg (eds), *Constitutions in Times of Financial Crisis* (Cambridge University Press 2019); Mark D. Rosen, 'Marijuana, State Extraterritoriality, and Congress' (2017) 58 B.C. L. Rev. 1013; Mark D. Rosen, 'Can Congress Play a Role in Remedying Dysfunctional Political Partisanship?' (2016) 50 Indiana L. Rev. 265.

130 Jorgen Pedersen, 'Habermas' Method: Rational Reconstruction' (2008) 38 Philosophy of the Social Sciences 457, 471–72.

131 See ibid. My methodology shares features with Habermas' methods of rational reconstruction and transcendental argumentation. See Pedersen (n 131).

One of the project's earlier articles, *The Special Norms Thesis*, unfolded without recourse to the concept of shared agency. It concluded that constitutional decisionmaking is appropriately taken pursuant to 'special norms,' in contrast to the much thinner norms that discipline ordinary politics. It reached that conclusion by interrogating the purposes that democratic constitutionalism aims to accomplish.[132] This chapter takes a different approach, assimilating democratic constitutionalism into the widespread human practice of shared agency to cash out how shared agency's generic properties can illuminate democratic constitutionalism.

Addressing a single topic by multiple investigatory paths can deliver epistemic payoffs. Here are two.

First, each investigatory path might carry distinctive insights that illuminate both the larger topic at hand and the other investigatory approach. To provide one such dual elucidation, *The Special Norms Thesis* lends this chapter's shared agency framework a powerful retort to the Unilateralist Objection. To coarsely compress *The Special Norms Thesis*' argument: democratic constitutionalism cannot work towards, much less accomplish, its foundational goals (of legitimating governmental authority, constituting a democratically apt political fraternity, and constructing a democratic polity's core identity) if participants treat constitutionalism as a mere extension of ordinary politics or the market.[133] While the Unilateralist Objection correctly expects that citizens in free societies will retain deeply conflicting values,[134] this is not inconsistent with democratic constitutionalism's being a domain where participants seek common ground in setting the terms by which they will decide their political relations and otherwise determine their political community's identity.[135] Treating democratic constitutionalism as a domain of unilateralism rather than shared agency not only risks undermining democratic constitutionalism, but may be so deeply incongruent with democratic constitutionalism as to be something other than democratic constitutionalism.

Here is a second epistemic payoff. If two distinct[136] methodologies generate a similar conclusion, such overlap itself may be confirmatory evidence of the

132 See Rosen (n 68) 2797–2812 and text accompanying note 134.

133 See Rosen (n 68) 2786–2859.

134 Compare John Rawls, *Political Liberalism* (Cambridge University Press 2005) xvi–xvii.

135 A crucial question this chapter flags but does not answer is the minimum value-overlap that a shared agency account of democratic constitutionalism presupposes. See text accompanying note 70.

136 To be more precise, while the argument in the 'Special Norms Thesis' proceeded wholly independently of the concept of shared agency, full specification of the Compatibility Norm's implications relied on 'The Special Norms Thesis' conclusions as to democratic constitutionalism's foundational purposes.

conclusion's validity.[137] For example, where Heisenberg's uncertainty principle and Schroedinger's equation generated similar predictions, the fact of overlap was seen by some scientists as evidence of the predictions' validity.[138] Likewise, because the norms constitutive of shared agency substantially overlap with the 'special norms' identified in *The Special Norms Thesis*, the two articles are mutually reinforcing.

13 Conclusion

The answer to the question that entitles this chapter – whether history is a limit or license in constitutional adjudication – is both. Whether history properly serves as limit or license turns on the constitutional question at hand, and is a function of the origin-account that best describes that question. Broadly speaking, history should limit agency vis-à-vis a constitution's definitive settlements.[139] But history properly licenses agency in relation to a constitution's partial settlements and open-ended commitments.

Yet even when history serves as a license, the license is only for a limited use. On the shared agency account, a constitution's partial settlements and open-ended commitments do not invite unconstrained agency, but a bounded agency. Like so many other important human endeavors, democratic constitutionalism is a project that calls for shared agency that both empowers and constrains its participants. Courts are not the sole participants in the project of democratic constitutionalism, which means that many non-judicial players also appropriately exercise agency when answering constitutional questions. All agents are subject to the norms of Interlock, Consistency, and Compatibility that are constitutive of shared agency.

So even where history licenses agency, a judge's agency is not limitless. Shared agency calls for bounded agency – a middle path between the extremes of agency-denial and legislating-from-the-bench.

---

137 Confirmatory evidence, not conclusive evidence.

138 See Benjamin Labatut, *When We Cease to Understand the World* 150–53, 159–62.

139 Even so, limiting is not the same thing as eliminating. See text accompanying notes 109–116.

Bibliography

Alexander L & Frederick Schauer F, 'On Extrajudicial Constitutional Interpretation' (1997) 110 Harv. L. Rev. 1359.

Avishai MA, *On Compromise and Rotten Compromises* (Princeton University Press 2013).

Baude W, 'Constitutional Liquidation' (2019) 71 Stan. L. Rev. 1.

Bradley CA & Morrison TW, 'Historical Gloss and the Separation of Powers' (2012) 126 Harv. L. Rev. 411.

Bratman ME, *Shared Agency: A Planning Theory of Acting Together* (Oxford University Press 2014).

Bratman ME, *Planning, Time, and Self-Governance: Essays in Practical Rationality* (Oxford Univ. Press 2018).

Casto WR, 'The Early Supreme Court Justices' Most Significant Opinion' (2003) 29 Ohio N.U. L. Rev. 173.

Dahl R, *How Democratic Is the Constitution?* (Yale University Press 2002).

Dennett DC, *From Bacteria to Bach and Back: The Evolution of Minds* (w.w. Norton & Company 2017).

Fallon RH Jr., 'The Many and Varied Roles of History in Constitutional Adjudication' (2015) 90 Notre Dame L. Rev. 1753.

Farrand M, *The Framing of the Constitution of the United States* (Yale University Press 1913).

Gardner J, 'Can There be a Written Constitution?' in Leslie Green and Brian Leiter (eds), *Oxford Studies in Philosophy of Law: Volume 1* (Oxford University Press 2011).

Green CR, 'Originalism and the Sense-Reference Distinction' (2006) 50 St. Louis U. L.J. 555.

Greenberg MD & Harry Litman H, 'The Meaning of Original Meaning' (1998) 86 Geo. L.J. 569.

Hansen H, 'Fallacies' in Edward N. Zalta (ed), *Stanford Encyclopedia of Philosophy* (Stanford University 2018), https://plato.stanford.edu/entries/fallacies [https://perma.cc/3RXN-W234].

Harari Y, *Sapiens: A Brief History of Humankind* (Harper 2015).

Idelman SC, 'A Prudential Theory of Judicial Candor' (1995) 73 Tex. L. Rev. 1307.

Jefferson Thomas, Letter from Thomas Jefferson to James Madison (Sept. 6, 1789) in *The Essential Jefferson* 176, 179 (Jean M. Yarbrough ed., 2006).

Klarman MJ, *The Framers' Coup: The Making of the Constitution* (Oxford University Press 2016).

Korsgaard CM, *Self-Constitution: Agency, Identity, and Integrity* (Oxford University Press 2019).

Labatut B, *When We Cease to Understand the World.*

Levinson DJ and Pildes RH, 'Separation of Parties, Not Powers' (2006) 119 Harv. L. Rev. 2311.

Margalit A, *On Compromise and Rotten Compromises* (*Princeton University Press* 2009).

Montesquieu, *Spirit of the Laws, Book XI* (1748).

Morgan ES, Inventing the People: The Rise of Popular Sovereignty in England and America (w.w. Norton & Company 1989).

Nachman Moshe ben, *Commentary of Nachmanides on Numbers 30:2* (Mossad Harav Kook 1986).

Pedersen J, 'Habermas' Method: Rational Reconstruction' (2008) 38 Philosophy of the Social Sciences 457.

Pinkard T, *Does History Make Sense? Hegel on the Historical Shapes of Justice* (Harvard University Press 2017).

Prakash SB, 'New Light on the Decision of 1789' (2006) 91 Cornell L. Rev. 1021.

Primus R, 'Unbundling Constitutionality' (2013) 80 U. Chi. L. Rev. 1079.

Rakove JN, Original Meanings: Politics and Ideas in the Making of the Constitution (Vintage 1997).

Rawls J, *Political Liberalism* (Cambridge University Press 2005).

Rosen, MD 'The Surprisingly Strong Case for Tailoring Constitutional Principles' (2005) 153 U. Pa. L. Rev. 1513.

Rosen, MD 'From Exclusivity to Concurrence' (2010) 94 Minn. L. Rev. 1051.

Rosen, MD 'When are Constitutional Rights Non-Absolute? McCutcheon, Conflicts, and the Sufficiency Question' (2015) 56 Wm. & Mary L. Rev. 1535.

Rosen, MD 'Can Congress Play a Role in Remedying Dysfunctional Political Partisanship?' (2016) 50 Indiana L. Rev. 265.

Rosen, MD 'Marijuana, State Extraterritoriality, and Congress' (2017) 58 B.C. L. Rev. 1.

Rosen, MD 'Legislatures and Constitutions in Times of Severe Financial Crisis' in Tom Ginsburg, Mark D. Rosen and Georg Vanberg (eds), *Constitutions in Times of Financial Crisis* (Cambridge University Press 2019).

Rosen, MD 'The Special Norms Thesis' (2019) 40 Cardozo L. Rev. 2769.

Rosen, MD 'Shared Agency and the Uncompleted Constitution' (manuscript on file with editors).

Schwartz DS, 'Coin, Currency and Constitution: Reconsidering the National Bank Precedent' (2020) 117 Mich. L. Rev. 1005.

Schwartzmann M, 'Judicial Sincerity' (2008) 94 Va. L. Rev. 987.

Shapiro SJ, *Legality* (Harvard University Press 2013).

Siegel NS, 'Umpires at Bat: On Integration and Legitimation' (2007) 24 Const. Comment. 701.

Solum LB, 'Originalism and Constitutional Construction' (2013) 82 Fordham L. Rev. 453.

Strauss D, *The Living Constitution* (Oxford University Press 2010).

Strevens LM, *The Knowledge Machine* (Liveright Publishing Corporation 2020).

Tomasello M, *Why We Cooperate* (The MIT Press 2009).

Tomasello M and Carpenter M, 'Shared Intentionality' (2007) 10 Developmental Science.

Vanderschraaf P and Giacomo Sillari G, 'Common Knowledge' in *The Stanford Encyclopedia of Philosophy* (Metaphysics Research Lab, Stanford University 2013) http://plato.stanford.edu/entries/common-knowledge.

Wilentz S, The Paradox of the American Revolution, *New York Review of Books* 26 (January 13, 2022).

Wittgenstein L, *Philosophical Investigations*.

Wurman I, A Debt Against the Living: An Introduction to Originalism (Cambridge University Press 2017).

Young EA, 'The Constitution Outside the Constitution' (2007) 117 Yale L. J. 407.

CHAPTER 2

When History Requires the Use of History in Constitutional Adjudication

Jorge M. Farinacci-Fernós

1 Introduction

While much has been written about using history in constitutional interpretation, construction, and adjudication,[1] there has been surprisingly less attention to developing a formal and comprehensive model for the appropriate use of history in deciding cases. Since history is an essential component of constitutional adjudication,[2] a general model is sorely needed. A useful model would account for (1) the different *types* of historical devices; (2) the diverse *roles* these devices play; (3) the different *stages* of constitutional analysis to which history may be applied; and (4) the *normative justifications* for the use of history in constitutional analysis, an issue that includes consideration of the different possible *interactions* between types, roles and stages. This chapter begins the task of developing a model by focusing on a particular normative proposal regarding the use of history in constitutional analysis: how history itself determines the use of history in constitutional interpretation.

The central claim of this chapter is that the history of the creation of a constitution directly impacts the choice of an interpretive method and that this choice, in turn, privileges or discards history as an interpretive tool. In particular, the chapter contends, the main normative justification for using history in

1 *See, for example,* Matthew J. Festa, 'Applying a Usable Past: The Use of History in Law' (2008) 38 Seton Hall L Rev 479 (proposing an evidence law approach); Rebecca L. Brown, 'History for the Non-Originalist' (2003) 26 Harv JL & Pub Pol'y 69; Richard A. Primus, 'Judicial Power and Mobilizing History' (2006) 65 Md L Rev 171; William E. Nelson, 'History and Neutrality in Constitutional Adjudication' (1986) 72 Va L Rev 1237; Jack L. Landau, 'A Judge's Perspective on the Use and Misuse of History in State Constitutional Interpretation' (2004) 38 Val U L Rev 451; Ethan Bercot, 'Forgetting to Weight: The Use of History in the Supreme Court's Establishment Clause' (2014) 102 Geo LJ 845, 864–74; Emil A. Kleinhaus, 'History as Precedent: The Post-Originalist Problem in Constitutional Law' (2000) 110 Yale LJ 121, 129.

2 *See* Jorge M. Farinacci-Fernós, 'Looking for the Correct Tool for the Job: Methodological Models of Constitutional Interpretation and Adjudication' (2018) 52 Rev Jur UIPR 213, 229 ('History cannot be so easily ignored in constitutional adjudication').

 | DOI:10.1163/9789004523739_004

constitutional adjudication stems from the process of constitutional creation itself. As such, history can serve two roles: (I) as an empirical source for identifying potentially determinative and authoritative constitutional meaning; and (II) by itself ascertaining the proper role of constitutional adoption history in constitutional analysis. The chapter argues that the more democratic, public, participatory, popular and socially transcendental the process of creation was, the stronger the justification for a model of constitutional interpretation and construction that privileges history, particularly adoption history, as an authoritative source of constitutional meaning. Indeed, under those circumstances, the chapter asserts, history tells us that we *must* use history in constitutional analysis. On the other hand, history also tells us that constitutions that were the result of undemocratic, secret, exclusionary, elite, or socially inconsequential processes of creation present a weaker case for using history, and particularly adoption history, in adjudication. Accordingly, history itself becomes the main normative source for the use of history as a methodological tool in constitutional interpretation.

An important dimension, then, of the approach this chapter offers is the issue of *legitimacy* and *authority*. The democratic, public, participatory, popular and socially transcendental characteristics of a constitutional creation process all promote a legitimacy and authority that require constitutional interpreters to take these founding elements into account. Beyond the conditions of creation, the chapter also pays close attention to existing levels of *connection* and *fidelity* to the original constitution. Two consequences follow. First, the normative force of the creation process is limited: a later democratic, public, participatory, popular and socially transcendental process might displace the process of origin.[3] When that happens, the normative justification for privileging the constitutional creation process disappears. The opposite may also be true: a constitution that was the result of a creation process that lacked legitimacy or authority can later acquire these traits if it survives and thrives and eventually gains connection and fidelity. Second, therefore, legitimacy and authority are never only backward looking. A process' democratic, public, participatory, public and socially transcendental nature is judged both with regards to the past and the present. What was legitimate in the past might not be so now. The issue of legitimacy is an ongoing and context-dependent phenomenon. In order for the creation process to determine the proper use of history in future interpretation, there needs to be sufficient continued

3 *See* Jorge M. Farinacci-Fernós, 'The Constitution is Dead! Long Live the Constitution!' (2020) 25 Barry L Rev 35.

acceptance of the process' legitimacy and authority in the present, in the form of connection and fidelity. As such, the main role for legitimacy and authority, as normative sources for using of history in constitutional analysis, occurs at the early stages of constitutional development. As time goes on, the importance of the legitimacy and authority generated by the creation process may give way to a new constitutional politics.

Part 2 sets out a taxonomy of relevant concepts for determining the proper use of history in constitutional analysis and it examines normative justifications for different combinations of those concepts in specific circumstances. Part 3 explores more particularly one of those normative justifications, the claim that the history of the process of constitutional creation should determine which method of constitutional interpretation is used, and it makes the argument that the more democratic, public, participatory, popular, and socially transcendental the processes of constitutional creation, the stronger the basis for use of creation history. Part 3 also uses some case studies – Bolivia, Puerto Rico, and Australia – to illustrate the argument. Part 4 offers some final thoughts.

2 A Taxonomy

As H. Jefferson Powell explains in discussing the U.S. Constitution, there is 'no general agreement on the proper role either of history in general, or of the history of the constitution's framing and ratification in particular'.[4] A common taxonomy might not be enough to produce general agreement about the proper role of history in constitutional analysis, but it can provide a shared conceptual language that facilitates productive scholarly debate on the issue. This part thus provides a taxonomy of concepts useful to modeling the role of history in constitutional analysis. The taxonomy includes: (1) the types of historical devices; (2) the roles of these historical devices; (3) the stages of constitutional analysis; and (4) the normative justifications for determining when and how historical devices should be used in constitutional analysis.

2.1 *Types of Historical Devices*

History comes in many shapes and sizes. *Types* of historical devices refers to the range of historical sources that might be used in constitutional adjudication, including their nature and scope, and their relationship to constitutional

4 H. Jefferson Powell, 'The Original Understanding of Original Intent' (1985) 98 Harv L Rev 885.

text. Two categories of historical devices are especially relevant: a society's general history and the constitution's own adoption history.

2.1.1 General History

Constitutions do not come out of nowhere.[5] Instead, they are part of the larger historical narrative of a particular society or community. As such, the historical development of that society or community is relevant to the process of constitutional interpretation. Such general history includes the

> history of constitutional development after adoption, traditions, historical changes in the organization of society itself, as well as its political, economic and cultural transformations, and so on. Particularly relevant to constitutional interpretation are issues relating to historical grievances, social conflict and inequalities, internal cohesion, national identity, among others.[6]

The general history of a society helps explain and contextualize its constitution and avoids isolating the constitutional text from the society that created it.[7] This is especially true of societies that have undergone important internal realignments, such as revolutions or independence movements. For example, it is impossible to understand the 1994 South African Constitution without reference to apartheid, the U.S. Constitution without reference to that country's War of Independence, or the 1978 Spanish Constitution without reference to the Franco era. Even more important than the specific events immediately prior to the constitutional process (which are part of its informal adoption history as described below) is a society's accumulated historical experience. The immediate antecedent events represent the culmination of a broader process or the latest link in a longer chain.

As such, the general history of a society provides an essential context for understanding its constitution. Importantly, general history includes non-legal history and takes account of national ethos, ideological foundations, and other broad elements of national identity and historical development. It should be

---

5 *See* Jorge M. Farinacci-Fernós, 'Post-Liberal Constitutionalism' (2018) 54 Tulsa L Rev 1, 46 ('Constitutions are not written in a historical vacuum'), cf Hanna Lerner, *Making Constitutions in Deeply Divided Societies* (Cambridge University Press 2011) 26 ('Constitutions are rarely, if ever, written on a clean slate').

6 Farinacci-Fernós, 'Looking for the Correct Tool for the Job' (n 2) 230.

7 Farinacci-Fernós, 'Post-Liberal Constitutionalism' (n 5) 46 ('Attention should also be given to the more general historical elements that shape the social process').

noted that many constitutions articulate a dominant national or popular *ethos* and render it enforceable constitutional law. That *ethos*, in turn, is the result of historical experiences and the impact of the dominant ideologies of a particular community. A society's deeply held policy preferences are not the product of spontaneous action or temporary passion. On the contrary, sometimes, they are the result of a historical and social process that was deeply influenced by a particular ideology, which now the people wish to entrench in their constitutional text.

In such circumstances, the history of that ideology will also be relevant in constitutional analysis, especially when it comes to constitutional provisions that are the direct result. History has the unique ability to travel outside the law, seek out meaning and content in the realm of politics and ideology, and then incorporate that meaning and content back into the law.

2.1.2 Adoption History

Adoption history refers to the events and circumstances directly related to and contemporaneous with the drafting and ratification of a constitution. It has both formal and informal elements.

The *formal* elements of adoption history comprise the official sources generated by the body that creates the constitution. This includes all of the deliberations and reports of the framing body and its committees and commissions, containing such things as drafts, revisions, debates, discarded proposals, and explanations.

Informal adoption history refers to the historical factors that led to the process of creating a constitution. This category includes the history of campaigns and other electoral processes that lead to the adoption of a constitution; the history of independence movements or other collapses of the pre-existing legal order; and the social forces that bring pressure for constitutional change.[8] Sources relevant to informal adoption history include public discussions and writings; the proposals, opinions and positions of key political and social groups; and the correspondence of important social and political actors. More generally, informal adoption extends to the 'entire historical context of the relevant political community that adopted the constitutional text, including economic factors, social relations [and] cultural assumptions'.[9]

Informal adoption history overcomes the limits of formal adoption history and thereby allows interpreters to identify and use other sources relevant to

8 ibid ('Finally, attention must also be given to the historical context in which the constitution was written, as well as the social forces that gave it life').

9 Farinacci-Fernós, 'Looking for the Correct Tool for the Job' (n 2) 229.

constitutional adjudication. Informal adoption history is not, however, necessarily separate from formal adoption history. In particular, non-legal sources can often provide context for what occurred during the deliberations of the constitutional body that produced a particular text.

Formal adoption history has three additional features that distinguish it from informal adoption history. First, the empirical accuracy and trustworthiness of the sources of formal adoption history tend to be more precise and reliable than sources in the informal context. For example, an official transcript of a constitutional assembly's deliberations is likely more accurate than handwritten annotations in a personal diary. Second, the main link with the normative justifications for using, or not using, adoption history is greater in the formal context than the informal one. This is because what gives adoption history most of its normative power is the legitimacy and authority generated by the official creation process. Third, formal adoption history, by its very nature, tends to be more closely related to the communicative, and above all legal, issues that are relevant to constitutional analysis. In most circumstances, therefore, formal adoption history will prove to be of greater analytical value.

2.2 *Roles of Historical Devices*

The *roles* of historical devices are the actual uses of historical sources and events in constitutional analysis. Five such roles are identifiable: authoritative, best evidence, persuasive, merely illustrative, and illegitimate.

2.2.1 Authoritative

A historical device is *authoritative* when it acts as the sole determinative source of constitutional meaning or effect or as the overriding element in constitutional analysis. In either instance, history displaces other possible sources. An authoritative role is the strongest role historical devices can play in constitutional analysis.

Authoritative historical devices require a particular result when ascertaining the meaning of the text or its purpose, or the intent of its drafters. As to text, an authoritative historical device acts as the only source that can be used to give meaning to the constitutional text, thereby displacing any role for other interpretive devices such as dictionaries or publicly accepted views regarding the text's communicative or legal meaning.

Arguably, when history is authoritative, it can even trump the actual text of the constitution itself if that text is in tension with historical sources. For example, if a particular word or concept used in the text of the constitution has a publicly accepted semantic meaning, it can give way to an authoritative historical device that points to a different, even otherwise erroneous, definition.

Likewise, history might serve to limit the application of a categorical textual provision.

The authoritative nature of a historical device can only derive from an uncontested normative source. As previewed, in the constitutional context, such sources are found in history itself. History must show that the historical process of constitutional creation generated sufficient legitimacy, and thus authority, to *require* giving historical devices authoritative status. When this happens, history displaces other possible sources of constitutional meaning. In part 3.2.1 we will analyze, for example, how the Bolivian and Puerto Rican constitutional courts treat formal adoption history as authoritative in constitutional analysis. Both of these countries had constitutional creation processes that gave formal adoption history normative force and that give rise, therefore, to its authoritative use.

2.2.2 Best Evidence

A historical device provides the *best evidence* when it acts as the primary or main source of constitutional meaning or effect. In such cases, history is given a higher hierarchical status over other possible sources regarding text and its purpose, and the intent of the text's drafters. However, historical evidence can be overridden when met with substantial contrary indications from other devices or sources. In other words, the historical device is open to challenge, since it is not the exclusive or overriding source of constitutional meaning. History provides a strong default position in many cases and can serve as a tiebreaker in close situations. Best evidence is the second strongest role a historical device can play in legal analysis. As a result, the use of historical devices as best evidence of meaning must be preceded by a constitutional creation process that generated substantial, though not incontestable, normative force.

2.2.3 Persuasive

A historical device is *persuasive* when it serves as a privileged, but not determinative or automatically binding, source of constitutional meaning or effect. In such instances, history is given great weight but not more than any other privileged source.[10] In other words, history becomes an equal part of a select group of devices or sources that can be used to analyze text, intent and purpose. A persuasive historical device plays only a moderate role in legal analysis.

---

10 *See* Primus (n 1) 177 (describing the persuasive power of historical devices as having 'justificatory force', though 'varied and diffuse even when it is powerful').

Therefore, it can be discarded if other privileged devices point in a different direction or to a different conclusion.

2.2.4 Merely Illustrative

A historical device is *merely illustrative* when it can be used as a source of constitutional meaning or effect but can just as easily be discarded. When this happens, history serves an auxiliary or confirmatory role. This is the weakest role a historical device can play in constitutional analysis. It reflects John G. Wofford's assertion that history 'should be merely one aid' in adjudication[11] and that of Christopher Eisgruber that history 'has a useful role to play in constitutional interpretation, but not, as if often thought, at the expense of our commitment to moral principle or justice'.[12]

2.2.5 Illegitimate

A historical device is *illegitimate* when its use runs contrary to the requirements of the constitution itself or to normative commitments. In such instances, the historical device must not even be consulted, let alone used. An express textual command in the constitution itself that forbids using historical devices can require this outcome. Likewise, history itself can also determine whether using history in constitutional analysis is illegitimate. As discussed in Part 3, when the constitutional creation process was plagued by undemocratic and exclusionary practices, using adoption history lacks normative justification.

2.3 *Stages of Constitutional Analysis*

Constitutional analysis has several *stages*: interpretation, construction and adjudication. These distinctions matter when determining the proper uses of historical devices. A single historical device can have one role at a particular stage of constitutional analysis, while playing a different role at a different stage.

2.3.1 Interpretation

As Jack Balkin explains, *interpretation* focuses on determining the communicative content of a constitutional provision.[13] This includes semantic meaning,

---

11 John G. Wofford, 'The Blinding Light: The Uses of History in Constitutional Interpretation' (1964) 31 U Chi L Rev 502, 532.

12 Christopher L. Eisgruber, 'The Living Hand of the Past: History and Constitutional Justice' (1997) 65 Fordham L Rev 1611.

13 Jack Balkin, 'The New Originalism and the Uses of History' (2013) 82 Fordham L Rev 641, fn. 3.

as well as issues related to syntax and context. Interpretation is mostly, though not exclusively, a text-based exercise. Through interpretation we ask the communicative question, *what does this mean?* Here, meaning is a linguistic proposition, not a legal one. In other words, interpretation is used to ascertain the semantic meaning of utterances, so as to provide a common frame of reference in terms of language between the different actors in any given communicative interaction. This is done to avoid linguistic anachronisms or to resolve communicative insufficiencies, such as ambiguities. Interpretation allows speaker and audience to share the same communicative information, so as to escape misunderstandings that result from communicative under-determinacy.

Historical devices, including formal and informal adoption history, can be useful in the search for communicative meaning, for example when ascertaining the semantic meaning of a word or phrase that is not currently in regular use or whose definition has changed over time. An obvious illustration: identifying the communicative content of the phrase 'domestic violence' as used in the U.S. Constitution, necessarily requires reference to historical devices given that the term has a quite different common use today.

2.3.2 Construction

As Lawrence Solum observes, constitutional *construction* is the process by which legal effect is given to a constitutional provision.[14] In contrast to communicative interpretation, construction is not limited by text but invites consideration of other sources relevant to constitutional analysis, including purpose, the subjective intent of the drafters, and history. Sometimes, there will exist a normative justification even for discarding communicative content as an element in determining legal effect. Once again, it will be history that determines if such reasons exist. In addition, history might also require that historical devices play the main role in both communicative interpretation and construction.

2.3.3 Adjudication

Adjudication has two key components: First, adjudication involves the actual application of communicative, and most importantly, legal content to a particular controversy; second, adjudication involves the development of legal, including constitutional, doctrine.[15] As Gary Lawson has emphasized, while

14 Lawrence B. Solum, 'The Interpretation-Construction Distinction' (2010) 27 Const Comment 95.

15 *See* Andras Sajo, 'Constitutional Adjudication in Light of Discourse Theory' (1996) 17 Cardozo L Rev 1193, 1197.

interpretation and construction deal with meaning (the former, communicative meaning; the latter, legal meaning), adjudication is related to 'the manner in which decisionmakers ... resolve disputes'.[16] In other words, adjudication is focused on the application of communicative and legal meaning to a specific set of facts.

2.4 *Next Steps*

So far, the discussion has focused on issues of how, when and where history can be used in constitutional analysis. There remains, of course, a vital question: *why should history be used at all?*[17] Resolving that issue allows for implementation of the elements analyzed in the preceding sections. Significantly, the completeness of any taxonomy requires careful attention to the normative justification for uses of history.[18] The chapter thus next takes up that issue.

3 How Process Determines Method

The question of the normative justification for uses of history in constitutional adjudication is directly related to the issue of how an interpretive methodology is chosen in the first place. That decision is not usually divorced from politics.[19] Michael McConnell is therefore right when he states that '[w]e can

16 Gary Lawson, 'On Reading Recipes and Constitutions' (1997) 85 Geo LJ 1823.

17 *See* Festa (n 1) 497–98 (identifying (1) the normative issue of *should* we use history in constitutional adjudication and (2) the methodological issue of *how* to do so. I propose to link these issues).

18 It is also worth mentioning that there are multiple potential interactions between the factors identified in the taxonomy – type, role and stage – and the resulting claim for uses of history. For example, there may be instances in which in determining both communicative and normative content authoritative weight *must* be given to formal adoption history. There may also be situations in which in identifying the purpose of constitutional provisions in order to adjudicate a controversy general history *can* be used as best evidence. In such circumstances the historical development of society at large helps identify the social ills that motivated the adoption of a particular constitutional provision and thus how broadly or narrowly it should be applied. Many other combinations, with varying results, are possible. *See, for example,* Jorge M. Farinacci-Fernós, 'South Africa's Forward-Looking Constitutional Revolution and the Role of Courts in Achieving Substantive Constitutional Goals' (2019) 53 Rev Jur UIPR 531 (discussing how the South African Constitutional Court rejects giving formal adoption history determinative status, but gives general history a privileged place in constitutional analysis).

19 *See* Farinacci-Fernós, 'Looking for the Correct Tool for the Job' (n 2) 216 ('From both a practical and theoretical standpoint, the actual selection of a particular model of constitutional interpretation is not a purely legalistic or mechanical decision').

determine the method to interpret the Constitution only if we are first clear about *why* the constitution is authoritative'.[20] In other words, there is necessarily a connection between method and authority; it is therefore essential to determine at the outset the basis on which a constitution is authoritative.

The central claim of this chapter is that history itself should determine whether and how historical sources are used in constitutional analysis. Specifically, when a constitution is adopted as the result of a highly democratic, public, participatory, popular and socially-transcendental process of creation, then history, particularly adoption history, can, should and must be used as an authoritative source of constitutional meaning.[21] On the contrary, constitutions that were the result of undemocratic, secret, exclusionary, elite and socially inconsequential processes of creation generate the weakest normative force as to the use of history in general, and adoption history in particular, in constitutional adjudication. This is so because that kind of creation process lacks legitimacy and, as a result, authority.[22] Recent experience has demonstrated that the processes for creating constitution have actually become more democratic and public than they were in the past.[23] A result of the trend is a stronger case for using adoption history in interpreting more recent constitutions.

---

20 (Emphasis added) Michael W. McConnell, 'Textualism and the Dead Hand of the Past' (1998) 66 Geo Wash L Rev 1127, 1128. *See also* Christopher J. Peters, 'What Lies Beneath: Interpretive Methodology, Constitutional Authority, and the Case of Originalism' [2013] BYU L Rev 1251 ('[T]he methods of interpretation must be defended by references to accounts of constitutional authority'); Eric Parnes, 'They the People: A Third-Party Beneficiary Approach to Constitutional Interpretation' (2003) 43 Santa Clara L Rev 495 ('[T]he method of interpretation must begin with, and derive from, and remain true to some source of the Constitution's legitimacy'); Richard S. Kay, 'Adherence to Original Intentions in Constitutional Adjudication: Three Objections and Responses' (1988) 82 Nw U L Rev 226, 285.

21 For an analysis of the different processes of constitutional creation, *see* Justin Blount, Zachary Elkins & Tom Ginsburg, 'Does the Process of Constitution-Making Matter' in Tom Ginsburg (ed), *Comparative Constitutional Design* (Cambridge University Press 2012).

22 Of course, as we will see later on, this normative situation can change in time, particularly if an individual constitution is able to acquire sufficient connection and fidelity through other means not associated with the adoption process itself. Yet, even in these circumstances, this does not automatically mean that adoption history should suddenly receive privileged status. Most likely, its use should cease being seen as an illegitimate enterprise. As with many things, time will tell.

23 Farinacci-Fernós, 'Post-Liberal Constitutionalism' (n 5) 44 ('As time has gone by, constitutional creation has been democratized and made more public. Participation has risen and popular attention to the process itself has become more heightened. As a result, the nature and role of the constitution-making process has changed dramatically').

This section advances the normative claim in more detail. The discussion necessarily has some limits. It focuses on the relation between the process of constitutional creation and uses of history, particularly adoption history, in constitutional analysis. The section also emphasizes the role of *legitimacy* and *authority* as the driving normative considerations in the choice of an interpretive method.

Legitimacy, as used here, refers to the public's approval of the process that generated the constitution. Authority exists when that approval generates popular acceptance of the constitution. This section contends that the principal source for legitimacy and authority is the constitutional creation process itself.

Importantly, however, legitimacy and authority in the constitutional creation process is not the only possible basis for a constitution's claim to validity. There can be instances in which a creation process that lacks legitimacy and authority will nonetheless produce a constitution accepted by the political community because, for example, the community agrees with the substantive content of the document. Accordingly, the normative claim advanced here, emphasizing the legitimacy and authority of the creation process, is limited to the issue of uses of history as a tool of constitutional analysis.

In addition, while a democratic process of constitutional creation (one that is likely to generate legitimacy and authority) can also produce a constitution that reflects the policy preferences of the social majority, a tight relationship between process and content is not inevitable. A socially accepted creation process might generate legitimacy and authority even if the constitutional text does not reflect popular preferences. Likewise, a creation process might lack acceptance but nonetheless produce a constitution that, because of its substantive content, garners support. In other words, connection and fidelity can exist even when the process of creation was defective. *Connection* in this sense refers to the level of substantive agreement between the current social majority and the content of the constitution. *Fidelity* is a result of connection: it refers to the level of allegiance that the current generation has to the constitution as an authoritative document.

Because the constitution is the primary governing document of a given society, its content will ideally reflect the policy preferences of the social majority. When this happens, the current social majority will continue to see the constitution as valid, even if its creation process failed to create legitimacy and authority. Significantly, the legitimacy and authority that a democratic creation process can generate eventually may run out. The eventual endurance or longevity of a constitution can thus come to depend more heavily upon connection and fidelity than on legitimacy and authority.

All of these features have implications for uses of history in constitutional adjudication. The initial decision to adopt a model that privileges or discards history results from the legitimacy and authority of the process that generated the constitution. In other words, legitimacy and authority determine the initial choice of a model of interpretation; fidelity and connection determine the validity of that model's continued usage (and whether there is a case for adopting a new model). Importantly, when a constitution gains social acceptance and reproduces its substantive content in the everyday operation of the body politic, the legitimacy and authority at creation may combine with connection and fidelity on the part of the current generation. In such circumstances, the normative force for using history in constitutional adjudication grows stronger.[24] In sum, '[t]he adequacy of a particular mode of interpretation will depend quite heavily on the prevailing social consensus as to the role of constitutional law, the role of the courts and the *legitimacy* of both the constitution itself and the adopted forms of interpretation and application. In particular ... it will depend on the degree of *fidelity* of the political community with its constitutional structure and project'.[25]

Finally, the approach offered here provides a robust response to the so-called 'dead-hand problem' of allowing previous generations to rule future ones without their consent or against their wishes. Prior commentators who have grappled with this problem have emphasized that (a) the whole point of constitutionalism is to generate legal norms that will transcend the generation that adopted them,[26] and (b) in the end, 'the dead cannot literally govern our choices [...] the living bear responsibility for continuing or discarding old arrangements'.[27] Recognizing that history itself generates the legitimacy and authority for uses of historical sources in constitutional adjudication has the added benefit that it is the *current* generation that is ultimately responsible for determining history's normative force. When the people recognize the

---

24 It should be recognized that in using history there are complex questions concerning the availability and reliability of historical sources. For present purposes, I note only that democratic, public, participatory, popular and socially transcendental processes of constitutional creation are likely to produce accurate and detailed historical records.

25 (Emphasis added and in original) Farinacci-Fernós, 'Looking for the Correct Tool for the Job' (n 2) 216.

26 Jamal Greene, 'Selling Originalism' (2009) 97 Geo LJ 657, 664 ('It is in the nature of a constitution to limit the will of a present majority'); McConnell (n 20) 1127 ('But in truth, the dead hand argument, if accepted, is fatal to *any* form of constitutionalism').

27 Adam M. Samaha, 'Dead Hand Arguments and Constitutional Interpretation' (2008) 108 Colum L Rev 606, 622; *See also* Bruce A. Ackerman, 'The Storrs Lectures: Discovering the Constitution' (1984) 93 Yale LJ 1013, 1051.

legitimacy and authority of a particular historical process, they accept, indeed require, a vital role for history in constitutional analysis.

3.1 *Elements of the Normative Model*

The normative approach this chapter offers is based on whether the creation process was democratic, public, participatory, popular, and socially transcendental. This section analyzes each of those components. While these elements are below treated individually, it remains important to recognize that they overlap and should be understood together.

3.1.1 Democratic

The key feature of a democratic process of constitution making is popular consent, in other words, that the political community recognizes that the framing process reflects the role of a self-governing people. In order to meet this requirement, the framing process cannot be, or even appear to be, a separate and remote event from current social and political reality, but rather one that flows directly from the exercise of constitutional politics by the people. When this happens, the framing body is not merely representative of the people: it is instead both the servant and direct embodiment of the people. In essence, the democratic character of the constitution-making process derives from the political connection between the people and the process itself.

Several specific factors are relevant to assessing how democratic a constitution-making process is: (1) the level of connection between the people and their representatives; (2) the nature of the selection process for the members of the framing body, including the level of public engagement in that process;[28] (3) the universe and actual number of individuals who were able to and actually did participate in the constitution-making process, including by selecting delegates and ratifying the constitution; (4) the accountability of the framing body and other key actors to the public; (5) the public's overall role as the driving force of the whole process by, for example, initiating reform, ratifying proposals, or even shutting down the framing process for failing to meet expectations; and (6) the extent to which the members of the framing body reflected the interests and preferences of the public.

---

28 *See* Blount, Elkins & Ginsburg (n 21) 35 (mentioning the 'mobilization of interests and counter interests prior to the preparation of a text'). *See also*, Jon Elster, 'Clearing and Strengthening the Channels of Constitution Making' in Tom Ginsburg (ed), *Comparative Constitutional Design* (Cambridge University Press 2012) 16–17 (identifying some of the issues related to the pre-drafting stage, including delegate selection).

The democratic nature of the creation process relates directly to the legitimacy of the process and the authority of the resulting constitution. As Andre Arato explains, 'non-democratic procedures of constitution making cannot be justified today'.[29]

3.1.2 Public

The public nature of a constitution-making process is a byproduct of its democratic character. Specifically, a public process is one that is open, transparent and accessible, with the deliberations of the framing body available and accessible to the public (for example, because the deliberations were broadcasted, covered by the press or witnessed by ordinary citizens).

A public process promotes legitimacy. If the process of creating a constitution is public, the people are not a passive entity waiting for a final result but are instead able to observe, react to, and even shape the procedures. Those opportunities are likely to generate support for the constitution that results. An open process also facilitates accountability. Secret deliberations are susceptible to self-dealing and other forms of corruption: elites meeting behind closed doors, free from popular supervision and democratic accountability, might well pursue their own narrow interests rather than those of the public at large. The resulting constitution is less likely to generate legitimacy.

3.1.3 Participatory

Participation refers to the role that the political community played in generating the actual content of the constitution.[30] Such participation can take different forms. In can be direct and formal, such as through opportunities for the public to introduce or consider specific constitutional provisions. It can also be indirect and informal, such as through popular pressure brought to bear upon the deliberations of the framing body.[31] Partial referenda, whether to consider particular issues or give popular assent to the progress made so far, are an important means of participation.

Popular participation reflects constitutional politics as distinguished from ordinary politics. As Ackerman explains, ordinary politics involves activity by political representatives on behalf of the people, with the members of the public themselves relatively disengaged. Constitutional politics, on the other

29 Andre Arato, 'Forms of Constitution Making and Theories of Democracy', (1995) 17 Cardozo L Rev 191, 192.

30 *See* Blount, Elkins & Ginsburg (n 21) 34 (on the issue of 'who is to be involved' in the creation process).

31 Ibid 46.

hand, involves a conscious and active self-governing people engaged in determining their fundamental law.[32] Constitutional politics directly reflects the popular preferences of the social majority[33] and allows the people to govern themselves rather than to be governed by intermediaries. A representative body becomes a direct embodiment of the people and not just a legislature composed of people who speak or act in their stead.

Public participation is a key legitimizing element for modern constitutions. As Elkins, Ginsburg and Blount observe, '[p]ublic involvement in constitution making is increasingly considered to be essential for the legitimacy and effectiveness of the process'.[34] Indeed, when the people are engaged in the creation of the constitution, eventual ratification is typically a foregone conclusion: participation in the process tends to give the resulting constitution legitimacy even before actual ratification.

The participatory and democratic nature of a process overlap but are nonetheless distinct elements. The democratic character of a process is largely reflected in events occurring before and after framing; participation deals with the involvement of the people in the actual formulation of the constitution's provisions.[35] Accordingly, a process might be democratic but not participatory. For example, there might be popular consent for initiating the drafting process, selecting the delegates, and ratifying their proposed text so that the process was democratic. Unless, however, there was also public involvement in generating the constitution's provisions, the process was not participatory.

3.1.4 Popular

A popular process is one that is reflective of the demographic composition and preferences of the existing social majority. While determining whether a process was participatory focuses on the extent to which the general public was involved, determining whether it was popular focuses on *who specifically* from the public was involved.

In this formulation, the social majority is the quantitatively dominant, and minimally cohesive, group within a particular society. It might be the working class, indigenous peoples, or a particular ethnicity or nationality. The social

32 *See* Ackerman (n 27).

33 (Emphasis added) Farinacci-Fernós, 'Post-Liberal Constitutionalism' (n 5) 35 ('[S]ocial majorities have more success in the exercise of constitutional politics than ordinary politics').

34 Zachary Elkins, Tom Ginsburg & Justin Blount, 'The Citizen as Founder: Public Participation in Constitutional Approval' (2008) 81 Temp L Rev 361.

35 *See* Farinacci-Fernós, 'Post-Liberal Constitutionalism' (n 5) 39–41.

majority stands in contrast to elites or the privileged. Importantly, while numerosity is essential, the social majority is not merely something more than 50% of the electorate. Instead, there is a qualitative aspect as well: a coalition that can be fairly characterized as the main embodiment of the political community. At the same time, a social majority need not be internally homogeneous: it can comprise a broad coalition of different groups of society, so long as they are minimally cohesive, and they share common objectives that can be transformed into a coherent constitutional project.

A popular process generates legitimacy and authority. Examples of social majorities in the creation process include the role of the indigenous majority in Bolivia in 2009, that of the poor urban and rural working class in 1950's Puerto Rico, and that of the black majority in South Africa in the early 1990s.

3.1.5 Socially Transcendental

Two factors bear on whether a constitution-making process was socially transcendental. The first is whether the process represented a pivotal event in a society's history. In other words, did the process change society in a meaningful way? The issue reflects the role of the constitution as a central pillar of society. Constitutions are not just law: they also reflect and shape political and social commitments and arrangements. The second factor is whether the process has a lasting effect, that is, whether the resulting constitution continues to reflect the preferences of the social majority over time. Examples of socially transcendental events include the achievement of national independence, the triumph of a revolutionary movement, and the attainment of other social realignments that represent a milestone in a society's history.

A transcendental process has a special claim to legitimacy. Popular perception that something new and meaningful occurred when the constitution was adopted is a powerful legitimizing force. Ongoing symmetry between the constitution's content and popular preferences stabilizes fidelity. In such circumstances, the constitution can become the main driving force of social development, reshaping society in accordance with the will of the social majority that may previously have been deprived of political power.

3.2 *Case Studies*

3.2.1 Puerto Rico and Bolivia

What do Puerto Rico and Bolivia have in common? First, their current constitutions were the result of democratic, public, participatory, popular and socially transcendental processes of creation. Second, and as a result, in both Puerto Rico and Bolivia, history in general, and adoption history in particular, play a key role in all stages of constitutional analysis. Third, the constitutions of Puerto Rico and Bolivia continue to reflect and shape the policy preferences of the social majority, thereby generating ongoing support for the constitutional order. Accordingly, Puerto Rico and Bolivia exemplify the role of history as a basis for constitutional authority and as the determinative source of constitutional meaning.

Puerto Rico's constitutional-creation process reflects all five elements identified in the preceding parts of this chapter.[36] First, the 1952 constitution, still in use today, was the first and only constitution ever written and adopted by the people of Puerto Rico: it reflects, therefore, a socially transcendental event.

Second, the creation process was democratic. The members of the constitutional convention were directly elected by the people of Puerto Rico through universal suffrage and convention members included delegates from three political parties. The convention's proposed constitution was approved by a popular referendum.

Third, the process was participatory. The convention was preceded by wide public debate about the type of constitution that should be adopted and the nature of the rights it should include. The delegates to the convention were elected after they had identified the proposals they would make at the convention. During the deliberations of the convention, between 1951 and 1952, several social, civic, labor, and other organizations had opportunities to make proposals of their own and some of those proposals were ultimately adopted.

Fourth, the process was public. The deliberations of the convention were covered extensively by media outlets. This resulted in lively interaction and engagement between members of the public and their elected delegates. All of the convention debates were readily accessible.

Finally, the process reflected the composition and views of the social majority. In particular, at the convention there was substantial cross-party representation of labor leaders and peasant-farmers (*campesinos*). The constitution itself reflected a socially-oriented view of government shared by broad sectors of the public.

These combined elements generate great normative pressure to use history in constitutional adjudication. Puerto Rican courts have obliged. They give formal adoption history almost complete authoritative force in interpretation, construction, and adjudication. Informal adoption history and general history

---

36 For an in-depth analysis of the constitutional creation process in Puerto Rico and how it has directly impacted the way Puerto Rican courts use history in constitutional adjudication, *see* Jorge M. Farinacci-Fernós, 'Originalism in Puerto Rico: Original Explication and its Relation with Clear Text, Broad Purpose and Progressive Policy' (2016) 85 Rev Jur UPR 203.

are given at least privileged weight at all three stages. These practices, dating to the first years after adoption of the constitution, continue to this day.[37]

The Bolivian experience is similar.[38] First, as the final step in an anti-colonial struggle, Bolivia's current (2009) constitution reflects a socially transcendental process. It is the first constitution that the majority indigenous population played a leading role in creating and it is widely viewed as the culmination of a broader revolutionary social movement seeking transformative legal change.

Second, the creation process was democratic. As the Bolivian Plurinational Constitutional Court has explained, the constitution 'was approved by the Constitutional Assembly in 2007, made compatible by the National Congress in 2008, approved by National Referendum on January 25, 2009, and promulgated on February 7, of the same year'.[39]

Third, the process was participatory. The constitutional assembly's work was carried out in the context of frequent social mobilizations demanding constitutional reform. Many of the proposals presented during the deliberations of the assembly came from mobilized social groups, such as labor and indigenous organizations.

Fourth, the process was public. As in Puerto Rico, the deliberations of the constitutional assembly were not secret discussions among elites but a public event under the watchful eye of an engaged social majority.

Finally, the Bolivian constitutional process of 2006–2009 was characterized by a leading role on the part of the country's indigenous population. Historically deprived of political power, this social majority mobilized to dominate a period of constitutional politics that resulted in the adoption of the 2009 constitution. The resulting constitution also reflects the policy preferences of that same social majority, including in provisions that incorporate indigenous principles and protect socioeconomic rights such as access to water.[40]

---

37 ibid.

38 For an in-depth analysis of the constitutional creation process in Bolivia and how it has directly impacted the way Bolivian courts use history in constitutional adjudication, *see* Jorge M. Farinacci-Fernós, 'When Social History Becomes a Constitution: The Bolivian Post-Liberal Experiment and the Central Role of History and Intent in Constitutional Adjudication' (2017) 47 Sw L Rev 101.

39 T.C.P., 4 Noviembre 2013, Sentencia Constitucional 1936/2013, at 6 (Bol.), <https://buscador.tcpbolivia.bo/_buscador/(S(ean2tdyOiefvizil331hzgxc))/WfrResolucionesl.aspx>; *see also* T.C.P., 9 Junio 2014, Sentencia Constitucional 1038/2014, at 8 (Bol.), https://buscador.tcpbolivia.bo/_buscador/(S(ean2tdyOiefvizil331hzgxc))/WfrResolucionesl.aspx (making reference to the 2006–2009 constitutional process), in Farinacci-Fernós, 'When Social History Becomes a Constitution' (n 55) 151.

40 *See, in general,* ibid.

In adjudicating constitutional cases, Bolivian courts place great emphasis on historical sources. They give formal adoption history almost complete authoritative force and give general history significant weight in all stages of judicial decision-making.[41]

3.2.2 Australia

Australia presents a quite different case. Its constitution, a framework document, was not adopted through the sort of democratic and participatory processes found in Puerto Rico and Bolivia. As Jeffrey Goldsworthy explains, '[t]he Constitution was drafted in Australia by representatives of the six colonies at constitutional conventions during the 1890's and subsequently approved by voters in separate referenda in each colony'.[42] Because at the time Australia was a colony, the constitution only took legal effect when approved by the British Parliament.

As to the text itself, the constitution is 'not a lengthy document',[43] since it has no Bill of Rights and 'does not include grand declarations of national values or aspirations'.[44] In that sense, the Australian constitution was hardly the result of a popular-driven, dynamic democratic process. At the same time, and in line with the pure framework model, 'the framers deemed it both unnecessary and unwise to fetter their legislatures' because 'democratically elected parliaments seemed to them the best possible guardians of liberty'.[45]

Moreover, the Australian framers saw a limited role for the constitution and for courts in interpreting it. '[T]he framers feared that judicial interpretations of abstract rights could have unpredictable and undesirable consequences'.[46] That assessment corresponds to the elite nature of the constitutional creation process: 'For one thing, they [the framers] did not want to be prevented from

---

41 *See* Farinacci-Fernós, 'When Social History Becomes a Constitution' (n 38) 155–56 and the decisions of the Bolivian Plurinational Constitutional Court referenced therein.

42 Jeffrey Goldsworthy, 'Australia: Devotion to Legalism' in Jeffrey Goldsworthy (ed), *Interpreting Constitutions: A Comparative Study* (Oxford University Press 2007) 106. *See also* Jamal Greene, 'On the Origins of Originalism' (2009) 88 Tex L Rev 1, 40–41. This section is partially based on a chapter of the author's S.J.D. Dissertation 'Original Explication and Post-Liberal Constitutionalism: The Role of Intent and History in the Judicial Enforcement of Teleological Constitutions' (SJD dissertation, Georgetown University Law Center 2017) and draws its analysis from Goldsworthy's excellent research into the Australian example. It is used it here as an example to illustrate its normative effects as to the model discussed in this chapter.

43 Goldsworthy (n 42) 109.

44 ibid.

45 ibid.

46 ibid.

discriminating against people of other races in order to protect the racial and cultural hegemony of their communities'.[47] The limited significance of the constitution persists. In particular, 'Australians remain wary of constitutionally entrenched rights'.[48]

In the case of the Australian constitution, history demonstrates that (1) the process of creation lacks the elements that confer a strong legitimizing force and therefore authority, and (2) that, as a result, adoption history should have a limited role, if any, in constitutional analysis. In addition, because of the relatively advanced age of the Australian constitution, many of its provisions have become anachronistic; some were premised on very different political and social circumstances than those that exist today.[49] Accordingly, there is no firm basis for fidelity on the part of present Australians to their constitution.

Although observers have long argued that historical sources and devices should not play an important role in constitutional analysis,[50] courts in Australia have taken a variable position on the matter. According to Goldsworthy, early courts, adjudicating constitutional cases, placed some emphasis on the views and work of the framers[51] but, keeping with the common law tradition, made use also of ordinary tools of statutory interpretation.[52] In constitutional interpretation, courts have relied upon sources related to adoption history, including draft versions of the constitutional text, and other materials found in the regularly-invoked volume, *The Annotated Constitution of the Australian Commonwealth* (*1901*).[53] Still, for many decades courts made no use of the debates associated with the creation process. That changed, however, in the late 1980s when Australian courts became willing to consult convention debates as informing meaning.[54] Nonetheless, 'the role of historical considerations should not be exaggerated'.[55] For the most part, and compared to practices in other jurisdictions, Australian courts make quite limited use of historical sources.[56]

47 ibid 109–10.
48 ibid 110.
49 ibid.
50 ibid.
51 ibid 116.
52 Ibid 117.
53 ibid.
54 ibid 124.
55 ibid 125.
56 For example, Goldsworthy states that, while there is a 'substantial increase in judicial references to the framers' intentions, and to the Convention Debates, […] [n]evertheless, it must be acknowledged that on many, and possibly most, contentious issues, historical evidence remains of little assistance, because either the framers did not discuss the issue,

4 Conclusion

This chapter has argued that historical experiences can provide normative justifications for using historical sources in legal analysis. In particular, the chapter has suggested that the process of constitutional creation is critical to determining how history, especially adoption history, should be used in constitutional interpretation. In other words, history itself tells us how to use history in constitutional analysis. The chapter has made a particular case for giving determinative status to historical devices, especially those from the adoption era, when a constitution is the product of a democratic and popular process that represents and incorporates the commitments of the social majority. In support of this idea, this chapter analyzed the experiences in three countries. With regards to Bolivia and Puerto Rico, their current constitutions were the result of democratic and popular creation processes. As a result, their courts have consistently used historical devices as authoritative in terms of constitutional meaning. With regards to Australia, its constitutional creation process lacked many of these characteristics, which has resulted in history having considerably less weight in constitutional analysis. Beyond its specific arguments, the overall goal of the chapter has been to emphasize the need for a common conceptual language that will permit constitutional decision-makers, in considering the role of history and other devices, to approach their roles from a shared starting point and an agreed-upon framework.

Bibliography

Ackerman BA, 'The Storrs Lectures: Discovering the Constitution' (1984) 93 Yale LJ 1013, 1051.

Arato A, 'Forms of Constitution Making and Theories of Democracy', (1995) 17 Cardozo L Rev 191, 192.

Balkin J, 'The New Originalism and the Uses of History' (2013) 82 Fordham L Rev 641.

Bercot E, 'Forgetting to Weight: The Use of History in the Supreme Court's Establishment Clause' (2014) 102 Geo LJ 845, 864–74.

Blount J, Elkins Z & Ginsburg T, 'Does the Process of Constitution-Making Matter' in Tom Ginsburg (ed), *Comparative Constitutional Design* (Cambridge University Press 2012) 34–35.

or what they said is itself unclear or divided'. ibid 127. This may be due both to the age of the constitution and the particular process of its creation, which differs from more modern experiences that tend to be considerably more deliberate.

Brown RL, 'History for the Non-Originalist' (2003) 26 Harv JL & Pub Pol'y 69.
Eisgruber CL, 'The Living Hand of the Past: History and Constitutional Justice' (1997) 65 Fordham L Rev 1611.
Elkins Z, Ginsburg T & Blount J, 'The Citizen as Founder: Public Participation in Constitutional Approval' (2008) 81 Temp L Rev 361.
Elster J, 'Clearing and Strengthening the Channels of Constitution Making' in Tom Ginsburg (ed), *Comparative Constitutional Design* (Cambridge University Press 2012) 16–17.
Farinacci-Fernós JM, 'Originalism in Puerto Rico: Original Explication and its Relation with Clear Text, Broad Purpose and Progressive Policy' (2016) 85 Rev Jur UPR 203.
Farinacci-Fernós JM 'Original Explication and Post-Liberal Constitutionalism: The Role of Intent and History in the Judicial Enforcement of Teleological Constitutions' (SJD dissertation, Georgetown University Law Center 2017).
Farinacci-Fernós JM, 'When Social History Becomes a Constitution: The Bolivian Post-Liberal Experiment and the Central Role of History and Intent in Constitutional Adjudication' (2017) 47 Sw L Rev 101, 151, 155–56.
Farinacci-Fernós JM, 'Looking for the Correct Tool for the Job: Methodological Models of Constitutional Interpretation and Adjudication' (2018) 52 Rev Jur UIPR 213, 229–230, 216.
Farinacci-Fernós JM, 'Post-Liberal Constitutionalism' (2018) 54 Tulsa L Rev 1, 35, 39–41, 44, 46.
Farinacci-Fernós JM, 'South Africa's Forward-Looking Constitutional Revolution and the Role of Courts in Achieving Substantive Constitutional Goals' (2019) 53 Rev Jur UIPR 531.
Farinacci-Fernós JM, 'The Constitution is Dead! Long Live the Constitution!' (2020) 25 Barry L Rev 35.
Festa MJ, 'Applying a Usable Past: The Use of History in Law' (2008) 38 Seton Hall L Rev 479, 497–98.
Goldsworthy J, 'Australia: Devotion to Legalism' in Jeffrey Goldsworthy (ed), *Interpreting Constitutions: A Comparative Study* (Oxford University Press 2007) 106, 109–10, 116–17, 124–25, 127.
Greene J, 'On the Origins of Originalism' (2009) 88 Tex L Rev 1, 40–41.
Greene J, 'Selling Originalism' (2009) 97 Geo LJ 657, 664.
Jefferson Powell H, 'The Original Understanding of Original Intent' (1985) 98 Harv L Rev 885.
Kay RS, 'Adherence to Original Intentions in Constitutional Adjudication: Three Objections and Responses' (1988) 82 Nw U L Rev. 226, 285.
Kleinhaus EA, 'History as Precedent: The Post-Originalist Problem in Constitutional Law' (2000) 110 Yale LJ 121, 129.

Landau JL, 'A Judge's Perspective on the Use and Misuse of History in State Constitutional Interpretation' (2004) 38 Val U L Rev. 451.
Lawson G, 'On Reading Recipes and Constitutions' (1997) 85 Geo LJ 1823.
Lerner H, *Making Constitutions in Deeply Divided Societies* (Cambridge University Press 2011) 26.
McConnell MW, 'Textualism and the Dead Hand of the Past' (1998) 66 Geo Wash L Rev 1127, 1128.
Nelson WE, 'History and Neutrality in Constitutional Adjudication' (1986) 72 Va L Rev 1237.
Parnes E, 'They the People: A Third-Party Beneficiary Approach to Constitutional Interpretation' (2003) 43 Santa Clara L Rev 495.
Peters CJ, 'What Lies Beneath: Interpretive Methodology, Constitutional Authority, and the Case of Originalism' [2013] BYU L Rev 1251.
Primus RA, 'Judicial Power and Mobilizing History', (2006) 65 Md L Rev 171, 177.
Sajo A, 'Constitutional Adjudication in Light of Discourse Theory' (1996) 17 Cardozo L Rev 1193, 1197.
Samaha AM, 'Dead Hand Arguments and Constitutional Interpretation' (2008) 108 Colum L Rev 606, 622.
Solum LB, 'The Interpretation-Construction Distinction' (2010) 27 Const. Comment. 95.
Wofford JG, 'The Blinding Light: The Uses of History in Constitutional Interpretation' (1964) 31 U Chi L Rev 502, 532.

CHAPTER 3

Memory as Mantle

Evil Pasts and Judges' Power in Germany and South Africa

Justin Collings

1 Introduction

Nothing favors constitutional courts like calamity – or so one might conclude after tracking the rise and spread of constitutional judicial review over the last seventy years. Constitutional courts have tended to emerge where disaster has struck. They have risen largely in the aftermath of oppression and misrule: after fascism in the 1950s, after authoritarianism in the 1970s, after communism in the 1990s, after colonialism at various times in the Global South. There are, of course, exceptions to this general trend. But the exceptions have followed the trend rather than inspired it. Historical causation is always uncertain, but the rise and reign of constitutional justice is unimaginable without the towering evils of the twentieth century.

Constitutional judges surely know this. In many jurisdictions, they realize that their institutional existence depends on past evils. They recognize, too, their constant need for institutional legitimacy, and they understand that such legitimacy is a delicate thing – often contested, always in flux, never to be taken for granted. Many have found in memory a powerful legitimating resource. Constitutional courts frequently invoke historical evil as an exercise in self-legitimation. They thus invert the famous dictum, variously attributed to Madame de Pompadour and Louis XIV: *Après nous le déluge*. Courts remind readers of the flood that came before. Without the justices' watchful care, they warn, it might return.

Although many courts wrap themselves in the mantle of memory, some do so with unusual frequency and force. This suggests that the past is central to such courts' self-understanding. Two of the world's most iconic constitutional courts – the German Federal Constitutional Court and the Constitutional Court of South Africa – have been particularly attuned to the past. Both courts have presented themselves as key to their countries' institutional response to historical evil – to Nazism in Germany, to settler colonialism and apartheid in South Africa. Of the two, the South African Court has been more fulsome in forging rhetorical links to a repudiated past. But the German Court's

 | DOI:10.1163/9789004523739_005

comparatively sparing invocations of Nazism have been no less effective in casting the Court as a symbol of renewal and a bulwark against recidivism. The connection, indeed, often goes without saying. Perhaps it might go without saying in South Africa as well.[1] But the Court there never tires of saying it. In any event, the ways in which the two courts invoke the evil past illuminate their self-understanding and highlight a core strategy of self-legitimation. These insights matter at a time when some find historical evil increasingly less persuasive as a basis for constitutional legitimacy. In South Africa, passionate voices object that the evils are not merely historic, and that the past has not yet passed.

The lessons from these two jurisdictions might be generalizable. Memory wars rage across the globe. An international populist insurgency fuels and exploits a widespread wish to honor prouder pasts – to celebrate ancient glories and make nations great again. That impulse is flatly at odds with a global constitutionalism aimed at righting recent (or now not-so-recent) wrongs. The self-understanding of the populists and the self-understanding of the courts are both informed by memory. But they are informed in diametrically opposing ways. This is one reason, among others, why populists rail against constitutional judges (excepting, of course, those appointed by populists in power). The clash is unlikely to subside soon. Whether memory as mantle will remain viable as a strategy of high-court self-legitimation is an open question.

This chapter seeks to illuminate such questions by exploring how the German and South African courts have invoked evil pasts to legitimate their present power. Legitimacy, of course, is a protean concept, elusive and slippery, with many meanings. I refer both to moral and rhetorical legitimacy and to a court's more basic capacity to get its judgments accepted and its authority recognized consistently over time.[2] When these two Courts invoke the memories of Nazism and apartheid, they are reaching beyond a narrow audience of expert insiders to persuade a broader public to accept both the outcome of a

1 See Jonathan Lewis, 'The Constitutional Court of South Africa: An Evaluation' (2009) 125 Law Quarterly Review 440, 442 ('It is supererogatory to remind lawyers in recent judgments that the introduction of the interim Constitution in 1994 heralded a new legal order. A habit of doing this is only explicable as unskilled prolixity or a manifestation of the idealist approach.').

2 For a sampling of the vast literature on judicial legitimacy, see Tara Leigh Grove, 'The Supreme Court's Legitimacy Dilemma' (2019) 132 Harv L Rev 2240; James L Gibson and Michael J Nelson, 'Is the U.S. Supreme Court's Legitimacy Grounded in Performance Satisfaction and Ideology?' (2015) 59 Am J Pol Sci 162; Brandon L Bartels and Christopher D Johnston, 'On the Ideological Foundations of Supreme Court Legitimacy in the American Public' (2013) 57 Am J Pol Sci 184.

given case and, more important, their own institutional authority writ large. By invoking evil pasts, the justices are arguing in an ethical mode.[3] They are making specific assertions about constitutional identity and constitutional values. And they are asserting a moral claim, often implicit, regarding their right to safeguard that identity and enforce those values.

Sometimes such invocations underwrite aggressive uses of judicial power. Both Courts have invoked the past to justify enforcing constitutional provisions in a robust, expansive, and purposive way. But they have also invoked the past to underwrite deference. The evil past can thus be invoked to support both aggression ('We know a rat when we see one …') and restraint (' … but this isn't a rat.'). Across the board in both jurisdictions, the constitution's pre-history has been central to the Court's self-understanding. In both cases, that self-understanding is under pressure. But neither Court shows any indication of backing down.

2 Germany

The (West) German Basic Law of 1949 was an overtly aversive,[4] never-again document. Its references to Nazism were muted and implicit. But its responses to Nazism were unmistakable and pronounced. Structurally, it was designed to remedy the Weimar constitution's putative flaws – those that made it vulnerable to demolition from within. This is the deep explanation for the Basic Law's 'militant democracy' provisions, which, among other things, allow for the exclusion of very small parties from Parliament and for the banning of anti-constitutional parties altogether. Similarly, in its rights catalogue, the Basic Law enshrines those rights that the Nazis had most flagrantly abused.

The Basic Law launched new institutions and new procedures, including a new court to guard and enforce it. The Federal Constitutional Court (*Bundesverfassungsgericht*) became the institutional face of the never-again constitution. Its early personnel confirmed the rupture with the past. Most early justices had suffered personally under Nazism. Some had lost jobs or even spouses; others had emigrated under duress. Some were of Jewish descent – the highest-ranking Jews in the postwar German state. Many had no prior judicial experience and were thus untainted by the Third Reich judiciary's

3 See Philip Bobbitt, *Constitutional Fate: Theory of the Constitution* (1982) 93–119.
4 See Kim Lane Scheppele, 'Aspirational and Aversive Constitutionalism: The Case for Studying Cross-Constitutional Influence through Negative Models' (2003) 1 Int l J Const L 296.

complicity in misrule.[5] The justices rarely mentioned their broadly anti-Nazi backgrounds. They didn't need to. It went without saying. But it was crucial to their collective identity and institutional self-understanding, and it provided a glaring contrast with some of the Court's most vocal early foes.

From the beginning, the Court stressed the Basic Law's repudiation of the past and the justices' role in preserving it. The State constituted by the Basic Law, the justices agreed, was the antithesis – designedly so – of the Third Reich. The Basic Law enshrined the values that Nazism perverted. It offered democracy for autocracy, the rule of law for the ruler's whim, and fundamental rights for state criminality. It was a bulwark against repetition, a project of redemption. The new constitutional order, the justices ruled in October 1952, was 'tied to values. It is the opposite of the total State, which as the exclusive governing power rejects human dignity, liberty, and equality.'[6]

Although they underscored the rule of law as a response to Nazism, the justices made clear that it wasn't synonymous with legal positivism. Indeed, the painful past warned against positivism's perils. As the justices wrote in a December 1953 judgment, 'Precisely the period of the National Socialist regime in Germany taught that even the Legislature can establish injustice [*Unrecht*].'[7] Accordingly, the legal system must, in extreme cases, grant greater weight to 'material justice' than to 'legal security.'[8] This meant, among other things, that even constitutional provisions were subject to the Court's review. The constitution itself made certain principles and provisions – those guaranteeing human dignity, federalism, and social democracy – unamendable.[9]

The Court stressed the constitution's core values even more dramatically in the *Lüth* judgment of January 1958. The politics of the past permeated *Lüth*. The case arose when its namesake, Erich Lüth, adjured his fellow citizens to boycott the first postwar film of Veit Harlan, Nazism's star filmmaker and creator of the venomously anti-Semitic movie *Jud Süss*.[10] Lüth thought Harlan's

---

5 On the first generation of German justices, see Richard Ley, 'Die Erstbesetzung des Bundesverfassungsgerichts' (1982) 13 *Zeitschrift für Parlamentsfragen* 528; Justin Collings, *Democracy's Guardians: A History of the German Federal Constitutional Court, 1951–2001* (2015) 5–9.

6 2 BVerfGE 1, 12 (1952).

7 See 3 BVerfGE 225, 232 (1953).

8 ibid.

9 Art. 79(3) GG.

10 Harlan was the only artist prosecuted after the War for crimes against humanity. He was acquitted in April 1949. On his trial, see Peter Reichel and Harald Schmid, *Von der Katastrophe zum Stolperstein* (2005) 34ff. On Harlan more generally, see Ingrid Buchloh, *Veit Harlan – Goebbels' Starregisseur* (Ferdinand Schöningh, 2010); Thomas Harlan, *Veit* (Rowohlt, 2011).

return would ruin German film and imperil (West) Germany's international rehabilitation. But when he called for a boycott, the new film's producers sued him for harming their financial interests in a manner averse to 'public morals' – a tortious offense under Section 823 of the Civil Code. Lüth lost, at trial and on appeal. He finally took his cause to Karlsruhe, where his complaint sat in the Constitutional Court's inbox for six years.

In reversing the judgments against Lüth, the Constitutional Court rebuked the lower courts for their jaundiced understanding of 'public morals.' Lüth's appeal for a boycott, the justices observed, did not offend public morals; in its concern for Germany's moral standing after Nazi misrule, it embodied them.[11] Lüth's campaign, the Court's First Senate insisted, must be considered in light of his 'general political and cultural-political efforts.'[12] Those efforts aimed at preventing the perception – especially among foreigners – that little had changed in German cultural life since 1945. 'Nothing,' the justices wrote, 'so damaged Germany's standing [in the world] as the savage persecution of Jews by National Socialism.' This being so, Germany had an overwhelming interest in reassuring a wary world 'that the German people have turned away from and condemn this mentality, not for reasons of political opportunism, but from an insight into its reprehensibility won through individual internal repentance.'[13]

The justices' sympathy for Lüth was obvious. They praised his efforts to improve relations between Christians and Jews and between West Germany and Israel.[14] Technically, the content of Lüth's statements was irrelevant to the Court's constitutional free-speech analysis (though the justices rebuked a lower-court finding that they offended the 'outlook of sensible ... and right-thinking citizens').[15] But implicit in the Court's judgment was the justices' conviction that, if free speech had any value at all, it was in protecting citizens' right to denounce the Nazi past and divide it from the Republican present. Elsewhere in the opinion, the justices quoted (in English) Benjamin Cardozo's observation that free speech constitutes 'the matrix, the indispensable condition of nearly every other form of freedom.'[16] That indispensable condition absorbed the anti-Nazi orientation inherent in the Basic Law's 'objective system of values.'[17]

11 7 BVerfGE at 221–230.
12 ibid 216.
13 ibid.
14 ibid 218.
15 ibid 230.
16 ibid 208.
17 ibid 205.

More than sixty years after it was decided, *Lüth* remains the largest landmark in the Court's history.[18] In *Lüth*, the Court characterized the constitution – especially its rights catalog – as an 'objective system of values' whose influence radiated throughout the legal order and encompassed all legal relations.[19] This meant that even relations between private parties were governed by fundamental rights protections and that all private law provisions must be construed in light of the constitution's spirit. On the Court's reading, fundamental rights were not merely defensive shields against the state; they were objective values that infused and informed the whole of legal life.

The passages that make *Lüth* famous did not invoke the Nazi past. But the case's context made the association obvious. Indeed, the row between Erich Lüth and Veit Harlan was a microcosm for the contrast between the Federal Republic and the Third Reich – between the democratic present and the evil past. It has always mattered, although it has rarely been spelled out, that the Constitutional Court founded its revolutionary rights jurisprudence while handing defeat to Nazism's most unsavory artist. It was the perfect setting for a judgment that did more than any other to expand the constitution's – and the justices' – breathtaking influence and power.

2.1 *Memory and the Rule of Law*

In time, *Lüth* would be hailed as a key contribution in the democratization of postwar German politics and society. And the perception that the Court helped democratize German politics and society has been central to its enduring legitimacy.[20] Early on, however, the Court was valued more for helping to restore the rule of law than for helping to revive democracy. The watchword of its early champions was *Rechtsstaat*, not *Demokratie*. In a host of early cases, the Court asserted rule-of-law principles against the explicit backdrop of their perversion by the Third Reich.

One such principle was the Court's own power of review. 'During the time of National Socialist rule,' the Court observed, less than six months after opening its doors, 'the right of the judge to examine laws and ordinances as

---

18 7 BVerfGE 198 (1958). For discussions of *Lüth*, see Thomas Henne and Arne Riedlinger (eds), *Das Lüth-Urteil aus (rechts-)historischer Sicht. Die Konflikte um Veit Harlan und die Grundrechtsjudikatur des Bundesverfassungsgerichts* (Berliner Wissenschafts-Verlag, 2005); Dieter Grimm, 'Die Karriere eines Boykottaufrufs' *Die Zeit* (27 September 2001); Friedrich Kübler, 'Lüth – eine sanfte Revolution' (2000) 83 Kritische Vierteljahresschrift für Gesetzgebung und Rechtswissenschaft 313.

19 ibid 205.

20 That, at least, is the argument of my own history of the Court. See Collings (n 6).

incompatible with the authoritarian conception of the state was generally denied.'[21] Under the Basic Law, things were different. Constitutional judicial review was central to the constitution's response to Nazism. Against that backdrop, the justices read their mandate broadly and with mounting confidence.

Such confidence was on display in the early Court's most powerful invocation of the Nazi past: a 1953 judgment dealing with Nazi-era civil servants, hosts of whom had challenged a law that granted them generous reintegration and partial back pay. The challengers claimed they had a right to *automatic* reintegration and *complete* back payment. They argued that civil servants were officers of the eternal German state, not of its transitory rulers. On this view, their relations with the state were perpetual; they survived regime change and even constitutional revolution; they endured seamlessly and without interruption across the Nazi avulsion.

The Court answered these claims with a bombshell. Its judgment was long – 104 printed pages flanked by seventeen headnotes, one with six subheadings.[22] But the Court answered the key question in single short sentence: 'All civil service ties were abolished on 8 May 1945,' the date of Germany's unconditional surrender. The implications were as dramatic as they were obvious. Nazi-era civil servants lost their jobs when Germany lost the War. Their claims dissolved when the State collapsed. On that State's successor they had no claims at all. Those dismissed at War's end had not been indefinitely suspended; they had been terminated for good and all. Whatever they received from the new Federal Republic in the way of recompense or reinstatement, they received only by Parliament's grace.

The Court's path to this stark conclusion was relentless, thorough, and, for the complainants, devastating. The conclusion rested on crucial observations about the Nazi State and its ties with the civil service.

Those relations, the justices said, were revolutionary. The Nazis had transformed the bureaucracy beyond recognition. National Socialism sought definitively to crush the traditional, non-partisan State.[23] It saw the State as 'an apparatus of power in the service of "the People" (*das Volk*),' and it equated the People's will with the Nazi party.[24] That the State was subservient to the People and that the People were embodied in the Party led naturally to a conception of the State as the instrument (*Werkzeug*) of the Party – the instrument, in

21 1 BVerfGE 184, 194 (1952).
22 See 3 BVerfGE 58 (17 December 1953).
23 ibid 85.
24 ibid 86.

practice, of the Führer's unfettered rule.[25] Legislation, administration, and even adjudication all centered on the *Führer*, as articulated in Carl Schmitt's 1934 article (which the justices cited), 'The Führer Protects the Law.'

'Thus,' the Court observed, 'the State became a dictatorship in which the Party Führer, endowed with limitless power which he at once stretched to its utmost technical possibilities, arbitrarily set in motion the state power apparatus toward the fulfillment of his plans.'[26] The State, in short, became Hitler's State – a 'centralized power state' (*zentraler Machtsstaat*) that allowed the *Führer* to 'pursue his political goals in the War against nearly every Great Power of the world.'[27]

This was the State that collapsed on 8 May 1945, and its collapse was total – militarily, financially, and economically.[28] (The Court might have added *morally*.) The debacle was so dramatic as to raise doubts whether the German Reich continued to exist.[29] Even assuming that it did, there were compelling reasons to conclude that the status of its civil servants did not.

Those civil servants, moreover, took their oath of loyalty not to the German State but to the person of Adolf Hitler. They swore they would 'be faithful and obedient to the Führer of the German Reich and [German] People, Adolf Hitler; honor the laws; and conscientiously fulfill the duties of my office, so help me God.'[30] That oath suggested, in the Court's view, that civil servants' status was 'utterly dependent on the continuance of the National Socialist form of rule embodied in Hitler.'[31] This suggestion was amply confirmed by Nazi-era civil service legislation, all of which stressed the civil servant's duty to serve the Party State.[32] Contemporary legal scholars had taken a similar view, and the Court marshaled quotations to that effect.[33] The same was true of the Nazi-era judiciary.[34] The Court concluded that the civil servants' legal status had morphed from partisan neutrality and loyalty to the State to 'personal loyalty to Hitler and … dependence on the NSDAP.'[35] It followed that their official status and legal rights endured only as long as Hitler remained in power and his Party

25 ibid.
26 ibid.
27 ibid.
28 ibid 87–88.
29 ibid 88.
30 ibid 99.
31 ibid 101.
32 ibid 101–103.
33 ibid 103–108.
34 ibid 94–95.
35 ibid 95.

ruled the State. It followed, that is, that their offices and rights were abolished on 8 May 1945. Q.E.D.

In its sweeping indictment, the Court spared no branch of the civil service. But universities came in for special censure,[36] and legal scholars, stung to the quick, attacked the judgment with full-throated ferocity. So did prominent judges. Both judges and jurists were among the civil servants whose allegiance to Hitler the Court had denounced.

The justices did not rush to answer their critics. But they did answer them eventually, with merciless assiduity, in a judgment dated 19 February 1957. In that later judgment, the Court chronicled in chilling detail just how pervasively and perniciously Nazism's spirit and aims had permeated the German administrative state.[37] The justices recanted nothing, and they added fuel to the flame. Some critics were answered with citations to their own Nazi-era publications. The Court thus discredited its detractors with reminders of their records.

The civil servants judgments forcefully distanced the Court from the old regime. By exposing the cancers of the Nazi-era administration, the justices brandished their own anti-Fascist credentials. It prepared them to assert the total constitution as a response to the total state, which they did a year later in *Lüth*.

2.2 *Memory and Restraint*

The early German Court wasn't always so bold, either in its encounters with the government or its engagement with the past. On many fronts, the Court began cautiously, upholding residual Nazi-era legislation whenever, under any plausible reading, the laws could be construed as pursuing 'system-neutral' goals through constitutional means.[38] The justices noted that some laws promulgated under the Nazi tyranny (*Gewaltherrschaft*) contained 'such a measure of injustice and general perniciousness' that 'any validity as law must be denied them,' but this was not true of every law passed from 1933 to 1945.[39] Although

36 ibid 141–143.

37 6 BVerfGE 132 (1957).

38 See Ulrich Löffler, *Instrumentalisierte Vergangenheit? Die nationalsozialistische Vergangenheit als Argumentationsfigur in der Rechtsprechung des Bundesverfassungsgerichts* (Peter Lang, 2004) 39.

39 ibid 414 (citing the *Gestapo* judgment).

the Court inevitably struck down laws it deemed 'typically National Socialist,'[40] there was no presumption against laws with an offending date of birth.

In some early cases, moreover, the Court might well have invoked the Nazi past but chose not to. The most dramatic was its 1957 judgment upholding a law that criminalized male (but not female) gay sex.[41] The judgment cited expert evidence about the dangers of male homosexuality but said nothing about the persecution of gay men under the Third Reich. That same year, the Court ruled that the Concordat between the Nazi regime and the Holy See was still in force, even though the treaty was concluded, on the German side, thanks to the notorious 'enabling law' (*Ermächtigungsgesetz*) of 1933; and even though the Nazi regime repeatedly violated the treaty's terms.[42] Nearly a decade later, in 1966, an evenly divided Court declined to condemn the arrest of editors at *Der Spiegel*, the country's most popular and provocative news weekly, during a midnight government raid that, for some, recalled oppressions of earlier times.[43]

Sometimes the past was invoked more forcefully by the advocates who opposed a law than by the Court that reviewed it. In December 1970, for instance, the Constitutional Court upheld a controversial set of 'Emergency Laws' (*Notstandsgesetze*), including a constitutional amendment, that allowed (during emergencies) state surveillance without judicial process.[44] The constitution envisioned, and the Court had earlier recognized, the possibility of unconstitutional constitutional amendments. But a majority deemed the challenged provisions merely 'system-immanent modifications of general constitutional principles' that otherwise retained full force.[45] The laws' opponents had invoked the Nazi precedent incessantly, branding the reforms 'NS Laws,' with 'NS' signaling 'National Socialist' as well as 'emergency' (*Notstand*). The majority never mentioned Nazism, whereas its reliance on the concept of 'militant democracy' pointed to the Weimar constitution's vulnerability to internal threats.

Even in matters of lesser public moment, the Court was mnemonically restrained. In 1973, for instance, the Court upheld a ban on *Mephisto*, a

40 In his comprehensive study of the Court's references to Nazism, Ulrich Löffler identified only five cases: 2 BVerfGE 307, 329 (1953); 8 BVerfGE 71, 78 (1958); 11 BVerfGE 6, 32 (1960); 13 BVerfGE 291, 301 (1962); 20 BVerfGE 150, 151, 160 (1966). See Löffler (n 39) 39.

41 6 BVerfGE 389 (1957).

42 6 BVerfGE 309, 334–5 (1957).

43 20 BVerfGE 162 (1966).

44 30 BVerfGE 1 (1970).

45 ibid 29.

roman-à-clef by Klaus Mann.[46] The novel was an acerbic and thinly-veiled portrait of Mann's onetime brother-in-law, Gustav Gründgens, whom Mann accused of prostituting his theatrical talents to serve the Third Reich. By a vote of 5-to-3, the Court ruled that, by enjoining the novel's publication, the lower court had not unreasonably balanced the conflicting values of personal honor and freedom of speech. Only one dissenter noted the relevance of Mann's role in the anti-Nazi resistance and of the novel's importance as a document of the German past.[47]

2.3 *Memory and Assertion*

The first time the German Constitutional Court invoked the Nazi past to support invalidating a national law came in 1975 when its First Senate quashed a statute legalizing abortion in the first trimester.[48] The invocation was intensely controversial. In response to government claims that West Germany's abortion reform was consistent with developments in other liberal democracies – with statutes in France and Britain, with judicial decrees in the U.S. – a majority of the Court's First Senate observed that in Germany the right to life was different and special. It was a right whose animating spirit and underlying principles could be explained only by reference to 'historical experience and the moral and spiritual contestation with the predecessor system of National Socialism.'[49] As an answer to a system in which an omnipotent State asserted 'unbounded power over all spheres of social life and in which regard for the life of the individual had no essential meaning in the pursuit of state objectives,' the postwar constitution had 'established a values-based order that placed the individual human being and his dignity at the center of all its regulations.'[50]

That value system rested on the proposition that 'within the order of creation, man possesses an independent worth, one that demands imperatively an unconditional respect for the life of every individual human ... and that therefore precludes, absent justifying reasons, the destruction of such life.'[51] The majority hastened to add that its comments on the relationship between the Nazi past and the right to life entailed no 'disparaging judgment about other legal orders that have not had these experiences with a tyrannical system, and that, on the basis of a different historical development, different political conditions, and different core philosophies of the state' have reached

46 30 BVerfGE 173 (1973).
47 ibid 225 (Rupp-von Brünneck J dissenting).
48 39 BVerfGE 1 (1975).
49 ibid 1, 67.
50 ibid.
51 ibid.

different conclusions.[52] But at the rhetorical climax of its judgment, the majority insisted that in Germany the right to life was different because German history was different. The justices in the Court's majority maintained that their judgment – which required the State to criminalize conduct that Parliament had tried to allow – was impelled and informed by the lessons of history.

In an impassioned dissent, Justices Wiltraut Rupp-von Brünneck and Helmut Simon insisted that the majority had gotten its history lesson precisely backward. The Nazis themselves, they noted, had criminalized advertisements for abortions or abortifacients, and had stiffened existing criminal sanctions for abortions.[53] For the dissenters, the Basic Law's 'decisive repudiation of the totalitarian National Socialist state' commanded caution in the context of criminal punishment, 'the misuse of which has already brought endless suffering to the history of humanity.'[54] The constitutional repudiation of Nazism also counseled a decent respect for other European constitutional traditions.[55] Some of those traditions were impressive and praiseworthy.[56] They, too, were informed by 'historical experience with a humanity-disdaining tyrannical system.'[57] These traditions' commitment to protecting human life was certainly not less than West Germany's. Their response to social and legal dilemmas like abortion should, the dissenters argued, prompt engaged discussion in the Federal Republic.[58] At the very least, similar reform provisions in other liberal states confirmed that the response of the West German legislature was reasonable, and that it honored the right to life.[59] By implication, one of the constitutional legacies of the past was the need for conscious, present-day engagement with, and membership within, the community of Western democracies.

The German Court's first abortion case makes clear that memory's mantle has multiple sides. The same past can be invoked in opposite directions and to different ends. The majority judgment also illustrates how an exquisitely intrusive exercise of judicial power – one that not only *prevented* the State from encroaching on individual rights but *required* the State to shield such rights against third-party threats and to do so with the backing of criminal

52 ibid 67–68 (internal citation omitted).

53 ibid.

54 ibid 77.

55 The dissenters pointed out that legislatures in Austria, France, Denmark, Sweden, and Great Britain had all adopted some form of a period solution. Ibid 94.

56 ibid.

57 ibid. In the German: 'einige von ihnen haben ebenfalls geschichtliche Erfahrungen mit einem menschenverachtenden Unrechtssystem.'

58 ibid 94–95.

59 ibid 94.

sanctions – can be bolstered by invoking an evil past. It also shows how memory can underwrite exceptionalism – how a court that wishes to chart a new path can draw support from a singular past.

The abortion judgment marked a flashpoint in the Court's mounting confrontation with a reformist government. The clash became a crisis, subsiding only when the Court unanimously upheld a landmark labor law in a deferential judgment of 1979.[60] Thereafter, the Court returned to a more deferential posture vis-à-vis the political branches, especially after 1982, when the reformist governing coalition (which had long since lost its reformist zeal) was replaced by a conservative one. The Court's invocations of the Nazi past became more sparing as well.

2.4 *Memory and Method*

Throughout its history, the German Court has occasionally brought the Nazi past to bear on questions of interpretive method. For example, the Court has invoked the Nazi past to reject rigid positivism. In a 1980 judgment, for instance, the Court noted that Article 116 of the Basic Law, which restored German citizenship to those who lost it under the Third Reich, was informed by 'the insight' that State acts did not become law merely by complying with established procedures. They must additionally honor 'fundamental principles of the idea of justice.'[61] Three decades previously, an earlier generation of justices had made the same point in the Court's very first judgment.[62]

The Court has also noted from time to time that a particular right must be read through the prism of the past. This often meant that the right must be understood broadly and robustly. In 1981, for instance, the Court ruled that constitutional guarantees of bodily integrity protected citizens against psychic as well as physical injuries.[63] A 'narrow construction,' the justices wrote, 'would not do justice to the fundamental right's function as a defensive right against government encroachments such as through psychic tortures, emotional torments, and their corresponding methods of interrogation. In any case,' they concluded, 'because the inclusion of this right arose in response to experiences during the Third Reich, this point of view may not be neglected entirely.'[64] In this and other cases, the past informed and sometimes expanded rights.

---

60 50 BVerfGE 290 (1979).

61 54 BVerfGE 53, 67–68 (1980).

62 1 BVerfGE 14, 61 (1951).

63 56 BVerfGE 54 (1981). Since 1981 (if not earlier), of course, the distinction between 'psychic' and 'physical' has been increasingly contested by scientists of numerous stripes.

64 ibid 75.

Sometimes, too, the Court has stressed that the Basic Law was designed as a global response to Nazism, and that its core values were the antithesis of Nazism's frenzied anti-values. In one 1983 judgment, the justices wrote that '[t]he Basic Law's *Rechtsstaat* differs from the National Socialist tyranny precisely in the fact that it regards respect for human dignity as its noblest duty (Art. 1(1) GG) and in this regard does not inquire into ancestry, race, religion, political views, or membership in other groups.'[65] No one could be denied such dignity, the justices added, not even the most heinously offending criminals.[66]

By contrast, the Court has sometimes highlighted how certain rights responded to the Nazi past, only to conclude that the relevant rights were nonetheless limited in scope or not implicated in the case at hand.[67] Elsewhere, the Court has invoked Nazi precedents to argue that rights enshrined in response to those precedents should not be unduly extended. The constitutional ban on forced labor, for example, was issued with a view to 'the forms of compulsory labor, with their degradation of the human personality, that became common in the National Socialist system,' as well as the 'compulsory measures then enforced in areas ruled by communism.'[68] With that concrete purpose in mind, the Court ruled in 1987 that the ban did not extend to work requirements levied by juvenile courts.

Most of the Court's invocations of Nazism have come in fundamental rights cases. But as it matured, the Court also invoked the evil past in cases about constitutional structure. One example is a 1988 judgment preserving a measure of municipal autonomy.[69] In its judgment, the Court noted 'that municipal constitutional law and reality have been defined since the collapse of the National Socialist regime by a tendency to push back against the bureaucratic-authoritative element and to give heightened application to the idea of municipal citizens' rights of self-determination.'[70] The past thus pointed to limits on the general, centralizing thrust that the Court at times had hastened or approved.

In structural cases as in fundamental rights cases, the Court has invoked Nazism to underwrite deference as well as intervention. Such deferential invocations have two aims. They signal that, even though the Court has stayed its hand, it has not abdicated its role as guardian; and they show respect for

65 64 BVerfGE 261, 284 (1983).
66 ibid.
67 See, e.g., 56 BVerfGE 22, 32 (1981).
68 74 BVerfGE 102, 116 (1987).
69 79 BVerfGE 127 (1988).
70 ibid.

political actors' own efforts to come to terms with the past. In this respect, the German Court has, with few exceptions, been consistently cautious and restrained in its invocations of the Nazi past. But the exceptions have been colossal. The Court, it might seem, has stored mnemonic capital for when it has really needed it.

As prominent examples of mnemonic deference, consider a pair of judgments, one from 1983 and one from 2005, in which the Court approved decisions by chancellors Helmut Kohl and Gerhard Schroeder to fake no-confidence votes to trigger snap elections.[71] In both judgments, the Court dwelt at some length on the Weimar-era crisis of parliamentary democracy – which enabled, of course, the Nazi demolition of democracy – but had little to say about the 'chancellor democracy' that had developed in the postwar era.[72] In both cases, the Court invoked the past to justify deferring to political decisions of dramatic importance but dubious constitutionality. In both cases, the Court conjured the past to justify staying its hand.

2.5 *Forever in the Shadow?*

The influence of the Nazi past has perhaps been most palpable when parties have invoked the anti-Nazi constitution to shield pro-Nazi speech. In such settings, the Court has sometimes carved exceptions to general constitutional guarantees. In an April 1994 judgment, for instance, the Court distinguished between expressions of opinion and factual assertions on which opinions might be based.[73] When expressions of opinion include demonstrably false assertions of fact, free speech must typically yield to personal honor. The complainants in the case had been denied a permit for a public assembly on the ground that speakers at the gathering would likely deny that the Holocaust happened. The case has come to be known as the 'Auschwitz Lie' (*Auschwitzlüge*) case, after the repulsive slogan of the complainants and their acolytes.

The justices acknowledged that Article 5 protected speech's form as well as its content, and the speakers didn't lose protection simply because their speech was sharp or hurtful.[74] But representations of fact, they added, were not expressions of opinion. Representations of fact that didn't foster public

---

71 62 BVerfGE 1 (1983); 114 BVerfGE 107 (2005).

72 See Florian Meinel, 'The Constitutional Miracle on the Rhine: Towards a History of West German Constitutionalism and the Federal Constitutional Court' (2016) 14 Int l J Const L 277, 290 ('The reader of the cases eventually learns more about pre-history than about history.').

73 90 BVerfGE 241 (1994).

74 ibid 247.

discourse or help shape public opinion enjoyed no constitutional protection.[75] Falsehood never contributed in this way and was, accordingly, unprotected speech.[76] Care must be taken, however, not to chill speech by threatening sanctions for bogus facts.[77] Furthermore, the line between expression of opinion and representation of fact is often hard to draw. Fact and opinion are often intertwined. In cases of mingling, the entire statement should be regarded as an expression of opinion, affording speech the fullest possible protection.[78] But when the 'facts' blended with opinion were demonstrably untrue, free speech must usually yield to personal honor. The relevant inquiry was fact- and context-specific.[79]

In subsequent years, constitutional challenges to prosecutions for Holocaust denial were nonstarters. In 1999, for instance, a three-justice panel of the First Senate rejected out of hand a complaint challenging an administrative court decision that found the complainant guilty of collective libel (*Beleidigung*) for denying the Holocaust. The complaint, the panel held, had no chance of success under Article 5(3) GG, and did not require review by the full Senate.[80]

In 2009, the First Senate reiterated dramatically the exceptional nature of pro-Nazi speech. In March 2005, just before the sixtieth anniversary of Nazism's collapse and the War in Europe's end, the Bundestag amended Section 130 of the Criminal Code – the section dealing with incitement (*Volksverhetzung*) – to include the following provision: 'Anyone who publicly or in a public gathering disrupts the public peace by approving, glorifying, or justifying the violent and tyrannical rule of National Socialism shall be punished with a prison sentence of up to three years or with a fine.'[81] A few months later, local officials in Wunsiedel – a small town in upper Franconia – banned a proposed demonstration in memory of Rudolf Hess, Hitler's 'Deputy Führer' from 1933 to 1941 and, before dying in custody in 1987, the last survivor among those convicted at Nuremberg. Hess was buried in Wunsiedel, and his gravesite became a shrine of Neo-Nazi pilgrimages and annual rallies on the anniversary of his death. The rally's organizers challenged the ban in a constitutional complaint.

In its judgment of 4 November 2009, the Court confirmed the constitutionality of Section 130 and upheld the ban on the Wunsiedel march.[82] In doing

75 ibid.
76 ibid.
77 ibid 248.
78 ibid.
79 ibid 248–249.
80 BVerfG, Beschluss der 1. Kammer des Ersten Senats vom 26. April 1999, 1 BvR 1047/96.
81 StGB s 130(4).
82 See 124 BVerfGE 300 (2009).

so, the justices declared emphatically that Nazi speech was exceptional within free speech law. The justices conceded at the outset that the amendment to the Criminal Code did not fit the traditional exemptions to Article 5 GG. It was not a neutral law of general application. It targeted certain kinds of expression about Nazism and only those.[83] It was, in American parlance, a quintessential content-based restriction. Even so, the justices held, the challenged provision was compatible with Article 5 because it expressed a principle inherent in the German constitutional order:

> In light of the injustice and horror – which defy general categories – that National Socialist rule visited upon Europe and on broad tracts of the world, and in light of the emergence of the Federal Republic, understood as the antithesis [*Gegenentwurf*] to National Socialism, an exception to the ban on content-based laws is inherent in Article 5(1) and (2) GG for provisions that place limits on the propagandistic approval of the National Socialist regime in the years between 1933 and 1945.[84]

Later in the judgment, the justices explained that the Basic Law as a whole should be understood as an antithesis to Nazism. The key passage merits full quotation:

> The humanity-hating regime of this time [1933 to 1945], which brought upon Europe and the world an immeasurable degree of pain, death, and oppression, has an antitypical, identity-forging significance for the constitutional order of the Federal Republic that is unique and cannot be captured solely on the basis of general statutory provisions. Historically, the deliberate repudiation of the tyrannical rule of National Socialism was a central concern of all the forces that took part in the creation and implementation of the Basic Law. Broadly speaking, the Basic Law can be interpreted as the antithesis of the totalitarian regime of National Socialism, and from its overall structure down to many of its details it is designed to learn from historical experiences and to foreclose, once and for all, any repetition of such injustices.[85]

This fundamentally anti-Nazi orientation had shaped 'the entire postwar order and the integration of the Federal Republic of Germany within the community

---

83 ibid 321.

84 ibid 327–28.

85 ibid 328.

of nations' down to the present day.[86] Against this backdrop, speech celebrating Nazism was worse than abhorrent; it was fundamentally destabilizing. 'The endorsement of such rule,' the justices wrote, 'is in Germany an attack on the identity of the polity from within' – an attack, moreover, 'with peace-menacing potential.'[87] This made such speech *sui generis*. Speech celebrating Nazism was 'not comparable with other speech and … can even provoke profound apprehension abroad.'[88] Because anti-Nazism supplied the core of German constitutionalism, pro-Nazi speech defied the general categories of Article 5. Such speech was unique and incomparable. Legislatures may, and courts must, regard it as exceptional.

The First Senate's *Wunsiedel* judgment is a paradigmatic statement of aversive mnemonic jurisprudence. It casts the entire constitutional project as a negative response to Nazism, and concludes on that basis that, where Nazism is concerned, the constitution itself contains inherent exceptions. As Andreas von Arnauld has noted, the Court's anti-Nazi narrative was 'not just employed to give meaning to a specific clause in the Basic Law, but instead to disregard Article 5.2 in favor of an implicit, historically inferred singular exception.'[89] In this particular case, the past's influence supported a deferential outcome. But the judgment's underlying logic was startling. Its core premise was that history doesn't just inform text; sometimes it trumps text. That logic implies stupendous powers for a Court that construes history as well as the constitution.

2.6 *The Waning Logic of* Vergangenheitsbewältigung?

The German Court's continued resort to the Nazi past has drawn criticism. As Florian Meinel has written:

> This tradition of constitutional reasoning is becoming increasingly problematic. As the constitutional logic of *Vergangenheitsbewältigung* (coming to terms with the past) itself is becoming historical, its rhetoric and motivation are increasingly unconvincing: Do the lessons of the past rather call for banning a fascist party or for having more confidence in democratic politics? Does a tough policy on hate speech follow from the past or is it rather the same past's lesson to adopt a more liberal approach? As the constitution endures, the precise meaning of the antithesis which it is supposed to embody, is more and more ambiguous

86 ibid 329.
87 ibid.
88 ibid.
89 Andreas von Arnauld, 'Norms and Narrative' (2017) 18 German Law Journal 309, 317.

> and inconclusive, which of course is as much a legal as a general political and cultural problem.[90]

There is an increasing sense among some observers that the Nazi experience has only limited lessons for the present-day work of the Constitutional Court. There is a sense, moreover, that the Court needs to do more to acknowledge its own historicity – including, as Meinel suggests, the historicity of its invocations of the past.

Recent years have witnessed some signs that the Court *is* taking stock of its own historicity and revisiting its own mnemonic traditions. The most recent episode in the Court's militant democracy jurisprudence provides an impressive example. Since at least 2001, the federal government has sought to ban the far-Right National Democratic Party (NPD). The Court rejected an early petition to ban the party after it was discovered that much of the party's inner circle –perhaps as many as 30 of the top 200 leaders – were undercover agents or informants for the German secret service.[91] The plot to ban the party persisted, however, and the most recent petition prompted full review by the Court's Second Senate in a judgment dated January 2017.

The Court rejected the petition unanimously.[92] It did so despite concluding that the party and its aims were in fact anti-constitutional – just like the German Communist Party that the Court had banned in 1956[93] and the Socialist Reich Party it had banned in 1952.[94] But, in a departure from those earlier cases, the justices declined to ban the NPD. The Second Senate reasoned that the power to ban anti-constitutional political parties was not the power to ban attitudes or worldviews. The Court should not ban a party merely because it embraces anti-constitutional goals; the party must also present some prospect of pursuing those goals successfully. This was clearly not the case with the NPD, a party the justices deemed too insignificant to ban. It was unimaginable that the party could achieve its aims, however repulsive. Under present circumstances, banning the NPD would merely prompt its devotees to regroup under altered guise.

In its *NPD* judgment, the Court spoke as the confident guardian of a mature democracy unthreatened by the NPD's puny and puerile rantings. The core credo of militant democracy had always been that the liberal state must be

90 Meinel (n 73) 289.
91 107 BVerfGE 339 (2003).
92 144 BVerfGE 20 (2017).
93 5 BVerfGE 85 (1956).
94 2 BVerfGE 1 (1952).

willing to fight fire with fire. But in the Federal Republic of 2017, the NPD was not a fire. It was a worm-eaten and soggy match.

Some international commentators saw in this judgment an end to a strand of German constitutional exceptionalism that was often presented as a response to the Nazi past. 'More than seven decades after Hitler,' observed the London *Economist*, 'German democracy and civic society are mature and robust enough to contain this pathogen.' *The Economist* hailed this assessment as 'a historical landmark, for it posits an official end to Germany's special and unique status within Europe in the treatment of right-wing radicalism.'[95] Whether the Court will distance itself from anti-Nazi exceptionalism in other contexts remains to be seen. Such a turn is hardly inevitable. After all, the *NPD* judgment did not renounce militant democracy; it merely found that the NPD was too puny to merit militancy. The judgment by no means forecloses the future banning of a less peripheral party. In any case, after nearly seven decades of mnemonic jurisprudence, it seems safe to predict that, for good or ill, the memory of Nazism will remain a touchstone of German constitutionalism and constitutional jurisprudence. And current events on the European stage, including in Germany itself, suggest that dark pasts may, all too soon, become newly relevant. In parts of Eastern Europe, they already have.

3 South Africa

Like the German Basic Law, South Africa's post-apartheid constitutions – its interim constitution of 1993 and its "permanent" constitution of 1996 – are expressly oriented toward the past. Indeed, they are even more explicit and emphatic in this regard than their German counterpart. 'We, the people of South Africa,' the 1996 document begins, 'recognise the injustices of our past … .'[96] A coda to the interim constitution speaks of building 'a historic bridge between the past of a deeply divided society . . . and a future founded on the recognition of human rights, democracy and peaceful co-existence and development opportunities for all South Africans ….'[97] When Nelson Mandela

95 'Too Peripheral to Matter: Germany's Supreme Court Decides Not to Ban the Neo-Nazi Party,' *The Economist* (London, 17 January 2017) <http://www.economist.com/news/europe/21714770-national-democratic-party-truly-nasty-not-strong-enough-be-able-fulfil-its>.

96 The Constitution of the Republic of South Africa (1996), Preamble.

97 Constitution of the Republic of South Africa Act 200 of 1993, 'National Unity and Reconciliation.'

became South Africa's first post-apartheid president in 1994, he made "never again" his explicit mantra. 'Never, never, and never again,' he thundered, 'shall it be that this beautiful land will again experience the oppression of one by another and suffer the indignity of being the skunk of the world.'[98]

As in Germany, a new constitutional court was created to enforce a constitution designed to repudiate the past. As in Germany, the first generation of justices personally symbolized a constitutional new beginning. In one way or another, the South African Court's first justices had all been prominent in the struggle against apartheid. They also reflected in microcosm something of the aspirational diversity of the rainbow nation. The first Court featured black justices, women justices, a justice of Indian descent, and two justices with physical disabilities. The Court looked at least a little like the country for which it would adjudicate.

This Court invoked the apartheid past volubly, frequently, and from the very beginning. In early cases, justice after justice wrote that the constitution marked 'a dramatic change,'[99] heralding 'a new dispensation.'[100] The constitution highlighted in bold relief the 'stark and dramatic' 'contrast between the past which it repudiates and the future to which it seeks to commit the nation.'[101] It represented 'the most fundamental change in the history of our country.'[102] It trumpeted 'a ringing and decisive break with a past which perpetuated inequality and irrational discrimination and arbitrary governmental and executive action.'[103]

Such phrases are merely illustrative. The apartheid past was the inexorable leitmotif of the Court's early jurisprudence.[104] Concurring in the Court's first judgment, Deputy President Ismail Mahomed wrote a rhetorically ambitious passage centered on a dyadic contrast, not between past and present or

98 Kader Asmal et al (eds), *Nelson Mandela: In His Own Words* (Little, Brown and Co., 2003) 70.

99 *S v Makwanyane* 1995 (3) SA 391 (CC) para 220 (Langa J concurring).

100 ibid.

101 ibid para 261 (Mahomed J concurring).

102 *S v Mhlungu and Others* 1995 (3) SA 867 (CC) para 89 (Kriegler J concurring).

103 ibid para 8.

104 See, e.g., *Shabalala and Five Others v The Attorney-General (Transvaal) and the Commissioner of South African Police* 1996 (1) SA 725 (CC) para 26 (The constitution 'constitutes a decisive break from a culture of Apartheid and racism to a constitutionally protected culture of openness and democracy and universal human rights for South Africans of all ages, classes and colours. There is a stark and dramatic contrast between the past in which South Africans were trapped and the future on which the Constitution is premised.').

present and future, but between 'the past' and 'the Constitution.'[105] The past meant apartheid; the constitution typified its opposite.

That contrast was central to the Court's many global descriptions of the constitution as a whole. The Court frequently referred to the new constitutional order as a new 'dispensation'[106] –deploying the term in a secular sense but with an unmistakable religious resonance. In a December 2014 judgment, Justice Johann van der Westhuizen called the constitution 'the credo that binds our nation together' – a document 'born from our sad history of the violation of virtually all human rights,' one that 'embodies our national vision of the future.'[107] A constitution, he added, has been described as the 'autobiography of the nation,' the 'window to a nation's soul,' and the 'mirror through which a society views itself.'[108] As guardian of the constitution, the Court too was something of a mirror, window, and national autobiographer.

Again and again in the Court's published decisions, one finds grand narratives that exalt the constitution and implicitly endorse the Court's aggressive role. The constitution, the justices never tire of stressing, was embraced in response to apartheid's evils. Through the constitution, proclaims a typical judgment from July 2012, South Africans 'committed ourselves to the building of a new society founded on the values of human dignity, the achievement of equality and the advancement of human rights and freedoms, non-racialism, non-sexism and the supremacy of the Constitution and the rule of law.'[109] The cornerstone of that society, the judgment added, 'is our Bill of Rights.'[110] Such an understanding placed the Constitutional Court – as definer of those values, enforcer of the Bill of Rights, guardian of the constitution, and guarantor of the rule of law – in an absolutely central role.

3.1 *Memory and Interpretation*

As in the German case, such exalted global readings had interpretive consequences. The Constitution, wrote Deputy President Mahomed in 1995, must be interpreted and applied 'against [its] historical background and ethos.'[111] This entailed limits, for instance, on deference to the legislature. In its first major

105 *Makwanyane* (n 100) para 262 (Mahomed DP concurring).

106 See, e.g., *In re Certification of the Constitution of the Republic of South Africa* 1996 (4) SA 744 (CC) para 10.

107 *De Lange v Presiding Bishop, Methodist Church of Southern Africa and Another*, 2016 (2) SA 1 (CC) para 75 (Van der Westhuizen J concurring).

108 ibid (footnotes and internal quotation marks omitted).

109 *Minister of Home Affairs and Others v Tsebe and Others* 2012 (5) SA 467 (CC) para 45.

110 ibid.

111 *Makwanyane* (n 100) para 263 (Mahomed DP concurring).

decision, the Court invalidated the death penalty despite popular support for it. This was an epochal judgment by any standard. But its tone was truly epic. All eleven justices wrote separate opinions. And all their trumpets sounded.

Several justices highlighted how the constitution required them to uphold enduring values against the whims of public opinion. They made this point by emphasizing the constitution's self-conscious response to an oppressive past.[112] 'The very reason for establishing a new legal order,' wrote Arthur Chaskalson, the Court's founding president, 'and for vesting the power of judicial review of all legislation in the courts, was to protect the rights of minorities and others who cannot protect their rights adequately through the democratic process … This Court cannot allow itself to be diverted,' Chaskalson concluded, 'from its duty to act as an independent arbiter of the Constitution by making choices on the basis that they will find favour with the public.'[113] The Court thus cast itself as the champion of minority rights. And it presented such protection as the very *raison d'être* of a new constitutional order that responded to an evil past.

The constitutional imperative to overcome the past required the Court not only to buck popular opinion at times, but to interpret the constitution in an expansive, purposive, teleological way.[114] This meant that individual provisions must not be read in isolation, but in conjunction with other provisions and 'in the broad context of a legal culture of accountability and transparency.'[115] In one of the Court's earliest decisions, its deputy president, Ismail Mahomed, wrote for the Court that narrow literalism would 'negate the very spirit and tenor of the Constitution and its widely celebrated objectives,' including 'the promise of the equal protection of the laws to all the people of this country and a ringing and decisive break with [the] past.'[116] Concurring in the same case, Justice Albie Sachs agreed that a 'narrow literal view' would clash with the unmistakable 'spirit' of an 'intensely valueladen' document. Drawing explicitly on the German example, Sachs added that narrow literalism 'would be as repugnant to the spirit, design and purpose of the [post-apartheid South African] Constitution as a purely technical, positivist and value-free approach to the post-Nazi Constitution in Germany would have been.'[117] It would

112 *Makwanyane* (n 100) para 89 (Chaskalson P for the majority); 256 (Madala J concurring); 265 (Mahomed J concurring); 305 (Mokgoro J concurring).

113 ibid para 89.

114 See, e.g., *Ferreira v Levin NO and Others* 1995 (2) SA 813 (W); *In re Certification of the Constitution of the Republic of South Africa* (n 107) para 34, 36.

115 *Shabalala and Others v Attorney-General of Transvaal and Another* 1995 (2) SACR 761 (CC) para 26.

116 *S v Mhlungu and Others* 1995 (3) SA 867 (CC) para 8.

117 ibid para 111 (Sachs J concurring).

'underplay[] the symbolical importance that a decisive break with the past has for millions of people, and flatten[] the [Constitution's] resonance for the public at large.'[118] The constitution carried a promise of renewal, and the Court must promote such renewal, even at the price of non-natural readings of some constitutional texts.

This pattern of promoting values and rejecting rigid formalism – all in the name of responding to the past – was persistent and pronounced. In another very early case, Justice Sachs wrote that the constitution required the Court to promote certain values, and that this duty had a particular bearing on questions of severability. In deciding whether to save the remainder of a partly unconstitutional act, the Court must 'posit a notional, contemporary Parliament dealing with the text in issue,' asking whether a democratic, post-apartheid legislature would wish to rescue any part of the offending act.[119]

The history of apartheid, moreover, demanded a non-formalistic understanding of equality. Equal treatment, the Court insisted, didn't always mean identical treatment.[120] In an April 2002 judgment, Justice Sandile Ngcobo wrote that because equality was part of the 'founding faith' of South Africa's constitutional democracy, it 'must not be subjected to a narrow approach' in the Court's jurisprudence.[121] Instead, it was 'especially significant in our country which has a history of injustice from past inequality' that the Court pursue a 'broad approach' similar to that of the Indian Supreme Court.[122] That meant flexibility for the legislature and flexibility for the Court. Frequently, the Court stressed the legislature's wide discretion when choosing the means with which to pursue constitutional transformation.[123]

In many early cases, the South African Court invoked apartheid memory to underwrite a robust interpretation of a particular constitutional right.[124] The justices held, for instance, that free speech enjoyed muscular protection, not least in light of its suppression under apartheid. Apartheid-era restrictions on speech were not only pernicious per se, wrote Deputy Chief Justice Langa, they 'also exacerbated the impact of the systemic violations of other fundamental

118 ibid para 137.

119 *Coetzee v Government of the Republic of South Africa* 1995 (4) SA 631 (CC) para 75.

120 *President of the Republic of South Africa and Another v Hugo* 1997 (4) SA 1 (CC).

121 *Van der Walt v Metcash Trading Ltd* 2002 (4) SA 317 (CC) para 35.

122 ibid.

123 See, e.g., *Bato Star Fishing (Pty) Ltd v Minister of Environmental Affairs and Tourism and Others* 2004 (4) SA 490 (CC).

124 See, e.g., *South African Transport and Allied Workers Union and Another v Garvas and Others* 2013 (1) SA 83 (CC) para 61 (on the right of assembly).

rights in South Africa.'[125] The memory of apartheid similarly undergirded the right to vote, even for prisoners. 'In the light of our history,' wrote Chief Justice Chaskalson, 'where denial of the right to vote was used to entrench white supremacy and to marginalise the great majority of the people of our country, it is for us a precious right which must be vigilantly respected and protected.'[126]

Sometimes, however, apartheid memory cut both ways. In a judgment upholding a conviction for contempt of court (called 'scandalising the court' in South Africa), Justice Johann Kriegler observed for the majority that the lessons of apartheid warned against threats to both freedom of thought and the rule of law.[127] In that particular case, the rule of law predominated.

3.2 *Memory and Legitimacy*

Apartheid memory, then, has been central to the South African Court's self-understanding and efforts at self-legitimation. Recalling the past has been key to the Court's institutional response to the counter-majoritarian difficulty. The alternative to constitutional supremacy, the justices have suggested, is parliamentary sovereignty – something the Court has frequently branded with the burdens of the past. Concurring in *Makwanyane*, the inaugural judgment that invalidated the death penalty, Justice Pius Langa stressed that the constitutional response to apartheid was also a constitutional rejection of parliamentary sovereignty – a tradition that in South Africa had 'meant, virtually, that the State could do anything, enact any law, subject only to procedural correctness.'[128] Parliamentary supremacy, on Langa's telling, was symptomatic of the bad old days. The new constitution had rightly ditched it. 'When the Constitution was enacted,' Langa observed, 'it signalled a dramatic change in the system of governance from one based on rule by parliament to a constitutional state in which the rights of individuals are guaranteed by the Constitution'[129] – and, of

125 *Islamic Unity Convention v Independent Broadcasting Authority and Others* 2002 (4) SA 294 (CC). On the other hand, Justice Langa continued, the constitution allowed reasonable limits on expression – largely in the name of fostering transition and transformation. In a later case, Justice Zak Yacoob wrote that in South Africa free speech 'must be all the more zealously guarded because the infringement of this right was used as an instrument … of thought control … to preserve apartheid and to impose a value system fashioned by a minority on all South Africans.' *Phillips and Another v Director of Public Prosecutions, Witwatersrand Local Division, and Others* 2003 (3) SA 345 (CC) para 23.

126 *Minister of Home Affairs v National Institute for Crime Prevention and the Reintegration of Offenders (NICRO) and Others* 2005 (3) SA 280 (CC) para 47.

127 *S v Mamabolo (E TV and Others Intervening)* 2001 (3) SA 409 (CC).

128 *Makwanyane* (n 100) para 219 (Langa J concurring).

129 ibid para 220.

course, the Constitutional Court. Linking parliamentary sovereignty to the bad past in this way was not a solitary gesture but a key perspective in the Court's self-understanding.[130]

The Court has always been selective in asserting this aspect of its self-understanding. Early on, the Court often invoked apartheid in easy cases and in controversial cases when it knew the ANC government was on its side. It also invoked apartheid memory in some highly controversial settings – such as the constitutional recognition of same-sex marriage when it knew it was ruling against the grain of popular opinion and on an issue that divided the ANC elite.[131] By contrast, the Court's mnemonic rhetoric has been muted or missing in socio-economic rights cases. Negative rights are often "never-again" rights, and aversive mnemonic discourse comes naturally to courts that vigorously enforce them. The South African Court has been most comfortable claiming memory's mantle in this context, when it most obviously acts as a Kelsenian negative legislature, rather than in contexts where aggressive action means telling the legislature what to do. The Court has also been cautious about invoking apartheid against the ANC. (In recent years, however, that has begun to change. More anon.)

Not only has the Court been reluctant to invoke apartheid against the government, it has frequently invoked it in the government's favor. The Court has argued from apartheid in crucial cases *upholding* government action. This has allowed the Court to maintain its anti-apartheid bona fides, and its reputation as guarantor of the constitutional response to apartheid, even as it affirms the deeds of the post-apartheid state. In many contexts, the Court has recited the evils of the past to underscore the complexities of the present – and to motivate, implicitly or explicitly, a jurisprudence of deference. This was true, for instance, in cases involving efforts to equalize schools. In some such cases, the Court highlighted the vastness and intractability of apartheid-induced educational conundrums, and a majority of the Court concluded that such

130 See, e.g., *President of the Republic of South Africa and Others v South African Rugby Football Union and Others* 1999 (4) SA 147 (CC) para 148; *Machele and Others v Mailula and Others* 2010 (2) SA 257 (CC).

131 *Minister of Home Affairs and Another v Fourie and Another; Lesbian and Gay Equality Project and Others v Minister of Home Affairs* 2006 (1) SA 524 (CC). See Theunis Roux, 'Principle and Pragmatism on the Constitutional Court of South Africa' (2009) 7 Int l J Const L 106, 122 (suggesting that, as a result on an intra-ANC split, the party was perhaps less likely than in the death penalty context to shield the Court from the political repercussions of its decision).

complexities demanded deference.[132] More broadly, the Court has always been highly deferential to race-conscious remedial legislation, and it has invariably invoked apartheid memory to justify such deference.[133]

This pattern has been especially prominent in the context of socio-economic rights. In socio-economic rights cases, the Court has often written in bracing tones of the stark economic equality that still mars South African society. It has laid blame for this squarely at apartheid's door. Redressing such inequities is an enormous task, and the Court has often underscored the challenge as a prelude to deference.[134] The Court did stress the apartheid-era origins of South Africa's housing shortage before sharpening its review of socio-economic rights in perhaps its most famous judgment on the matter.[135] But even its boldest socio-economic rights decisions deferred significantly to the government's discretion.[136]

There have been other cases, too, in which the Court has simply deferred to government and made only passing reference to the apartheid past – and sometimes made no reference at all – even in cases involving rights that apartheid flagrantly violated, such as the right to vote,[137] and risks that apartheid glaringly raised, such as the parliamentary stranglehold of a dominant party.[138] The Court has also drawn ambivalent conclusions about the right to property. On the one hand, property has to be protected – not least because it is in the constitution and because property rights were systematically abused during the colonial and apartheid eras. On the other hand, redressing inequities of housing and land is central, on the Court's telling, to the Constitution's transformative mission.[139]

---

132 See, e.g., *Bel Porto School Governing Body and Others v Premier, Western Cape, and Another* 2002 (3) SA 265 (CC).

133 See, e.g., *Minister of Finance and Another v Van Heerden* 2004 (6) SA 121 (CC).

134 See, e.g., *Soobramoney v Minister of Health, KwaZulu-Natal* 1998 (1) SA 765 (CC).

135 *Government of the Republic of South Africa and Others v Grootboom and Others* 2001 (1) SA 46 (CC).

136 See, e.g., *Minister of Health and Others v Treatment Action Campaign and Others* (No 2) 2002 (5) SA 721 (CC).

137 See *New National Party of South Africa v Government of the Republic of South Africa and Others* 1999 (3) SA 191 (CC). In this case, invoking apartheid memory to vindicate the right to vote would have been ironic and aesthetically odd: the main plaintiff was the refurbished party of apartheid, and the defendant was the ANC government that had first opposed and then displaced it.

138 See *United Democratic Movement v President of the Republic of South Africa and Others*, 2003 (1) SA 495 (CC).

139 See, e.g., *Mkontwana v Nelson Mandela Metropolitan Municipality and Another* 2005 (1) SA 530 (CC) para 82 (O'Regan J concurring); *Shoprite Checkers (Pty) Limited v Member of the*

In its formative years, then, the South African Court mingled caution and commitment. For every full-throated 'argument from apartheid,'[140] there was a deferential or pragmatic judgment that invoked the past only briefly or not at all. These tended to come in cases in which the Court had reason to fear government opposition or inertia. Even in these deferential judgments, however, the Court underscored – repeatedly and relentlessly – apartheid's enduring impact.[141] By casting the constitution and themselves as a remedial response to apartheid, the justices suggested that apartheid's ongoing impact highlights an ongoing need for the Constitutional Court. By implication, the Court's intervention *vel non* is legitimate so long as redressing the past remains a legitimate need.

3.3 *Memory in a Minor Key: The Zuma Years*

After around 2008 – beginning, perhaps, with a notorious scandal involving improper efforts to intimidate or influence the justices – the Court could no longer assume that the government would comply unquestioningly with its decisions. Nor, it turned out, could the government count on consistent deference from the Court. The government had, of course, lost several cases during the Court's early years – some of them quite important. But government defeats in the Court's early years were rare. That changed after Jacob Zuma became president in 2009. The new president and his cabinet faced one defeat after another before the Constitutional Court. The Zuma years (2009–2018) were years in which politicians criticized the Court with unprecedented persistence. They were years in which the Court, for the first time, invoked apartheid memory against the ANC and its rulers in political office.

Perhaps fittingly, this chapter of the Court's history unfolded in a new, mnemonically-redolent building. Built on the site of the Old Fort Prison complex – a prison with the dubious distinction of having housed as inmates both Nelson Mandela and Mahatma Gandhi – the new building was designed as a memorial to apartheid's victims and a herald of South Africa's future. 'We

---

Executive Council for Economic Development, Environmental Affairs and Tourism, Eastern Cape and Others 2015 (6) SA 125 (CC).

140 James Fowkes, *Building the Constitution: The Practice of Constitutional Interpretation in Post-Apartheid South Africa* (Cambridge University Press, 2016) 63.

141 See, e.g., *Fedsure Life Assurance Ltd and Others v Greater Johannesburg Transitional Metropolitan Council and Others* 1999 (1) SA 374 (CC) para 121; *First National Bank of SA Limited t/a Wesbank v Minister of Finance* 2002 (4) SA 768 (CC) para 49; *Democratic Alliance and Another v Masondo NO and Another* 2003 (2) SA 413 (CC) para 56; *President of the Republic of South Africa and Another v Modderklip Boerdery (Pty) Ltd* 2005 (5) SA 3 (CC) para 36.

have built a new Constitutional Court,' wrote Justice Albie Sachs, 'right in the heart of what had been Johannesburg's most notorious prison. In a highly visible way, it symbolizes the "never again" principle coupled with the redemptive possibilities of national life.'[142]

During the Zuma era, the Court began to invoke apartheid memory in two new contexts: enforcing socio-economic rights and chastening executive power. The Court had always viewed apartheid memory as a commission for judicial activism. 'Fidelity to the Constitution,' wrote Justice Sachs in a 2006 concurrence, 'requires us to do more than we have done in the past.'[143] But in the Zuma years, the Court assumed a new and unfamiliar role: checking the excesses of single-party rule. The justices undertook this new role delicately, perhaps with heavy hearts. In many respects, the Court remained deferential, regularly praising (and vigorously enforcing) anti-apartheid remedial legislation.[144] But the Court had now become both partner and watchdog. In that ambiguous role, the Court invoked the past selectively – honoring government attempts to reverse apartheid's legacies while striking a softer, but pointed, mnemonic stance when protecting democratic structures and processes.

The Court's increased role in enforcing democratic rights pre-dated Zuma's presidency by a couple years. In *Doctors for Life*, the Court ruled that the constitution required Parliament to hold public hearings on a raft of controversial bills, and it rooted such rights of popular participation in apartheid memory.[145] The Court similarly invoked apartheid to vindicate the right of individual parliamentarians to introduce bills without prior permission.[146] Both of these judgments ran against the ANC's immediate interests and wishes.

The Court confronted the ANC even more directly in a December 2012 judgment invalidating a regional meeting of the party's Provincial Executive Committee.[147] The Court did so on participatory-rights grounds, stressing that

142 Albie Sachs, *The Strange Alchemy of Life and Law* (Oxford University Press, 2009) 89.

143 *South African Broadcasting Corporation Limited v National Director of Public Prosecutions and Others* 2007 (1) SA 523 (CC).

144 See, e.g., *Van Vuren v Minister of Correctional Services and Others* 2012 (1) SACR 103 (CC) para 48; *Competition Commission of South Africa v Senwes Ltd* 2012 (7) BCLR 667 (CC) para 3; *Sebola and Another v Standard Bank of South Africa Ltd and Another* 2012 (5) SA 142 (CC) para 39; *Agri SA v Minister for Minerals and Energy* 2013 (4) SA 1 (CC) para 73; *Nkata v Firstrand Bank Limited and Others* 2016 (4) SA 257 (CC) paras 95–96; *Bakgatla-Ba-Kgafela Communal Property Association v Bakgatla-Ba-Kgafela Tribal Authority and Others* 2015 (6) SA 32 (CC) para.1.

145 *Doctors for Life International v Speaker of the National Assembly and Others* 2006 (6) SA 416 (CC) paras 108, 112, 116, 174.

146 *Oriani-Ambrosini v Sisulu, Speaker of the National Assembly* 2012 (6) SA 588 (CC) para 49.

147 *Ramakatsa and Others v Magashule and Others* 2013 (2) BCLR 202 (CC).

its interpretation of the relevant constitutional provision 'must be informed by a context that is both historical and constitutional' and thus attuned to a time when 'the majority of people in our country were denied political rights which were enjoyed by a minority.'[148] The judgment even highlighted, gently, the need for democratic opposition and competition among parties.

Subsequent rebukes were less gentle. By quashing government initiatives with mounting frequency, the Court aroused the ruling party's ire. In 2011, the ANC's chief parliamentary whip, Mathole Motshekga, warned the justices to leave Parliament's laws alone.[149] Around the same time Gwede Mantashe, the party's general secretary, lambasted the judiciary as a counterrevolutionary force marked by 'hostility … towards the executive and Parliament.'[150] Zuma himself told courts to back off. The people's democratic will, he intoned, 'must not be subverted, simply because those who disagree with the ruling party politically, and who cannot win the popular vote during elections, feel other arms of the State are avenues to help them co-govern the country.'[151] 'Political battles,' the president added, 'must be fought on political platforms.'[152]

But the battles in the courts continued, and the Constitutional Court increasingly invoked apartheid memory against the party of liberation.

The Court's most dramatic invocation of apartheid against the ANC top brass came in its celebrated *Nkandla* judgment of 2016. Underlying the dispute was the expenditure of 246 million Rand of public funds on a putative 'security upgrade' – which included such safety essentials as a visitor's center, an amphitheater, a cattle enclosure, a chicken run, and a swimming pool – to President Zuma's estate near Nkandla, a town in rural KwaZulu-Natal. The story broke in December 2009.[153] After an investigation, the public protector's report of March 2014 denounced the president's fiscal malfeasance and called for fair repayment. The National Assembly, however, absolved Zuma of any need to comply with the charge. Opposition parties challenged the resolution, and Zuma's refusal to repay, in a constitutional complaint.

In a related matter, the Court invalidated the arrests of opposition MPs who had repeatedly interrupted Zuma's February 2015 State of the Nation address to

148 ibid para 64.

149 See Wyndham Hartley, 'Moseneke Speaks Up Against Attacks on Constitution' *Business Day* (Johannesburg, 30 September 2011).

150 ibid.

151 Jacob Zuma, 'Keynote Address to Access to Justice Conference' (8 July 2011), http://www.presidency.gov.za/speeches/keynote-address-president-jacob-zuma-ocassion-3rd-access-justice-conference%2C-pretoria.

152 ibid.

153 See 'Zuma's R65m Nkandla Splurge' *Mail & Guardian* (Johannesburg, 4 December 2009).

ask when the president would repay his share of the Nkandla funds.[154] In doing so, the justices sounded squarely in apartheid memory. South Africa's '[h]ard-won democracy,' wrote Justice Mbuyiseli Madlanga, 'came at a huge cost to many; a cost that included arrest, detention, torture and – above all – death at the hands of the apartheid regime.'[155] Such memories motivated a universal duty 'jealously to safeguard that democracy,' whose 'very notion' would be 'warped' if all MPs did not 'enjoy the right to full and meaningful contribution' to uninhibited parliamentary debate.[156]

Thirteen days later, on 31 March 2016, the justices reached the merits of the Nkandla case. Their judgment was unanimous and unsparing. For President Zuma, it was an unqualified and total defeat. Writing for the Court, Chief Justice Mogoeng Mogoeng opened with a ringing invocation of apartheid and a blistering rebuke of corruption. 'One of the crucial elements of our constitutional vision,' the chief justice began, 'is to make a decisive break from the unchecked abuse of State power and resources that was virtually institutionalised during the apartheid era.'[157] It was a striking prologue. The Court had often invoked the "decisive break" motif but never so prominently in the context of official venality and abuse of state power. This was apartheid memory in a new context and in a new key.

The chief justice's next statements were even stronger. In order to reverse apartheid abuses, he continued, 'we adopted accountability, the rule of law and the supremacy of the Constitution as values of our constitutional democracy.'[158] In a State founded on such values, 'public office-bearers ignore their constitutional obligations at their peril.'[159] The chief's warning words were like tumbrels rattling through Parisian streets. In the lines that followed, the guillotine dropped its blade.

'[C]onstitutionalism, accountability and the rule of law,' Chief Justice Mogoeng wrote, 'constitute the sharp and mighty sword that stands ready to chop the ugly head of impunity off its stiffened neck.'[160]

The prose was purple, but the point was clear. South Africa's anti-apartheid constitution would not tolerate apartheid-style official abuses. By clear

154 *Democratic Alliance v Speaker of the National Assembly and Others* 2016 (3) SA 487 (CC).
155 ibid para 11.
156 ibid.
157 *Economic Freedom Fighters v Speaker of the National Assembly and Others; Democratic Alliance v Speaker of the National Assembly and Others* 2016 (5) BCLR 618 (CC) para 1.
158 ibid.
159 ibid.
160 ibid.

implication, Zuma and his enablers had acted in a manner characteristic of their apartheid-era predecessors and unworthy of the new dispensation. In response, the justices must swing their sharp and mighty sword.

They did so for another 104 paragraphs. But apart from an oblique nod to 'the painful divisions of the past,'[161] there was no further mention of apartheid. After such a preamble, there didn't need to be. Instead, the judgment hammered home its central finding that president and Parliament had both traduced their solemn oaths. Accordingly, the justices ordered Zuma to comply with the public protector's order. He must repay the embezzled funds, and Parliament must assist in the effort.

The winning parties were jubilant. 'All is not lost,' crowed Julius Malema, the victorious plaintiff. 'This judgment seeks to rescue our constitution and our country.'[162] The vindicated public protector, Thuli Madonsela, observed that South Africa's democracy 'was built with the understanding that there would be ways to compensate for failure in parts of the system. Today,' she rejoiced, 'was that day.'[163]

But the rejoicing reached beyond the victors to the masses of disillusioned South Africans. Former Justice Albie Sachs, by then seven years into retirement, recounts an illustrative episode:

> I was rushing to catch my plane at the airport when a middle-aged African man blocked my path and flung his arms around me. 'Thank you, thank you,' he kept repeating. 'It wasn't me,' I interrupted, 'I left the Court some years ago.' But he kept his grip and carried on offering thanks. I had to pull myself away to reach the gate in time. But then as the plane lifted off my heart swelled with emotion. The Constitutional Court had ordered the President to pay back the public funds overspent on his private home. There was hope.[164]

By any measure, the judgment was daring and bold. It was the sternest rebuke the Court had ever given to a sitting government and head of state. Against the liberation party's boss, the Court had invoked the mantle of redemptive, transformative, anti-apartheid memory. In doing so, it had inverted the pattern of its early years. Back then, the Court had prominently invoked apartheid memory against public opinion when the justices knew they would be backed by the

161 ibid para 26.
162 'Payback Time' *The Economist* (London 1 April 2016).
163 ibid.
164 Albie Sachs, *We, the People: Insights of An Activist Judge* (Wits University Press 2016) vii.

ruling elite. Now the Court had invoked the nation's past against the country's present rulers – and the people at large were dancing in the streets.

In June 2017, the Court handed Zuma another defeat when it ruled that the Speaker of the National Assembly had the power to prescribe voting by secret ballot.[165] Once again, the Court rooted its ruling 'in a history which involves a transition from a society based on division, injustice and exclusion from the democratic process to one which respects the dignity of all citizens, and includes all in the process of governance.'[166] A no-confidence vote was held against Zuma on 8 August 2017. The president narrowly survived: 177 MPs voted for Zuma's removal, 198 against. Removal required 201 votes in favor. But it was a dismal showing for a president whose party held 249 seats. At least sixteen ANC rebels voted against him. Many more abstained. The dissidents were surely emboldened by a secret ballot enabled by the Constitutional Court.

The years of Zuma's presidency engulfed the Court in a remarkable sequence of high-profile confrontations with the ruling party and the executive branch. In the process, the Court was anything but deferential and retiring. For our purposes, the most salient feature of these cases was the Court's consistent invocation of apartheid to underwrite its watchdog role. After an inaugural decade in which the Court rarely asserted apartheid memory against the government, the Zuma-era Court did so repeatedly, emphatically, and in cases of the highest political moment. It did so, moreover, notwithstanding unprecedented official criticism. These were gestures of both confidence and desperation. An embattled Court called on its own reserves of public trust and invoked the legacy of a traumatic past to undergird the legitimacy of its unprecedented institutional assertion.

3.4 *Speak, Memory*

As South Africa emerged from the Zuma years, the Court was as vocal about apartheid as ever. It continued to invoke apartheid memory in a wide variety of cases and in a dizzying array of circumstances. Across these recent cases run two contrasting themes. The first is that constitutional memory is inescapably limited; the second, that it is nonetheless inescapable. Efforts to redress the past will always be modest and incremental. But they must continue all the same.

An exemplary articulation of the first theme appears in the opening paragraph of an August 2014 judgment by Justice van der Westhuizen. 'If only,' he

165 *United Democratic Movement v Speaker of the National Assembly and Others* 2017 (5) SA 300 (CC).

166 ibid para 29 (internal citations omitted).

sighed, 'we could repeat, re-run or re-shape history to avoid the injustices of the apartheid era. But we cannot.'[167] The wounded present held only humbler options. 'Perhaps the best that can be done,' Justice van der Westhuizen continued, 'is to try to redress past injustices by enacting and applying legislation under the Constitution of our young democracy to deal with some of the consequences of the apartheid regime's treatment of the majority of South Africans.'[168] But the remedies would always be incomplete. '[E]ven restoration,' Justice van der Westhuizen observed later on, 'could not knit together the bones of history. The brutality of apartheid irreparably smashed them.'[169]

And yet the Court must go on working to repair the irreparable. It must continue invoking apartheid memory and highlighting its pernicious fallout. It must persist in reminding the country, as Justice Cameron put it in a May 2017 concurrence, 'that the past is not done with us; that it is not past; that it will not leave us in peace until we have reckoned with its claims to justice.'[170]

All signs suggest that the Court will continue to cast itself as an agent of that reckoning, invoking apartheid memory to reinforce the legitimacy of its enterprise.

4 Conclusion

These overviews of mnemonic jurisprudence in Germany and South Africa make clear that the memory of Nazism in the one case and of apartheid in the other have been central to the courts' self-understanding and central to their countries' constitutional identity. Both courts have invoked the past repeatedly and in prominent places. Both have done so in both activist and deferential ways. As noted in the introduction, this malleability of memory suggests affinities between the evil past in these two jurisdictions and the anticanon in the United States.[171] As described by Jamal Greene, the anticanon – a set of four universally discredited decisions of the U.S. Supreme Court: *Dred Scott*,[172] *Plessy*,[173] *Lochner*,[174] and *Korematsu*[175] – is a valuable rhetorical resource for

167 *Florence v Government of the Republic of South Africa* 2014 (6) SA 456 (CC) para 1.
168 ibid.
169 ibid para 41.
170 *Daniels v Scribante and Another* 2017 (4) SA 341 (CC) para 154.
171 See Richard A. Primus, 'Canon, Anti-Canon, and Judicial Dissent' (1998) 48 Duke LJ 243.
172 *Dred Scott v Sandford*, 60 U.S. 393 (1857).
173 *Plessy v Ferguson*, 163 U.S. 537 (1896).
174 *Lochner v New York*, 198 U.S. 45 (1905).
175 *Korematsu v United States*, 323 U.S. 214 (1944).

judges precisely because it is so protean.[176] It can be invoked by all sides in a dizzying array of cases. Historical evil exhibits a similar 'pluripotency.'[177] Judges can invoke it or not with consummate discretion. They can do so to buttress vigorous enforcement of constitutional provisions or to justify deference to the government. They can do so to underwrite methodological innovations or to ground new theories of interpretation. They can do so to reinforce global statements about the nature of the constitution, the values of the polity, or the identity of the people. They can do so to bolster grand pronouncements about ultimate constitutional ethics. They can do so in all of these ways and many more.

Always the tactical goal is persuasion, the strategic aim legitimacy. Much has been said and written in the twenty-first century – by both lawyers and political scientists, from both theoretical and empirical perspectives – on the question of judicial legitimacy. Many writers agree that legitimacy is a normative concept centered on an institution's legal and moral right to make decisions that bind others.[178] Judicial legitimacy entails the broadly accepted authority to issue judgments for a political community.[179] It commands citizen loyalty, not mere acquiescence, and it gives courts leeway to counter public opinion.[180] It is a stock of political capital, a reservoir of popular good will.[181] To preserve it, judges must convince the populace that they are unlike other political actors. Legitimated courts must be recognized as different from bureaucrats and legislators.[182]

One leading model of judicial legitimacy, positivity theory, posits that judges preserve legitimacy through the symbols of judicial authority.[183] Exposure to such symbols seems to enhance legitimacy.[184] Exposure to such symbols can

176 Greene (n 4) 435.

177 ibid 460.

178 See, e.g., Michael J Nelson and James L Gibson, 'U.S. Supreme Court Legitimacy: Unanswered Questions and an Agenda for Future Research' in Robert M Howard and Kirk A Randazzo (eds), *The Routledge Handbook of Judicial Behavior* (Routledge 2018) 132, 133.

179 ibid 133.

180 ibid 133–134.

181 ibid.

182 ibid 135.

183 See James L. Gibson and Michael J. Nelson, 'Reconsidering Positivity Theory: What Roles do Politicization, Ideological Disagreement, and Legal Realism Play in Shaping U.S. Supreme Court Legitimacy?' (2017) 14 Journal of Empirical Legal Studies 592, 593.

184 See James L Gibson, Milton Lodge, and Benjamin Woodson, 'Losing, But Accepting: Legitimacy, Positivity Theory, and the Symbols of Judicial Authority' (2014) 48 Law and Society Review 837.

even neutralize citizen disappointment with particular decisions.[185] There is, it would seem, something intoxicating about robes and gavels, benches and books, pillars of marble and stone – something that inspires awe, reverence, compliance.[186]

I suggest, in closing, that the past provides another powerful symbol for both of the courts I have studied. To be sure, the judges in Karlsruhe and Johannesburg don robes and swing gavels and pronounce solemn judgments in the name of We the People. But they also inhabit buildings that reflect in architecture the polity's rejection of its past. The German Constitutional Court sits in a boxlike modernist building with abundant glass windows suggesting openness and transparency.[187] It looks more like a public library than the home of a powerful court. As noted earlier, the South African Court resides in a building even more redolent of the past and even more evocative of its rejection. Both buildings are visual symbols of a new dispensation.

In their mnemonic jurisprudence, both courts have gone much further in claiming the mantle of memory. Both have made opposition to the past central to the nation's constitutional identity and to their own institutional self-understanding. By doing so, both courts have not only defined themselves in opposition to the past, they have differentiated themselves from the politicians whose acts they review. Politicians are notoriously shortsighted – obsessively focused on passing the next bill or surviving the next election (or the next no-confidence vote or impeachment proceedings). By invoking the past, courts highlight their capacity to take a longer view. They emphasize their role as guardians of a new order – as preservers of collective memory and enforcers of common commitments. They seek to ensure their legitimacy and uphold their power by wrapping themselves in memory's evocative mantle.

All signs suggest that both courts will continue to do so. But it is also clear that they will do so in the face of mounting contestation. Loud voices in South Africa bemoan the post-apartheid constitution's ostensible failures.[188] Some

185 See James L Gibson and Michael J Nelson, 'Change in Institutional Support for the U.S. Supreme Court: Is the Court's Legitimacy Imperiled by the Decisions it Makes?' (2016) 80 Public Opinion Quarterly 622.

186 The link between symbols and legitimacy has been suspected intuitively and tested empirically for a long time now. See Gregory Casey, 'The Supreme Court and Myth: An Empirical Investigation' (1974) 8 Law & Soc'y Rev 385.

187 See, e.g., Klaus Jan Philipp, 'Das Bundesverfassungsgericht in Karlsruhe – Prolegomena zu einer Stilgeschichte der Nachkriegsarchitektur' [2018] Insitu 131; Falk Jaeger (ed), *Transparenz und Würde. Das Bundesverfassungsgericht und seine Architektur* (JOVIS 2014).

188 See, e.g., Joel M Modiri, 'Conquest and Constitutionalism: First Thoughts on an Alternative Jurisprudence' (2018) 34 S Afr J Hum Rts 300; Gideon van Riet 'The Limits of Political Development and Donstitutionalism in South Africa' (2016) 75 New Contree

deny that it is 'post'-apartheid in any meaningful sense.[189] Still others call for its abolition.[190] In Germany, by contrast, the Basic Law is much feted, as during its seventieth-anniversary jubilee in 2019. But those very celebrations have been haunted by a sense of persistent unease. Many suspect that the constitution has passed its zenith. Others fear the encroachments of illiberal forces – among European neighbors most obviously, but at home as well. In both Germany and South Africa, though for very different reasons, the future looks to be very uncertain. Perhaps that means the past will be as well.

Bibliography

Asmal K, et al (eds), *Nelson Mandela: In His Own Words* (Little, Brown and Co., 2003) 70.

Bartels B L, Johnston C D, 'On the Ideological Foundations of Supreme Court Legitimacy in the American Public' (2013) 57 Am J Pol Sci 184.

Bobbitt P, *Constitutional Fate: Theory of the Constitution* (1982) 93–119.

Bond P, 'Constitutionalism as a Barrier to the Resolution of Widespread Community Rebellions in South Africa' (2014) 41 Politikon 461–482; Terblanche Delport 'An Ethical (Anti-) Constitutionalism? Transformation for a Transfigured Public' (2014) 46 Acta Academica 104–121.

Buchloch I, *Veit Harlan – Goebbels' Starregisseur* (Ferdinand Schöningh, 2010).

Casey G, 'The Supreme Court and Myth: An Empirical Investigation' (1974) 8 Law & Soc'y Rev 385.

Collings J, *Democracy's Guardians: A History of the German Federal Constitutional Court, 1951–2001* (2015) 5–9.

Fowkes J, *Building the Constitution: The Practice of Constitutional Interpretation in Post-Apartheid South Africa* (Cambridge University Press, 2016) 63.

98–115; Patrick Bond 'Constitutionalism as a Barrier to the Resolution of Widespread Community Rebellions in South Africa' (2014) 41 Politikon 461–482; Terblanche Delport 'An Ethical (Anti-) Constitutionalism? Transformation for a Transfigured Public' (2014) 46 Acta Academica 104–121.

189 See, e.g., Lewis Nkosi, 'The Ideology of Reconciliation: Its Effects on South African Culture' in Lindy Stiebel and Michael JF Chapman (eds), *Writing Home: Lewis Nkosi on South African Writing* (University of KwaZulu-Nata Press 2016); Lewis Nkosi, 'The Republic of Letters after the Mandela Republic' in Lindy Stiebel and Michael JF Chapman (eds), *Writing Home: Lewis Nkosi on South African Writing* (University of KwaZulu-Natal Press 2016).

190 Noted in Joel M Modiri, 'Introduction to Special Issue: Conquest, Constitutionalism, and Democratic Contestations' (2018) 34 S Afr J Hum Rts 295, 296.

Gibson J L, Lodge M, and Woodson B, 'Losing, But Accepting: Legitimacy, Positivity Theory, and the Symbols of Judicial Authority' (2014) 48 Law and Society Review 837.

Gibson J L and Nelson M J, 'Is the U.S. Supreme Court's Legitimacy Grounded in Performance Satisfaction and Ideology?' (2015) 59 Am J Pol Sci 162.

Gibson J L and Nelson M J, 'Change in Institutional Support for the U.S. Supreme Court: Is the Court's Legitimacy Imperiled by the Decisions it Makes?' (2016) 80 Public Opinion Quarterly 622.

Gibson J L and Nelson M J,'Reconsidering Positivity Theory: What Roles do Politicization, Ideological Disagreement, and Legal Realism Play in Shaping U.S. Supreme Court Legitimacy?' (2017) 14 Journal of Empirical Legal Studies 592, 593.

Grimm D, 'Die Karriere eines Boykottaufrufs' *Die Zeit* (27 September 2001).

Grove T L, 'The Supreme Court's Legitimacy Dilemma' (2019) 132 Harv L Rev 2240.

Harlan T, *Veit* (Rowohlt, 2011).

Hartley W, 'Moseneke Speaks Up Against Attacks on Constitution' *Business Day* (Johannesburg, 30 September 2011).

Henne T, and Riedlinger A (eds), *Das Lüth-Urteil aus (rechts-)historischer Sicht. Die Konflikte um Veit Harlan und die Grundrechtsjudikatur des Bundesverfassungsgerichts* (Berliner Wissenschafts-Verlag, 2005).

Kübler F, 'Lüth – eine sanfte Revolution' (2000) 83 Kritische Vierteljahresschrift für Gesetzgebung und Rechtswissenschaft 313.

Lewis J, 'The Constitutional Court of South Africa: An Evaluation' (2009) 125 Law Quarterly Review 440, 442.

Ley R, 'Die Erstbesetzung des Bundesverfassungsgerichts' (1982) 13 *Zeitschrift für Parlamentsfragen* 528.

Löffler U, *Instrumentalisierte Vergangenheit? Die nationalsozialistische Vergangenheit als Argumentationsfigur in der Rechtsprechung des Bundesverfassungsgerichts* (Peter Lang, 2004) 39.

Meinel F, 'The Constitutional Miracle on the Rhine: Towards a History of West German Constitutionalism and the Federal Constitutional Court' (2016) 14 Int l J Const L 277, 290.

Modiri J M, 'Conquest and Constitutionalism: First Thoughts on an Alternative Jurisprudence' (2018) 34 S Afr J Hum Rts 300.

Modiri J M, 'Introduction to Special Issue: Conquest, Constitutionalism, and Democratic Contestations' (2018) 34 S Afr J Hum Rts 295, 296.

Nelson M J and Gibson J L, 'U.S. Supreme Court Legitimacy: Unanswered Questions and an Agenda for Future Research' in Robert M Howard and Kirk A Randazzo (eds), *The Routledge Handbook of Judicial Behavior* (Routledge 2018) 132, 133.

Nkosi L, 'The Ideology of Reconciliation: Its Effects on South African Culture' in Lindy Stiebel and Michael JF Chapman (eds), *Writing Home: Lewis Nkosi on South African Writing* (University of KwaZulu-Nata Press 2016).

Nkosi L, 'The Republic of Letters after the Mandela Republic' in Lindy Stiebel and Michael JF Chapman (eds), *Writing Home: Lewis Nkosi on South African Writing* (University of KwaZulu-Natal Press 2016).

Philipp KJ, 'Das Bundesverfassungsgericht in Karlsruhe – Prolegomena zu einer Stilgeschichte der Nachkriegsarchitektur' [2018] Insitu 131; Falk Jaeger (ed), *Transparenz und Würde. Das Bundesverfassungsgericht und seine Architektur* (JOVIS 2014).

Primus R A., 'Canon, Anti-Canon, and Judicial Dissent' (1998) 48 Duke LJ 243.

Reichel P, Schmid H, *Von der Katastrophe zum Stolperstein* (2005) 34ff.

Roux T, 'Principle and Pragmatism on the Constitutional Court of South Africa (2009) 7 Int l J Const L 106, 122.

Sachs A, *The Strange Alchemy of Life and Law* (Oxford University Press, 2009) 89.

Sachs A, *We, the People: Insights of An Activist Judge* (Wits University Press 2016) vii.

Scheppele K L, 'Aspirational and Aversive Constitutionalism: The Case for Studying Cross-Constitutional Influence through Negative Models' (2003) 1 Int l J Const L 296.

van Riet G, 'The Limits of Political Development and Donstitutionalism in South Africa' (2016) 75 New Contree 98–115.

von Arnauld A, 'Norms and Narrative' (2017) 18 German Law Journal 309, 317.

PART 2

Historical Precedents and Inter-constitutional Interpretation

CHAPTER 4

Comparing Constitutional Historicities

The Case of Precedents in Canada and the United States

Jean-Christophe Bédard-Rubin

1 Introduction*

When Canada adopted the Canadian Charter of Rights and Freedoms in 1982 and 'patriated' its constitution, many commentators feared it would import north-of-the-border debates that generate puzzles in American constitutional law. How can judges interpret abstract constitutional rights? What weight should judges assign to the intent of the framers or the original public meaning in the interpretation of constitutional provisions? Given that the Constitution would become very difficult to amend, would judges become the main actors in charge of constitutional change? And how could one know that judges change their minds on principled grounds rather than simply on a whim, following public opinion, or their own political preferences? Yet, thirty years after the 'charter revolution' it seems clear that, despite some limited convergence, Canadian and American constitutional cultures have not merged.[1] Looking back 'from the new normal'[2] allows us to see how the evolution of constitutional law through judicial interpretation has been 'problematized'[3] differently in Canada and the United States. In particular, the American debates

* I would like to thank Jason Mazzone, Justin Frosini, Francesco Biagi and the participants in the 2019 Constitutional History: Comparative Perspectives conference in Chicago for their comments, questions and suggestions. I would also like to thank David Schneiderman, Konstanze von Schütz and four anonymous reviewers for comments and suggestions on the larger project from which this chapter is drawn. Of course, all remaining errors are mine.

1 See generally David Schneiderman, *Red, White, and Kind of Blue: The Conservatives and the Americanization of Canadian Constitutional Culture* (University of Toronto Press 2015); Samuel V LaSelva, *Canada and the Ethics of Constitutionalism: Identity, Destiny, and Constitutional Faith* (McGill-Queen's UP 2018).

2 Peter McCormick, *The End of the Charter Revolution: Looking Back From the New Normal* (University of Toronto Press 2015).

3 I understand 'problematization' as 'the totality of discursive and non-discursive practices that introduces an object into the game of truth and falsity and constitutes it as an object of thought'. Michel Foucault, *Dits et écrits t.IV* (Gallimard 1994) n. 350. My translation.

 | DOI:10.1163/9789004523739_006

concerning the place of constitutional precedents in adjudication have gained little traction in Canada.

Constitutional precedents underscore 'the unique problem of constitutional theory [which] is to explain how self-government is possible under the conditions of temporality within which the state exists'.[4] Precedents can be thought of as knots, as dense points of tension between constitutional law and democratic self-government. Every constitutional culture tries to mediate this tension with what the historian François Hartog calls a 'regime of historicity'.[5] Hartog defines the concept of regime of historicity in two ways. In a narrow sense, it is 'the way in which a given society approaches its past and reflects upon it'. In a broader sense, it refers to all the 'modalities of self-consciousness that each society adopts in its construction of time and its perceptions'. Since 'every cultural order has its own historicity, even its own regime of historicity',[6] the concept is capacious enough 'as a heuristic tool [to] help us reach a better understanding of […] moments of crisis of time, as they have arisen whenever the way in which past, present, and future are articulated no longer seems self-evident'.[7]

The chapter focuses on constitutional precedents as a specific form of engagement by constitutional actors with a Hartog-style articulation of past, present and future. The chapter thereby provides an entry point into Canadian and American constitutional historicities. Other authors have contrasted the importance of originalism in American constitutional discourse with its marginal role in Canada.[8] Focusing on originalism, however, obscures additional

---

4 Paul W Kahn, *Legitimacy and History: Self-Government in American Constitutional Thought* (Yale UP 1992) 4.

5 François Hartog, *Regimes of Historicity: Presentism and the Experience of Time* (Saskia Brown tr, Columbia UP 2015). See also François Hartog, *Évidence de l'histoire* (Gallimard, 2005); François Hartog, *Croire en l'histoire* (Flammarion 2016).

6 François Hartog, *Regimes of Historicity: Presentism and the Experience of Time* (Saskia Brown tr, Columbia UP 2015) 56.

7 François Hartog, *Regimes of Historicity: Presentism and the Experience of Time* (Saskia Brown tr, Columbia UP 2015) 16. Hartog's project is to understand the transition, since the 1980s, to a 'presentist' regime of historicity in the Western world that differs from the classical and modern regimes. He thus uses the concept resolutely at the macrolevel. Hartog's conceptual framework has been deployed in constitutional studies to explore the 1948 Italian Constitution. See Maurizio Cau, 'La Costituzione nel tempo. Regimi di storicità di un progretto storico-politico' (2018) 36 Giornale di Storia Costituzionale 147.

8 See Bradley W Miller, 'Beguiled by Metaphors: The 'Living Tree' and Originalist Constitutional Interpretation in Canada' (2009) 22 CJLJ 331; Bradley W Miller, 'Origin Myth: The Persons Case, The Living Tree and the New Originalism' in Grant Huscroft and Bradley W Miller (eds), *The Challenge of Originalism: Theories of Constitutional Interpretation* (CUP 2013); Jamal Greene and Yvonne Tew, 'Comparing Approaches to

dimensions of the ways in which constitutional discourse articulates historicity. Politicians and judges, in their reconstruction of historical materials and the normative content that they believe they can derive from it, illuminate the ways in which the tension between law, judicial power, and democratic self-government are mediated whenever changes are brought about or resisted in judicial decisions as small-scale moments of 'crisis of time'.[9]

In a classic study of precedents, A.L. Goodhart wrote that '[t]he prior case, being directly in point is no longer one which may be used as a pattern; it is one which must be followed in the subsequent case. It is more than a model; it has become a fixed and binding rule'.[10] On the surface, Canada and the United States have moved away from this model and have adopted similarly flexible approaches to precedent. *Stare decisis* is not an 'inexorable command'[11] anymore and 'constitutional decisions are not immutable, even in the absence of constitutional amendment'.[12] Even if in most cases, 'it is more important that the applicable rule of law be settled than that it be settled right', as Louis Brandeis wrote,[13] that principle does not hold in the case of constitutional adjudication, since the stakes of 'getting it right' are increased by the fact that a wrong interpretation cannot be corrected by the legislative branch but only via constitutional amendment.[14] At the same time, constitutional adjudication

---

Constitutional History' in Erin F Delaney and Rosalind Dixon (eds), *Comparative Judicial Review* (Edward Elgar 2018). Generally, on the unrecognized use of originalism in Canada, see Leonid Sirota and Benjamin Oliphant, 'Has the Supreme Court Rejected 'Originalism'?' (2016) 42 Queen's L.J. 107; Leonid Sirota and Benjamin J Oliphant, 'Originalist Reasoning in Canadian Constitutional Jurisprudence' (2017) 50 UBC L Rev. 505.

9 In general, on 'crisis' as a moment of decision, see Myriam Revault-d'Allonnes, 'De l'autorité à l'institution: la durée publique' (2004) 307 Esprit 42.

10 A.L. Goodhart, *Precedent in English and Continental Law* (Stevens and Sons 1934) 9.

11 See, e.g., *Payne v Tennessee* 501 US 808 (1991) (Rehnquist, CJ); *Hohn v United States* 524 US 236, 251, (1998); *Pearson v Callahan* 555 US 223, 233 (2009). See also *Lawrence v Texas*, 539 US 558, 577 (2003); *State Oil* Co. *v Khan* 522 US 3, 20 (1997); *Agostini v Felton*, 521 US 203, 235 (1997); *Seminole Tribe of Fla. v Florida* 517 US 44, 63 (1996).

12 *Clark v Canadian National Railway Co.* [1988] 2 SCR 680, para 44. See also the discussion of Justice Binnie in *R v Henry* 2005 SCC 76, [2005] 3 SCR 609, para 44 and *Canada v Craig* 2012 SCC 43, [2012] 2 SCR 489, para 24–31.

13 *Burnet v Coronado Oil & Gas Co.* 285 US 393, 406–407 (1932) (Brandeis J, dissenting).

14 For one of the most influential articles on the subject, see Henry Paul Monaghan, '*Stare Decisis* and Constitutional Adjudication' (1988) 88 Colum. L Rev. 723. In the United States, the Supreme Court has thus elaborated a doctrine holding *stare decisis* to be 'at its weakest when [it] interpret[s] the Constitution because [its] interpretation can be altered only by constitutional amendment or by overruling [its] prior decisions'. *Agostini v Felton* 521 US 203, 235 (1997). However, empirical analysis suggests that, in fact, there is 'only a modicum of evidence suggesting that constitutional precedents are more vulnerable to departure'. Lee Epstein, William M Landes and Adam Liptak, 'The Decision to Depart (Or

involves the interpretation of laconic provisions that refer to vague and highly disputed moral ideas.[15] Popular conceptions about such notions change over time even while constitutional text remains the same. Should judges keep pace with society? Or are too frequent departures from precedents likely to break the spell of judges as simply applying the law? Would casting aside precedents endanger the rule of law in general?[16] Precedents seem both *necessary* for a court to be perceived as *applying* the law, but at the same time *problematic* because the application of outdated precedents might reduce the institutional legitimacy of the court if they conflict with contemporary understandings about the requirements of justice.

Surprisingly, this tension, which has constituted the core of the American debate about the value of constitutional precedents, has received little attention in Canada. Despite a surface resemblance between American and Canadian doctrines of *stare decisis*, constitutional precedents partake in a larger 'web of signification'[17] that gives them different meaning in each constitutional culture. '[T]he term 'constitutional culture'', Reva Siegel writes, 'refers to the understandings of role and practices of argument that guide interactions among citizens and officials in matters concerning the Constitution's meaning'.[18] Robert C. Post describes constitutional culture as 'a specific subset of culture that encompasses extrajudicial beliefs about the substance of the Constitution'.[19] For my purposes, the concept of constitutional culture can be broadly defined as a subset of a general culture that is composed of attitudes and beliefs about the constitutional institutions of a given society, as well as the nature and source of legally-warranted public authority within the society.

Not) From Constitutional Precedent: An Empirical Study of The Roberts Court' (2015) 90 N.Y.U. L. Rev. 1115, 1146. The Supreme Court of Canada does not adhere to such a distinction between constitutional and statutory/Common Law precedent. See *Ontario (Attorney General) v Fraser* 2011 SCC 20, [2011] 2 S.C.R. 3.

15 The importance of 'getting it right' is higher for morally contentious provisions such as fundamental rights and freedoms than it is for other more procedural provisions. On this question, see David A Strauss, *The Living Constitution* (OUP 2008) ch. 5.

16 Some scholars have suggested that a certain level of adherence to precedent is a necessary component for the rule of law in general. On the binding force of precedents as a manifestation of the rule of law rather than as a necessary component of the rule of law, see, Jeremy Waldron, 'Stare Decisis and the Rule of Law: A Layered Approach' (2012) 111 Mich. L Rev. 1.

17 Clifford Geertz, *The Interpretation of Cultures* (Basic Books 1973) 182.

18 Reva B Siegel, 'Constitutional Culture, Social Movement Conflict and Constitutional Change: The Case of the de facto ERA' (2006) 94 CLR 1323, 1325.

19 Robert C Post, 'The Supreme Court 2002 Term – Foreword: Fashioning the Legal Constitution: Culture, Courts, and Law' (2002) 117 Harv. L Rev. 4, 8.

It is not limited to the text of the constitution and includes the meaning and the conception of the proper functioning of constitutional institutions.

My analysis, aimed at understanding the meaning associated with precedents and history, focuses on the official constitutional culture exhibited by the 'the characteristic rhetorical strategies' and the 'repertoire of recurring argumentative moves'[20] of the actors who are most concerned with articulating that culture: judges and politicians. While the use of precedents and history more generally certainly respond to strategic considerations, in my analysis I bracket for now questions of motivations because, as Epstein and Knight explain, '[i]nvoking precedent will be effective only if … others believe in its importance. This follows from the fact that the strategic use of norms depends on the acceptance of the norm by some segment of a community'.[21]

The chapter has four parts. The first part briefly describes the place that precedents have had in the mainstream constitutional culture of Canada and the United States over the past twenty years. It shows that while precedents and their possible overruling have been a central topic of discussion and concern in the United States, the same is not true in Canada. The second part of the chapter traces the origins of the different roles precedents play in the United States and Canada by focusing on what American scholars have called 'super-precedents'. The third part of the chapter moves to an interpretive account of the role of history in constitutional culture. It argues that Canada's dominant constitutional narrative is elusive and illustrates that claim by focusing on metaphors of incompleteness and openness used to describe the Canadian constitutional project. The fourth part of the chapter contrasts this incompleteness with the 'narrativization' of American constitutional discourse and shows how the American narrative brings closure to the meaning of American constitutional law.

To borrow from Hayden White, the difference between Canadian and American constitutional historicity is as important as that 'between a historical discourse that narrates, on the one side, and a discourse that narrativizes, on the other; between a discourse that openly adopts a perspective that looks out on the world and reports it and a discourse that feigns to make the

20 Karl E Klare, 'Legal Culture and Transformative Constitutionalism' (1998) 14 SAJHR 146, 166.

21 Lee Epstein and Jack Knight, *The Choices Justices Make* (Brookings Institute 1998) 177. On the necessity to adapt attitudinal and strategic study of judicial behavior to different cultural settings, especially when comparing Canada and the United States, see Matthew E Wetstein and others, 'Ideological Consistency and Attitudinal Conflict: A Comparative Analysis of the U.S. and Canadian Supreme Courts' (2009) 42 Comp. Pol. Stud. 763.

world speak itself and speak itself *as a story*'.[22] Narratives, which are central in American constitutional law and marginal and elusive in Canada, also invert 'the effect of contingency, in the sense of that which could have happened differently or which might not have happened at all, by incorporating it in some way into the effect of necessity or probability exerted by the configuring act'. Integrated in an intelligible whole, contingent events and judicial decisions are presented as if they were necessary. Yet, this 'necessity is a narrative necessity'. It only 'comes from the configurating act […]'.[23] While Canadian judges and politicians certainly narrate their constitutional history, they do not *narrativize* it in the way Americans do. Precedents are generally given an 'illustrative' or 'privileged' role in Canada, they are 'authoritative' in the United States.[24] The rhetorical force of precedents and the intensity of the justification required to overrule them is therefore much higher in the U.S. than in Canada.

2 Constitutional Precedents in the Foreground and Background

Under the leadership of Chief Justice Beverley McLachlin (2000–2017), the Supreme Court of Canada came to revisit many of its previous rulings reached in cases of first impression during the immediate years after the adoption of the *Canadian Charter of Rights and Freedoms* in 1982.[25] Many of these cases involved sensitive moral issues such as physician-assisted suicide, sex workers rights or a general right to strike. The first generation of *Charter* decisions had been justified on the basis that it was politicians, not judges, who had decided to entrench fundamental rights and freedoms enforceable through judicial review. 'We didn't volunteer' wrote one Supreme Court Justice in an article of that name.[26] The same justification was not available in the McLachlin era because it was the Court itself expanding the reach of the Charter.[27] Still, the

22 Hayden White, 'The Value of Narrativity in the Representation of Reality' (1980) 7:1 Critical Inquiry 5, 6-7.

23 Paul Ricoeur, *Oneself as Another* (Kathleen Balmey tr, University of Chicago Press 1992) 142.

24 On these categories and the different roles that history – in this case precedents – can play in constitutional adjudication, see in this volume Jorge M Farinacci Fernos, 'When History Requires the Use of History in Constitutional Adjudication'.

25 *Canadian Charter of Rights and Freedoms*, Part I of the *Constitution Act, 1982*, being Schedule B to the *Canada Act 1982* (UK), 1982, c 11, [*Charter*].

26 Bertha Wilson, 'We didn't volunteer' (April 1999) Policy Options 8.

27 I leave aside the question of *stare decisis* in other areas of law. In the context of federalism, see *R v Comeau* 2018 SCC 15, [2018] 1 SCR 342. In administrative law, see *Canada (Minister of Immigration and Citizenship) v Vavilov* 2019 SCC 65.

decisions of the Supreme Court overruling its earlier cases have not stirred much controversy nor generally been condemned as a grab of judicial power. In the public understanding, overruling precedent appears to fit within the regular functioning of courts in the Canadian constitutional system.

In 2013, in the *Bedford* decision,[28] the Supreme Court of Canada overruled its 1990 decision, the *Prostitution Reference*.[29] Before 2013, the *Criminal Code* forbade public solicitation for the purpose of selling sexual services, keeping a common bawdyhouse and living on the avails of prostitution. In the *Prostitution Reference*, the Court had upheld the constitutionality of these provisions of the Criminal Code. Even if they limited the right to freedom of expression, the Court explained, the limitation was justifiable 'in a free and democratic society'.[30] Between 1990 and 2013, numerous social science studies showed that sex workers, whose activity itself was lawful, were endangered by the criminal restrictions on provision of their services. When in 2002 it was discovered that a serial killer in Vancouver had murdered 49 women, most of whom were sex workers, their precarious situation gained heightened national public attention. In *Bedford*, the Court retreated from its earlier conclusion in the *Prostitution Reference* and ruled that the provisions of the Criminal Code were unconstitutional because they limited the rights to life, liberty and security protected under section 7 of the Canadian Charter of Rights and Freedoms. The Court in *Bedford* also identified two elements that could justify a lower court itself revisiting a Supreme Court decision: (1) if a new legal issue is raised or (2) if there has been 'significant developments in the law, […] in the circumstances or evidence that fundamentally shifts the parameters of the debate'.[31] Even as it examined the vertical strength of *stare decisis*, i.e. the doctrine that lower courts are generally strictly bound by the precedents of higher courts in the judicial hierarchy, *Bedford* avoided questions of horizontal *stare decisis*, i.e. how a court should treat its own past decisions.[32]

28 *Bedford v Canada (Attorney General)* 2013 SCC 72, [2013] 3 SCR 1101.

29 *Reference re ss. 193 and 195.1(1)(C) of the Criminal Code (Man.)* [1990] 1 SCR 1123. This was not technically a decision but an advisory opinion pursuant to section 53 of the *Supreme Court Act*, (1985) RSC c. S-26.

30 *Charter*, s. 1.

31 *Bedford v Canada (Attorney General)* 2013 SCC 72, [2013] 3 SCR 1101, para 42.

32 For a good discussion of recent developments in light of the cases discussed here, see Debra Parkes, 'Precedent Revisited: Carter v. Canada (AG) and the Contemporary Practice of Precedent' (2016) 10 MJLH 123. See also Debra Parkes, 'Precedent Unbound? Contemporary Approaches to Precedent in Canada' (2006) 32 Man. L.J. 135; Michelle Bloodworth, 'A Fact Is A Fact Is A Fact: *Stare Decisis* and The Distinction Between Adjudicative and Social Facts in *Bedford* and *Carter*' (2014) 32 NJCL 193.

In 2015 in *Saskatchewan Federation of Labour,*[33] the Court overruled a trilogy of precedents from 1987.[34] In this trilogy, the Supreme Court had restrictively interpreted the freedom of association. The Court had determined that labour legislation was not required to provide for a collective bargaining mechanism nor for a right to strike. That trilogy had been weakened by a line of subsequent cases;[35] the *Saskatchewan* ruling was the final step to holding that the freedom of association includes a general right to strike.[36] The decision is one of the very few instances where the question of the horizontal strength of *stare decisis* in cases of fundamental rights and freedoms was discussed at any length at the Supreme Court of Canada.[37] Justices Marshall Rothstein and Richard Wagner dissented in *Saskatchewan* and their criticism of the majority's reasoning had two components. First, they criticized the majority for constitutionalizing a specific model of labour law that, they said, involves balancing conflicting interests of unions, employees and employers in a way best left to the political process. Second, they criticized the majority for overturning the labour law trilogy. They based their opinion on the fact that, even if the doctrinal context had evolved since the labour law trilogy in 1987, no new social facts (as in *Bedford*) had emerged.

The two criticisms levelled by Rothstein and Wagner are related. Throughout their dissent, the dissenting justices imply that there is a connection between disregarding a previous ruling and reaching a decision that requires a political balancing of conflicting interests. That sort of criticism, linking an overreach of judicial power in the terrain of policymaking to a weak application of *stare decisis*, is much more common in response to decisions of the U.S. Supreme

---

33 *Saskatchewan Federation of Labour v Saskatchewan* 2015 SCC 4, [2015] 1 SCR 245.

34 *Reference re Public Service Employee Relations Act (Alta.)* [1987] 1 SCR 313; *PSAC v Canada* [1987] 1 SCR 424, *RWDSU v Saskatchewan* [1987] 1 SCR 460.

35 *Dunmore v Ontario (Attorney General)* 2001 SCC 94, [2001] 3 SCR 1016; *Health Services and Support – Facilities Subsector Bargaining Association v British Columbia* 2007 SCC 27, [2007] 2 SCR 391; *Ontario (Attorney General) v Fraser* 2011 SCC 20, [2011] 2 SCR 3, *Mounted Police Association of Ontario v Canada (Attorney General)* 2015 SCC 1, [2015] 1 SCR 3, *Meredith v Canada (Attorney General)* 2015 SCC 2, [2015] 1 SCR 125.

36 That right can be limited in some circumstances. Justice Abella writes for the majority: 'Where strike action is limited in a way that substantially interferes with a meaningful process of collective bargaining, it must be replaced by one of the meaningful dispute resolution mechanisms commonly used in labour relations'. *Saskatchewan Federation of Labour v Saskatchewan* 2015 SCC 4, [2015] 1 SCR 245, para 24.

37 Justice Rothstein's dissent in *Ontario (Attorney General) v Fraser* 2011 SCC 20, [2011] 2 SCR 3 also discussed *stare decisis* at length. However, he advocated overruling instead of following a previous decision.

Court.[38] *Saskatchewan* appears to be the first time in Canada that members of the Court have attacked the majority for its disregard of precedential authority in a case of fundamental rights and freedoms. Still, the criticism did not generate any sort of political reaction and it has remained the exception rather than the rule, with little lasting effect on Canadian constitutional culture.

In fact, a few months after *Saskatchewan*, Justice Rothstein and Wagner joined a unanimous Court in the *Carter*[39] decision to strike down the criminal prohibition on physician-assisted suicide. The decision also implicitly overruled the Court's 1993 decision in *Rodriguez* which had upheld the same provisions of the Criminal Code.[40] In *Carter* the Court considered issues of vertical *stare decisis* in eight short paragraphs but made no mention of horizontal *stare decisis*; the concerns that Rothstein and Wagner had voiced in *Saskatchewan* had apparently faded. *Carter* and *Bedford* were unanimous decisions, authored either by 'the Court' or the Chief Justice.[41] Precedent did not prove a dividing line between majorities and minorities on the Court. Both decisions were momentous, with considerable ripple effects in the political realm, but the fact that the Court had changed its mind and overruled a previous decision garnered little attention.

In most instances the Supreme Court of Canada avoids explicitly overruling its previous decisions. It relies instead on narrow technical grounds to avoid revisiting them. It uses coded language or hints such as that 'there are compelling reasons for declining to follow' a precedent,[42] or that even if the 'the basic tenets have not changed […] their application in particular cases' tilts the balance in the opposite direction.[43] Sometimes the exclusion of certain elements from the scope of a constitutional right 'can no longer stand'[44] or the result of a case needs to be 'revisited'.[45] Sometimes the Court avoids the question of *stare decisis* entirely by resolving a case on different grounds.[46] At other times,

38 The best example is perhaps Justice Scalia's dissent in *Lawrence* discussed below in section IV.

39 *Carter v Canada (Attorney General)* 2015 SCC 5, [2015] 1 SCR 331.

40 *Rodriguez v British Columbia (Attorney General)* [1993] 3 SCR 519.

41 The same was true for an earlier decision regarding extradition to face the death penalty that overruled a decision barely ten years old. See *United States v Burns* 2001 SCC 7, [2001] 1 SCR 283.

42 *R v Henry* 2005 SCC 76, [2005] 3 SCR 609, para 45.

43 *United States v Burns* 2001 SCC 7, [2001] 1 SCR 283, para 144.

44 *Health Services and Support – Facilities Subsector Bargaining Association v British Columbia* 2007 SCC 27, [2007] 2 SCR 391, para 20, 36.

45 *Mounted Police Association of Ontario v Canada (Attorney General)* 2015 SCC 1, [2015] 1 SCR 3, para 127.

46 *Bedford v Canada (Attorney General)* 2013 SCC 72, [2013] 3 SCR 1101, para 47.

judges justify a decision that seems to contradict a precedent on the basis that the 'historical, international, and jurisprudential landscape [...] has arrived at the destination sought'[47] by the dissenters in the earlier case.

Meanwhile, in the United States, the question of the strength of constitutional precedents has been a central topic of debate in the academic literature, in the decisions of the Supreme Court, and in political forums. Since *Planned Parenthood* v. *Casey*[48] in 1992 'reaffirmed' – while limiting – 'the central holding' of *Roe* v. *Wade*[49] on the basis of *stare decisis*, constitutional precedents have become the main argumentative move both in favour of and against constitutional change. In highly sensitive cases, *stare decisis* has been a constant dividing line between majorities and minorities. Members of the Court have accused each other of having 'so little regard for the usual principles of *stare decisis*' that they 'subvert all known principles of *stare decisis*',[50] of being 'manipulative in invoking the doctrine [of stare decisis]'[51] and of making an 'appeal to *stare decisis* [that] rings particularly hollow'.[52] Dissenters have written that '[t]he majority's decision is an act of will, not legal judgment [because it] has no basis in the Constitution or this Court's precedent'.[53] At other times, dissenters have complained that '[h]ow any of these ruminations weakens the force of stare decisis, escapes my comprehension'.[54]

Interest in precedent in the United States likely has a political dimension. According to Mark Tushnet, since the 1980s, the focus on precedent has intensified because '[l]iberals who formerly admired courts for rejecting restrictive precedents began to see the wisdom of adhering to the beleaguered rulings of the Warren Court, whereas conservatives began to say that it was all right to turn the clock back (and overrule recent decisions) if the clock was telling the wrong time'.[55] As the Supreme Court shifted more and more to the

---

47 *Saskatchewan Federation of Labour v Saskatchewan* 2015 SCC 4, [2015] 1 SCR 245, para 75.

48 *Planned Parenthood of Southeastern Pa.* v *Casey* 505 US 833 (1992).

49 *Roe v Wade* 410 US 113 (1973).

50 *Janus v American Federation of State, County and Municipal Employees, Council 31, no 16–1466*, 585 U.S. ___, 138 S. Ct. 2448, 2487, 2497 (2018) (Kagan J, dissenting).

51 *Lawrence v Texas* 539 US 558, 123 S. Ct. 2472, 2488 (2003) (Scalia J, dissenting).

52 *Parents Involved In Community Schools v Seattle School District No. 1* 551 US 701, 127 S. Ct. 2738, 2764 (2007) (Roberts CJ).

53 *Obergefell v Hodges* 576 US 644, 135 S. Ct. 2584, 2612 (2015) (Roberts CJ, dissenting).

54 *Citizens United v Federal Election Commission* 558 US 310, 130 S. Ct. 876, 939 (2010) (Stevens, J. dissenting).

55 Mark Tushnet, *Red, White, and Blue: A Critical Analysis of Constitutional Law* (Harvard UP 1988) 21. This diagnosis is also shared by others, including Lawrence B Solum, 'The Supreme Court in Bondage: Constitutional Stare Decisis, Legal Formalism, and the Future of Unenumerated Rights' (2006–2007) 9 U. Pa. J. Const. L. 155.

right of the political spectrum, liberals also came to appreciate the virtues of a loose application of *stare decisis* as the Court issued new 'beleaguered rulings'. Indeed, in *Citizens United,*[56] a 2010 decision that overruled a previous line of cases[57] and invalidated key provisions of federal campaign finance law on First Amendment grounds, liberals found their own *Roe* v. *Wade*. Hillary Clinton, the 2016 democratic candidate for the U.S. presidency, promised that overruling *Citizens United* would be a litmus test for her potential Supreme Court nominees;[58] Joe Biden promised in his 2020 presidential campaign to introduce a constitutional amendment to overrule the case.[59]

The significance of precedents in the American system is illustrated by the close attention to the issue in judicial confirmation hearings. Beginning with the appointment of Sandra Day O'Connor in 1981, broadcasting of hearings has greatly increased the length and the level of engagement of Senators in the confirmation process.[60] Confirmation hearings have become an important element of American constitutional culture. Future judges and justices appear before the Senate judiciary committee, which can thereby channel to the nominee the concerns of the American electorate. Although the confirmation process is decried by many scholars as highly dysfunctional, others have praised it because it allows elected representatives to weigh in on the Court's work on behalf of 'we the people'.[61]

Despite the inherently political nature of the confirmation process, nominees strive to present themselves as neutral arbiters distinct from political actors. They stress repeatedly how their work is to be understood through a legal frame, not a political one, emphasizing necessity rather than contingency in decision-making.[62] Tellingly, since 1981 all nominees to the United States

---

56 *Citizens United v Federal Election Commission* 558 US 310 (2010).

57 *Austin v Michigan Chamber of Commerce* 494 US 652 (1990); *McConnell v Federal Election Commission* 540 US 93 (2003).

58 Matea Gold and Anne Gearan, 'Hillary Clinton's litmus test for Supreme Court nominees: a pledge to overturn Citizens United' *Washington Post* (Washington, 14 May 2015) <https://www.washingtonpost.com/news/post-politics/wp/2015/05/14/hillary-clintons-litmus-test-for-supreme-court-nominees-a-pledge-to-overturn-citizens-united/> accessed 2 December 2020. One can also think of the importance of gun rights since *District of Columbia v Heller* 554 US 570, 128 S. Ct. 2783 (2008).

59 Biden for President, 'The Biden Plan to Guarantee Government Works for the People' (*Biden Harris*) <https://joebiden.com/governmentreform/#> accessed 2 December 2020.

60 Dion Farganis and Justin Wedeking, *Supreme Court Confirmation Hearings in the U.S. Senate: Reconsidering the Charade* (University of Michigan Press 2014) 80.

61 Paul M Collins and Lori A Ringhand, *Supreme Court Confirmation Hearings and Constitutional Change* (CUP 2013) 225–230.

62 In their analysis of public support for the Supreme Court during the Alito confirmation hearings, Gibson and Caldeira find that the framing effect of 'judiciousness' rather

Supreme Court have been questioned extensively about their views on precedent and *stare decisis*, making that issue among the most important nominees must address.[63]

In Canada, since 2004, the successive Conservative and Liberal Governments have experimented with a more open appointment process for members of the Supreme Court. One step has been to hold hearings for nominees before an ad hoc parliamentary committee. Many observers initially feared that such hearings would result in an Americanization and politicization of the appointment process.[64] However, Lawlor and Crandall report that participating Members of Parliament have focused on 'little beyond what could be gleaned from a biographical document' and that '[t]he questions asked by the committee were largely devoid of the level of interrogation of policy preferences and personal beliefs that may impact judicial decision making'.[65] Discussion of particular decisions, when it has occurred at all, has remained casual. In no instances have parliamentarians sought to gauge the adherence of appointees to *stare decisis* in general much less their commitment to specific court

---

than party affiliation or ideology is a difficult one to replace. They analyze the situation thus: 'The job of the opposition to a nominee is to try to substitute an alternative frame through which the debate can be conducted. That frame of course focuses on ideology, issues, and partisanship. We have seen, however, just how difficult it is for substitute frames to be effective. We attribute this to the wellspring of legitimacy enjoyed by the Supreme Court, and the consequence of this legitimacy, which is the belief that judges are different from ordinary politicians, and that therefore nominees ought to be evaluated on the basis of legal, not political, criteria. As long as the Supreme Court maintains its reservoir of goodwill – and if presidents are cagey enough to nominate candidates for whom an easy prima facie case for judiciousness can be made – it seems unlikely that political forces can be effectively mobilized to deny presidents their choices'. James L Gibson and Gregory A Caldeira, *Citizens, Courts and Confirmations: Positivity Theory and The Judgments Of The American People* (Princeton UP 2009) 94–95.

63 Jason J Czarnecki, William K Ford and Lori A Ringhand, 'An Empirical Analysis of the Confirmation Hearings of the Justice of the Rehnquist Natural Court' (2007) 24 Const. Comment. 127. For an interesting contrast with the Canadian experience, see Andrea Lawlor and Erin Crandall, 'Questioning Judges With a Questionable Process: An Analysis of Committee Appearances by Canadian Supreme Court Candidates' (2015) 48 Can. J. Pol. Sci. 863.

64 For a review of the arguments, see Peter McCormick, 'Selecting the Supremes: The Appointment of Judges to the Supreme Court of Canada' (2005) 7 J. App. Prac. & Process 1. From an empirical perspective, see Matthew E Wetstein and others, 'Ideological Consistency and Attitudinal Conflict: A Comparative Analysis of the U.S. and Canadian Supreme Courts' (2009) 42 Comp. Pol. Stud. 763, 785–786.

65 Andrea Lawlor and Erin Crandall, 'Questioning Judges With a Questionable Process: An Analysis of Committee Appearances by Canadian Supreme Court Candidates' (2015) 48 Can. J. Pol. Sci. 863, 880.

decisions. In his analysis of the media coverage of the new appointment process, Schneiderman concludes that '[o]verall coverage might best be described as a big 'love-in''.[66] These features set the Canadian process apart from what occurs in the United States. There, confirmation hearings are often divisive affairs, not least because of the intense focus on whether and when a nominee will vote to overturn a prior judicial decision. One result is the American notion of 'super-precedents'.

3 Super-Precedents

In American constitutional culture, certain judicial decisions have come to constitute fixed points of agreement about the meaning and the legitimacy of the constitutional project. This process of entrenchment of certain fundamental constitutional decisions plays out at different levels: doctrinal, political, sociological. These 'super-precedents' are decisions that are so entrenched that they are very unlikely to be revisited or reconsidered.

Michael Gerhardt defines super-precedents as 'fixtures of the legal framework' that 'seep deep into the public consciousness'. They are 'constitutional decisions whose correctness is no longer a viable issue for courts to decide'. In a nutshell, 'super precedents take on a special status in constitutional law as landmark opinions, so encrusted and deeply embedded in constitutional law that they have become practically immune to reconsideration and reversal'.[67] In this sense, it is particularly their sociological rather than doctrinal dimension that distinguishes American decisions from Canadian ones.[68] The invocation of 'Miranda rights' in American TV shows provides perhaps the best example of the omnipresence of landmark decisions in the legal consciousness of the American public. When they become entrenched not only in legal textbooks but also in popular constitutional culture, super-precedents form what Sanford Levinson and Jack Balkin call 'canonical' decisions of constitutional

66 David Schneiderman, *Red, White, and Kind of Blue: The Conservatives and the Americanization of Canadian Constitutional Culture* (University of Toronto Press 2015) 279.

67 Michael J Gerhardt, 'Super Precedent' (2006) 90 Minn L Rev 1204, 1205, 1217–1218.

68 Michael Gerhardt distinguishes three types of super-precedents: precedents establishing a doctrine, precedents establishing a practice, and foundational precedents or precedents that settle an important constitutional dispute and are accepted by the public and the other branches. Michael J Gerhardt, *The Power of Precedent* (OUP 2008) ch. 6. See also, Michael J Gerhardt, 'Super Precedent' (2006) 90 Minn L Rev 1204.

law.[69] These canonical decisions are central elements of constitutional literacy which play an important role in civic life because they give citizens a way to address the defects of their legal system in terms that are compatible with the system as a whole. '[C]ultural literacy in constitutional matters', Levinson and Balkin write, 'is important because it fosters pride in and attachment to the American political community. At least some cases may form part of the canon because they seem to promote an appealing portrait of 'America-the-good''.[70]

Super-precedents have been a recurring theme of confirmation hearings since 2005 when nominee John G. Roberts Jr. appeared before the Senate Judiciary Committee. Committee Chairman Arlene Spector asked Roberts if he believed in 'super-precedent' or what Spector called 'super-duper-precedent'. Roberts answered that he considered *stare decisis* to be a very important doctrine, but he otherwise dodged the question of 'super-precedent'.[71] Similar exchanges occurred in the confirmation hearings for Samuel Alito,[72] Sonia Sotomayor,[73] Neil Gorsuch[74] and Amy Coney Barrett.[75] Barrett, tellingly, had written articles on the subject of precedent and *stare decisis* before her appointment to the bench.[76]

---

69 Sanford Levinson and Jack Balkin, 'The Canons of Constitutional Law' (1998) 111 Harv L Rev 963.

70 ibid 977.

71 Senate Committee on the Judiciary, *Confirmation Hearing on the Nomination of John G. Roberts Jr. to be Chief Justice of the Supreme Court of the United States* 109th Cong (United States Government Printing Office, 2005) 145. See also, Jeffrey Rosen, 'So, Do You Believe in Superprecedent?' *New York Times* (New York, 30 October 2005) <http://www.nytimes.com/2005/10/30/weekinreview/so-do-you-believe-in-superprecedent.html> accessed 2 December 2020.

72 Senate Committee on the Judiciary, *Confirmation Hearing on the Nomination of Samuel A. Alito, Jr. to be an Associate Justice of the Supreme Court of the United States*, 109th Cong (United States Government Printing Office 2006) 321.

73 Senate Committee on the Judiciary, *Confirmation Hearing on the Nomination of Hon. Sonia Sotomayor, To Be An Associate Justice of the Supreme Court of the United States*, 111th Cong (United States Government Printing Office 2009) 15, 376.

74 Senate Committee on the Judiciary, *Confirmation Hearing on the Nomination of Hon. Neil M. Gorsuch To Be An Associate Justice of the Supreme Court of the United States*, 115th Cong (United States Government Printing Office 2017) 7, 77, 78, 84, 258.

75 Siobhan Hughes, 'Barrett: Why Roe Isn't a Super Precedent' *Wall Street Journal* (New York, 13 October 2020) <https://www.wsj.com/livecoverage/amy-coney-barrett-supreme-court-confirmation-hearing-day-two/card/mvQLaARCKTb3gS16iE1z?mod=e2twp> accessed 2 December 2020. While questioned extensively about precedents generally, the expression 'super-precedent' has not been used during the confirmation hearing of Elena Kagan and Brett Kavanaugh.

76 See, e.g., Amy Coney Barrett, 'Stare Decisis and Due Process' (2003) 74 U Colo L Rev 1011; Amy Coney Barrett, 'Statutory Stare Decisis in the Court of Appeals' (2005) 73 Geo Wash

Confirmation hearings do not simply reveal pre-existing norms. They also participate in the creation and crystallization of those norms.[77] The discussion of specific constitutional cases may secure a commitment to core decisions that the public in general or the senators in particular view as non-negotiable and beyond reconsideration. By determining fixed points of agreement, the process creates for the public legal consciousness and for the justices themselves a coherent constitutional narrative.[78]

Nominees who question the super-precedents constitutive of this narrative risk being rejected. That is what happened in 1987 to Supreme Court nominee Robert H. Bork, whose hearing outcome influenced the candor with which all subsequent nominees have answered committee questions.[79] Many senators (and other observers) viewed Bork's originalism as extreme. At his hearing, senators questioned Bork about the compatibility of his originalist methodology to the outcome in *Brown* v. *Board of Education*, the landmark decision holding racially segregated public schooling unconstitutional. Although Bork said that *Brown* was rightly decided, he failed to convince senators that the decision was consistent with his own originalism. Bork also stated that *Griswold*[80] – which recognized a right of privacy that included the right of married couples to use contraception and provided a basis for the right to abortion recognized in *Roe* v. *Wade* – was wrongly decided.[81] Finally, when Senator Hatch, a supporter of Bork, asked him to identify the most controversial case in American constitutional law, Bork said it was *Brown*. Hatch interrupted with, "Or perhaps Dred Scott?", but the attempted rescue came too late.[82] Linda Greenhouse explains that '[a]s Senator Hatch immediately grasped, the nominee had violated a cardinal rule of modern judicial confirmation hearings, which is that *Brown*

L Rev 317; Amy Coney Barrett, 'Precedent and Judicial Disagreement' (2013) 91 Tex L Rev 1711; Amy Coney Barrett, 'Originalism and Stare Decisis' (2017) 92 Notre Dame L Rev 1921.

77 The point is underscored by Michael J Gerhardt, *The Power of Precedent* (OUP 2008) 191–198 and by Paul M Collins and Lori A Ringhand, *Supreme Court Confirmation Hearings and Constitutional Change* (CUP 2013) 264–266.

78 See the discussion in David Schneiderman, *Red, White, and Kind of Blue: The Conservatives and the Americanization of Canadian Constitutional Culture* (University of Toronto Press 2015) 252–258.

79 Senate Committee on the Judiciary, *Nomination of Robert H. Bork To Be Associate Justice Of The Supreme Court Of The United States* 100th Cong (United States Government Printing Office 1989).

80 *Griswold v Connecticut* 381 US 479 (1965).

81 Senate Committee on the Judiciary, *Nomination of Robert H. Bork To Be Associate Justice Of The Supreme Court Of The United States* 100th Cong (United States Government Printing Office 1989) 117–118.

82 ibid 186.

v. *Board of Education* is beyond debate'.[83] Michael Gerhardt provides a complementary explanation. In addition to his 'candid criticism of *Brown*',[84] Bork's nomination to the Supreme Court failed because of 'his candid declaration that *Griswold* was wrongly decided, reinforcing the impression he may have lacked a sufficient regard for precedent generally'.[85] Bork's comments not only questioned some decisions of constitutional law, but the very decisions that give meaning to the American constitutional project as a whole, i.e. to fixed points of agreement in the dominant constitutional narrative that provide 'an appealing portray of 'America-the-good''.[86]

Viewed from Canada, super-precedents appear a distinctively American phenomenon. While Canada does have important decisions that are cited repeatedly, such decisions are not constituted as a coherent body exhibiting the historical unfolding of a single and coherent narrative. American judges invoke *Marbury* v. *Madison*, *Brown* v. *Board of Education*, *Loving* v. *Virginia* and even *Lawrence* v. *Texas* as the proof of the slow unfolding of the liberal egalitarian promise at the heart of the American constitutional project. Canadian judges do not have a comparable dominant constitutional narrative to draw upon and thus lack the rhetorical resources to explain the value (or flaws) of their prior decisions.

4 Dominant or Elusive Constitutional Narrative

The principal difference between the Canadian and the American approach to constitutional precedents concerns the embeddedness of precedents within a constitutional narrative. The narrativization of constitutional history in the United States and its use by judges and other legal officials influence the

83 Linda Greehouse, 'Robert Bork's Tragedy' *The New York Times Opiniator* (New York, 9 January 2013) <http://opinionator.blogs.nytimes.com/2013/01/09/robert-borks-tragedy/> accessed 2 December 2020.

84 Michael J Gerhardt, *The Power of Precedent* (OUP 2008) 184.

85 ibid 186. See also the discussion in David Schneiderman, *Red, White, and Kind of Blue: The Conservatives and the Americanization of Canadian Constitutional Culture* (University of Toronto Press 2015) 252–258. Compare Robert H. Bork's comments on *Griswold* with the future Chief Justice John G. Roberts Jr.'s comments about the entrenchment of this decision in the settled core of American constitutional law, see Senate Committee on the Judiciary, *Confirmation Hearing on the Nomination of John G. Roberts Jr. to be Chief Justice of the Supreme Court of the United States* 109th Cong (United States Government Printing Office 2005) 261–263.

86 Sanford Levinson and Jack Balkin, 'The Canons of Constitutional Law', (1998) 111 Harv L Rev 963, 977.

importance and function of precedents. Given that there is no such dominant narrative about Canada's political identity, constitutional precedents do not provide meaningful orientation beyond their central holding.

Many scholars have sought to describe the Canadian constitutional and political identity. These efforts have had only limited success. As sociologist Seymour Martin Lipset writes in his seminal comparative political and sociological analysis of Canada and the United States, '[n]ational identity is the quintessential Canadian issue. Almost alone among modern developed countries, Canada has continued to debate its self-conception to the present day'.[87] In fact, as Charles Taylor puts, the question that has haunted Canada since its inception is 'what is a country for? That is, what ought to be the basis of unity around which a sovereign political entity can be built? This is a strange question, in a way; it is not one that would likely be asked in many countries. But it arises here because there are alternatives and, therefore, need for justification'.[88] Uncertainty about the constitutional project itself means that Canadians have failed to develop a dominant and comprehensive narrative to explain and justify their own constitutional institutions. In 2002, Samuel LaSelva observed 'Canadians seem increasingly unable even to live under a common constitution, let alone recognize a constitutional faith'.[89] In 2018, even with the decline of Quebec separatism efforts, LaSelva could still write that '[c]ompared to the American version, Canada's constitutional faith seems both elusive and unrealized'.[90]

The question of Canada's constitutional origin feeds an existential ambivalence. While the American founding has a date, 1776 or, alternatively, 1787, Canada's origin point is much harder to pin down. The Sesquicentennial of the 1867 Constitution in 2017 generated little enthusiasm and instead raised questions about whether 1867 actually represented Canada's beginning.[91] Paul Kahn observed that in the United States the legal order is conceptually envisaged as succeeding to the state of nature and marks as such the beginning of history: 'This state of nature exists before history begins. It is without any

87 Seymour Martin Lipset, *Continental Divide: The Values and Institutions of the United States and Canada* (Routledge 1991) 42.

88 Charles Taylor, 'Can Canada Survive the Charter?' (1992) 30 Alta. L. Rev. 427, 427–428.

89 Samuel V LaSelva, 'Federalism, Pluralism, and Constitutional Faith: Canada In Question' (2002) 7 Rev. Const. Stud. 204, 205.

90 Samuel V LaSelva, *Canada and the Ethics of Constitutionalism: Identity, Destiny, and Constitutional Faith* (McGill-Queen's UP 2018) 133.

91 In general, see the articles collected in the special edition of *Canadian Issues*, (2016). See especially Jack Jedwab, 'The Politics of Founding Canada: Then and Now' (2016) Canadian Issues 17.

sense of time at all, except a constantly repeating cycle of desire and satisfaction. We speak of 'foundings' and 'origins' – the 'birth of the nation' – as if the time before our legal order did not exist in the same historical dimension'.[92] Uncertainty about Canada's founding date makes a comparable account in Canada far more difficult.

Canada's Constitution Act, 1867 also does not reflect much of a political ideology. Canadian constitutional drafters were less interested than the American founders had been in proclaiming democratic and republican ideals.[93] Constitutional drafters in Canada were instead largely focused on reassuring colonial authorities that the constitutional design would be acceptable to the French Canadiens and the North American British alike.[94]

For much of its history the Supreme Court of Canada was itself limited in its capacity to issue ground-breaking and inspirational rulings because it only became the country's final court of appeal in 1949, and until 1975 its institutional role was more oriented towards correcting the errors of lower courts than developing the law.[95] The limited role of the Court helps explain the relatively marginal role of symbolic legal figures and important judicial decisions in Canadian constitutional culture. Pierre Elliott Trudeau himself recognized rather cheerfully this situation early in his career. Writing in 1969, Trudeau captured an essential difference between the Canadian and the American constitutional project. He observed that in reading the British North America Act, 1867, Canada's main constitutional document, 'one is struck by its absence of

---

92 Paul W Kahn, *The Cultural Study of Law: Reconstructing Legal Scholarship* (University of Chicago Press 1998) 16.

93 Peter H Russell, *Constitutional Odyssey: Can Canadians Become A Sovereign People?* (2nd edn, University of Toronto Press, 1992) 3–6. Some scholars, like Janet Ajzenstadt, have questioned Russell's reading of Confederation and helped to recast the views of the framers of the British North America Act, 1867 in a more intellectually sophisticated light. However, Ajzenstadt herself recognizes that the dominant scholarly tradition has been to attribute such little value to the views of the framers to the point of ignoring their debates up until very recently. She writes that 'American scholars and the American public are constantly engaged in the study of origins. […] How very different is the situation in this country! Some of the documents pertaining to Confederation have never been published; many that were once available are out of print. Canadians are relentlessly future-oriented. The idea of turning to the past for instruction strikes us as futile – absurd'. See Janet Ajzenstadt, *The Canadian Founding: John Locke and Parliament* (McGill Queen's UP 2007) 20.

94 Peter H Russell, *Constitutional Odyssey: Can Canadians Become A Sovereign People?* (2nd edn, University of Toronto Press 1992) ch. 2 and 3.

95 James Snell and Frederick Vaughan, *The Supreme Court of Canada: History of the Institution* (University of Toronto Press 1985) 238–241. See also, Emmett MacFarlane, *Governing from the Bench: The Supreme Court of Canada and the Judicial Role* (UBC Press 2013) 42–43.

principles, ideals, or other frills; even the regional safeguards and minority guarantees are pragmatically presented, here and there, rather than proclaimed as a thrilling bill of rights'. Trudeau added that while the idea of liberty is the 'binding force' of the United States and is proclaimed in all its constitutional documents, 'the Canadian nation seems [by comparison] founded on the common sense of empirical politicians who had wanted to establish some law and order over a disjointed half-continent'.[96] During his political career, Trudeau championed the idea of providing Canada with its own constitutional founding moment, an effort that culminated in the 1982 Patriation of the Constitution from the United Kingdom and the adoption of the Canadian Charter of Rights and Freedoms.[97] However, the struggle between Ottawa and the Provinces in the process that led to Patriation[98] and the fact that the package was never put to the people for a vote[99] made for an uncertain foundational document.

The Charter itself was also of limited significance. As a renowned academic wrote contemporaneously to the adoption of the Charter, 'the Charter of Rights broke no significant new ground in comparison to the classical bills of rights such as those of the United States and France [and] no doubt stemmed in measure from the dominant role of technocrats and bureaucrats generally in the actual drafting (poets and philosophers-state-men were influential in the elaboration of the American and French charters)'.[100] When the Charter was adopted, the title of a book captured the anti-climatic nature of the moment: 'And No One Cheered'.[101]

Further, Quebec never even formally signed onto patriation. That provoked two rounds of constitutional renegotiation in which Canada's very existence

96 Pierre Elliott Trudeau, *Federalism and the French Canadians* (Macmillan 1969) 197.

97 On the *Charter* as intended primarily for nation-building, see Rainer Knopff and FL Morton, *Charter Politics* (Nelson Canada 1992) 73–78. See also, Peter H Russell, 'The Political Purposes of the Canadian Charter of Rights and Freedoms' (1983) 61 Can. Bar Rev. 30.

98 See, among others, Alan C Cairns, 'The Politics of Constitutional Renewal in Canada' in Alan C Cairns and Douglas E Williams (eds), *Disruptions: Constitutional Struggles, from the Charter to Meech Lake* (McLelland and Stewart 1991); Roy Romanow, John Whyte and Howard Leeson, *Canada … Notwithstanding: The Making of the Constitution 1976–1982* (Carswell 1984); Frédéric Bastien, *La Bataille de Londres. Dessous, secrets et coulisses du rapatriement constitutionnel* (Boréal 2013).

99 Bruce A Ackerman and Robert E Charney, 'Canada at the Constitutional Crossroads' (1984) 34 U.T.L.J. 117.

100 Edward McWhinney, *Canada and the Constitution 1979–1982* (University of Toronto Press 1982) 55–56.

101 Keith Banting and Richard Simeon (eds), *And no One Cheered: Federalism, Democracy and the Constitution Act* (Methuen 1983).

was in play.[102] The failed constitutional amendments stemming from the Meech Lake Accord (1987–1990) and the Charlottetown Accord (1991–1992) worsened the condition of incompleteness of the Canadian constitution and created an 'internal exile within the federation' for Quebecers.[103] Moreover, Canada's recent reckoning with its colonial past, exemplified by the report of the Truth and Reconciliation Commission of 2015, has called into question the place of Indigenous peoples within Canada with accompanying demands for changes of a constitutional magnitude.[104]

Yet it is not that Canada has failed to develop narrations of its past at all. What Canada lacks is a single dominant and coherent constitutional narrative. Canada's constitutional culture is entangled in contradictions and tensions. One possible narrative candidate is liberal multiculturalism. But as a narrative multiculturalism has significant limitations. First, a large part of the population rejects it.[105] For example, many in Quebec are suspicious of multiculturalism, condemning it as a strategy to displace Quebec nationalism and the compact theory of federalism by diluting Quebec's cultural identity.[106]

---

102 Former Quebec Premier, Philippe Couillard, said in 2013 when he became the leader of the Quebec Liberal Party that he hoped Quebec could come back in the Confederation, thereby alluding to a possible symbolic signature of the 1982 Constitution Act for the 150th anniversary of the B.N.A. Act in 2017. This did not occur, but the Government released a new constitutional policy. Gouvernement du Québec, *Quebecers, Our Way of Being Canadian*, (Gouvernement du Québec 2017).

103 Guy Laforest, *Interpreting Quebec's Exile Within the Federation* (Peter Lang 2014) ch. 1.

104 Truth and Reconciliation Commission of Canada, *Honouring the Truth, Reconciling for the Future* (TRC 2015).

105 According to a 2015 poll by the Environics Institute, 'multiculturalism' (54%) ranks far below the Health Care System (88%) as a very important symbol of Canadian identity. Quebecers are the least likely to find multiculturalism to be a very important Canadian symbol (39%). The Environics Institute for Survey Research, *Focus Canada 2015: Canadian Public Opinion about Immigration and Multiculturalism*, (Environics Institute 2015) <https://www.environicsinstitute.org/docs/default-source/project-documents/focus-canada-2015-survey-on-immigration-and-multiculturalism/final-report.pdf?sfvrsn=71f7c79e_2> accessed 2 December 2020. Quebecers are also much less prone to identify the Canadian Charter (which constitutionally entrenches multiculturalism) as a defining characteristic of Canadian identity. Statistics Canada, *Perception of national symbols as very important to the Canadian identity, by province, 2013* (General Social Survey 2013) <https://www150.statcan.gc.ca/n1/pub/89-652-x/2015005/t/tbl01-eng.htm> accessed 2 December 2020.

106 See, e.g., Joseph Facal, *Quelque chose comme un grand peuple* (Boréal 2012) ch. 5; Mathieu Bock-Côté, *Le multiculturalisme comme idéologie politique* (Cerf 2016). See also the discussion in Gérard Bouchard, *L'interculturalisme: Un point de vue québécois* (Boréal 2012) 93–107.

No Quebec Premier, federalist or separatist, has ever endorsed multiculturalism.[107] Likewise, for many Indigenous groups the multicultural liberal framework is simply incompatible with their traditional ways of life or tone-deaf to their constitutional claims.[108]

Second, multiculturalism has had a slow impact on Canadian constitutional culture because it is a somewhat recent creation that coincides with the initial steps that led towards the adoption of the Canadian Charter of Rights and Freedoms. Multiculturalism and the Charter were two projects of the same generation, the same party, even the same person, i.e. Pierre Elliott Trudeau. There is still resistance among the political elites to this conception of Canadian constitutional culture. The Conservative Government of Stephen Harper (2006 - 2015) attempted to rebrand a more 'Tory' conception of Canadian identity and to move away from the liberal-multicultural script.[109] As such, multiculturalism lacks the kind of multi-generational and consensual character that, for example, the Declaration of Independence or the Reconstruction Amendments have acquired in the American constitutional narrative.[110]

Understood in a broader historical context, the Patriation of the Constitution and the adoption of the Charter were more projects of self-government that empowered Canada to amend its own constitution than they were aspirational moments.[111] Even the metaphors employed to justify the exercise of judicial

107 Gérard Bouchard, *L'interculturalisme: Un point de vue québécois* (Boréal 2012) 93.

108 See, e.g., Glen Sean Coulthard, *Red Skin, White Masks: Rejecting the Colonial Politics of Recognition* (University of Minnesota Press 2014). On the topic of multiculturalism and the place of First Nations within Canada's constitutional faith, see Samuel V LaSelva, *Canada and the Ethics of Constitutionalism: Identity, Destiny, and Constitutional Faith* (McGill-Queen's UP 2018) ch. 8.

109 See Ian McKay and Jamie Swift, *Warrior Nations: Rebranding Canada in an Age of Anxiety* (Between the Lines 2012) 269–271; Raymond B Blake, 'A New Canadian Dynamism? From Multiculturalism and Diversity to History and Core Values' (2013) 26 Brit J Can Stud 79; Yasmeen Abu-Laban, 'Reforms by Stealth: the Harper Conservatives and Canadian Multiculturalism' in Jack Jedwab (ed), *The Multiculturalism Question: Debating Identity in 21st-Century Canada* (McGill-Queens UP 2014) 149. As Garth Stevenson notes, however, "[a]lthough occasional grumbling is still heard in the media, there is no longer any politically significant opposition to the word [multiculturalism] in Anglophone Canada". Garth Stevenson, *Building Nations from Diversity: Canadian and American Experience Compared* (McGill-Queen's UP 2014) 223.

110 In the Oxford Handbook on the Canadian constitution published in 2017, multiculturalism does not even get a chapter. See Peter Oliver, Patrick Macklem and Nathalie Des Rosiers (eds), *Oxford Handbook of Canadian Constitutional Law* (OUP 2017).

111 On the historical development that led to the adoption of the Charter, told from an insider's perspective, see Barry L Strayer, *Canada's Constitutional Revolution* (University of Alberta Press, 2013).

power since the adoption of the Charter underscore this dimension. The metaphor of dialogue offers an image of the Charter that fits within Canada's 'demos-enabling', not 'demos-constraining', constitutional institutions.[112] Rather than forestalling constitutional change, the Charter is thus seen as a complement to other institutions of strong self-government easy to maneuver like parliamentarianism and cabinet government. These institutions provide 'flexibility' and 'muscularity' to the state and stand in contrast to the general anti-statism of the American constitutional system of strict separation of powers designed to limit the possibilities of political change.[113] The 'dialogue' metaphor, which scholars and judges alike have used as a justification for the Canadian model of judicial review, portrays the Charter as a tool of self-government rather than a program or an ideal to be reached.[114] But the 'dialogue' metaphor is also a phenomenon of high legal culture meant as a response to critics of judicial activism. And while it might have assuaged the fears of some majoritarian democrats, the metaphor has not produced popular attachment to any single and coherent constitutional vision.[115] The theory of dialogue provides neither the reason nor the explanation for adoption of the Charter but only a justification for the new institutional function of the Supreme Court since 1982.[116]

In addition to the 'dialogue' metaphor, the Supreme Court has regularly invoked the notion of the constitution as a 'living tree'. The Court revived this metaphor in the early 1980s, a time when 'originalism' was gaining traction in American constitutional theory, both in academia and on the bench.[117] As the

---

112 See, in general, the discussion in David Schneiderman, *Red, White, and Kind of Blue: The Conservatives and the Americanization of Canadian Constitutional Culture* (University of Toronto Press 2015) 27–41. On anti-statism as a distinctively American cultural trait, see Seymour Martin Lipset, *Continental Divide: The Values and Institutions of the United States and Canada* (Routledge 1991) 20–22.

113 David Schneiderman, *Red, White, and Kind of Blue: The Conservatives and the Americanization of Canadian Constitutional Culture* (University of Toronto Press 2015) 67.

114 For the first formulation and the main exposition of the theory of dialogue, see Peter Hogg and Alison Bushell, 'The Charter Dialogue Between Courts and Legislatures (Or Perhaps the Charter Isn't Such a Bad Thing After All)' (1997) 35 Osgoode Hall L.J. 75; Kent Roach, *The Supreme Court on Trial: Judicial Activism of Democratic Dialogue* (Irwin Law 2001). See also *Vriend* v. *Alberta*, [1998] 1 R.C.S. 493.

115 See Stéphane Bernatchez, 'Les traces du débat sur la légitimité de la justice constitutionnelle dans la jurisprudence de la Cour Suprême du Canada' (2005–06) 36 R.D.U.S. 165.

116 On the poor explanatory power of the theory of constitutional dialogue, see generally Jean-Christophe Bédard-Rubin, 'Des Causes et des Conséquences du Dialogue Constitutionnel' (2018) 23 Rev. Const. Stud. 287.

117 Justice Antonin Scalia, undoubtedly the most prominent proponent of originalism in the United States, was appointed to the Supreme Court of the United States in 1986. A series of speeches by then-Attorney General Edwin Meese promoting originalism in 1985 helped

first Charter cases made their way to the Supreme Court, Canadian justices had to position themselves on the importance of the intentions of the 'drafters' of the Charter for purposes of constitutional interpretation.[118] The 'living tree' signalled the justices' refusal to import originalism and its denial of judicial agency into Canada.[119] But, in addition to the rejection of originalism, the living tree doctrine also reinforced a conception of the Canadian constitutional project as incomplete, indeterminate and open to change.[120]

As Hugo Cyr observes, the Canadian constitutional imagination is animated by the idea that the Canadian constitution is still to be made.[121] Individuals involved in bringing the project to full fruition should be understood as engaged in constitutional meaning-making rather than as expounding a constitution given to them. 'The Constitution is thus not only found', writes Cyr, 'it is not a mere object of knowledge, it is also made – it is the product of some ongoing process'. Instead of looking at the constitution as the object of reverence for something that was handed down, '[r]especting the Constitution thus implies not only following it, but may also imply helping it move towards its destination'.[122] Cyr explains that, given this kind of narration, courts, and

---

give it wider public attention. On the beginnings of originalism as a mainstream doctrine of constitutional interpretation, see Steven G Calabresi, *Originalism: A Quarter-Century of Debate* (Regnery Publishing 2007).

118 On the use of the *Persons* case in early charter jurisprudence and the rejection of originalism, see Bradley W Miller, 'Origin Myth: The Persons Case, The Living Tree and the New Originalism' in Grant Huscroft and Bradley W Miller (eds), *The Challenge of Originalism: Theories of Constitutional Interpretation* (CUP 2013). See, in particular, *Re B.C. Motor Vehicle Act* [1985] 2 SCR 486.

119 On originalism and history as a denial of agency, see in this volume Mark D Rosen, 'History: Limit or License in Constitutional Adjudication'.

120 See, among others, Seymour Martin Lipset, *Continental Divide: The Values and Institutions of the United States and Canada* (Routledge 1990); Charles Taylor, *Rapprocher les solitudes: Écrits sur le fédéralisme et le nationalisme au Canada* (Presses de l'Université Laval 1992); Roderick A MacDonald, 'Three Centuries of Constitution Making in Canada: Will there be a fourth?' (1996) 30 UBC L Rev 211; Jocelyn Létourneau, *Passer à l'avenir: histoire, mémoire, identité dans le Québec d'aujourd'hui* (Boréal 2000); Samuel V LaSelva, 'Federalism, Pluralism, and Constitutional Faith: Canadian Question' (2002) 7 Rev. Const. Stud. 204; Hugo Cyr, 'Conceptual Metaphors for an Unfinished Constitution' (2014) 19 Rev. Const. Stud. 1; David Schneiderman, *Red, White, and Kind of Blue: The Conservatives and the Americanization of Canadian Constitutional Culture* (University of Toronto Press 2015); Peter H Russell, *Canada's Odyssey: A Country Based on Incomplete Conquest* (University of Toronto Press 2017).

121 Hugo Cyr, 'Conceptual Metaphors for an Unfinished Constitution' (2014) 19 Rev. Const. Stud. 1.

122 Hugo Cyr, 'Conceptual Metaphors for an Unfinished Constitution' (2014) 19 Rev. Const. Stud. 1, 7. For an analysis of Canada's metaphorical vocabulary as caught between the

especially the Supreme Court, have relied heavily on a series of metaphors – in particular the 'living tree' metaphor – to illustrate their own perception of their institutional role in making the Constitution more complete.

In the United States, the fate of the nation seems on the contrary to be tied to its constitutional history. As the historian Hans Kohn writes, the United States Constitution is 'so intimately welded with the national existence itself that the two have become inseparable'.[123] The creation of the American nation involved a severance of legal ties to England, with the Declaration of Independence, and constituted Americans as a people.[124] Moreover, the ratification of the proposed constitution by the states in the years between 1787 and 1790 still makes this founding moment, i.e. the adoption of a constitution by 'we the people', a landmark achievement even by contemporary standards.[125] As Paul Kahn observes of the American people,

> [l]ife under the rule of law is a way of imagining history, the state, and the self – their changes and continuities. The rule of law may be our deepest political myth. It is the foundation of our beliefs about our community as a single people with a unique history, as well as our view of our individual obligations to the state.[126]

Given the important symbolic force of the American constitution, referring to its drafters or its early expounders is very useful and has powerful rhetorical force. Contemporary constitutional decisions are replete with rhetorical references to early constitutional decisions, the *Federalist Papers*, or great justices like John Marshall.[127] American judges present themselves as heirs of a

---

image of the 'unfinished' and the 'endangered' constitution, see Étienne Cloutier, 'A Tale of Two Metaphors: A Narrative Take on the Canadian Constitution' (2019) 64 McGill L.J. 447. For an assessment of the silences of Canada's constitution testifying to its condition of incompleteness, see Dave Guénette, 'Le silence des textes constitutionnels canadiens – expression d'une constitution encore inachevée' (2015) 56 C. de D. 411.

123 Hans Kohn, *American Nationalism: An Interpretive Essay* (Macmillan 1957) 8.

124 Sanford Levinson, *Constitutional Faith* (Princeton UP 1988) 11.

125 See Zachary Elkins, Tom Ginsburg and Justin Blount, 'The Citizen as Founder: Public Participation In Constitutional Approval' (2008) 81 Temp. L. Rev. 361.

126 Paul W Kahn, *The Reign of Law: Marbury v. Madison and the Construction of America* (Yale UP 1997) XI.

127 See, for example, the concurrence of Justice Stevens in *Roper* v. *Simmons*, where the Court adopted a decisively 'evolutionary' reading of the protection against 'cruel and unusual punishment'. Stevens filed a concurring opinion of one paragraph only to celebrate this evolutionary approach, but he could not help but conclude by referring to two founding fathers and early expounders of the constitution. He writes: 'In the best tradition of the common law, the pace of [the] evolution [of the law] is a matter for continuing

tradition that transcends them, that was wholly given at the moment of origin, and that they must interpret; instances of constitutional change are presented as exercises of retrieval rather than creation, in which the law, not the individual judge, speaks.

5 Narratives of Constitutional History

Constitutional thought in the United States generally involves a narrativization of constitutional history that 'feigns to make the world speak itself and speak itself *as a story*'.[128] The narrative is rooted in clear beginnings and pictured as the progressive unfolding of the liberal egalitarianism at the core of the American constitutional project.

This kind of narrativization has many effects that are of interest to a study of constitutional precedents and constitutional historicity more generally. It gives historical arguments (including originalism) a preeminent place in arguments about constitutional meaning.[129] It also portrays current decisions as necessary, i.e. as the ineluctable next step in a process in which the judges simply recognize the pre-existing law but play no (or only a minimal) role in its creation. The narrative suppresses the contingency of judicial decisions and makes them appear fully determined by constitutional history. Finally, the narrative influences the way in which constitutional change is understood; change is seen as a way of going back to the correct interpretation, as recovering the true meaning of the constitutional project, rather than as the creation of new constitutional meaning.

Consider, for example, *Parents Involved in Community Schools* v. *Seattle School District No. 1*.[130] In that case, the US Supreme Court held unconstitutional school districts' use of student race in making assignments to public

---

debate; but that our understanding of the Constitution does change from time to time has been settled since John Marshall breathed life into its text. If great lawyers of his day – Alexander Hamilton, for example – were sitting with us today, I would expect them to join Justice Kennedy's opinion for the Court. In all events, I do so without hesitation'. *Roper v Simmons* 543 US 551 (2005) (Stevens J, concurring).

128 Hayden White, 'The Value of Narrativity in the Representation of Reality', (1980) 7 Critical Inquiry 5, 7.

129 Mark Tushnet refers to the historical modality of interpretation as the most important in constitutional interpretation in the United States. Mark Tushnet, 'The United States: Eclectism in the Service of Pragmatism' in Jeffrey Goldsworthy (ed), *Interpreting Constitutions* (OUP 2006) 7.

130 *Parents Involved in Community Schools v Seattle School District No. 1* 551 US 701 (2007).

schools in order to maintain racial balance within individual schools and to prevent *de facto* segregation. The case generated close attention to the meaning of *Brown* v. *Board of Education*.[131] Chief Justice Roberts, writing for the majority, concluded,

> [W]hen it comes to using race to assign children to schools, history will be heard. […] Before *Brown*, schoolchildren were told where they could and could not go based on the color of their skin. The school districts in these cases have not carried the heavy burden of demonstrating that we should allow this once again – even for very different reasons. […] The way to stop discrimination on the basis of race is to stop discrimination on the basis of race.[132] (Emphasis added)

In his dissent, Justice Breyer argued that the majority had corrupted *Brown*'s legacy. He wrote that the majority opinion

> distorts precedent, it misapplies the relevant constitutional principles, it announces legal rules that will obstruct efforts by state and local governments to deal effectively with the growing resegregation of public schools, it threatens to substitute for present calm a disruptive round of race related litigation, and it undermines *Brown*'s promise of integrated primary and secondary education that local communities have sought to make a reality.[133] (Emphasis added)

Roberts and Breyer did not disagree about what *Brown* had decided, but only what *Brown* meant, or, as Justice Breyer put it, what *Brown* 'promised'. The disagreement demonstrates that what a decision means depends on the broader narrative of which it is a part.

There is no comparable idea of precedent in Canadian constitutional culture. Even if some precedents have acquired a strong doctrinal status because of their entrenchment in the Canadian legal fabric, none gives meaning to the

131 *Brown* v. *Board of Education of Topeka*, 347 U.S. 483 (1954). This is a point explored by Mark Tushnet in his Jerome Hall Lecture at Maurer School of Law, Indiana University. Mark Tushnet, '*Parents Involved* and the Struggle for Historical Memory', (Jerome Hall Lecture delivered at the Maurer School of Law, Indiana University Bloomington, 25 September 2014). The presentation I give here of this decision is influenced by Tushnet's analysis.

132 *Parents Involved in Community Schools v Seattle School District No. 1* 551 US 701 (2007) (Roberts, CJ).

133 ibid (Breyer, J, dissenting).

Canadian constitutional project as a whole in the way that *Brown* does in the United States. This is true even of the famous decision in the *Persons* case of 1929.[134] Today, that case is mostly remembered because it recognized women to be 'persons' for the purposes of the British North America Act, 1867 such that women could in consequence be appointed to the Canadian Senate. The case is also remembered because Viscount Sankey used the 'living tree' metaphor for the first time to describe the Canadian constitution. Regardless of the symbolic status the *Persons* case may have in today's legal circles, its historical importance hardly influenced the Canadian constitutional narrative.[135] Women had obtained the right to vote in 1918 and they could run for office in the House of Commons beginning in 1919; Agnes Macphail was the first woman to be elected to the House of Commons in 1921.[136] The metaphor of the 'living tree' was barely even mentioned by commentators in 1929.[137] As Robert Sharpe and Patricia MacMahon highlight, 'it was not until the revival of the feminist movement in the 1970s […] that the Canadians renewed their interest in the [*Persons*] case and its legacy'. Interpreting the meaning of 'persons' in the 1867 Act was a recognition that women had already been integrated into political life, not a cause of that integration.

In a similar vein, the *Secession Reference*,[138] the landmark decision in which the Supreme Court of Canada passed judgment on the legality of Quebec's threat of unilateral secession, does not have in Canadian constitutional culture the tutelary status that *Brown* holds in the United States. The Reference was a response to a 'failed constitutional moment',[139] i.e. the 1995 referendum on the secession of Quebec in which the "No" option won by the narrowest of margins. Three years after the referendum, various technical questions related to it

134 *Edwards v A.G. Canada* [1930] A.C. 124.

135 As Robert Sharpe and Patricia MacMahon write: 'The broader constitutional legacy of the *Persons* case, like its cultural legacy, is of relatively recent origin'. Robert J Sharpe and Patricia I MacMahon, *The Persons Case: The Origin and Legacy of the Fight for Legal Personhood* (University of Toronto Press 2007) 202.

136 Tabita Marshal and David A. Cruickshank, 'Persons Case' *The Canadian Encyclopedia* (6 November 2020) <http://www.thecanadianencyclopedia.ca/en/article/persons-case/> accessed 2 December 2020.

137 Bradley Miller, reviewing the comments from the legal community at the time, writes that only one of them mentioned the 'living tree' metaphor. See Bradley W. Miller, 'Origin Myth: The Persons Case, The Living Tree and the New Originalism' in Grant Huscroft and Bradley W. Miller (eds), *The Challenge of Originalism: Theories of Constitutional Interpretation* (CUP 2013) fn. 69.

138 *Reference re Secession of Quebec* [1998] 2 SCR 217.

139 See Sujit Chouhdry, 'Ackerman's Higher Lawmaking in Comparative Constitutional Perspective: Constitutional Moments as Constitutional Failures?' (2008) 6 ICON 193.

were litigated, and the federal government asked the Supreme Court to intervene. The Court had to find a way out of a politically untenable situation. It ruled that under both Canadian and international law Quebec lacked the right to unilaterally secede from the rest of Canada. However, the Court recognized that if a clear democratic majority in Quebec expressed a will to leave Canada, this expression would trigger a duty to negotiate an amicable separation. The Court further found four unwritten constitutional principles in Canada that would guide any such negotiations: federalism, democracy, constitutionalism and the rule of law, and the protection of minorities. Examining the legacy of the *Secession Reference* in Canadian constitutional law, David Schneiderman argues, 'the Court's invocation of unwritten constitutional principles … was not intended to determine constitutional outcomes going forward. It was not meant, in other words, to harden into doctrinal precedent. In short, the justices were being legally disingenuous'.[140] Notably, the complex constitutional claims of Indigenous groups, only marginally discussed in the *Secession Reference*, have become increasingly important and central concerns of Canadian constitutional law and politics since the mid-1990s.[141] The four unwritten principles identified in the *Secession Reference* have proven ill-suited to making sense of these claims.[142]

Compared to American precedents like *Brown* v. *Board of Education*, the *Persons* case and the *Secession Reference* represent more a judicial confirmation of a process that was already underway and a response to a threat that had already passed than the imposition of requirements reflected in a constitutional narrative.[143] It is difficult to see in Canadian constitutional history any decision that has cemented around it the national political *status quo* as much as *Brown* v. *Board of Education*[144] did. Rulings that define and sharpen political cleavages in the United States recede rapidly to the background in Canada.

140 David Schneiderman, 'Unwritten Constitutional Principles in Canada: Genuine or Strategic?' in Rosalind Dixon and Adrienne Stone (eds), *The Invisible Constitution* (CUP 2018) 517, 519.

141 See, e.g., John Borrows, *Canada's Indigenous Constitution* (University of Toronto Press 2010).

142 On this point, see Martin Papillon, 'Les traités avec les peuples autochtones : un 5e pilier de l'ordre constitutionnel canadien?' in Félix Mathieu and Dave Guénette (eds), *Réimaginer le Canada : Vers un État multinational?* (Presses de l'Université Laval 2019) 395.

143 There is controversy about this thesis. Michael Klarman, for example, argues that *Brown* was already a product of the growing civil rights movement. Michael J Klarman, 'Rethinking the Civil Rights and Civil Liberties Revolution' (1996) 82 Va L Rev 19; Michael J Klarman, 'How *Brown* Changed Race Relations: The Backlash Thesis' (1995) 81 J Am Hist 81.

144 *Brown v Board of Education of Topeka* 347 US 483 (1954).

Here, the contrast between *Morgentaler*[145] and *Roe* v. *Wade*[146] is revealing. The former ended controversy over abortion in Canada; the latter has fueled controversy over abortion in the United States, becoming one of the 'beleaguered rulings' in American constitutional law.[147] More generally, in Canada, 'it is surprisingly rare that a Supreme Court decision will define a ballot box question at the federal or provincial levels'.[148] Further, the notwithstanding clause of the Canadian Charter allows legislatures to override judicial interpretations of certain rights and freedoms. This mechanism, which gives politicians an effective means to respond to controversial rulings of the Supreme Court,[149] makes it exceedingly unlikely that a Canadian decision will ever crystallize into a super-precedent of the kind found in the United States.

A further consequence of the narrativization of constitutional reasoning and the accompanying faith the narrative promotes is the way in which constitutional change is justified. Discussing the faith of Americans in their constitutional project, Sanford Levinson writes:

> Justification is found in existing materials rather than in claims of new revelation, but change (or what Marshall in *McCulloch v. Maryland* termed 'adaptation') occurs regardless. Significantly, such adaptation is almost always justified by reference to its non-deviation from the genuine foundation or true essence of the faith community and, indeed, the utility of any changes to preserving what is most central to the faith community.[150]

Levinson shows that, in a given community of faith, the justification for change is found *in the past*, not in the future. Historical justification for change as a return to a more genuine understanding of the constitutional project is a cornerstone of American constitutional reasoning. Thus, as discussed, in overruling earlier decisions the US Supreme Court may explain that the decision was wrong the day it was decided.[151] The Supreme Court of Canada has generally

145 *R v Morgentaler* [1988] 1 SCR 30.

146 *Roe v Wade* 410 US 113 (1973).

147 Mark Tushnet, *Red, White and Blue: A Critical Analysis of the Constitutional Law* (Harvard UP 1988) 21.

148 David Schneiderman, *Red, White and Kind of Blue: The Conservatives and the Americanization of Canadian Constitutional Culture* (University of Toronto Press 2015) 237.

149 See, e.g., *Ford v Quebec (Attorney General)* [1988] 2 SCR 712.

150 Sanford Levinson, *Constitutional Faith* (Princeton UP 1988) 152.

151 See Michael J Gerhardt, *The Power of Precedent* (OUP 2008) 19. Gerhardt's analysis is not focused exclusively on constitutional law cases. However, overruling previous decisions as 'wrong the day they were decided' is used in constitutional law cases. See the discussion

avoided any similar characterization of its prior decisions in Charter cases; previous decisions are either overruled *sub silentio* or they are carefully distinguished.[152] As such, the Supreme Court of Canada has been able to make the constitutional project move forward all the while avoiding the constraining nature of constitutional precedents.

In *Lawrence* v. *Texas*,[153] the US Supreme Court was asked to revisit its 1986 decision in *Bowers* v. *Hardwick*[154] rejecting a constitutional challenge to a Georgia criminal sodomy statute. In his concurring opinion in *Bowers*, Chief Justice Burger invoked Roman law, the English eighteenth-century treatise writer William Blackstone, the Bible, and other evidence of Western moral thought to conclude that the Fourteenth Amendment did not protect a right to homosexual intimacy because no such right had ever been recognized in Western civilization. Writing for the majority in *Lawrence*, however, Justice Kennedy criticized Burger's use of history and concluded that '*Bowers* was not correct when it was decided, and it is not correct today. It ought not to remain binding precedent. *Bowers* v. *Hardwick* should be and now is overruled'.[155] Three elements of Kennedy's opinion shed important light on the Court's use of precedents.

First, Kennedy does not set aside the historical mode of argumentation used by Burger in *Bowers*. Rather Kennedy criticizes the historical reconstruction in *Bowers* and proposes an alternative account of Western civilization that is more accepting of homosexuality. His purpose is not to demonstrate that the Court has changed its mind or that it is relying on a different kind of argument in order to reach a different result. Kennedy's argument aims simply to correct the historical record. Like the *Bowers* majority, Kennedy embraces the historical mode of reasoning.

A second significant element of Kennedy's majority opinion in *Lawrence* is that setting the historical record straight means that the precedent, *Bowers*, was wrong *the day it was decided*.[156] Kennedy does not try to show how the constitution has evolved during the 17 years between *Bowers* and *Lawrence*. Instead, he views the earlier decision as wrong; *Lawrence* therefore simply recovers the correct constitutional understanding. That approach has an

---

in *Planned Parenthood of Southeastern Pa. v Casey* 505 US 833 (1992) and *Lawrence v Texas* 539 US 558 (2003).

152 See, e.g., *United States v Burns* 2001 SCC 7, [2001] 1 SCR 283.

153 *Lawrence v Texas* 539 US 558 (2003).

154 *Bowers v Hardwick* 478 US 186 (1986).

155 *Lawrence v Texas* 539 US 558, 578 (2003).

156 *Lawrence v Texas* 539 US 558 (2003).

important implication. As Jack Balkin writes: 'our belief that a case was always wrong (or always right) is important because it supports or coheres with other beliefs we have about how to understand our constitutional tradition and how to give meaning to the constitutional project today'.[157]

A third aspect of Kennedy's opinion in *Lawrence* is that it explicitly overrules *Bowers*. As noted, the Supreme Court of Canada generally does not overrule Charter precedents in such an open fashion. When it does overrule precedents, it does so using coded language or indirect hints. *Lawrence's* statement that *Bowers* was wrong when decided and must be overruled has no comparison in Canadian jurisprudence.

Justice Scalia's dissent in *Lawrence* illustrates a further aspect of American constitutional law and culture. In his dissent Scalia accuses Kennedy of reading his own political preferences into the Constitution and overruling *Bowers* because it did not comport with Kennedy's political views.[158] In Canada, where there is very little discussion of the horizontal strength of *stare decisis* with respect to issues of fundamental rights and freedoms, willingness to overrule precedent is not a mark of judicial activism; a commitment to *stare decisis* is simply not the dividing line between judges who apply the law and those who are doing politics.

6 Conclusion

Constitutional cultures articulate in different ways the relationship between past, present, and future. Constitutional precedents are special sites where this articulation occurs. They make visible the ways in which constitutional actors who contemplate or criticize constitutional change problematize the tension between constitutional law and democratic self-government. Metaphors, institutions, and rhetorical strategies partake in conferring different historical meaning to small-scale moments of crisis in the present when alternative constitutional futures are envisioned. In this chapter, close examination

157 Jack M. Balkin, *Constitutional Redemption: Political Faith in an Unjust World* (Harvard UP 2011) 184. *Lawrence* is not the only decision where the Court said that the prior decision was wrong the day it was decided. See also *Trump v Hawaii* 138 S Ct 2392, 2423 (2018) (Roberts CJ) in which Roberts for the majority stated in *obiter dictum* that '*Korematsu* was gravely wrong the day it was decided, has been overruled in the court of history and – to be clear – has no place in law under the Constitution'. For another example see the majority opinion in *Ramos v Louisiana* 140 S Ct 1390 (2020) (Gorsuch J).

158 *Lawrence v Texas* 539 US 558, 602–605 (2003) (Scalia J, dissenting).

of the ways in which constitutional precedents are treated in contemporary Canadian and American constitutional cultures has revealed that both countries problematize precedents differently. Their respective constitutional cultures are animated by different constitutional historicities.

The narrative dimension of the American constitutional project is at the heart of American constitutional thought. The use of precedents in the United States illustrates the slow unfolding of the promises of America's founding constitutional documents. Retelling the story of 'America-the-good' requires using precedents to justify change as well as permanence; change itself is always a retrieval, a movement backward towards the true America that always was. Super-precedents not only orient the narrative reconstruction of America's constitutional past, but they are also largely taken to determine that reconstruction.

Canada's historical condition is markedly different. Without a clear or complete political identity, Canada has also no clear constitutional beginning and seems to remain in a state of constitutional pre-history. Without a dominant constitutional narrative, historical events and constitutional precedents provide little intelligibility to Canada's constitutional project beyond the specific dispute that they settled. The constraining effect of constitutional precedents appears small, and their configurative force on historical narratives negligible. Moving the constitution forward means bringing Canada closer to its founding at some point in the future.

The Canadian constitution set sails on new seas with the adoption of the Charter in 1982. The attraction of American constitutional law never ceased, but, North and South of the border, the wind of change has blown in noticeably different directions.

Bibliography

Balkin, Jack M, *Constitutional Redemption: Political Faith in an Unjust World* (Harvard UP 2011).

Collins, Paul M, and Lori A Ringhand, *Supreme Court Confirmation Hearings and Constitutional Change* (CUP 2013).

Cyr, Hugo, 'Conceptual Metaphors for an Unfinished Constitution' (2014) 19 Rev. Const. Stud. 1.

Gerhardt, Michael J, *The Power of Precedent* (OUP 2008).

Hartog, François, *Regimes of Historicity: Presentism and the Experience of Time* (Saskia Brown tr, Columbia UP 2015).

Kahn, Paul W, *The Cultural Study of Law: Reconstructing Legal Scholarship* (University of Chicago Press 1998).

LaSelva, Samuel V, *Canada and the Ethics of Constitutionalism: Identity, Destiny and Constitutional Faith* (McGill-Queen's UP 2018).

Levinson, Sanford, *Constitutional Faith* (Princeton UP 1988).

Lipset, Seymour Martin, *Continental Divide: The Values and Institutions of the United States and Canada* (Routledge 1991).

Parkes, Debra, 'Precedent Revisited: Carter v. Canada (AG) and the Contemporary Practice of Precedent' (2016) 10 MJLH 123.

Schneiderman, David, *Red, White and Kind of Blue: The Conservatives and the Americanization of Canadian Constitutional Culture* (University of Toronto Press 2015).

Sharpe, Robert J, and Patricia I MacMahon, *The Persons Case: The Origin and Legacy of the Fight for Legal Personhood* (University of Toronto Press 2007).

White, Hayden, 'The Value of Narrativity in the Representation of Reality' (1980) 7:1 Critical Inquiry 5.

CHAPTER 5

Inter-constitutional Interpretation

A Case Study of the Articles of Confederation

Cem Tecimer

1 Introduction: Reviving Dead Constitutions?*

Countries replace their constitutions time and again. One frequently cited statistical study has found the average lifespan of a constitution to be nineteen years.[1] In certain regions of the world, for example in Latin America, the overall rate at which constitutional replacement occurs appears to be higher, shortening the nineteen-year lifespan.[2] Regardless of whether the constitutional transformation in question results in progressive or regressive outcomes, most episodes of constitutional replacement take place under conditions of national vulnerability or crisis. Scholarship has ably compiled many factors that singularly or collectively occasion episodes of constitution-making, ranging from social and economic crises to revolution, from regime collapse to fear thereof, and from post-war to post-colonial negotiations between nations and

* This chapter was enabled by thought-provoking discussions with Francesco Biagi, Justin Frosini, Jason Mazzone, and participants at the conference on *Constitutional History: Comparative Perspectives* held in Chicago on April 29–30, 2019. For helpful comments and suggestions, I thank Jennifer Allison, Vicki Jackson, Mark Jia, Il-Young Jung, Rama Hyeweon Kim, Laurence Tribe, Dinan Wu, and Dan Zhou. I am grateful to Jane Fair Bestor for graciously providing comments and critiques at every stage of my writing. Special thanks to the participants of the workshop titled *The Art of the Response Paper* for critiquing my work. I must single out Jason Mazzone, whose incisive comments and contributions, beyond my count, have been essential to the improvement of the manuscript. This chapter benefitted from the generous support of the Harvard Law School Graduate Program. Needless to say, all remaining errors and shortcomings are my own.

1 Tom Ginsburg, 'Constitutional endurance' in Tom Ginsburg and Rosalind Dixon (eds), *Comparative Constitutional Law* (Edward Elgar Publishing 2011) 112. See also Zachary Elkins, Tom Ginsburg, and James Melton, *The Endurance of National* Constitutions (CUP 2009) 129. For some of the prominent methodological challenges accompanying this statistical study see ibid 126–29.

2 See eg Gabriel L Negretto, 'Replacing and Amending Constitutions: The Logic of Constitutional Change in Latin America' (2012) 46 Law & Society Review 749, 752–53.

 | DOI:10.1163/9789004523739_007

emerging nations.[3] Because of the undesirable conditions under which nearly all episodes of constitutional replacement take place,[4] framers of new constitutions tend to draft these documents with the hope that they will endure. In most instances, the drafting of a new constitution is accompanied by statements from political and legal elites influential in the drafting process that criticize the previous constitution, partly because the prior document is perceived as tainted with the vices that occasioned the drafting of the new document in the first place. Another reason for criticizing the previous constitution is to provide the document about to be birthed with a degree of legitimacy – especially in polities where the legitimacy of the new constitution stands in a zero-sum relationship with the previous constitution, and perhaps that is the case, to varying degrees, in every country.

All of this should be familiar to an American audience. The much-celebrated *Federalist Papers*, published in the late 18th century and figuring prominently in the jurisprudence of the US Supreme Court,[5] are essentially a collection of articles that simultaneously criticize the many perceived vices of the Articles of Confederation while promoting the then-new US Constitution. 'The great and radical vice in the construction of the existing Confederation,'[6] 'the principle defects of the Confederation,'[7] and '[t]he (…) most palpable defect of the subsisting Confederation'[8] are among the many instances in which *The Federalist Papers* portray the Articles as in need of rectification through replacement.

More than two centuries after the publication of *The Federalist Papers*, the strategy of delegitimizing the previous constitution in favor of the new constitution remains largely unchanged. Fast-forward to 2011's Hungary: János Lázár, then-leader of the Fidesz parliamentary group – the dominant political party in Hungary to this day – told the Hungarian Parliament, immediately before voting on the new Hungarian Constitution, 'that the [new] Constitution

3 For a classic statement on the causes of constitution-making see Jon Elster, 'Forces and Mechanisms in the Constitution-Making Process' (1995) 45 Duke Law Journal 364, 370–71. For a similar but more expansive list see Elkins, Ginsburg and Melton (n 1) 95.

4 See also Kim Lane Scheppele, 'Aspirational and aversive constitutionalism: The case for studying cross-constitutional influence through negative models' (2003) 1 ICON 296, 300: 'After all, constitutions are rarely written when political life is uneventful. Constitutions are typically drafted or substantially modified at moments of rupture, when there is a crisis, or change of regime, or opportunity of history.'

5 See eg John Manning, 'Textualism and the Role of *The Federalist* in Constitutional Adjudication' (1998) 66 The George Washington Law Review 1337.

6 *The Federalist Papers* 15 (Hamilton).

7 ibid.

8 *The Federalist Papers* 21 (Hamilton). For similar references see Jason Mazzone and Cem Tecimer, 'Interconstitutionalism' (2022) 132 The Yale Law Journal 3000, 3020 (forthcoming).

represented something fundamental: a break with Hungary's communist past.'[9] In similar vein, in his annual state of the nation address, about a year after the enactment of the new Constitution, Hungarian Prime Minister Viktor Orbán defended the new document: 'I am proud of the new and modern Constitution.'[10] He added that it was 'the first [constitution] in Europe to prescribe decreasing public debt and keeping the balance of the budget.'[11]

Other examples abound. The most recent Nepalese Constitution of 2015, for instance, in the quite generous characterization of the Nepalese government, has been described as a 'historic achievement' and the realization of a 'decades-long dream of Nepali people to have a constitution made through an elected representative body.'[12] As Kenya passed its new Constitution in 2010 with a striking 67 percent of Kenyans behind it, then energy minister Kiraitu Murungi stated: 'Kenya has been reborn.'[13] Kenya's President at the time, Mwai Kibaki, in similar fashion, characterized the new document as '[Kenya's] shield and defender as [Kenya] strive[s] to conquer poverty, disease and ignorance.'[14] More generally, the new Constitution was lauded as 'a cornerstone of the effort to correct longstanding imbalances of power and prevent the kind of upheaval that followed deeply flawed elections,'[15] an expression of widespread popular dissatisfaction with the prior constitutional order.

Stripping the old constitution of its legitimacy, be it in the eyes of politicians, scholars, or the public at large, also involves, from the standpoint of the new constitution's framers, a rhetoric that presents the old and soon-to-be-abrogated constitution as no longer carrying any legal import. Simply put, framers of new constitutions strive *rhetorically* to portray antecedent

9 Judy Dempsey, 'Hungarian Parliament Approves New Constitution' *The New York Times* (New York, 18 April 2011) <https://www.nytimes.com/2011/04/19/world/europe/19iht-hungary19.html?searchResultPosition=12> accessed 4 September 2019. See also Mazzone and Tecimer (n 8) 3024.

10 Palko Karasz, 'Leader of Hungary Defends New Constitution' *The New York Times* (New York, 7 February 2012) <https://www.nytimes.com/2012/02/08/world/europe/viktor-orban-defends-hungarys-new-constitution.html?searchResultPosition=4> accessed 4 September 2019.

11 ibid.

12 Government of Nepal, 'History of Nepal' (*Ministry of Foreign Affairs*) <https://mofa.gov.np/about-nepal/history-of-nepal/> accessed 4 September 2019.

13 Jeffrey Gettleman, 'Kenyans Approve New Constitution' *The New York Times* (New York, 5 August 2010) <https://www.nytimes.com/2010/08/06/world/africa/06kenya.html?searchResultPosition=4> accessed 4 September 2019. See also Mazzone and Tecimer (n 8) 3024.

14 ibid.

15 Jeffrey Gettleman, 'Kenyan Constitution Opens New Front in Culture Wars' *The New York Times* (New York, 13 May 2010) <https://www.nytimes.com/2010/05/14/world/africa/14kenya.html?searchResultPosition=1> accessed 4 September 2019.

constitutions as having been consigned to the ash heap of history. And through the enactment of the new constitution, they strive to do the same *legally*. An extreme example comes from the Hungarian case, where the preamble to the new Constitution of 2011 declares: 'We do not recognize the communist constitution of 1949, since it was the basis for tyrannical rule; therefore we proclaim it to be invalid.' Even when the drafting of a new constitution is less acrimonious than was the case in Hungary, the process is more or less universally understood as one of abrogating and legally superseding the previous constitution.[16] Perhaps in an effort to accentuate this reality as a textual matter, some framers choose to include abrogation articles in their newly enacted constitutions.[17] Even in the absence of such articles, judicial opinions sometimes reflect a widely shared understanding that the new constitution replaces its older counterpart.[18]

Despite many framers' attempts to the contrary, abrogated constitutions nonetheless make various appearances in the new constitutional order, even after they have been ousted by their successors, casting doubt on the political rhetoric that promises a "clean slate" once the old constitution is replaced. In a strikingly prevalent manner, yet to be studied in detail by domestic and comparative constitutional law scholarship alike, courts (and interpreters more generally) in countries with a history of constitutional replacement invoke their replaced constitutions to generate meaning for their in-force constitutions. I call this practice "inter-constitutional interpretation."[19]

Inter-constitutional interpretation is ubiquitous. Understanding the practice sheds light on the meaning of constitutionalism, the role of courts, and

16 The timing of abrogation can vary. In the US, for instance, some have argued that the Articles of Confederation were not entirely and immediately abrogated by the enactment of the Constitution. See especially Vasan Kesavan, 'When Did the Articles of Confederation Cease to Be Law?' (2002) 78 Notre Dame Law Review 35, 42.

17 See eg Constitution of Honduras art 378 (1982); Constitution of Liberia art 95(a) (1986); Constitution of Iraq art 143 (2005). For other examples see Mazzone and Tecimer (n 8) 3024.

18 In one US Supreme Court case, on the relationship between the Articles of Confederation and the US Constitution, it was reasoned in dicta that 'the new Constitution [had] superseded the old.' See *Michelin Tire Corporation v Wages*, 423 US 276, 284 (1976), approvingly citing Max Farrand (ed), *The Records of the Federal Convention of 1787*, vol 3 (OUP 1911) 542.

19 To my knowledge, I am the first to use the word 'inter-constitutional' in this context (of interpretation). The word has made appearances in the literature as in the case of 'inter-constitutional collisions,' which one author has coined to refer to normative clashes between various domestic and transnational constitutional regimes, especially with regard to their 'norms of organization and fundamental rights.' See generally Gunther Teubner, *Constitutional Fragments: Societal Constitutionalism and Globalization* (OUP 2012) 150–73.

the way in which the legal past influences the present. Consider some examples: in 1819, the US Supreme Court invoked a textual difference between the Articles of Confederation and the US Constitution to rule that Congress, under the latter document, had implied powers to incorporate a federal bank.[20] In its reasoning, the Court relied on the fact that the Articles of Confederation had included the word 'expressly' to enumerate congressional powers. That is, the Articles were power-conferring to the extent that they had *expressly* provided for a congressional power in the document. The new Constitution, by contrast, 'omit[ted] the word,'[21] thereby conceding the possibility of Congress having implied powers and not merely those enumerated in Article I of the US Constitution. Thus, Chief Justice John Marshall was able to infer an implied congressional power to incorporate a federal bank.

In 1971, the French Constitutional Council recognized a constitutional right of association even though the 1958 Constitution (in force at the time) contained no such specific protection.[22] In its analysis the Council first referenced the Preamble to the Constitution, which, in turn, alluded to the Preamble to the previous (and abrogated) Constitution of 1946. The 1946 Preamble referenced 'the fundamental principles acknowledged in the laws of the Republic.' The Council reasoned that the right to association was one of those 'fundamental principles.' It was therefore protected by the Constitution of 1958.[23]

In 1995, the South African Constitutional Court decided a case involving the issue of whether, under the Interim Constitution, a provincial or local division of the Supreme Court could inquire into the constitutionality of acts of Parliament. The case raised questions of what an 'act of Parliament' precisely was and whether acts of parliaments preceding the adoption of the Interim Constitution were acts subject to judicial review under it.[24] In his concurring opinion, Justice Trengove reasoned that the Interim Constitution '[made] provision for constitutional continuity, treating the 1983 Constitution of the Republic of South Africa as the previous Constitution,' and from that, concluded that laws passed by parliaments prior to the enactment of the Interim Constitution were also considered 'Acts of Parliament' within the meaning of Article 102(8) of the Interim Constitution, and thus were immune from constitutional review by divisions of the Supreme Court.[25]

---

20 *McCulloch v Maryland*, 17 US (4 Wheat) 316, 406 (1819).

21 ibid. See also Mazzone and Tecimer (n 8) 3017–18.

22 Decision of the French Constitutional Council 44–71 (1971).

23 For a summary see Liav Orgad, 'The preamble in constitutional interpretation' (2010) 8 ICON 714, 727. See also Mazzone and Tecimer (n 8) 3011.

24 *Zantsi v Council of State, Ciskei & Others* 1995 (4) SA 615 (CC) (S Afr).

25 ibid para 35. See also Mazzone and Tecimer (n 8) 3024–25.

In 2004, in an individual complaint decision, the German Federal Constitutional Court ruled that two state laws on institutionalizing criminals with 'a special propensity for recidivism' violated the German Basic Law because the laws regulated an area of criminal law in which the federal government had already exercised its concurrent regulatory power.[26] To bolster its ruling and show that the federal government's power to regulate in the domain of criminal law traditionally included regulating the institutionalization of criminals, the Court invoked the Weimar Constitution of 1919, and explained that the term 'criminal law' had also been used in that previous constitution to cover 'guarding and preventive consequences of wrongdoing.'[27]

In 2018, a case involving the non-delegation doctrine came before the Turkish Constitutional Court: a 2018 law passed by the Turkish Parliament authorized the executive branch to make changes to and repeal a number of specified laws in order to adjust the Turkish legal landscape to the country's recent transition into a presidential system. The law also contained a provision granting the executive the power to make changes to and repeal 'other laws,' without enumerating them. The Court ultimately ruled that that vague formulation was not a violation of the non-delegation doctrine and therefore consistent with the in-force Turkish Constitution of 1982.[28] In its decision, the Court cited the absence in the current Constitution of a provision that had existed in the previous Constitution of 1961: Article 64 of the abrogated 1961 Constitution had explicitly required Parliament to enumerate all laws which it authorized the executive to repeal. The Court concluded that the absence of a similar provision in the current Constitution showed that no such enumeration was necessary. The law granting the executive to make changes to and repeal certain enumerated laws as well as 'other laws' was thus upheld.[29]

There are numerous examples of the phenomenon of inter-constitutional interpretation in the jurisprudence of various apex courts across the globe, and as the cases described above indicate, referencing an antecedent constitution is a common strategy not only across polities with vast differences, but also across time. Both the US Supreme Court and the Turkish Constitutional Court have employed this interpretive practice, for instance: following the examples mentioned above, the former did so in 1819, the latter in 2018, with almost two centuries intervening in between.

---

26 2 BvR 834/02 (10 February 2004).

27 ibid. See also Mazzone and Tecimer (n 8) 3025–26.

28 Turkish Constitutional Court, E 2018/100, K 2018/79 (5 July 2018).

29 ibid para 25. See also Mazzone and Tecimer (n 8) 3044–45.

This chapter takes a close look at the spatially and temporally pervasive but understudied phenomenon of inter-constitutional interpretation. The chapter is divided into three parts. Following this Introduction, Part 2 focuses on conceptualizing and more precisely defining the contours of inter-constitutional interpretation by contrasting it with other methods of cross-constitutional engagement. Part 3 focuses on inter-constitutional interpretation in the United States with a close study of the US Supreme Court's uses, in interpreting the existing US Constitution, of the predecessor national charter (or constitution), the Articles of Confederation. By engaging in both a quantitative and qualitative analysis of Supreme Court precedents, Part 3 highlights such issues as the frequency of references to the Articles; the types of opinions that reference the former constitution, with an eye to whether distinct types of opinions (such as dissenting opinions) invoke the antecedent constitution more often than do others; the manner in which the old constitution is invoked, whether approvingly or disapprovingly; whether an invocation serves to establish a narrative of continuous constitutional tradition or of rupture; whether the old constitution is invoked by reference to its text or in other non-textual ways; and whether there are, as a matter of substantive constitutional law doctrine, recurring themes that trigger invocations of the Articles more frequently than others do. (An appendix presents the raw data that forms the basis for the analysis in Part 3.) Part 3 thus offers a thorough analysis of the phenomenon of inter-constitutional interpretation in a particular domestic constitutional context. As such, it represents the methodological approach of comparative constitutional law scholarship that one scholar has usefully labeled 'constitutional ethnography.'[30] The chapter concludes in Part 4.

2 What Inter-constitutional Interpretation Is and Is *Not*: A Typology of Constitutional Engagement

Inter-constitutional interpretation, in its most basic formulation, is the interpretive practice of referring to a polity's antecedent constitution(s), textually or otherwise, to generate meaning for the same polity's in-force, that is, current, constitution.

Three attributes of this formulation merit highlighting: (1) First, I intentionally refer to inter-constitutional interpretation as an interpretive 'practice' as

---

30 See Kim Lane Scheppele, 'Constitutional Ethnography: An Introduction' (2004) 38 Law & Society Review 389; cf Ran Hirschl, 'The Question of Case Selection in Comparative Constitutional Law' (2005) 53 American Journal of Comparative Law 125, 126–27.

opposed to a method of constitutional interpretation. The invocation of an abrogated constitution usually centers around a comparison of the text of that document with its new counterpart (textualism), a comparison of the different or similar constitutional structures built into the two documents (structuralism), an inquiry into the intentions of the framers of the new constitution in light of the perceived virtues and vices of the abrogated constitution(s) (a variant of originalism), or a combination of some or all of the foregoing. There is, accordingly, no need to obfuscate extant taxonomies on the various methods of constitutional interpretation;[31] inter-constitutional interpretation can easily be classified under one or multiple established instantiations of constitutional interpretation already set out in the literature; I therefore refer to it as a 'practice' rather than a 'mode' (or 'method') of constitutional interpretation. (2) Second is the inter-temporal dimension embedded in my formulation: inter-constitutional interpretation, as I define it, is inevitably a retrospective endeavor of looking back at the replaced constitution (the antecedent constitution) to gain insights into the meaning of the replacer constitution (the current constitution). (3) Third, the retrospection described under (2), that is, the inter-temporality, occurs between constitutions of the *same* polity, as occurs in invoking the Articles of Confederation to generate meaning for the US Constitution, or invoking the French Constitution of 1946 to generate meaning for the French Constitution of 1958. Consequently, in my formulation, inter-constitutional interpretation has a domestic tilt. In other words, it is two or more constitutions of the *same* polity, at least one abrogated and at least one in force, that form the object of inter-constitutional interpretation. That domestic tilt, however, does not exclude outsiders, that is, nonmembers of the polity whose constitutions are being compared, from engaging in inter-constitutional interpretation – a possibility that I consider below.[32]

In what follows, I compare and contrast inter-constitutional interpretation with six other well-identified interpretive practices that bear some resemblance to it (and to each other) but are ultimately conceptually distinct.[33] In doing so, I aim to clarify the various instances of constitutional engagement by distinguishing them from one another by dimensions of *time* (ie whether the engagement is intertemporal or current), *number* (whether the engagement

31 For a classic statement on the different methods of constitutional interpretation in the US see Philip Bobbitt, *Constitutional Fate: Theory of The Constitution* (OUP 1982); see also Richard H Fallon Jr, 'A Constructivist Coherence Theory of Constitutional Interpretation' (1987) 100 Harvard Law Review 1189, 1194–1209. For a similar discussion of the three attributes of inter-constitutional interpretation see Mazzone and Tecimer (n 8) 3008.

32 See below, part 2.7.

33 I do not purport to provide an exhaustive catalog of interpretive practices. For a similar typology see Mazzone and Tecimer (n 8) 3008–10.

TABLE 5.1 A typology of constitutional engagement

Interpretive practice		Key feature	Distinctions from inter-constitutional interpretation
(1)	Cross-constitutional interpretation	Comparison of two or more constitutions of different countries	– One of the constitutions compared need not be abrogated – Constitutions compared belong to different countries
(2)	Intra-constitutional interpretation	Comparison between parts of the same constitution	– Comparison and analysis occur within a single constitution
(3)	State constitutions	Comparison between state constitutions and a federal constitution	– The constitutions compared need not be abrogated – State constitutions are not the functional and hierarchical equivalent of a federal constitution
(4)	Bi- or multi-lingual comparisons	Comparison between linguistically different versions of the same constitution	– Units compared are variants of the same constitution; thus, comparison and analysis occur within a single constitution
(5)	Comparisons involving constitutional documents	Comparison between a constitution and a constitutive document	– Constitutive documents are not the functional and hierarchical equivalent of a federal constitution – The constitutive document need not be abrogated
(6)	Inter-draft comparisons	Comparison between drafts of the same constitution (or between a draft and the final version)	– Comparison and analysis occur within a single constitution

involves a single constitution or multiple constitutions), and *function* (whether the document engaged is a constitution proper or the constitution of a federal subunit or merely a document of constitutive and ceremonial significance). This approach to constitutional engagement elucidates some distinct ways of engaging with a single constitution or with two or more constitutions – practices often erroneously lumped under the same (and admittedly unrevealing) category of 'constitutional dialogue' or 'constitutional engagement' in comparative constitutional scholarship. (Table 5.1 summarizes the principal ways in which the six other methods identified differ from inter-constitutional interpretation.)

2.1 *Cross-constitutional Interpretation*

Cross-constitutional interpretation describes the well-documented practice of invoking a *different* polity's constitution to generate meaning for another constitution, usually one's *own*.[34] Consider one paradigmatic example from US Supreme Court jurisprudence: in *Roper v Simmons*,[35] the Court held that the Eighth Amendment prohibited the imposition of the death penalty on juvenile offenders. The Court took notice of the domestic constitutional situation in a multitude of countries, and especially in England, to arrive at the conclusion that the evolving consensus across the globe was abolition of the death penalty for juveniles under the age of eighteen.[36] Thus, in *Roper*, English constitutional law, and that of other countries, provided Supreme Court Justices (at least those in the majority) with insights into understanding their own US Constitution.

Inter-constitutional interpretation differs from the practice of cross-constitutional interpretation primarily because in the former practice, the objects of comparison are of the *same* polity (eg the Articles of Confederation and the US Constitution), whereas in the latter approach the objects belong to *different* polities (eg the uncodified British Constitution and US Constitution). Admittedly, in some instances there might be no sharp line between belonging to the same polity and belonging to different polities. For US courts, for example,

34 The literature on this well-studied phenomenon of transnational constitutional influence is voluminous. For a general statement see Vicki C Jackson, *Constitutional Engagement in a Transnational Era* (OUP 2010).

35 543 US 551 (2005).

36 For these comparative references see ibid 575–78. See also Mazzone and Tecimer (n 8) 3008 n 13. For a study documenting the US Supreme Court's foreign law references more generally see Steven Calabresi and Stephanie Dotson Zimdahl, 'The Supreme Court and Foreign Sources of Law: Two Hundred Years of Practice and The Juvenile Death Penalty Decision' (2005) 47 William & Mary Law Review 743.

English constitutional law, from which much of early American constitutional law was drawn, is considered less 'other'[37] than is, say, the constitutional law of Zimbabwe.[38] Viewed in this light, documents that are thought to constitute the central pieces of English constitutional law – such as the English Bill of Rights – and the Articles of Confederation might both be considered equally acceptable materials for what may be termed a 'genetic' form of constitutional interpretation.[39] In fact, numerous cases of the US Supreme Court make reference to British constitutional documents and the Articles of Confederation in the same decision, justifying their uses on grounds that these materials contain similar or identical phraseology to the text of the US Constitution.[40] Be that as it may, national borders can still serve as a proxy for delineating what counts as the constitution(al law) of another polity, and by implication, what is properly deemed cross- or inter-constitutional interpretation.

But why is this distinction relevant, and why should inter-constitutional interpretation as I define it merit separate treatment? One persuasive reason for conceptualizing inter- and cross-constitutional interpretations as different interpretive practices lies in the legal, political, and scholarly controversies over (and, in the US case, perhaps the fixation on) the permissibility of courts invoking the (constitutional) law of foreign countries, a topic that has

37 See eg *Roper v Simmons* (n 35) 577: 'The United Kingdom's experience bears particular relevance here in light of the historic ties between our countries and in light of the Eighth Amendment's own origins.' Justice Scalia also stated that British constitutional law is of more relevance when the source of a constitutional provision can be found in British law. See Norman Dorsen, 'The relevance of foreign legal materials in US constitutional cases: A conversation between Justice Antonin Scalia and Justice Stephen Breyer' (2005) 3 ICON 519, 525, 540.

38 Justice Breyer, for example, once noted: 'I may have made what one might call a tactical error in referring to a case from Zimbabwe – not the human rights capital of the world.' Dorsen (n 37) 528.

39 See Rosalind Dixon and Vicki C Jackson, 'Constitutions Inside Out: Outsider Interventions in Domestic Constitutional Contests' (2013) 48 Wake Forest Law Review 149, 167 and ibid 167 n 65.

40 For US Supreme Court cases citing both the Articles of Confederation and British constitutional law see eg *Tenney v Brandhove*, 341 US 367, 372 (1951): 'Article V of the Articles of Confederation is quite close to the English Bill of Rights[.]'; *United States v Johnson*, 383 US 169, 177 (1966): 'The language of that Article, of which the present clause is only a slight modification, is in turn almost identical to the English Bill of Rights of 1689[.]'; *Furman v Georgia*, 408 US 238, 243 (1972) (Douglas, J, concurring): 'The English Bill of Rights […] stated that […] These were the words chosen for our Eighth Amendment.'; *United States v Brewster*, 408 US 501, 547 (1972) (Brennan, J, dissenting): '[…] by revising Article V of the Articles of Confederation […] This wording derived in turn from the provision of the English Bill of Rights […]'.

occupied much of the discussion of references to the constitutions of other polities for purposes of domestic constitutional adjudication.[41] Presumably, inter-constitutional interpretation, which involves juxtaposing the constitutions of the *same* polity, will not be subject to the same flood of criticism, triggered by a group of motivations ranging from constitutional parochialism to ideas about judicial restraint and democratic theory, that cross-constitutional interpretation has generated.[42]

A second reason for distinguishing the two practices is that a polity's former constitution is presumably better known by its members and thus used more accurately by those same people, as opposed to uses of a foreign constitution as to which outsider expertise might be more limited. Thus, for example, the chances of American judges "getting it right" with respect to the Articles of Confederation are likely higher than with respect to, say, the Zimbabwean Constitution.[43]

A third reason lies in the virtual absence, if not for analytical reasons at least for practical reasons, of "cherry-picking concerns" in inter-constitutional interpretation.[44] French judges, for instance, are less likely to be questioned for selection bias when they quote from the 1946 French Constitution in

41 See also Dixon and Jackson (n 39) 149.

42 See also Mazzone and Tecimer (n 8) 3083. On the arguments against citations to foreign law see Richard A Posner, 'Foreword: A Political Court' (2005) 119 Harvard Law Review 32, 85–90. To be sure, forceful responses have been formulated against these strains of criticism, drawing on the benefits of engaging with foreign law. See representatively Vicki C Jackson, 'Constitutional Comparisons: Convergence, Resistance, Engagement' (2005) 119 Harvard Law Review 109, 116–20.

43 See also Mazzone and Tecimer (n 8) 3084. Of course, here, the inter-temporal aspect of inter-constitutional interpretation might work against that very same assertion: in an ever more connected world, it might be easier for American judges (or interpreters more generally) to learn more about the Zimbabwean Constitution than the Articles of Confederation, of which only limited historical evidence exists. On the other hand, cross-constitutional interpretation can be inter-temporal as well: if we control for time, the likelihood of an American judge knowing more about their own abrogated constitution (eg Articles of Confederation) could be higher than the (hypothetical) abrogated Zimbabwean Constitution from, more or less, the same date. Additionally, if the subject of inter-constitutional interpretation, that is the interpreter who compares the same polity's constitutions, is an outsider (eg a foreign government or court), a possibility that I consider below (see part 2.7), the domestic expertise argument in favor of inter-constitutional interpretation may simply not hold up.

44 On the so-called 'cherry picking' problem in comparative constitutional law see Ran Hirschl, *Comparative Matters: The Renaissance of Comparative Constitutional Law* (OUP 2014) 19, 187–88. See also Mazzone and Tecimer (n 8) 3084 n 482 and accompanying text.

their opinions than they would be when they quote from the Constitution of Mongolia.[45]

Fourth, the functionalist argument in favor of looking at foreign constitutions,[46] summarized by the idea that constitutionalist systems are designed to address similar problems and that judges across different countries are confronted with similar interpretive questions, also, and arguably more forcefully, exists when a polity looks to its previous constitution. A new constitution inevitably responds to the perceived deficiencies of its predecessor and simultaneously continues in the tradition of its predecessor in areas in which the former constitution is understood to have regulated successfully.[47] Hence, an antecedent constitution might possess more functional relevance to the successor constitution than any other constitution.

Fifth, the supposedly anti-democratic nature of looking to foreign constitutional jurisdictions will not necessarily bedevil an inter-constitutional inquiry. The opponents of citing foreign (constitutional) law have argued that the self-given character of a constitution renders looking to *foreign* law inconsistent with the democratic character of constitutions.[48] That particular concern does not exist when a polity looks to its *own* former constitution. Of course, there might be other reasons to resist use of an earlier constitution. Especially in constitutional systems whose former constitutions were racially or otherwise discriminatory or the product of anti-democratic constitution-making processes, references to the abrogated constitution might also provoke democratic

45 There could be, of course, instances in which the French judge's invoking the Constitution of Mongolia would be more pertinent to the resolution of the dispute at hand than France's former constitution. As a general matter, however, constitutional parochialism still seems a prominent reason why the French judge would garner more support when citing a past French constitution than citing the constitution of any other foreign state in the absence of special circumstances rendering that foreign constitution of particular relevance. For a brief discussion of the same hypothetical see Mazzone and Tecimer (n 8) 3084.

46 See eg Jackson (n 42) 116–17.

47 However, looking at foreign constitutions may also enhance understandings of one's own constitutional system and its functioning. See ibid 117. The new constitution may simply repeat too many features of its antecedent, rendering the possibility of expressivist conclusions that differentiate the new constitutional order from the previous one slim. For an argument that constitution-making and amendment processes too often result in repetitive outcomes that mimic the prior document see Ozan O Varol, 'Constitutional Stickiness' (2016) 49 University of California Davis Law Review 899. The case of stickiness, however, will be relatively offset in the case of so-called 'transformative' constitutions characterized by a striking breaking away from the previous order. For a general discussion of the functionalist argument in favor of looking at a polity's own past constitution see Mazzone and Tecimer (n 8) 3084.

48 Jackson (n 42) 120–21. For a concise summary of arguments made from this standpoint see also Sujit Choudry, 'Migration as a new metaphor in comparative constitutional law' in Sujit Choudry (ed), *The Migration of Constitutional Ideas* (CUP 2006) 6–13. See also Mazzone and Tecimer (n 8) 3084 n 487 and accompanying text.

concerns. Additionally, and independent of how the former constitution is perceived by the current polity, the intrinsically inter-temporal and historic outlook that accompanies the practice of invoking a past constitution might trigger more general anxieties associated with the anti-democratic nature of historical methods of constitutional interpretation: invoking an out-of-force constitution to generate meaning for an extant constitution arguably binds the present democratic polity to 'the dead hand of the past' and is therefore anti-democratic per se.[49]

All of this, then, suggests that inter-constitutional interpretation has the potential to secure higher rates of buy-in from potential interpreters, including judges, both normatively and as a practical matter.[50] If that assertion holds true, that is, if inter-constitutional interpretation is understood to be both normatively more desirable than other forms of constitutional engagement (especially those that invoke what are perceived to be foreign constitutions) and more widely practiced as an empirical matter, there is merit in thinking of it as different from cross-constitutional interpretation (and the other modes of engagement outlined below) and therefore deserving of separate scholarly treatment.

2.2 *Intra-constitutional Interpretation*

More easily distinguishable from inter-constitutional interpretation is the interpretive practice of *intra*-constitutional interpretation, which generates meaning for an in-force constitution by self-referential means, textually or otherwise.[51] The main difference between the two practices lies primarily in the number of objects under study: while intra-constitutional interpretation

---

49 See also Mazzone and Tecimer (n 8) 3084–85. For a forceful critique of the characterization of cross-constitutional interpretation as being anti-democratic see Jackson (n 42) 121.

50 In polities where the use of foreign law does not occasion the same kinds of controversies as in the US, this assertion might be less valid or simply wrong. However, while anxieties against the use of foreign law in the US are indeed 'heightened,' I see no reason not to expect other polities making similar arguments against the use of foreign law in constitutional adjudication. South Africa, whose constitution expressly enables interpreters to look to foreign law ('may consider foreign law'), is a prominent exception. See the Constitution of South Africa, § 39(1) (1996).

51 The term intra-constitutional has also been used in the literature to refer to the differences between domestic constitutional law and comparative constitutional law analyses. Constitutional law, it has been argued, 'focuses on intra-constitutional analysis,' meaning its intended audience is stakeholders within a single constitutional polity. Ran Hirschl, 'Comparative Methodologies' in Roger Materman and Robert Schütze (eds), *The Cambridge Companion to Comparative Constitutional Law* (CUP 2019) 14.

conventionally relies on a single constitution, inter-constitutional interpretation requires at least two constitutions to compare.

In its pure form, intra-constitutional interpretation operates within a single constitution. The right to privacy jurisprudence of the US Supreme Court provides a case in point. In *Griswold v Connecticut*,[52] Justice Douglas, writing for the majority, ruled that the US Constitution contains an implied right to privacy, located in the 'penumbras' of various provisions of the Bill of Rights. His conclusion was thus primarily drawn from a collection of references intrinsic to a single constitution.

Another example can be found in Justice Blackmun's majority opinion in *Freytag v Commissioner*,[53] where he argued that the phrase 'Heads of Departments' in the Appointments Clause of Article II of the US Constitution must be understood as referring solely to divisions under the executive branch – an interpretive outcome that also accorded, he argued, with other provisions of the Constitution, including the Opinion Clause of Article II. Blackmun, referencing the Court's own caselaw, reasoned: '[…] this Court noted that the phrase "Heads of Departments" in the Appointments Clause must be read in conjunction with the Opinion Clause of Art. II, § 2, cl. 1.'[54] These types of intra-constitutional analyses often go hand in hand with a textual method of constitutional interpretation aptly labeled 'intratextualism' by one scholar, who defines the practice as 'read[ing] a contested word or phrase that appears in the Constitution in light of another passage in the Constitution featuring the same (or a very similar) word or phrase.'[55]

To be sure, the intrinsic attributes of a constitution, for example, its plain text or even its structure, might invite the use of history in constitutional interpretation, and more specifically, the very use of predecessor constitutions.[56] In those cases, there can occur both inter- and intra-constitutional interpretation.

52 381 US 479 (1965).

53 501 US 868 (1991).

54 ibid 886. See also Mazzone and Tecimer (n 8) 3009 n 14.

55 Akhil Reed Amar, 'Intratextualism' (1999) 112 Harvard Law Review 747, 748. This practice, of course, imputes a higher degree of coherence to the document than its framers might have thought of in the first place. See generally Adrian Vermeule and Ernest A Young, 'Hercules, Herbert, and Amar: The Trouble with *Intratextualism*' (2000) 113 Harvard Law Review 730.

56 Renata Uitz, *Constitutions, Courts, and History: Historical Narratives in Constitutional Adjudication* (Central European University Press 2005) 116–36. There are references in the US Constitution to the Articles of Confederation, including the following mention in art VI: "All debts contracted and engagements entered into, before the adoption of this Constitution, shall be as valid against the United States under this Constitution, as under the Confederation." For other interconstitutionalist references in the US Constitution see Mazzone and Tecimer (n 8) 3012.

One example comes from the German Basic Law. Article 140 regulating the law of religious denominations provides: 'The provision of Articles 136, 137, 138, 139 and 141 of the German Constitution of 11 August 1919 shall be an integral part of this Basic Law.' Thus, the text of the German Basic Law itself can be said to demand inter-constitutional analysis.

Another example is the US Supreme Court's decision in *United States Steel Corp v Multistate Tax Commission*.[57] In ruling that the Compacts Clause of the US Constitution did not require congressional approval for inter-state compacts that did not enhance state power in relation to federal power, Justice Powell's majority opinion invoked the Articles of Confederation to support the conclusion (*inter*-constitutional interpretation). In his textual analysis of Article VI of the Articles of Confederation, Powell noted that while states were, absent congressional approval, prohibited from entering into any 'conference, agreement, alliance or treaty' with any *foreign* power, the same article, in the subsequent paragraph that dealt with relations between states, merely subjected inter-state 'treat[ies], confederation[s] or alliance[s],' and not agreements, to congressional approval. Powell inferred from this textual difference between the first two paragraphs of Article VI of the Articles of Confederation (*intra*-constitutional interpretation of the Articles) that while agreements states made with foreign powers were always subject to congressional approval, inter-state agreements were not necessarily so, given the exclusion of the word 'agreement' from the part of Article VI regulating relations between states.[58] Justice Powell's opinion, therefore, can be said to employ both inter- (comparing the US Constitution and the Articles) and intra-constitutional (comparing two different texts within the Articles) interpretive practices.[59]

2.3 *State Constitutions / the Constitutions of Federal Subunits*

In federal systems, federal subunits (eg states in the US, *Länder* in Germany) typically have their own constitutions. In the US, primarily because of textual similarities and the fact that the framers of the US Constitution drew inspiration from existing state constitutions, state constitutions and state constitutional law are considered relevant resources for interpreting the

57 434 US 452 (1978).

58 ibid 460 n 10.

59 I recognize that sometimes the line separating two constitutions might be subject to debate. For example, some scholars contend that the Reconstruction Amendments so significantly altered the original Constitution that they ushered in a new constitution. See Mitchell Franklin, 'Concerning the Influence of Roman Law on the Formulation of the Constitution of the United States' (1964) 38 Tulane Law Review 621, 643.

federal Constitution.[60] Certain state constitutions are deemed particularly relevant: the Massachusetts Constitution of 1780, for instance, has a special place among state constitutions because of its age and influence upon the framers of the US Constitution. Among other things, the Massachusetts Constitution reflected an influential Montesquieuan conception of separation of powers.[61]

The US Supreme Court has often referred to state constitutions. In *District of Columbia v Heller*,[62] for example, Justice Scalia, writing for the majority, argued that his interpretation of the Second Amendment to the US Constitution as guaranteeing an individual right to possess arms was 'confirmed by analogous arms-bearing rights in state constitutions that preceded and immediately followed adoption of the Second Amendment.'[63]

In line with the 'genetic' mode of interpretation[64] that conceives of English constitutional law, state constitutions, the Articles of Confederation, and the US Constitution as having sprung from the same roots, the US Supreme Court has also referenced state constitutions *and* the Articles together on numerous occasions.[65]

Invoking a state constitution bears certain similarities to invoking a past constitution designed for the entire polity such as the national constitution in a federal system. In both instances the constitution serves as a historical reference. (Of course, if the referenced state constitution is still in force, as is often true when the US Supreme Court looks to state constitutions, its invocation lacks the inter-temporal element of uses of an abrogated national constitution.) However, a major difference between inter-constitutional interpretation and the comparison of state constitutions and the US Constitution lies in the fact that, in the former case, the objects of comparison are understood as functional equivalents rather than as standing in a hierarchical relationship; state constitutions, by contrast, are inferior to the federal Constitution rather than its functional counterpart.

---

60 See eg the assertion that '[The US Constitution] cannot be understood or activated without reference to the state constitutions.' John Kincaid, 'State Constitutions in the Federal System' (1988) 496 The Annals of the American Academy 12, 13. See also Mazzone and Tecimer (n 8) 3009 n 15.

61 See eg Mark Tushnet, *The Constitution of the United States of America: A Contextual Analysis* (2nd ed, Hart Publishing 2015) 89. See also Mazzone and Tecimer (n 8) 3009 n 15.

62 554 US 570 (2008).

63 ibid 600–601. See also Mazzone and Tecimer (n 8) 3009 n 15.

64 See (n 39) and accompanying text.

65 See eg *Murdock v Pennsylvania* 319 US 105 (1943); *Furman v Georgia* (n 40); *United States v Brewster* (n 40); *Marsh v Chambers* 463 US 783 (1983); *Freytag v Commissioner* (n 53); *United States Term Limits v Thornton* 514 US 779 (1995).

Moreover, the fact that in virtually all cases past national constitutions are fewer in number than state constitutions can give rise to cherry-picking problems when invoking state constitutions. Why, for example, does the Supreme Court look to the Constitution of Massachusetts but omit any discussion of the Constitution of Rhode Island? If the predecessor of the US Constitution is accepted to be the Articles, there is no cherry-picking problem.[66] But if a provision being interpreted exists in, say, twenty other state constitutions with small differences in phrasing, the problem of justifying invoking and not invoking some of those twenty constitutions for purposes of constitutional interpretation intensifies.

2.4 *Bi- or Multi-lingual Constitutional Interpretation*

In polities with multiple officially recognized languages, the very same constitution may have various versions – translations of the same document. While drafters presumably go to great lengths to make sure that translations are as faithful as possible to the original version, linguistic differences between versions might exist. Uncovering the meaning of a constitution might thus require comparing and contrasting versions of the same constitution in different languages. Consider the case of *Du Plessis*[67] from South Africa. There, the issue was whether the Interim Constitution applied to common law defamation. Article 7 of the document provided: 'This Chapter [ie Fundamental Rights] shall apply to all law in force […].' The question the court faced was whether the common law, which regulated defamation, fell within the term, 'all law,' in the same way as statutory law. Justice Kentridge, while recognizing that the English version of the Interim Constitution, which was at best ambiguous on the matter, was the binding version, invoked the version of the document in Afrikaans to arrive at the conclusion that the term 'all law' indeed encompassed both statutory and common law.[68]

In bi- or multi-lingual constitutional interpretation the comparison essentially involves different linguistic version of the *same* document, whereas inter-constitutional interpretation requires at least two inter-temporally distinguishable constitutions belonging to the same polity, one abrogated and one in force.

66 In polities with multiple past constitutions, however, (eg Brazil and France) the problem of cherry-picking may nonetheless arise.

67 *Du Plessis v De Klerk*, CCT 8/95; 1996 (3) SA 850 (CC); 1996 (5) BCLR 658 (CC) (S Afr).

68 For a similar discussion of the case see Uitz (n 56) 71. See also Mazzone and Tecimer (n 8) 3009 n 16.

2.5 *Comparisons to Other Documents* (*of Constitutional or Quasi-constitutional Importance*)

Consider one of the 'anti-canonical' cases in US constitutional law,[69] *Dred Scott v Sandford.*[70] There, in ruling that blacks (free or enslaved) could not be United States citizens, Chief Justice Taney relied on a multitude of sources other than the US Constitution:

> We have the language of *the Declaration of Independence* and of *the Articles of Confederation*, in addition to the plain words of *the Constitution* itself; we have the legislation of the different States, before, about the time, and since, the Constitution was adopted; we have the legislation of Congress, from the time of its adoption to a recent period; and we have the constant and uniform action of the Executive Department, all concurring together, and leading to the same result.[71]

Taney's use of the Declaration of Independence is just one example of a pervasive phenomenon in constitutional interpretation: referring to foundational materials that carry special significance in generating meaning for that polity's in-force constitution. While scholars have debated the precise status that should be given to the Declaration of Independence,[72] it is surely not the predecessor of the US Constitution in the same sense as the Articles of Confederation. Constitutive documents such as the Declaration state aspirational goals – much like constitutional preambles – but constitutions *proper* are heavily regulative in content. Furthermore, the general character of and the aspirational tone that pervades most constitutive documents make their invocation largely rhetorical; references to past constitutions are typically more substantive.

---

69 Jamal Greene, 'The Anticanon' (2011) 125 Harvard Law Review 379, 436–42.

70 60 US (19 How) 393 (1857).

71 ibid 426 (emphasis added). For a brief discussion see Mazzone and Tecimer (n 8) 3010 n 17.

72 For instance, Professor Tushnet argues that the Preamble to the US Constitution and the Declaration of Independence collectively form America's 'thin constitution' as opposed to its 'thick constitution' found in the various provisions of the US Constitution. Tushnet further argues that the most basic constitutional principles enshrined in the thin, and not thick, constitution are what guide US constitutional law. Mark Tushnet, *Taking the Constitution Away from the Courts* (Princeton University Press 1999) 9–14. See also Mazzone and Tecimer (n 8) 3010 n 17.

2.6 *Inter-draft Comparisons*

A final possibility is the comparison of various drafts of the *same* constitution.[73] On occasion, the US Supreme Court invokes drafts prepared and submitted to the Constitutional Convention (tasked initially with proposing amendments to the Articles of Confederation) to generate meaning for the US Constitution.[74] The difference here is, very much like in the case of a comparison between bi- or multi-lingual interpretation and intra-constitutional interpretation, the absence of two objects of inquiry (ie two *different constitutions*). In that sense, inter-draft comparisons of the same constitution are similar to more general forms of statutory interpretation that make use of legislative drafts.[75]

2.7 *Inter-constitutional Interpretation Gone Global?*

It bears noting that none of the above-mentioned ways of engaging with constitutions requires the interpreter, that is, the actor who engages in any of the listed interpretive practices, to be domestic. The people or institutions engaging in any and all of these practices, including inter-constitutional interpretation, need not be the courts or politicians of the polity whose constitutions are being compared. As recent scholarship has shown, outsider intervention in domestic constitutional contests is an increasingly visible phenomenon,[76] and inter-constitutional interpretation as well as the other above-mentioned interpretive practices can be utilized by domestic and international actors alike.

For example, a comparison between the current German Basic Law and its predecessor, the Weimar Constitution of 1919 (an example of inter-constitutional interpretation), is found in a decision of the German Constitutional Court[77] (a domestic actor/insider) as well as in a decision of the South African Constitutional Court (a foreign actor/outsider). In 1997, in *President of the Republic of South Africa and Another v Hugo*,[78] the South African Constitutional Court examined the constitutionality of Presidential

73 An interesting possibility might arise when an in-force constitution is compared with the draft of an abrogated constitution or when an abrogated constitution is compared to the draft of an in-force constitution. Those two instances are both inter-temporal and involve two different constitutions (one in enacted and one in draft form), and therefore might be considered a form of inter-constitutional interpretation.

74 See eg *Reid v Covert* 354 US 1, 21 n 40 (1957). See also Mazzone and Tecimer (n 8) 3010 n 18.

75 On legislative history in statutory interpretation, including references to legislative drafts, see generally William N Eskridge, Jr, 'Legislative History Values' (1990) 66 Chicago-Kent Law Review 365.

76 See Dixon and Jackson (n 39).

77 For an example already discussed see (n 26–27) above and accompanying text.

78 (CCT11/96) [1997] ZACC 4; 1997 (6) BCLR 708; 1997 (4) SA 1 (18 April 1997) (S Afr).

Act no. 17, which pardoned certain classes of prisoners, including mothers of children below the age of 12. The respondent, a male prisoner and father to a child younger than 12, alleged that the Act in question unconstitutionally discriminated against fathers. Focusing initially on the broader question of whether the president had constitutional authority to grant pardons and whether those pardons were subject to constitutional review – two questions ultimately answered in the affirmative – Justice Goldstone referred to the German constitutional law of presidential pardons, invoking both the Basic Law and its predecessor, the Weimar Constitution of 1919:

> The German courts have also approached the power of pardon and reprieve as a prerogative power originating at the commencement of the German monarchy and taken over into the Weimar Constitution. Whether that power can be reviewed under the present constitution by the Federal Constitutional Court was an issue which led to one of the few tied decisions of that court. In BVerfGE 25, 352 (1969) four of the justices were of the opinion that the Basic Law (Comprehensive Judicial Review of all Acts of Public Authority) did not apply to acts of mercy [...] The other four justices held that the historical tradition could not live within the framework of the Basic Law and that the arbitrary exercise of public power was not exempt from the basic requirements of the constitution.[79]

In sum, while the *object* of comparison matters in distinguishing among different methods of constitutional engagement, the *subject* of comparison, that is, the person or institutions interpreting the constitution(s) in question, can be an insider or outsider.

3 Uses of the Articles of Confederation in Interpreting the US Constitution

This part examines how the highest court in the US makes use of the Articles of Confederation in constitutional adjudication. The focus here is on courts, indeed a single court, but it would be wrong to conclude that only courts engage in inter-constitutional interpretation.[80] Indeed, inter-constitutional interpretation might be most prevalent and established outside of the

79 ibid para 25.

80 It has been rightly pointed out that much of American constitutional law is defined and interpreted by the operation of ordinary politics and not by federal courts. That is

judiciary. Members of the political branches might engage in less legalistic forms of inter-constitutional interpretation than does the judiciary but their invocations of past constitutions remain important. Compared to courts, inter-constitutional statements by politicians might reach broader audiences and provide general guidance to other branches responsible for interpreting specific provisions of a constitution.[81] It would also be wrong to think that extra-judicial instances of inter-constitutional interpretation lack legal consequence. Consider Abraham Lincoln's First Inaugural Address in 1861. There, in arriving at the political and legal conclusion that states were constitutionally prohibited from seceding from the Union, Lincoln, a lawyer himself, invoked the Articles of Confederation:

> Descending from these general principles, we find the proposition that in legal contemplation the Union is perpetual confirmed by the history of the Union itself. The Union is much older than the Constitution. It was formed, in fact, by the Articles of Association in 1774. It was matured and continued by the Declaration of Independence in 1776. It was further matured, and the faith of all the then thirteen States expressly plighted and engaged that it should be perpetual, by the Articles of Confederation in 1778. And finally, in 1787, one of the declared objects for ordaining and establishing the Constitution was 'to form a more perfect Union.'[82]

In addition, while the focus here is on the US Supreme Court, it bears noting that other American courts engage in inter-constitutional interpretation as well. Lower federal courts refer to the Articles to generate constitutional meaning. State courts also make use of the Articles (and make use of prior

---

generally why extra-judicial inter-constitutional interpretation might be equally, if not more, important than judicial uses of the same. See Tushnet (n 61) 154.

81 Opponents of extra-judicial constitutional interpretation argue that judicial supremacy and the definitive settlement of disputes is an essential feature of constitutionalism. Larry Alexander and Frederick Schauer, 'On Extrajudicial Constitutional Interpretation' (1997) 110 Harvard Law Review 1359, 1371. cf Keith E Whittington, 'Extrajudicial Constitutional Interpretation: Three Objections and Responses' (2002) 80 North Carolina Law Review 773.

82 'First Inaugural Address of Abraham Lincoln' (*The Avalon Project*, 2008) <https://avalon.law.yale.edu/19th_century/lincoln1.asp> accessed 11 September 2019. See also Gregory E Maggs, 'A Concise Guide to the Articles of Confederation as a Source for Determining the Original Meaning of the Constitution' (2017) 85 The George Washington Law Review 397, 429. In this part of his speech, Lincoln also refers to the Declaration of Independence and the Articles of Association, both of which can be considered materials of constitutional importance mentioned earlier. See part 2.5 above. For other examples of extra-judicial inter-constitutional interpretation see Mazzone and Tecimer (n 8) 3005.

state constitutions in interpreting the current state constitution). References to the Articles appear also in briefs submitted to courts; sometimes courts then make use of such references, sometimes they do not.[83]

3.1 *The Status of the Articles of Confederation*

In the US context, it may be objected that the Articles of Confederation were not a constitution and that the first and only constitution of the nation is the Constitution of 1789. On this account, use of the Articles to interpret the 1789 Constitution is not a form of inter-constitutional interpretation as I have defined it.

The legal status of the Articles has indeed been debated in scholarship, largely in relation to a particular question of constitutional replacement: whether it was lawful for the US Constitution to replace the Articles given that under Article 13 any amendment required congressional approval and unanimous agreement by the legislatures of the states[84] and the delegates to the Philadelphia Convention were tasked with offering amendments to the Articles not replacing them altogether. Some scholars argue that the US Constitution, derived from the sovereign people, did not need to follow the internal procedures of change contained in the Articles, which lacked a comparable democratic legitimacy. The Articles, then, were at most a multilateral treaty, one 'conveniently dishonored on all sides,'[85] and so by the time of the Philadelphia Convention had lost any binding quality. This assessment is not

83 For some US Supreme Court cases that do *not* discuss the Articles, although invoked in the attorney briefs, see *Talbot v Jansen* 3 US (3 Dall) 133 (1795); *Fletcher v Peck* 10 US (6 Cranch) 87 (1810); *Gibbons v Ogden* 22 US (9 Wheat) 1 (1824); *Groves v Slaughter* 40 US (15 Pet) 449 (1841); *Cummings v Missouri* 71 US (4 Fall) 277 (1867); *Atlantic Coast Line R Co v Mazursky* 216 US 122 (1910); *Missouri v Holland* 252 US 416 (1920); *United States v Sprague* 282 US 716 (1931); *Edwards v California* 314 US 160 (1941).

84 Articles of Confederation art XIII, in relevant part, provides: 'nor shall any alteration at any time hereafter be made in any of them; unless such alteration be agreed to in a Congress of the United States, and be afterwards confirmed by the legislatures of every State.'

85 Akhil R Amar, 'Of Sovereignty and Federalism' (1987) 96 The Yale Law Journal 1425, 1447–48. Amar describes the Articles' status as 'a fallen treaty.' ibid 1448. Similarly, David Strauss rightly points out that '[t]he Constitution enjoys a legal status in our society that the Articles of Confederation-or, for that matter, the Declaration of Independence-does not.' David Strauss, 'What is Constitutional Theory?' (1999) 87 California Law Review 581, 583. I do not consider this, per se, to be an objection to the (although abrogated) constitutional status of the Articles from the perspective of constitutional actors of the present day. I take Strauss's assertion to be a conventional statement on the enhanced legitimacy of the US Constitution when compared to the Articles, given the traditional narrative that the former perfected deficiencies in the latter.

just a modern view: James Madison described the Articles as merely '[a] compact between independent sovereigns.'[86]

Regardless of issues of legality, there is consensus that the US Constitution *replaced* the Articles,[87] and that point suffices for treating both documents as constitutions for purposes of this chapter. In other words, it is sufficient that from a sociological perspective, interpreters view the Articles as having constitutional status.[88] As the discussion below shows, when the US Supreme Court invokes the Articles it assumes their status as a constitution.[89]

3.2 *Methodology and Analysis*

My study provides insights into how the Supreme Court has invoked the Articles of Confederation from the Court's inception in 1789 until September 2019 – a period spanning 230 years. The raw data for my analysis comes from a search in legal databases for all Supreme Court cases that refer to the Articles.[90] During the period of study the Court referred to the Articles in a total of 169 cases,[91] and within those 169 cases, in a total of 199 opinions. The sheer number

86 *The Federalist Papers* 43 (Madison). It bears noting here that the formal label of a document is of some, but not conclusive, relevance to determining its status as a constitution or not ('The German Basic Law,' which is not formally stylized as a constitution is a prime example).

87 Akhil Amar, for instance, concedes this. See Akhil Reed Amar, 'America's Lived Constitution' (2011) 120 The Yale Law Journal 1734, 1743: '[T]he Constitution had sprung to life, a process in which "We, the People" had altered various state laws and institutions in force prior to the Constitution's ratification and had abolished the old Articles of Confederation.' See also Mazzone and Tecimer (n 8) 3019 n 69 and accompanying text.

88 Rosalind Dixon and Tom Ginsburg, 'Introduction' in Tom Ginsburg and Rosalind Dixon (eds), *Comparative Constitutional Law* (Edward Elgar Publishing 2011) 5: 'A fourth approach is more sociological and open-textured, and linked to the way in which national actors understand domestic legal norms as constitutional.' See also Mazzone and Tecimer (n 8) 3019 n 71 and accompanying text.

89 For some textual indications that this is indeed the perception among the members of the Court see eg *Federal Power Commission v Tuscarora Indian Nation*, 362 US 99, 135 n 16 (1960) (Black, J, dissenting): 'the original'; *National Federation of Independent Business v Sebelius*, 567 US 519, 599–600 (2012) (Ginsburg, J, dissenting): 'the Constitution's precursor.' See also Mazzone and Tecimer (n 8) 3019 n 70.

90 I have searched for 'articles of /3 confederation' in two prominent databases, Lexis Nexis and Westlaw, and then cross-compared results, reading through each case to make sure the Articles were indeed mentioned, and to analyze their uses.

91 It is possible my research has overlooked a small number of cases but, if so, they are not likely to alter significantly the conclusions the chapter draws. cf Maggs (n 82) 398, n 1: 'A Westlaw search of "articles of confederation" in the Supreme Court database yields 175 cases.' cf also ibid 431: 'The Supreme Court has cited the Articles of Confederation in more than 180 cases.'

of times the Court has invoked the Articles is, however, only a small part of the story. The remainder of this section discusses other key results of the study.

3.2.1 The Articles Have Been Referenced More Often in Recent Times

The earliest mention of the Articles is in *Chisholm v Georgia*[92] – a case in which the Court ruled that Article III, Section 2 of the Constitution abrogated states' sovereign immunity (later superseded by the Eleventh Amendment). In his dissenting opinion, Justice Iredell invoked the Articles in a way that would set the stage for a still-continuing debate about the nature of the Articles and how the Constitution differs from them:

> The powers of the general Government, either of a Legislative or executive nature, or which particularly concerns Treaties with Foreign Powers, do for the most part (if not wholly) affect individuals, and not States: They require no aid from any State authority. This is the great leading distinction between the old *articles of confederation*, and the present constitution.[93]

Justice Iredell distinguished the Articles from the current Constitution, asserting that the Constitution, unlike the Articles, regulates individuals and not states. Therefore, he reasoned, the Constitution could not be said to have abrogated sovereign immunity, because that would be tantamount to regulating the states. A second reference in the same case came from Justice Wilson, who initiated what can usefully be termed "aversive references" to the Articles, a topic discussed further below.[94] After acknowledging that the 'thirteen States […] were connected by articles of confederation,' Wilson gave a critique of the document: 'To the purposes of public strength and felicity, that confederacy was totally inadequate. A requisition on the several States terminated its Legislative authority: Executive or Judicial authority it had none.'[95]

Fast-forward to 2019: 226 years later, the Court was still referencing the Articles, as it did in *Tennessee Wine & Spirits Retailers Association v Thomas*.[96] There, writing for the majority, Justice Alito invoked the Articles twice, in both instances to draw attention to how under the Articles, which lacked a workable Commerce Clause, states enacted legislation that discriminated against

92 2 US (2 Dall) 419 (1793).

93 ibid 435 (Iredell, J, dissenting) (emphasis added).

94 See below, part 3.2.6.

95 *Chisholm v Georgia* (n 92) 463 (Wilson, J).

96 139 S Ct 2449 (2019).

TABLE 5.2 References to the Articles by the Supreme Court (1789 – September 2019)

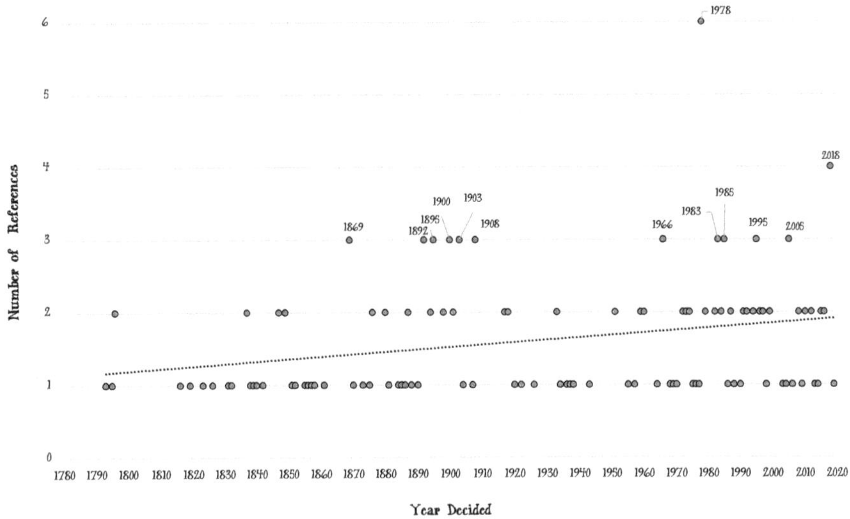

sister states. Alito wrote that '[u]nder the Articles of Confederation, States notoriously obstructed the interstate shipment of goods'[97] and that 'economic Balkanization […] had plagued relations among the Colonies and later among the States under the Articles of Confederation.'[98]

As Table 5.2 shows, the number of cases invoking the Articles has varied over time. 1978 witnessed the highest number of cases invoking the Articles with a total of 6, followed by 2018, in which the Articles were mentioned in a total of 4 cases. On the other hand, there have been years in which the Articles were never invoked: most recently in 2017, 2011, 2007, 2002, 2001, and 2000. However, the general trend shows a small but steady *increase* in the number of references to the Articles over the years. Simply put, the Articles have been mentioned more times in recent Supreme Court cases than in older cases, which may be understandable given especially that in its early years the Court did not decide many cases to begin with. But considering also that the Court's docket has shrunk significantly in recent years, the increase in cases referring to the Articles might be all the more impressive. During the Court's first century of operations, from 1789 to 1889 (inclusive), there were only 44 cases in which the Articles received mentioned. Over the next one hundred years, from 1890 to 1990 (inclusive), the Articles were referenced in 85 cases. And in the

97 ibid 2460.

98 ibid 2461 (citations omitted).

first decades of the Court's third century of operations, from 1991 to 2019 (a period of 29 years), 40 cases invoked the Articles, nearly as many cases as in the Court's entire first century.

The increase, over time, in the number of references the Court makes to the Articles is significant. The finding cuts against any theory that courts invoke historical materials more often when the constitutional order is still at a nascent stage, on an assumption that once central questions of constitutional significance become settled (because precedents start to accumulate and basic interpretive queries are answered through textual or other methods) recourse to historical materials will start to decline as an interpretive practice. The increasing popularity of the Articles supports the opposite conclusion.

Three potential explanations account for the increased number of references to the Articles in more recent years. The first is what one scholar has termed the 'canonizing influence of time' hypothesis to explain the rise of originalism as a – or even *the* – favored method of interpretation in US constitutional law.[99] Similarly, it is entirely plausible that the rise in the number of cases invoking the Articles is associated with the passage of time, and the simultaneous endurance of the Articles in the Court's imagination as a document – with its flaws and virtues – relevant to understanding the Constitution.

A second explanation is that the increased influence of originalism has itself been accompanied by increased attention to the Articles. Especially for variants of originalism that emphasize original intent, the phenomenon of what may be termed "framer overlap" is a curious feature of American constitutional law: some of the individuals who influenced the drafting of the Articles later helped write the US Constitution, a phenomenon with few counterparts in other polities across the world where constitution writing episodes are usually temporally far removed from each other. Because of framer overlap, the Articles are directly relevant to discovering the intentions of the framers of the US Constitution, not least because some of the framers of the US Constitution who had also authored the antecedent document had lived, happily and unhappily, under that antecedent document, so that original intent includes the intent to change (or preserve) the model of governance under the Articles.

At the same time, these two hypotheses alone might not accurately capture the entire reality. For example, how can we explain multi-year breaks during which the Court did not invoke the Articles? Between 1796 and 1816, the Court never mentioned the Articles, the longest such period. The second longest period without reference to the Articles was between 1908 and 1917; the third, between 1943 and 1951. Since 1982, by contrast, the Articles were invoked at least

99 See Jamal Greene, 'On the Origins of Originalism' (2009) 88 Texas Law Review 1.

once every year until 2019, except in 1989, 1993, 2000, 2001, 2002, 2007, 2011 and 2017. Perhaps a relatively consistent use of the Articles since the early 1980s reflects changes in the Court's membership. Or perhaps the explanation lies in greater attention to historical materials as part of a conservative response to the liberal orientations of the Warren and Burger Courts.[100] Regardless, it is difficult to account for the observed ebbs and flows in the Court's references to the Articles.

A third explanation, therefore, is that there is no logical explanation, and that to insist on one is to impose order on what is in fact a messy reality. There might indeed be no discernable reason for periods during which the Court makes no mention of the Articles. One response might insist that the cases that came before the Court in those gap years, as a matter of substance, did not have anything to do with the Articles, but that explanation is not satisfactory: the Articles have been used in many cases involving varied subjects. Subject matter and the content of the Court's docket in a given year cannot realistically account for the presence or lack of references to the Articles.

3.2.2 Court Opinions Have Invoked the Articles More Often than Individual Opinions

Cases from 1851 onward in which the Articles were mentioned readily lend themselves to an analysis based on the type of opinion that refers to the Articles.[101] Since 1851, the Articles have been invoked in a total of 149 cases and 171 opinions. Table 5.3 shows the distribution of these 171 opinions by type.

TABLE 5.3 Distribution of opinion types

Opinion type	**Number of opinions invoking the articles**
Court opinion (unanimous, majority, plurality)	91
Concurring	16
Dissenting	55
Concurring in part, dissenting in part	9

100 ibid 69.

101 Because of inconsistent designation of opinion type and the issuance of seriatim opinions, cases pre-1851 do not readily lend themselves to a comparable analysis. See Linda Greenhouse, *A Very Short Introduction: The U.S. Supreme Court* (OUP 2000) 11.

Most invocations of the Articles have occurred in opinions by the Court, followed by dissenting opinions. Relatively few concurrences have made use of the Articles.

3.2.3 Some Justices Refer to the Articles More than Others

Some Justices have cited the Articles frequently while other members of the Court have not cited them at all. Table 5.4 shows the top 5 Justices in terms of their opinions referencing the Articles. Justice Thomas, still on the Court, has authored the most opinions citing the Articles.

Making sense of these numbers, of course, requires attention to context. For example, Justice Stevens, in third place, is also the third-longest-serving member of the Court (he served for 35 years). Many members of the Court served previously on a lower court: counting just Supreme Court cases misses references to the Articles they may have made in lower court opinions.

Nonetheless, these figures are instructive. Perhaps first and foremost, Justice Thomas is the most outspoken proponent of originalism on the Court, and particularly of referring to the meaning of the Constitution at the time of its adoption.[102] Justice Thomas's many references to the Articles suggest their particular relevance to originalist approaches.

TABLE 5.4 Justices who have most often cited the Articles

Justice	Number of opinions invoking the articles
Clarence Thomas	12
William Brennan, Jr	10
John Paul Stevens	9
Anthony Kennedy Edward Douglas White (tied)	8
David Souter John Marshall Harlan (I) (tied)	7

102 On Thomas's strong support for originalism see eg Clarence Thomas, 'Judging' (1996) 45 The University of Kansas Law Review 1, 6: 'For example, I have said in my opinions that when interpreting the Constitution, judges should seek the original understanding of the provision's text, if that text's meaning is not readily apparent.'

At the same time, the numbers show that it is not just originalists who are interested in the Articles. During the period examined, Justice Stevens invoked the Articles in just 3 fewer cases than did Justice Thomas. Sometimes Stevens did so in opinions that had an originalist flavor, as in his dissent in *DC v Heller*;[103] at other times Stevens invoked the Articles in non-originalist opinions.[104]

Consider, too, Justices Ginsburg and Scalia. They are typically viewed as located on opposite ends of the political spectrum and while Justice Scalia identified himself as an originalist,[105] Justice Ginsburg never used that appellation to describe herself. Yet both invoked the Articles in an equal number of cases: 3. This may very well mean that the decision to invoke the Articles is largely a matter of personal choice rather than constitutional ideology, and dependent upon the individual justice and their familiarity with and willingness to look to the Articles as an interpretive guide. To put it differently, an originalist justice need not look to the Articles and non-originalist justices should not be presumed to not invoke the Articles in their opinions.

3.2.4 The Justices Seldom Justify Their Use of the Articles

How, then, do the Justices justify their uses of the Articles?[106] Unsurprisingly, most of the time, the Justices do not justify their uses of the Articles at all – just as they do not justify referring to certain previous cases, the structure of the Constitution, or the practical consequences of decisions. The fact that the Justices seldom justify their invocation of the Articles may reflect a certain cultural embeddedness of the interpretive practice of referring to the Articles. If use of the Articles is uncontroversial and commonplace, the perceived necessity to justify their use in any particular instance may simply not arise. Consider Justice Kennedy's dissenting opinion in *United States v IBM*:[107] 'In interpreting constitutional restrictions on the taxing power, we must recall that the want of this power in the National Government was one of the great weaknesses of the Articles of Confederation.'[108] Other than this conclusory 'we must recall,' Justice Kennedy did not explain why it was appropriate to consider the state of the federal taxing power under the Articles.

103 See *District of Columbia v Heller* (n 62) 636–80 (Stevens, J, dissenting).
104 See eg *Gonzales v Raich*, 545 US 1 (2005).
105 See eg Antonin Scalia, 'Originalism: The Lesser Evil' 57 (1989) University of Cincinnati Law Review 849.
106 I use the word 'justify' only to refer to explanations as to why a particular practice is suited to constitutional interpretation.
107 517 US 843 (1996).
108 ibid 874 (Kennedy, J, dissenting).

An alternative explanation lies in the fact that referring to the Articles is an interpretive practice that often works in tandem with broader historical and originalist methods of interpretation and the latter two, as dominant and pervasive methods in constitutional practice, rarely need justification. As one scholar has put it, '[a]lthough arguments invoked in constitutional reasoning are not self-legitimating, the legitimacy of references to history is hardly ever questioned.'[109]

Even so, occasionally the Justices do explain their invocation of the Articles. Such justifications can be divided into three broad categories. First, sometimes the Justices flesh out the connection between originalism and the use of the Articles. In other words, they will explicitly articulate the relevance of looking to the Articles as a means to explicate original intent,[110] based on the assumption that the framers had the vices and virtues of the Articles in mind when drafting the new Constitution. The paradigmatic example here is Justice O'Connor's concurring opinion in *Federal Energy Regulatory Commission v Mississippi*.[111] In explaining that the Constitution permits the national government to regulate individuals directly and thus avoids the problem, under the Articles, of state legislatures impeding the implementation of federal law, O'Connor wrote: '*Experience under the Articles of Confederation taught the Framers that* multiple state legislatures, unchecked by any central power, "[threaten] danger not to the harmony only, but to the tranquility of the Union."'[112] Another example within this first category is Justice Brennan's dissent in *Allied Structural Steel Company v Spannaus*,[113] invoking the Articles to trace the origins of the Constitution's Contract Clause:

> *The widespread dissatisfaction with the Articles of Confederation and, thus, the adoption of our Constitution*, was largely a result of the mass of legislation enacted by various States during our earlier national period to relieve debtors from the obligation to perform contracts with their creditors.[114]

109 Uitz (n 56) 93.

110 Notwithstanding the fact, of course, that there exists a sophisticated literature on originalism and its varieties, which have moved beyond original intent to discussions of original public meaning.

111 456 US 742 (1982).

112 ibid 795 n 33 (O'Connor, J, concurring in part and dissenting in part) (citations omitted) (emphasis added).

113 438 US 234 (1978).

114 ibid 256 (Brennan, J, dissenting) (emphasis added).

Second, sometimes the Justices preface invocations of the Articles by noting that a historical exposition of the origins of some feature of the Constitution (also found, in antecedent form, in the Articles) may generally be helpful for understanding its meaning. Consider, for example, Justice McLean's dissenting opinion in *Prigg v Pennsylvania*,[115] in which the majority ruled that a Pennsylvania law prohibiting the return of fugitive slaves was invalid under Article IV, Section 2 of the Constitution and, as inconsistent with the federal Fugitive Slave Act of 1793, under the Supremacy Clause of Article VI. In arguing that the Fugitive Slave Clause of Article IV, Section 2 was intended to address the federal government, and not the states, Justice McLean first resorted to the Articles of Confederation to trace the origins of the Constitution's Fugitive Slave Clause:

> *A law is better understood by a knowledge of the evils which led to its adoption. And this applies most strongly to a fundamental law.*
>
> At an early period of our history, slavery existed in all the colonies; and fugitives from labour were claimed and delivered up under a spirit of comity or conventional law among the colonies. The articles of confederation contained no provision on the subject, and *there can be no doubt that the provision introduced into the Constitution was the result of experience and manifest necessity*. A matter so delicate, important, and exciting, was very properly introduced into the organic law.[116]

Justice McLean thought it important to go back to the Articles, not – at least, not only – because he wished to exhibit punctilious reverence for the framers, but because he believed in the general importance of the historical context that paved the way for the adoption of certain parts of the document he was tasked with interpreting.

A third justification the Justices sometimes employ in invoking the Articles of Confederation is the notion of textual – and less frequently, purposive – similarity between the Articles and the Constitution. The underlying assumption is an easily cognizable one: if identical or similar language has been used elsewhere before, the Justices will take notice of it as it might shed light on the origins of the language employed in the current document and may thus assist in ascertaining the intended meaning of the words used therein. Conversely, even minor textual differences, as observed by Chief Justice

---

115 41 US 539 (1842).

116 ibid 660 (McLean, J, dissenting) (emphasis added).

Marshall in *McCulloch*,[117] may aid the interpretive process by bolstering assertions that the meaning under the successor document must differ from that of its predecessor.

Consider here Justice Harlan's majority opinion in *United States v Johnson*,[118] holding that an intensive judicial inquiry into whether a congressman was engaged in corruption that heavily relied on the congressman's speeches and statements made in the House of Representatives violated the constitutional protections afforded to him by the Speech and Debate Clause of the Constitution. In tracing the origin of the Clause to the Articles of Confederation – and eventually to the English Bill of Rights of 1689 – Justice Harlan noted that the Clause 'repeated *almost verbatim* the language of Article v of the Articles of Confederation.'[119]

A few years earlier, in *Kinsella v United States*,[120] which held that military courts did not enjoy jurisdiction over civilian dependents of military personnel, Justice Whittaker's opinion employed a similar technique. In interpreting Article I, Section 8, Clause 14, which empowers Congress to 'make Rules for the Government and Regulation of the land and naval Forces,' Justice Whittaker observed: 'That *language was taken straight from* the Articles of Confederation.'[121] An additional example is Justice Douglas's dissent in *New York v O'Neill*,[122] a case that held it constitutional for states to adopt a uniform law for extraditing witnesses to other states when needed to testify in criminal proceedings. In asserting that the majority's conclusion, in his view erroneously, excepted witnesses from the constitutional guarantee of the right to travel, Justice Douglas turned to the Articles as the source of this right: 'The right to free ingress and egress within the country and even beyond the borders is a basic constitutional right, though it is not contained *in haec verba* in the Constitution. It had been included in the Articles of Confederation, Article IV […].'[123]

On occasion, the Justices invoke similarity not of text but of purpose: the Articles and the Constitution shared a goal but the Articles fell short in achieving it. The majority opinion authored by Justice Douglas White in *United States*

117 See (n 20–21) above and accompanying text.
118 383 US 169 (1966).
119 ibid 177 (emphasis added).
120 361 US 234 (1960).
121 ibid 269 (Whittaker, J, concurring in part and dissenting in part) (citations omitted) (emphasis added).
122 359 US 1 (1959).
123 ibid 2 (Douglas, J, dissenting) (emphasis original).

v Wheeler[124] is illustrative. After pointing to the textual similarity between the Privileges and Immunities Clause in Article IV, Section 2 of the Constitution and Article IV of the Articles of Confederation, and quoting an earlier precedent, Justice Douglas White concluded:

> There can be but little question that *the purpose of both these provisions is the same*, and that the privileges and immunities intended are the same in each. In the article of the Confederation we have some of these specifically mentioned, and enough perhaps to give some general idea of the class of civil rights meant by the phrase.[125]

It is important to underscore that in general the Justices do not offer any justification for their uses of the Articles. That such justifications are quite rare suggests a taken-for-granted relevance of the Articles, and more generally, of historical inquires in elucidating the Constitution. It is useful, then, to contrast the assumed relevance of the Articles with the recent controversy over the question of whether foreign law is ever relevant to domestic constitutional adjudication. The assumed relevance of the Articles might suggest constitutional parochialism: despite their flaws and status as a defunct constitution the Articles are *ours*; they belong to *our* constitutional heritage; they were drafted by some of the very same men who framed *our* Constitution. Foreign law, on the other hand, emphatically does *not* belong to *us*.

One last point that bears mention is that some cases show an observable 'socialization effect' in which one Justice's use of the Articles produces a use of the Articles by another Justice, sometimes in reaching a different conclusion. The best example of this phenomenon in the entire caselaw of the Court comes from Justice Thomas's dissenting opinion in *Central Virginia Community College v Katz*.[126] In that case, Justice Stevens, writing for the Court, ruled that the Bankruptcy Clause of the Constitution in Article I, Section 8 waived state sovereign immunity; accordingly, states could not invoke a sovereign immunity defense in bankruptcy proceedings. In arriving at this conclusion, Justice Stevens relied in part on the experiences under the Articles of Confederation, in which some state courts did not respect others' discharge orders.[127] Justice Thomas took issue with that presentation by his colleague, and invoked the Articles *precisely to respond to Justice Stevens*:

124 254 US 281 (1920).
125 ibid 296 (quoting *Slaughter-House Cases* 83 US (16 Wall) 36, 75 (1872)) (emphasis added).
126 546 US 356 (2006).
127 See ibid 368–69.

> The majority attempts to bolster its historical argument by making three additional observations about the bankruptcy power [...] (2) the inability of debtors, first in the American Colonies and then under the Articles of Confederation, to enforce in one state court a discharge order issued by another state court [...].
>
> The majority's second observation – that the Framers were concerned that, under the Articles of Confederation, debtors were unable to obtain discharge orders issued by the court of one State that would be binding in the court of another State – implicates nothing more than the application of full faith and credit, as is apparent from the majority opinion itself. Accordingly, it has nothing to do with state sovereign immunity from suit.[128]

In essence, Justice Thomas objected to the relevance of the Articles to the point Justice Stevens sought to make. Justice Thomas understood the Articles to be supportive of the conclusion that the Constitution, via its Full Faith and Credit Clause, provided a remedy for the problems that arose under the Articles when states refused to recognize judgments of the courts of sister states. But he was skeptical of his colleague's further claim that the remedying of that problem also limited state sovereign immunity in cases of bankruptcy, so that debtors could enforce a discharge order issued by a state court in another state's court. Justice Thomas thus invoked the Articles to refute Justice Stevens's own characterization of them. In essence, use of the Articles can be a result of judicial dialogue.[129]

3.2.5 The Articles Are Rarely Outcome Determinative

The Articles are rarely outcome determinative: invocation of the Articles alone hardly ever resolves a constitutional dispute one way or another. The point may help explain why the Justices spend little time justifying their reliance on the Articles: because the Articles do not determine the outcome of the case.[130]

---

128 ibid 388–90 (Thomas, J, dissenting).

129 A socialization effect might similarly occasion invocations of Articles by Justices when the Articles are mentioned in the briefs before the Court.

130 Similar reasoning suggests that the Court does not need constitutional license to cite to foreign law and that the controversy over invocations of foreign law is overstated given that while the Justices may *mention* foreign law it is not the basis on which cases are decided. See eg Mark Tushnet, *Weak Courts, Strong Rights: Judicial Review and Social Welfare Rights in Comparative Constitutional Law* (Princeton University Press 2009) 3.

Outcome-determinative, however, is a tricky adjective in constitutional adjudication. Debate exists on what determined the outcome in many of the Court's landmark cases such as *Brown v Board of Education*,[131] which held that racial segregation in public schools violates the Equal Protection Clause of the Fourteenth Amendment. Perhaps *Brown* is explained by textualism or by a particular version of originalism. Perhaps it only makes sense on policy or moral grounds. It at least seems clear that some factors did not explain the outcome in the case. Established precedent was not determinative: *Plessy v Fergusson*,[132] with its infamous 'separate but equal' doctrine, had licensed racial segregation in public facilities. An unyieldingly staunch variant of originalism did not determine the outcome in *Brown* either. But explaining what did not produce an outcome does not necessarily explain what did, particularly if a result is the product of multiple factors that make difficult identifying an exact interpretive determinant.[133]

Indeed, it is easier to see when the Articles have *not* determined the outcome in the cases in which they have been invoked. The Articles serve as one means for engaging with the past and not even the preferred or most salient mechanism. They are usually invoked for expository purposes, to contextualize and historicize the constitutional question before the Court, in a manner that does not drive the actual resolution of the case.[134] There are many examples. Consider, for instance, Justice Ginsburg's opinion for the Court in *Baker v GMC*,[135] holding that the Full Faith and Credit Clause did not bar an employee bound by an injunction as part of a settlement agreement from testifying in the court of another state. In a footnote to her first reference to the Clause, Ginsburg referred to the Articles to draw attention to the Clause's historical origins:

> Predating the Constitution, the Articles of Confederation contained a provision of the same order: 'Full faith and credit shall be given in each

131 347 US 483 (1954).

132 163 US 537 (1896).

133 Richard Fallon refers to this phenomenon as 'constructivist coherence,' by which he suggests that Justices are inclined to rely on a multitude of sources and interpret them agreeably and in line with one another to arrive at constitutional outcomes. See especially Fallon (n 31) 1268–85 for examples of cases that employ this strategy.

134 cf. Greene (n 69) 398, which describes neutral citations of so-called anticanonical Supreme Court cases that 'occur in the course of historical discussion that is tangential to the normative arguments at issue in the citing case.'

135 522 US 222 (1998).

of these States to the records, acts and judicial proceedings of the courts and magistrates of every other State.' Articles of Confederation, Art. IV. For a concise history of full faith and credit, see Jackson, Full Faith and Credit: The Lawyer's Clause of the Constitution, 45 Colum. L. Rev. 1 (1945).[136]

This invocation of the Articles was not even minimally dispositive of the issue presented in the case.

Why, then, would Justices invoke the Articles if they do not determine outcomes? Justice Scalia remarked on the issue of citing foreign law: '[I]f you don't want it to be authoritative, then what is the criterion for citing it?'[137] The same question might be raised with respect to the Articles. Of course, there might be a difference. Perhaps members of the Court consider the Articles authoritative (or aim to make them so), whereas there is broad consensus that foreign law is not authoritative. A less gracious explanation is that invocation of the Articles, and of historical sources more generally, bespeaks education and a proficient command of history, thereby elevating the credibility of the author. This explanation is very much in line with some suggested reasons for Justices' references to foreign law in domestic constitutional adjudication: to 'decorate' their opinions, for 'window-dressing' purposes, and so forth.[138] Additionally, using the Articles, and thereby invoking 'the wisdom of the ages,' might function as a rhetorical trump, aimed at blocking further discussion on the subject.

3.2.6 The Justices Cite the Articles Approvingly and Disapprovingly, Rendering Them a Malleable Interpretive Tool

Commentators, likely influenced by *The Federalist Papers*,[139] take a decidedly negative view of the Articles of Confederation.[140] According to one observer, 'serious problems developed under the Articles of Confederation.'[141]

---

136 ibid 231 n 3.

137 Dorsen (n 37) 522.

138 See generally Ran Hirschl, 'Judicial review and the politics of comparative citations: theory, evidence and methodological challenges' in Erin Delaney and Rosalind Dixon (eds), *Comparative Judicial Review* (Edward Elgar Publishing 2018).

139 See references in (n 5–8) above and accompanying text.

140 See Maggs (n 82) 399: '[M]ost lawyers and judges have received little instruction about them [ie the Articles]. They typically know that the Articles of Confederation set up a weak union whose shortcomings became apparent in the 1780s and led to adoption of the Constitution.'

141 Erwin Chemerinsky, *Constitutional Law: Principles and Policies* (5th ed, Walters Kluwer Press 2015) 10.

To another, '[i]n part, it was flaws in the Articles of Confederation that were responsible for the crisis, which in turn paved the way for the Constitution.'[142] In another's formulation, '[a]s swiftly became clear, the government created by the Articles of Confederation was too weak.'[143] The general understanding is that the Constitution sensibly replaced the weak and ineffective system of government the Articles had created.[144]

Do the Justices' opinions reflect a similarly negative perspective on the Articles? My close reading of the 199 opinions invoking the Articles showed an almost even split between disapproving references[145] and approving or neutral references. I categorized as a disapproving reference an invocation of the Articles prefaced or followed by negative words or phrases. These included 'the […] economic Balkanization that had plagued relations […] among the States,'[146] 'Congress lacked authority,'[147] 'unsatisfactory,'[148] 'the inability of the

142 Michael J Klarman, *The Framers' Coup: The Making of the United States Constitution* (OUP 2016) 13. For the best recent restatement on the flaws in the Articles see ibid 11–72.

143 Richard H Fallon Jr, *The Dynamic Constitution: An Introduction to American Constitutional Law and Practice* (CUP 2012) 3.

144 See eg Charles C Thach Jr, *The Creation of the American Presidency, 1775–1789: A Study in Constitutional History* (The John Hopkins Press 1922) 16: 'the complete inability of the government set up by the Articles of Confederation to function.' To be sure, some scholars are more skeptical about this presentation of the Articles. See eg Eric M. Freedman, 'The United States and the Articles of Confederation: Drifting Toward Anarchy or Inching Toward Commonwealth?' (1978) 88 The Yale Law Journal 142. Freedman suggests that 'the early Constitution Period owed a very substantial debt to those of the Articles Period.' ibid 143. See also Max Farrand, *The Framing of the Constitution of the United States* (Yale University Press 1913) 42–45.

145 In an insightful analysis of how constitutional engagement – defined broadly – involves not only aspirational but also 'aversive' stances toward certain constitutions, Professor Kim Lane Scheppele has drawn attention to the phenomenon of 'aversive constitutionalism.' See Scheppele (n 4) 301–07. My use of the words 'aversion' and 'disapproving,' however, slightly differs from her use of the terms. Professor Scheppele uses the word 'aversion' to denote strong repulsion towards a particular constitutional experience that exceeds the level of finding a constitutional experience unsatisfactory or marginally undesirable when compared to others. My use is more expansive and would include instances of mere undesirability as well. See eg ibid 303: 'Looking an option over and saying "this won't work here" in a constitutional debate is quite different from saying "this would be horrifying to adopt."' Further, Professor Scheppele's work focuses largely on constitution drafting episodes, rather than later instances of constitutional interpretation (including, by judges).

146 See eg *Tennessee Wine & Spirits Retailers Association v Thomas* (n 96) 2461.

147 *Murphy v NCAA*, 138 S Ct 1461, 1476 (2018).

148 *Jesner v Arab Bank, PLC* 138 S Ct 1386, 1396 (2018).

TABLE 5.5 Disapproving and approving references to the Articles

Type of reference	Number of opinions
Non-disapproving/approving	104
Disapproving	95

central government,'[149] 'existential threat,'[150] 'unable to provide redress'[151] 'the shortcomings of,'[152] 'ability to paralyze the National Legislature,'[153] 'unworkable,'[154] 'substantially frustrated,'[155] 'defects,'[156] 'the central problem,'[157] 'lacked the effective capacity'[158] 'structural ills,'[159] 'principal defect,'[160] 'widespread dissatisfaction,'[161] 'want of all coercive authority,'[162] and 'not entitled to the dignified appellation of government,'[163] among many others. I categorized other references to the Articles, those without such words or phrases, as approving or neutral invocations.[164] Table 5.5 reports the results of this analysis.[165]

Of the total 199 opinions, 95 refer to the Articles with disapproving words or phrases. The remaining 104 opinions are either non-disapproving, that is, neutral, or approving in terms of the way in which they invoke the Articles. Given that the Articles are invoked approvingly and disapprovingly at an almost equal

149 ibid.
150 ibid 1416 (Gorsuch, J, concurring in part and concurring in the judgment).
151 ibid 1426 (Sotomayor, J, dissenting).
152 *Evenwel v Abbott*, 136 S Ct 1120, 1137 (2016) (Thomas, J, concurring).
153 ibid.
154 *National Federation of Independent Business v Sebelius* (n 89) 600 (Ginsburg, J, concurring in part and dissenting in part).
155 *Medellín v Texas*, 552 US 491, 543 (2008) (Breyer, J, dissenting).
156 *Central Virginia Community College v Katz* (n 126) 384 (Thomas, J, dissenting).
157 *Gonzales v Raich* (n 104) 16.
158 *Alden v Maine*, 527 US 706, 809 n 39 (1999) (Souter, J, dissenting).
159 *Quill Corporation v North Dakota*, 504 US 298, 312 (1992).
160 *FERC v Mississippi*, 456 US 742, 791 (1982) (O'Connor, J, concurring in part and dissenting in part).
161 *Allied Structural Steel Company v Spannaus* (n 113) 256 (Brennan, J, dissenting).
162 *Ex parte Virginia*, 100 US 339, 356 (1879) (Field, J, dissenting).
163 *Thurlow v Massachusetts*, 46 US (5 How) 504, 587 (1847) (McLean, J, dissenting).
164 For a similar methodology see Greene (n 69) 397–98.
165 I recognize some limits to the approach employed here: mere usage of negative words does not necessarily mean a disapproving use of the Articles; the Articles might be used disapprovingly but without negative adjectives; and an opinion might be disapproving of the Articles in one aspect but approving in another.

rate they appear to be a malleable tool at the disposal of the Justices[166] – not unlike nearly all historical material, some would argue.[167] At the same time, the even split suggests the Justices may view the Articles more favorably than do academics, who take a generally negative view of the Articles. For the Justices, the Articles had problems that were remedied by the Constitution but there exists also an important element of continuity between the two documents.

3.2.7 References to the Articles Can Be Textual and Non-textual

I also examined the extent to which the Justices specifically quote from the text of the Articles. References to text, as opposed to more general notions of the vices and virtues of the Articles, may reveal more detailed and serious engagement with a document. Textual references also involve *direct* engagement with a document, as opposed to mere repetition of standard accounts of it, and thus a greater measure of independence in analysis.

My criteria for separating textual references from the non-textual are two-fold. I considered those references textual that (1) expressly identified a provision of the Articles (eg 'Article 4,' 'the sixth article,' 'Full Faith and Credit Clause of the Articles of Confederation,' etc.) *or* (2) directly quoted from the Articles. In some cases, both criteria were satisfied. References that did not satisfy either of the two criteria were deemed non-textual references.[168] Table 5.6 summarizes the results.

TABLE 5.6 Textual versus non-textual references

Type of reference	Number of opinions
Textual	86
Non-textual	113

166 Professor Scheppele has noted a changing popular attitude toward the Articles: historically they were initially regarded positively, in the sense of drawing 'a strong and negative constitutional lesson from the abuses of Britain,' but shortly prior to the adoption of the Constitution, they 'themselves were the leading negative models.' Scheppele (n 4) 309.

167 See generally Uitz (n 56).

168 Of course, this methodology has some limitations. For example, a discussion of the Articles may engage with a certain part of its text without either expressly mentioning which article is being referenced or without directly quoting from it.

There are more non-textual than textual references. This finding perhaps suggests that the Articles are more often invoked in ways that reflect preconceptions about them, rather than independent analysis. Non-textual references that invoke the Articles alongside other sources (such as *The Federalist Papers*) might be especially likely to perpetuate pre-existing ideas about the Articles.

At the same time, textual references take different form. Three types stand out:[169] (1) comparisons between identical or similar textual provisions in both the Articles and the Constitution; (2) attention to a word or phrase that exists in the Articles but not in the Constitution; and (3) attention to a word or phrase that exists in the Constitution but not in the Articles. Sometimes there is also combination of (2) and (3).

An example of the first type is the Court's treatment of Article IV in the Articles and the Constitution alike as protecting a similar right to travel.[170] Justice Scalia's separate opinion in *Arizona v United States*,[171] in which the Court held parts of Arizona's immigration laws preempted by federal law, exemplifies the second and third types. Scalia compared the Privileges and Immunities Clause in Articles IV of both documents by focusing on words in each clause that did not appear in the other. He reasoned that the Articles' use of the word 'inhabitants' as the addressee of privileges and immunities effectively meant that 'an unwelcome alien could obtain all the rights of a citizen of one State simply by first becoming an *inhabitant* of another.'[172] 'To remedy this,' he continued, 'the Constitution's Privileges and Immunities Clause provided that "[t]he *Citizens* of each State shall be entitled to all Privileges and Immunities of Citizens in the several States."'[173] In his detailed analysis of the two texts, Scalia drew attention to the use of 'inhabitants' in the Articles but 'citizens' in the Constitution – a change in phraseology he considered significant although, as one commentator has observed, Scalia did not seem to consider the possibility that 'the variation in wording might simply reflect an alternative manner of drafting.'[174]

EEOC v Wyoming[175] provides a further example of types two and three. In his opinion concurring in the majority's holding that the extension of the Age Discrimination in Employment Act to state government employment was a

169 For a similar typology see Maggs (n 82) 420–24.

170 See eg *Zobel v Williams*, 457 US 55 (1982).

171 567 US 387 (2012).

172 ibid 418 (Scalia, J, concurring in part, dissenting in part) (emphasis original).

173 ibid (emphasis original).

174 Maggs (n 82) 421.

175 460 US 226 (1983).

valid exercise of Congress's Commerce Clause power, Justice Stevens took notice of:

> [T]he dramatic contrast between the Articles of Confederation, which had declared explicitly that each "[each] State retains its sovereignty, freedom, and independence," Art. 2, and the new Constitution, which contained not a word respecting the sovereignty, freedom, and independence of the States, but rather conveyed an unequivocal message in the Supremacy Clause, Art. VI, cl. 2. The role of the States in the Confederation was repeatedly contrasted with their role in the proposed Constitution, both by supporters and by opponents of ratification.[176]

Justice Stevens then used this contrast – the Constitution contains a Supremacy Clause but lacks a state sovereignty provision – to bolster his conclusion that the federal statute permissibly regulated the states.

Importantly, in comparing the text of the Articles and the Constitution the Justices have not been consistent in determining what counts as a similarity and what represents a difference.[177] For example, in *McCulloch*, the Court emphasized the difference between 'delegated' (in the Constitution) and '*expressly* delegated' (in the Articles). By contrast, in cases in which the Court has compared Article IV of the Articles and Article IV of the Constitution it has deemed them similar despite textual differences. Among other differences, Article IV of the Articles protects 'free ingress and regress' but Article IV of the Constitution does not include that phrase. But in *Zobel v Williams*,[178] for example, Justice O'Connor's concurrence reiterated the longstanding view that 'this Article [ie Article IV of the Constitution] was formed exactly upon the 4th article of the present Confederation.'[179]

176 ibid 248 n 8 (Stevens, J, concurring) (citations omitted).

177 See also Maggs (n 82) 422. In fact, *McCulloch* itself contrasted the Articles with the Constitution inconsistently. While Chief Justice Marshall emphasized the difference between '*expressly* delegated' in the former and 'delegated' in the latter to conclude that Congress had implied powers under the Constitution, he did not mention that the Articles expressly state, in Article IV: 'provided also that no imposition, duties or restriction shall be laid by any state, on the property of the united states, or either of them.' This textual limit, absent from the Constitution, could have been dispositive on the question of whether the State of Maryland could tax the Federal Bank, a query the Chief Justice ultimately answered principally on structural rather than textual grounds. See also ibid 434. On the difficulty of determining what constitutes textual similarity and difference see also Mazzone and Tecimer (n 8) 3039.

178 (n 170).

179 ibid 79 (O'Connor, J, concurring) (citations omitted). Professor Maggs has also recognized this inconsistency with respect to the *Zobel* case. See Maggs (n 82) 422.

TABLE 5.7 Number of textual references to individual articles

Article number	Number of overall mentions
Preamble	2[a]
Article I	4
Article II	5
Article III	4
Article IV	31
Article V	8
Article VI	12
Article VII	0
Article VIII	3
Article IX	36
Article X	1
Article XI	3
Article XII	0
Article XIII	1

a In *United States v Curtis-Wright*, 299 US 304, 307 (1936), Justice Sutherland invoked the Articles' reference to the Union as 'perpetual' but he did not identify whether his source was the preamble or the 13th article (or both). I have counted the reference as to the preamble.

It is also helpful to consider, within the set of 86 opinions with textual references to the Articles, the frequency with which individual articles are cited. In approaching this issue, I grouped references by article number; I also counted references to different parts of the same article as unique references. Table 5.7 summarizes the results.[180]

Article IX tops the list followed by Article IV. It is instructive that these two provisions are the most often invoked. Article IX deals with an aggregate of matters, including Congress' powers. Article IV grants 'free inhabitants' all privileges and immunities that 'citizens in the several States' enjoy, and also deals with inter-state extradition, full faith and credit to state court judgments, state representation in Congress, and freedom of speech and debate therein.

180 See also Appendix, Table 5.9.

3.2.8 The Articles Are Invoked More Frequently in Connection to Certain Constitutional Law Subjects

The Justices invoke the Articles more often with respect to some subject areas of constitutional law than others. Table 5.8 reports on the number of cases referring to the Articles by issue presented.[181] The remainder of this section explores in more detail the four issues that generated the largest number of references.

3.2.8.1 *Commerce Clause*

In contrast to the Constitution, the Articles famously lacked a provision empowering Congress to regulate interstate commerce, an important source of federal power in the modern era. There are three main periods in the Court's history in which the Justices have invoked the Articles in conjunction with the Constitution's Commerce Clause. The first consists of scattered references in three cases from the mid-1800s. One example here is Justice McLean's dissent in *Thurlow v Massachusetts*[182] comparing the Articles to the Constitution and writing that the Constitution's Commerce Clause is '[a]mong the delegated functions'[183] of the federal government.

The second period overlaps with the *Lochner* era (in which the Court invalidated numerous laws on grounds of economic freedom) in the late 19th and early 20th century. One example here is Justice Harlan's dissent in *New York v Roberts*,[184] invoking the Articles to warn against state government regulation that could result from a restrictive interpretation of Congress's power under the Commerce Clause:

181 Again, there are certain limitations to my own approach. Other researchers might categorize cases differently than I did. For example, I have grouped issues dealing with the Indian Commerce Clause as well as relations between either the federal government or the state governments and the Indian tribes under the single heading of 'Indians.' Some cases also raise more than one constitutional issue; I have focused on the dominant issue raised. From my set of 169 cases, I excluded one case, *United States v American Library Association*, 539 US 194, 237 (2003) (rejecting First Amendment challenge to filtering software requirement in the Children's Internet Protection Act) in which Justice Souter, in his dissenting opinion, invoked the Articles not substantively but in discussing uses of public library computers: 'Since it makes no difference to the cost of Internet access whether an adult calls up material harmful for children or the Articles of Confederation, blocking (on facts like these) is not necessitated by scarcity of either money or space.'

182 See above (n 163).

183 ibid 587.

184 171 US 658 (1898).

TABLE 5.8 Cases referencing the Articles by subject matter

Substantive theme	Number of cases invoking the articles
Commerce Clause	29
Inter-State Disputes	21
State Sovereignty	20
Privileges and Immunities	18
Foreign Relations	9
Indians	8
Taxation	8
Full Faith and Credit	7
Admiralty	7
Courts Martial	4
Elections	4
Legislative Immunity	4
Contracts Clause	4
Citizenship	4
Import-Export Clause	3
Paper Money	3
Postal Service	2
Religion	2
Public Nature of Federal Lawmaking	1
Appointments	1
Legislative Veto	1
War Powers	1
Statement and Account Clause	1
National Sovereignty (National Flag)	1
Free Speech	1
Cruel and Unusual Punishment	1
Removal Power	1
Military Conscription	1
Public Domain	1

> If each State in the Union should enact a statute exempting from taxation the franchise and business of corporations of companies wholly engaged in carrying on manufacture within its limits, but taxing the franchise or business of corporations or companies whose manufacturing is carried on in other States, it is easy to see that commerce among the States would be as much at the mercy of discriminating state legislation as it was under the Articles of Confederation […].[185]

The third period runs from the late 1970s to the present day. It differs from the prior two because it involves majority opinions characterizing the Commerce Clause as the single most important remedy for anemic federal power under the Articles. Consider Justice Blackmun's confident language in the majority opinion he authored in *Department of Revenue v Washington Stevedoring Companies*:[186] 'Two of the chief weaknesses of the Articles of Confederation were the lack of power in Congress to regulate foreign and interstate commerce, and the presence of power in the States to do so.'[187] Fast-forward to 2019, to Justice Alito's opinion in *Tennessee Wine & Spirits Retailers Association*,[188] and the sentiment is unchanged: the Articles' lack of a commerce power caused 'economic Balkanization.'[189] Indeed, *almost all* of the opinions citing the Articles and the Commerce Clause together in this third period involve 'disapproving' references to the Articles. There is no reason to think that this current pattern is likely to change anytime soon.

3.2.8.2 *Inter-state Disputes*

Two types of inter-state disputes have triggered the Court's invocation of the Articles: (1) disputes concerning inter-state boundaries and (2) disputes involving inter-state compacts.

In contrast to the pattern under the Commerce Clause, references to the Articles in inter-state disputes have occurred almost entirely in the Court's pre-1900 cases. Both the Articles and the Constitution provide for federal settlement of state boundary disputes: Congress under Article IX of the Articles and the federal judiciary under Article III, § 2, of the Constitution. Accordingly, the Court has pointed to a continuity. In *Rhode Island v Massachusetts*,[190] for

185 ibid 679–80 (Harlan, J, dissenting).
186 435 US 734 (1978).
187 ibid 754 n 19 (citations omitted).
188 See (n 96).
189 ibid 2461.
190 37 US 657 (1838).

example, Justice Baldwin observed that because the Constitution emanates from the people, with respect to inter-state boundary disputes, it 'could not have been intended to give to the judicial power a less extended jurisdiction, or less efficient means of final action, than the articles of confederation'[191] gave to Congress. Justice McLean's dissent two years later in the second iteration of *Rhode Island v Massachusetts*,[192] picked up on the same idea: 'The articles of confederation formed by the new government' he reasoned, 'made special provision for the settlement of disputed boundaries between states.'[193] Other opinions in have also emphasized this continuity.[194]

Use of the Articles in cases involving inter-state compacts is more complex. This is mostly because the Articles and the Constitution treat inter-state compacts similarly in some respects but differently in others. Article VI of the Articles prohibited states from entering into 'any treaty, confederation, or alliance whatever in between them,' absent congressional consent 'specifying accurately the purposes for which the same is to be entered into, and how long it shall continue.' The Constitution, in Article I, Section 10, provides: 'No State shall, without the Consent of Congress […] enter into any Agreement or compact with another State […].' In other words, with requisite congressional consent, under the Articles, state could enter into treaties, confederations or alliances, whereas under the Constitution, only agreements and compacts that receive congressional approval are permitted. In addition, under the Articles, with congressional consent, states could enter into 'any conference, agreement, alliance or treaty' with *foreign* governments but the Constitution wholly prohibits such arrangements.

Some cases note the similarities between the Articles and the Constitution while still recognizing the stronger prohibitions in the Constitution's text. Justice Story's opinion in *Green v Biddle*[195] is a case in point. He wrote:

> Both by the original articles of confederation, and the existing national constitution, the States are prohibited from treating or contracting with each other, without the consent of Congress. The terms of the prohibition in the constitution, are very strong[.] […] It extends to all agreements or

191 ibid 728.

192 39 US 210 (1840).

193 ibid 278 (McLean, J, dissenting).

194 See eg *Howard v Ingersoll*, 54 US (13 How) 381, 403 (1852); *Florida v Georgia*, 58 US (17 How) 478, 521–22 (1855) (Campbell, J, dissenting); *Coffee v Grover*, 123 US 1, 30 (1887); *United States v Texas*, 143 US 621, 639, 645 (1892); *Georgia v South Carolina*, 257 US 516 (1922).

195 21 US (8 Wheat) 1 (1823).

> compacts, no matter what is the subject of them. It is immaterial, therefore, whether that subject be harmless or dangerous to the Union. There is here no room for interpretation.[196]

A decade later, in *Poole v Fleeger's Lessee*,[197] Justice Baldwin took an equally forceful position. 'From these provisions,' he explained, 'it is most manifest, that the framers of the constitution had the whole subject-matter directly before them, and substituted the prohibitions in the tenth section of the first article, for those in the sixth article of confederation, with [...] *important changes*.'[198] Justice Field revisited the issue in *Wharton v Wise*,[199] a case concerning an inter-state compact made between Virginia and Maryland in 1785 (before the Constitution took effect). Field noted: '[T]he meaning of the clause of the Constitution of the United States which is similar, in one particular, with that in the Articles of Confederation, and broader in another [...]'[200] He continued: 'The article of the confederation inhibits "any treaty, confederation, or alliance" between two or more States without the consent of Congress. The Constitution of the United States prohibits, without such consent, any agreement or compact of one State with another.'[201]

The most recent case concerning inter-state compacts and the Articles is *United States Steel Corporation v Multistate Tax Commission* in which the Court upheld a commission formed by states, without congressional approval, to assist in enacting and administering tax laws with respect to multistate businesses.[202] In his majority opinion, Justice Powell compared two provisions of Article VI of the Articles: the first, absent congressional consent, prohibited states from entering into any 'conference, agreement, alliance, or treaty' *with foreign states*.[203] The second, dealing exclusively with inter-state relations, subjected to congressional approval any inter-state 'treaty, confederation, or alliance.'[204] Powell next contrasted the language of the Articles with that of the Constitution. The Articles, he observed, did not contain the limitation on inter-state 'agreements' or 'compacts' that appears in the Constitution. He therefore concluded: 'Congressional consent clearly was required [under the

196 ibid 39–40.
197 36 US 185 (1837).
198 ibid 212 (emphasis added).
199 153 US 155 (1894).
200 ibid 168.
201 ibid.
202 See (n 57).
203 Articles of Confederation, art VI, § 1.
204 ibid art VI, § 2.

Articles] before a State could enter into an "agreement" with a foreign state or power or before two or more States could enter into "treaties, alliances, or confederations,"' but not for mere 'agreements' among States.[205] Accordingly, the Constitution imposed a new requirement: 'any Agreement or Compact with another State' is subject to congressional consent. Nonetheless, Powell ruled in favor of the Tax Commission, holding that inter-state agreements that do not encroach upon federal power do not need congressional consent. In his dissent, Justice White also compared the Articles to the Constitution and concluded that '[t]he Constitution adopted an absolute prohibition against treaties, alliances, or confederations by the States; and imposed the requirement of congressional approval for "any Agreement or Compact with another State, or with a foreign Power."'[206] Because he viewed the constitutional rule to be absolute, White would have invalidated the commission for lacking congressional authorization.

3.2.8.3 *State Sovereignty*

The Articles have been invoked by the Justices in cases involving issues of state sovereignty, including the "anti-commandeering" doctrine. As with the Commerce Clause, these invocations of the Articles have gained steam since the late 1970s.

Most observers accept a basic distinction between the Articles and the Constitution: that while under the Articles federal power operated only through the states (and so required their cooperation), under the Constitution the federal government has power to regulate individuals directly. *Chisholm v Georgia*[207] is an early case recognizing this distinction. Justice Iredell wrote:

> The powers of the general Government, either of a Legislative or executive nature, or which particularly concerns Treaties with Foreign Powers, do for the most part (if not wholly) affect individuals, and not States: They require no aid from any State authority. This is the great leading distinction between the old articles of confederation, and the present constitution.[208]

Similarly, Justice Wilson observed that '[t]he People of the United States' were 'the first personages introduced,'[209] and continued: 'The articles of

205 *United States Steel Corporation v Multistate Tax Commission* (n 57) 460 n 10.
206 ibid 482 n 3.
207 See (n 92).
208 ibid 435.
209 ibid 463.

confederation, it is well known, did not operate upon individual citizens, but operated only upon States. This defect was remedied by the national Constitution, which, as all allow, has an operation on individual citizens.'[210]

Recognizing this distinction between the Articles and the Constitution still leaves open many questions about the relationship between the national government and the states. Consider Justice Field's dissent in *Ex parte Virginia*[211] which held that the Fourteenth Amendment empowered Congress to bar states from excluding African Americans from juries. Field thought that because, in contrast to the Articles, the Constitution gave Congress power to regulate individuals, it was barred from imposing its laws upon the states themselves. Field wrote:

> Nothing, in my judgment, could have a greater tendency to destroy the independence and autonomy of the States; reduce them to a humiliating and degrading dependence upon the central government; engender constant irritation; and destroy that domestic tranquillity [*sic*] which it was one of the objects of the Constitution to insure, than the doctrine asserted in this case, that Congress can exercise coercive authority over judicial officers of the States in the discharge of their duties under State laws.[212]

A similar notion appears in Justice McReynolds' dissent in *Steward Machine Company v Davis*,[213] in which the Court upheld provisions of the federal Social Security Act of 1935 that taxed employers to fund an unemployment compensation scheme but allowed for a tax credit for payments to a federally approved state-operated fund. In his dissent, McReynolds acknowledged that compared to the Articles, the Constitution had made state powers 'much restricted'[214] but he thought the federal law intruded too far upon the authority of the states, as reflected in the Tenth Amendment: 'the perpetuity and indissolubility of the Union, by no means implies the loss of distinct and individual existence, or of the right of self-government, by the States.'[215]

More recent federalism cases have also invoked the Articles. Consider Justice O'Connor's partial dissent in *FERC v Mississippi*[216] in which she thought provisions of the Public Utility Regulatory Policies Act of 1978 requiring states

210 ibid 464.
211 See (n 162).
212 ibid 358 (Field, J, dissenting).
213 301 US 548 (1937).
214 ibid 599 (McReynolds, J, dissenting).
215 ibid.
216 See (n 160).

to consider certain regulatory standards according to federally specified procedures unconstitutionally infringed state sovereignty. She wrote: 'Under the Articles of Confederation, the National Legislature operated through the States. […] The Framers, however, eschewed this course, choosing instead to allow Congress to pass laws directly affecting individuals […]. This product of the Constitutional Convention, I believe, is fundamentally inconsistent with a system in which either Congress or a state legislature harnesses the legislative powers of the other sovereign.'[217]

Justice O'Connor reiterated this position in her majority opinion in *New York v United States*,[218] which invalidated the 'take title' provision of a federal law that required states to purchase low-level radioactive waste if they had not regulated its disposal. She noted that '[u]nder the Articles of Confederation, Congress lacked the authority in most respects to govern the people directly,'[219] but that once the Constitution gave Congress such power it could not commandeer the operations of state legislatures. Describing the Commerce Clause, Justice O'Connor explained:

> The Constitution established Congress as "a superintending authority over the reciprocal trade" among the States, The Federalist No. 42, p. 268 (C. Rossiter ed. 1961), by empowering Congress to regulate that trade directly, not by authorizing Congress to issue trade-related orders to state governments.[220]

Dissenting in *New York v United States*, Justice Stevens took issue with Justice O'Connor's characterization of the Articles and the implication she attributed to them. Stevens took the view that the Constitution enhanced and added to existing federal power already granted under the Articles. In his view, just because the federal government gained power to regulate individuals directly did not mean it lost power to compel state governments to act. Stevens wrote:

> Under the Articles of Confederation, the Federal Government had the power to issue commands to the States. See Arts. VIII, IX. Because that indirect exercise of federal power proved ineffective, the Framers of the Constitution empowered the Federal Government to exercise legislative authority directly over individuals within the States, even though that direct authority constituted a greater intrusion on state sovereignty.

217 ibid 795 (O'Connor, J, concurring in part and dissenting in part).
218 505 US 144 (1992).
219 ibid 163.
220 ibid 180.

> Nothing in that history suggests that the Federal Government may not also impose its will upon the several States as it did under the Articles. The Constitution enhanced, rather than diminished, the power of the Federal Government.[221]

3.2.8.4 *Privileges and Immunities*

In both the Articles of the Confederation and the Constitution, Article IV protects privileges and immunities. The Court has taken the position that these provisions safeguard the same rights. In *The Slaughter House Cases*,[222] for instance, Justice Miller for the Court wrote that '[t]he first occurrence of the words "privileges and immunities" in our constitutional history, is to be found in the fourth of the articles of the old Confederation,' and continued: 'There can be but little question that the purpose of both these provisions is the same, and that the privileges and immunities intended are the same in each.'[223] (Miller took a very different view of the scope of privileges and immunities protected from state infringement under the Fourteenth Amendment.) Other cases have made a similar point.[224] At the same time, Article IV in the Articles of Confederation and the Constitution are not textually identical. Notably, Article IV of the Articles of Confederation specifically protects a right of travel: 'the people of each state shall have free ingress and regress to and from any other state.' The Constitution does not contain a comparable provision. Nonetheless, based on an understanding of continuity between the two documents, the Court has held that that the Constitution implies the same right of travel that the Articles made explicit.[225]

Sometimes, however, textual differences have mattered. Article IV of the Articles excepted from the enjoyment of privileges and immunities 'paupers, vagabonds, and fugitives from Justice.' The Constitution makes no such exception. The difference was relevant to Justice Douglas in his dissent from the Court's dismissal of the writ of certiorari in *Hicks v District of Columbia*,[226] a case that challenged as unconstitutionally vague a Washington DC statute criminalizing vagrancy. Deeming the exception in the Articles a British

221 ibid 210 (Stevens, J, concurring in part and dissenting in part).
222 See (n 125).
223 ibid 75.
224 See eg *Maxwell v Dow*, 176 US 581, 588 (1900); *The Lottery Case*, 188 US 321, 373–74 (1903) (Fuller, J, dissenting).
225 See eg *United States v Wheeler* (n 124); *New York v O'Neill* (n 122); *United States v Guest*, 383 US 745, 758 (1966); see also ibid 764 (Harlan, J, dissenting).
226 383 US 252 (1966).

'superimposi[tion],' that represented an 'incongruity' with American values, and one the Constitution had renounced, Douglas urged the Court to invalidate the challenged law.[227]

3.2.9 The Justices Often Make Mediated Uses of the Articles

When the Justices invoke the Articles, they often make use of interpretations provided by other sources, including previous cases, rather than considering the Articles afresh. One example is the repeated description of the Constitution's Commerce Clause as responding to state economic protectionism or what the Justices often refer to as 'economic Balkanization.'[228] The most recent use of that term is in Justice Alito's opinion for the Court in *Tennessee Wine & Spirits Retailers Association v Thomas*.[229] Alito relied on *Granholm v Heald*[230] as authority for the claim; *Heald* had relied upon *Hughes v Oklahoma*.[231] Notably, though, *Hughes* is not entirely reliable authority for the claim that the Articles produced economic balkanization. Justice Brennan's use in *Hughes* of the term 'balkanization' was inspired by Justice Black's dissenting opinion, 30 years earlier, in *HP Hood & Sons v Du Mond*.[232] It made no mention of the Articles. Instead, discussing the dormant commerce clause doctrine and referencing law review articles,[233] Black wrote:

> Some people believe in this philosophy because of fear that judicial toleration of any state regulations of local phases of commerce will bring about what they call "Balkanization" of trade in the United States – trade

227 ibid 255–56 (Douglas, J, dissenting).

228 At least 11 cases use this phrase: *Hughes v Oklahoma*, 441 US 322, 325–26 (1979); *South-Central Timber Development v Wunnicke*, 467 US 82, 92 (1984); *Wardair Canada v Florida Department of Revenue*, 477 US 1, 7 (1986); *CTS Corporation v Dynamics Corporation of America*, 481 US 69, 100 (1987) (White, J, dissenting); *Oregon Waste Systems v Department of Environmental Quality*, 511 US 93, 98–9 (1994); *Oklahoma Tax Commission v Jefferson Lines*, 514 US 175, 179–80 (1995); *Granholm v Heald*, 544 US 460, 472 (2005); *Department of Revenue of Kentucky v Davis*, 553 US 328, 338 (2008); *Comptroller of the Treasury v Wynne*, 135 S Ct 1787, 1794 (2015); *South Dakota v Wayfair*, 138 S Ct 2080, 2089 (2018); *Tennessee Wine & Spirits Retailers Association v Thomas* (n 96) 2461. cf Mark Tushnet, *Red, White, and Blue: A Critical Analysis of Constitutional Law* (Harvard University Press 1988) 78: 'When scholars write about the commerce clause they routinely invoke the framers' fear of economic balkanization [...].'

229 See (n 96).

230 See (n 228).

231 See ibid.

232 336 US 525 (1949).

233 Justice Black cites first and foremost Frank Bane, 'Interstate Trade Barriers' (1949) 16 Indiana Law Journal 121, which does not explicitly use the term 'Balkanization' but criticizes trade barriers erected by states, and interestingly, mentions the Articles: 'For 150 years we have blandly assumed that the United States is a nation and that the constitutional

> barriers so high between the states that the stream of interstate commerce cannot flow over them.[234]

In sum, a term, 'economic balkanization,' appearing in legal scholarship, is used in a dissenting opinion in a case making no reference to the Articles of Confederation. The term is later used, in *Hughes*, to describe a defect of the Articles. Since then, other cases, quoting either *Hughes* or later cases that cite *Hughes*, have said the Constitution's Commerce Clause responded to the problem of 'economic Balkanization' that the Articles generated.

In other cases, different sources have played a mediating role: the Justices have invoked the Articles through references to *The Federalist Papers*,[235] other law review articles,[236] and Story's *Commentaries on the Constitution of the United States*,[237] among other materials.

4 Conclusion

Kenneth Wheare has written that '[i]f we investigate the origins of modern constitutions, we find that, practically without exception, they were drawn up and adopted because people wish to make a new start,' and that 'countries have a constitution for the very simple and elementary reason that they wanted, for some reason, to begin again.'[238] This chapter has demonstrated that the start made by a new constitution is rarely entirely new. Although inter-constitutional interpretation is an understudied phenomenon, abrogated constitutions regularly play a role in the new constitutional order and are relevant to contemporary constitutional adjudication.

Inter-constitutional interpretation occurs in most polities with a history of constitutional replacement. The United States is no exception. The chapter's case study has examined the ways in which the Supreme Court invokes the Articles of Confederation as an interpretive tool in deciding cases under the Constitution. The Articles are no longer law, but they remain a source of legal authority. Still, the Articles do not rule from their grave. Even when invoked

fathers by scrapping the Articles of Confederation had discarded the post-revolutionary theory that the United States was a confederation of independent sovereign nations.' ibid.

234 *HP Hood & Sons v Du Mond* (n 232) 554 (Black, J, dissenting) (citations omitted).

235 See eg *Medellín v Texas* (n 155) 543 (Breyer, J, dissenting), quoting *The Federalist 42* (Madison); *Murphy v NCAA* (n 147) 1476, quoting *The Federalist 15* (Hamilton).

236 See eg *City of Sherrill v Oneida Indian Nation*, 544 US 197, 204 n 2 (2005), quoting a law review article that deals with 'Indian relations under the Articles of Confederation and the Constitution.'

237 See eg *New York v Roberts* (n 184) 680 (Harlan, J, dissenting).

238 Kenneth Clinton Wheare, *Modern constitutions* (2nd ed, OUP 1966) 6.

they tend not to determine the outcomes of cases. They are amenable to multiple and even contradictory interpretations. And they are often deployed along with other sources and alongside other interpretive approaches. Just as the Articles of Confederation deserve recognition for their continued significance to constitutional practices in the United States, attention to the past constitutions of other nations can shed important light on their existing legal and political arrangements.

Bibliography

Alexander L and Schauer F, 'On Extrajudicial Constitutional Interpretation' (1997) 110 Harvard Law Review 1359.

Amar AR, 'America's Lived Constitution' (2011) 120 The Yale Law Journal 1734.

Amar AR, 'Intratextualism' (1999) 112 Harvard Law Review 747.

Amar AR, 'Of Sovereignty and Federalism' (1987) 96 The Yale Law Journal 1425.

Bane F, 'Interstate Trade Barriers' (1949) 16 Indiana Law Journal 121.

Bobbitt P, *Constitutional Fate: Theory of The Constitution* (OUP 1982).

Calabresi S and Zimdahl SD, 'The Supreme Court and Foreign Sources of Law: Two Hundred Years of Practice and The Juvenile Death Penalty Decision' (2005) 47 William & Mary Law Review 743.

Chemerinsky E, *Constitutional Law: Principles and Policies* (5th ed, Walters Kluwer Press 2015).

Choudry S, 'Migration as a new metaphor in comparative constitutional law' in Sujit Choudry (ed), *The Migration of Constitutional Ideas* (CUP 2006).

Dempsey J, 'Hungarian Parliament Approves New Constitution' *The New York Times* (New York, 18 April 2011) <https://www.nytimes.com/2011/04/19/world/europe/19iht-hungary19.html?searchResultPosition=12> accessed 4 September 2019.

Dixon R and Ginsburg T, 'Introduction' in Tom Ginsburg and Rosalind Dixon (eds), *Comparative Constitutional Law* (Edward Elgar Publishing 2011).

Dixon R and Jackson VC, 'Constitutions Inside Out: Outsider Interventions in Domestic Constitutional Contests' (2013) 48 Wake Forest Law Review 149.

Dorsen N, 'The relevance of foreign legal materials in US constitutional cases: A conversation between Justice Antonin Scalia and Justice Stephen Breyer' (2005) 3 ICON 519.

Elkins Z, Ginsburg T and Melton J, *The Endurance of National* Constitutions (CUP 2009).

Elster J, 'Forces and Mechanisms in the Constitution-Making Process' (1995) 45 Duke Law Journal 364.

Eskridge WN, 'Legislative History Values' (1990) 66 Chicago-Kent Law Review 365.

Fallon RH, 'A Constructivist Coherence Theory of Constitutional Interpretation' (1987) 100 Harvard Law Review 1189.

Fallon RH, *The Dynamic Constitution: An Introduction to American Constitutional Law and Practice* (CUP 2012).

Farrand M, *The Framing of the Constitution of the United States* (Yale University Press 1913).

Farrand M, *The Records of the Federal Convention of 1787*, vol 3 (OUP 1911).

Franklin M, 'Concerning the Influence of Roman Law on the Formulation of the Constitution of the United States' (1964) 38 Tulane Law Review 621.

Freedman EM, 'The United States and the Articles of Confederation: Drifting Toward Anarchy or Inching Toward Commonwealth?' (1978) 88 The Yale Law Journal 142.

Gettleman J, 'Kenyan Constitution Opens New Front in Culture Wars' *The New York Times* (New York, 13 May 2010) <https://www.nytimes.com/2010/05/14/world/africa/14kenya.html?searchResultPosition=1> accessed 4 September 2019.

Gettleman J, 'Kenyans Approve New Constitution' *The New York Times* (New York, 5 August 2010) <https://www.nytimes.com/2010/08/06/world/africa/06kenya.html?searchResultPosition=4> accessed 4 September 2019.

Ginsburg T, 'Constitutional endurance' in Tom Ginsburg and Rosalind Dixon (eds), *Comparative Constitutional Law* (Edward Elgar Publishing 2011).

Government of Nepal, 'History of Nepal' (*Ministry of Foreign Affairs*) <https://mofa.gov.np/about-nepal/history-of-nepal/> accessed 4 September 2019.

Greene J, 'On the Origins of Originalism' (2009) 88 Texas Law Review 1.

Greene J, 'The Anticanon' (2011) 125 Harvard Law Review 379.

Greenhouse L, *A Very Short Introduction: The U.S. Supreme Court* (OUP 2000).

Hirschl R, *Comparative Matters: The Renaissance of Comparative Constitutional Law* (OUP 2014).

Hirschl R, 'Comparative Methodologies' in Roger Materman and Robert Schütze (eds), *The Cambridge Companion to Comparative Constitutional Law* (CUP 2019).

Hirschl R, 'Judicial review and the politics of comparative citations: theory, evidence and methodological challenges' in Erin Delaney and Rosalind Dixon (eds), *Comparative Judicial Review* (Edward Elgar Publishing 2018).

Hirschl R, 'The Question of Case Selection in Comparative Constitutional Law' (2005) 53 American Journal of Comparative Law 125.

Jackson VC, 'Constitutional Comparisons: Convergence, Resistance, Engagement' (2005) 119 Harvard Law Review 109.

Jackson VC, *Constitutional Engagement in a Transnational Era* (OUP 2010).

Karasz P, 'Leader of Hungary Defends New Constitution' *The New York Times* (New York, 7 February 2012) <https://www.nytimes.com/2012/02/08/world/europe/viktor-orban-defends-hungarys-new-constitution.html?searchResultPosition=4> accessed 4 September 2019.

Kesavan V, 'When Did the Articles of Confederation Cease to Be Law?' (2002) 78 Notre Dame Law Review 35.

Kincaid J, 'State Constitutions in the Federal System' (1988) 496 The Annals of the American Academy 12.

Klarman MJ, *The Framers' Coup: The Making of the United States Constitution* (OUP 2016).

Lincoln A , 'First Inaugural Address of Abraham Lincoln' (*The Avalon Project*, 2008) <https://avalon.law.yale.edu/19th_century/lincoln1.asp> accessed 11 September 2019.

Maggs GE, 'A Concise Guide to the Articles of Confederation as a Source for Determining the Original Meaning of the Constitution' (2017) 85 The George Washington Law Review 397.

Manning J, 'Textualism and the Role of *The Federalist* in Constitutional Adjudication' (1998) 66 The George Washington Law Review 1337.

Mazzone J and Tecimer C, 'Interconstitutionalism' (2022) 132 The Yale Law Journal 3000 (forthcoming)

Negretto GL, 'Replacing and Amending Constitutions: The Logic of Constitutional Change in Latin America' (2012) 46 Law & Society Review 749.

Orgad L, 'The preamble in constitutional interpretation' (2010) 8 ICON 714.

Posner RA, 'Foreword: A Political Court' (2005) 119 Harvard Law Review 32.

Scalia A, 'Originalism: The Lesser Evil' 57 (1989) University of Cincinnati Law Review 849.

Scheppele KL, 'Aspirational and aversive constitutionalism: The case for studying cross-constitutional influence through negative models' (2003) 1 ICON 296.

Scheppele KL, 'Constitutional Ethnography: An Introduction' (2004) 38 Law & Society Review 389.

Strauss D, 'What is Constitutional Theory?' (1999) 87 California Law Review 581.

Teubner G, *Constitutional Fragments: Societal Constitutionalism and Globalization* (OUP 2012).

Thach CC, *The Creation of the American Presidency, 1775–1789: A Study in Constitutional History* (The John Hopkins Press 1922).

The Federalist Papers.

Thomas C, 'Judging' (1996) 45 The University of Kansas Law Review 1.

Tushnet M, *Red, White, and Blue: A Critical Analysis of Constitutional Law* (Harvard University Press 1988).

Tushnet M, *Taking the Constitution Away from the Courts* (Princeton University Press 1999).

Tushnet M, *The Constitution of the United States of America: A Contextual Analysis* (2nd ed, Hart Publishing 2015).

Tushnet M, *Weak Courts, Strong Rights: Judicial Review and Social Welfare Rights in Comparative Constitutional Law* (Princeton University Press 2009).

Uitz R, *Constitutions, Courts, and History: Historical Narratives in Constitutional Adjudication* (Central European University Press 2005).

Varol OO, 'Constitutional Stickiness' (2016) 49 University of California Davis Law Review 899.

Vermeule A and Young EA, 'Hercules, Herbert, and Amar: The Trouble with *Intratextualism*' (2000) 113 Harvard Law Review 730.

Wheare KC, *Modern constitutions* (2nd ed, OUP 1966).

Whittington KE, 'Extrajudicial Constitutional Interpretation: Three Objections and Responses' (2002) 80 North Carolina Law Review 773.

Appendix*

TABLE 5.9 Supreme Court cases invoking the Articles

Case	Year	Number of opinions with reference	Type(s) of opinion (author)	Aversive (AV) / aspirational (AS)	Textual (T) / non-textual (NT)	Substantive theme for reference
Tenn. Wine & Spirits Retailers Ass'n v. Thomas	2019	1	Maj (Alito)	AV	NT	Commerce Clause (dormant cc)
Ortiz v. United States	2018	1	Maj (Kagan)	AS	NT	Courts martial
South Dakota v. Wayfair, Inc.	2018	1	Maj (Kennedy)	AV	NT	Commerce Clause (dormant cc)
Murphy v. NCAA	2018	1	Maj (Alito)	AV	NT	State sovereignty (anti-commandeering)
Jesner v. Arab Bank, PLC	2018	3	Maj (Kennedy); Con (Gorsuch); Diss (Sotomayor)	AV; AV; AV	NT; NT; NT	Foreign relations (foreign grievances)
Puerto Rico v. Sánchez Valle	2016	1	Diss (Breyer)	AS	NT	State sovereignty (source)
Evenwel v. Abbott	2016	1	Con (Thomas)	AV	T	Elections (minority rule)
Zivotofsky v. Kerry	2015	1	Con/Diss (Thomas)	AS	T	Foreign relations (diplomatic relations) (passports)

* Key: Maj (majority); Con (concurring opinion); Diss (dissenting opinion); Una (unanimous); Con/Diss (concurring in part, dissenting in part); OP (opinion with no other identifying label); AV (aversive); AS (aspirational); T (textual); NT (non-textual).

TABLE 5.9 Supreme Court cases invoking the Articles (*cont.*)

Case	Year	Number of opinions with reference	Type(s) of opinion (author)	Aversive (AV) / aspirational (AS)	Textual (T) / non-textual (NT)	Substantive theme for reference
Comptroller of the Treasury v. Wynne	2015	1	Maj (Alito)	AV	NT	Commerce Clause (dormant cc)
Bond v. United States	2014	1	Con (Thomas)	AS	T	Foreign relations (treaty power)
Adoptive Couple v. Baby Girl	2013	1	Con (Thomas)	AV	T	Indians
NFIB v. Sebelius	2012	1	Con/Diss (Ginsburg)	AV	NT	Commerce Clause (general)
Arizona v. United States	2012	1	Con/Diss (Scalia)	AV	T	Privileges and Immunities (state power to exclude aliens)
McDonald v. City of Chicago	2010	1	Con (Thomas)	AS	NT	Privileges and Immunities (general)
Doe v. Reed	2010	1	Diss (Thomas)	AS	T	Public nature of federal lawmaking
Haywood v. Drown	2009	1	Diss (Thomas)	AV	NT	Full Faith and Credit Clause (general)
Department of Revenue of KY v. Davis	2008	2	Maj (Souter); Diss (Kennedy)	AV; AV	NT; NT	Commerce Clause (dormant cc)
Medellín v. Texas	2008	1	Diss (Breyer)	AV	NT	Foreign relations (treaty power) (supremacy clause)
Central Virginia Community College v. Katz	2006	2	Maj (Stevens); Diss (Thomas)	AV; AV	T; NT	Full Faith and Credit Clause (bankruptcy)

Case	Year	Number of opinions with reference	Type(s) of opinion (author)	Aversive (AV) / aspirational (AS)	Textual (T) / non-textual (NT)	Substantive theme for reference
Gonzales v. Raich	2005	1	Maj (Stevens)	AV	NT	Commerce Clause (general)
Granholm v. Heald	2005	1	Maj (Kennedy)	AV	NT	Commerce Clause (dormant cc)
City of Sherrill v. Oneida Indian Nation	2005	1	Maj (Ginsburg)	AS	NT	Indians
US Postal Service v. Flamingo Indus.	2004	1	Una (Kennedy)	AS	T	Postal service
United States v. American Library Association	2003	1	Diss (Souter)	N/A	NT	N/A (no substantive use)
Alden v. Maine	1999	2	Maj (Kennedy); Diss (Souter)	AV; AV	NT; NT	State sovereignty
Saenz v. Roe	1999	2	Maj (Stevens); Diss (Thomas)	AS; AS	T; T	Privileges and Immunities (right to travel)
Baker v. GMC	1998	1	Una (Ginsburg)	AS	T	Full Faith and Credit Clause (general)
Printz v. United States	1997	2	Maj (Scalia); Diss (Stevens)	AV; AV	NT; NT	State sovereignty (anti-commandeering)
Camps Newfound/ Owatonna v. Town of Harrison	1997	1	Diss (Thomas)	AV	T	Commerce Clause (dormant cc)
United States v. IBM	1996	1	Diss (Kennedy)	AV	NT	Import-Export (tax)
Seminole Tribe v. Florida	1996	1	Diss (Souter)	AV	T	State sovereignty
United States Term Limits v. Thornton	1995	2	Maj (Stevens); Diss (Thomas)	AV; AS	T; T	Elections (Qualifications)

TABLE 5.9 Supreme Court cases invoking the Articles (*cont.*)

Case	Year	Number of opinions with reference	Type(s) of opinion (author)	Aversive (AV) / aspirational (AS)	Textual (T) / non-textual (NT)	Substantive theme for reference
Oklahoma Tax Commission v. Jefferson Lines	1995	1	Maj (Souter)	AV	NT	Commerce Clause (dormant cc)
Jerome B. Grubart v. Great Lakes Dredge & Dock Co.	1995	1	Maj (Souter)	AV	NT	Admiralty
C & A Carbone v. Town of Clarkstown	1994	1	Diss (Souter)	AV	NT	Commerce Clause (dormant cc)
Oregon Waste Systems v. Department of Environmental Quality	1994	1	Maj (Thomas)	AV	NT	Commerce Clause (dormant cc)
New York v. United States	1992	2	Maj (O'Connor); Con/ Diss (Stevens)	AV; AV	NT; T	State sovereignty (anti-commandeering)
Quill Corp. v. North Dakota	1992	1	Maj (Stevens)	AV	NT	Commerce Clause (dormant cc)
Freytag v. Commissioner	1991	1	Con (Scalia)	AS	T	Appointments Clause
Dennis v. Higgins	1991	1	Diss (Kennedy)	AV	NT	Commerce Clause (dormant cc)
Port Authority Trans-Hudson Corp. v. Feeney	1990	1	Con (Brennan)	AS	T	State sovereignty
Regents of University of California v. Public Employment Relations Bd.	1988	1	Maj (O'Connor)	AS	NT	Postal service
Welch v. Texas Dept. of Highways and Public Transp.	1987	1	Diss (Brennan)	AS	NT	State sovereignty

Case	Year	Number of opinions with reference	Type(s) of opinion (author)	Aversive (AV) / aspirational (AS)	Textual (T) / non-textual (NT)	Substantive theme for reference
CTS Corp. v. Dynamics Corp. America	1987	1	Diss (White)	AV	NT	Commerce Clause (dormant cc)
Wardair Canada, Inc. v. Florida Department of Revenue	1986	1	Maj (Brennan)	AV	NT	Commerce Clause (dormant cc)
Atascadero State Hospital v. Scanlon	1985	1	Diss (Brennan)	AV	NT	State sovereignty
Supreme Court of New Hampshire v. Piper	1985	1	Maj (Powell)	AS	T	Privileges and Immunities (general)
County of Oneida v. Oneida Indian Nation	1985	1	Maj (Powell)	AV	NT	Indians
South-Central Timber Dev., Inc. v. Wunnicke	1984	1	Maj (White)	AV	NT	Commerce Clause (dormant cc)
United Bldg. & Constr. Trades Council v. Camden	1984	1	Diss (Blackmun)	AS	T	Privileges and Immunities (general)
Marsh v. Chambers	1983	1	Diss (Brennan)	AS	NT	Religion Clauses (establishment)
INS v. Chadha	1983	1	Diss (White)	AS	NT	Legislative veto
EEOC v. Wyoming	1983	2	Con (Stevens); Diss (White)	AV; AV	T; T	Commerce Clause (general)
Zobel v. Williams	1982	1	Con (O'Connor)	AS	T	Privileges and Immunities (general)
FERC v. Mississippi	1982	1	Con/Diss (O'Connor)	AV	NT	State sovereignty (anti-commandeering)

TABLE 5.9 Supreme Court cases invoking the Articles (*cont.*)

Case	Year	Number of opinions with reference	Type(s) of opinion (author)	Aversive (AV) / aspirational (AS)	Textual (T) / non-textual (NT)	Substantive theme for reference
Hughes v. Oklahoma	1979	1	Maj (Brennan)	AV	NT	Commerce Clause (dormant cc)
Nevada v. Hall	1979	1	Diss (Rehnquist)	AV	T	State sovereignty
Allied Structural Steel Co. v. Spannaus	1978	1	Diss (Brennan)	AV	NT	Contracts Clause
Hicklin v. Orbeck	1978	1	Una (Brennan)	AS	T	Privileges and Immunities (general)
Exxon Corp. v. Governor of Maryland	1978	1	Con/Diss (Blackmun)	AV	NT	Commerce Clause (dormant cc)
Baldwin v. Fish and Game Commission of Montana	1978	2	Maj (Blackmun); Con (Burger)	AS; AS	T; T	Privileges and Immunities (general)
Department of Revenue of State of Washington v. Association of Washington Stevedoring Companies	1978	1	Maj (Blackmun)	AV	NT	Commerce Clause (dormant cc)
U.S. Steel Corp. v. Multistate Tax Commission	1978	2	Maj (Powell); Diss (White)	AS; AV	T; T	Inter-state disputes (Interstate compacts)
Vendo Company v. Lektro-Vend Corporation	1977	1	Diss (Stevens)	AV	NT	Commerce Clause (general)
Michelin Tire Corporation v. Wages, Tax Commissioner	1976	1	Maj (Brennan)	AV	NT	Import-Export (tax)
Austin v. New Hampshire	1975	1	Maj (Marshall)	AS	T	Privileges and Immunities (general)

Case	Year	Number of opinions with reference	Type(s) of opinion (author)	Aversive (AV) / aspirational (AS)	Textual (T) / non-textual (NT)	Substantive theme for reference
United States v. Richardson	1974	1	Diss (Douglas)	AV	NT	Statement and Account
Smith v. Goguen	1974	1	Con (White)	AS	NT	Sovereignty (union flag)
United States v. 12 200-Foot Reels of Super 8mm Film	1973	1	Diss (Douglas)	AS	NT	1st amendment (obscenity)
Ohio v. Kentucky	1973	1	Maj (Blackmun)	AS	NT	Inter-state dispute (boundary)
United States v. Brewster	1972	1	Diss (Brennan)	AS	T	Parliamentary immunity (speech and debate clause)
Furman v. Georgia	1972	1	Con (Douglas)	AS	NT	Cruel and unusual punishment
Oregon v. Mitchell	1970	1	Con/Diss (Harlan-II)	AS	T	Privileges and Immunities (general)
O'Callahan v. Parker	1969	1	Diss (Harlan-II)	AS	T	Courts martial
Zschernig v. Miller	1968	1	Con (Harlan-II)	AV	NT	Foreign relations (treaty power)
United States v. Guest	1966	2	Maj (Stewart); Con/ Diss (Harlan-II)	AS; AS	T; T	Privileges and Immunities (right to travel)
Hicks v. District of Columbia	1966	1	Diss (Douglas)	AV	T	Privileges and Immunities (vagrancy)
United States v. Johnson	1966	1	Maj (Harlan-II)	AS	T	Parliamentary immunity (speech and debate clause)

TABLE 5.9 Supreme Court cases invoking the Articles (*cont.*)

Case	Year	Number of opinions with reference	Type(s) of opinion (author)	Aversive (AV) / aspirational (AS)	Textual (T) / non-textual (NT)	Substantive theme for reference
Wesberry v. Sanders	1964	1	Maj (Black)	AV	NT	Elections (voting district population)
Federal Power Commission v. Tuscarora Indian Nation	1960	1	Diss (Black)	AS	T	Indians
Kinsella v. United States	1960	1	Con/Diss (Whittaker)	AS	NT	Courts martial
New York v. O'Neill	1959	1	Diss (Douglas)	AS	T	Privileges and Immunities (right to travel)
Romero v. International Terminal Operating Co.	1959	1	Maj (Frankfurter)	AS	NT	Admiralty
Reid v. Covert	1957	1	Maj (Black)	AS	NT	Foreign relations (treaty power) (supremacy clause)
United States ex. rel. Toth v. Quarles	1955	1	Diss (Reed)	AS	T	Courts martial
Hughes v. Fetter	1951	1	Diss (Frankfurter)	AS	T	Full Faith and Credit Clause (general)
Tenney v. Brandhove	1951	1	Maj (Frankfurter)	AS	T	Parliamentary immunity (speech and debate clause)
Murdock v. Pennsylvania	1943	1	Diss (Reed)	AS	T	Religion Clauses (free exercise)
Hinderlider v. La Plata River & Cherry Creek Ditch Co.	1938	1	Maj (Brandeis)	AS	NT	Inter-state disputes (Interstate compacts)

Case	Year	Number of opinions with reference	Type(s) of opinion (author)	Aversive (AV) / aspirational (AS)	Textual (T) / non-textual (NT)	Substantive theme for reference
Steward Machine Co. v. Davis	1937	1	Diss (McReynolds)	AS	NT	State sovereignty
United States v. Curtiss-Wright Export Corp.	1936	1	Maj (Sutherland)	AS	T	Foreign relations
Home Bldg. & Loan Ass'n v. Blaisdell	1934	1	Diss (Sutherland)	AV	NT	Contracts Clause
Vermont v. New Hampshire	1933	1	Maj (Stone)	AS	NT	Boundary dispute
United States v. Flores	1933	1	Una (Stone)	AS	T	Admiralty
Myers v. United States	1926	2	Maj (Taft); Diss (McReynolds)	AV; AS	NT; NT	Removal power
Georgia v. South Carolina	1922	1	Una (Clarke)	AS	NT	Inter-state dispute (boundary)
United States v. Wheeler	1920	1	Maj (Douglas White)	AS	T	Privileges and Immunities (right to travel)
Virginia v. West Virginia	1918	1	Una (Douglas White)	AV	T	State sovereignty
Selective Draft Law Cases	1918	1	Una (Douglas White)	AS	NT	Military conscription
Biddinger v. Commissioner of Police of City of New York	1917	1	Una (Clarke)	AS	NT	Extradition
Southern Pacific Company v. Jensen	1917	1	Diss (Pitney)	AV	NT	Admiralty
Dick v. United States	1908	1	Una (Harlan-I)	AV	NT	Indians
Williamson v. United States	1908	1	Maj (Douglas White)	AS	T	Parliamentary immunity (freedom from arrest)

TABLE 5.9 Supreme Court cases invoking the Articles (*cont.*)

Case	Year	Number of opinions with reference	Type(s) of opinion (author)	Aversive (AV) / aspirational (AS)	Textual (T) / non-textual (NT)	Substantive theme for reference
Employers' Liability Cases	1908	1	Diss (Moody)	AV	NT	Commerce Clause (general)
Kansas v. Colorado	1907	1	Maj (Brewer)	AS	T	inter-state dispute (boundary)
Northern Security Company v. United States	1904	1	Maj (Harlan-I)	AV	NT	Commerce Clause (general)
Kean v. Calumet Canal and Improvement Company	1903	1	Diss (Douglas White)	AS	NT	Public domain
Lottery Case	1903	1	Diss (Fueller)	AS	T	Privileges and Immunities (general)
Caldwell v. North Carolina	1903	1	Una (Shiras)	AV	NT	Commerce Clause (general)
Downes v. Bidwell	1901	3	Maj (Brown); Con (Douglas White); Diss (Harlan-I)	AV; AS; AV	T; T; NT	State sovereignty
Missouri v. Illinois	1901	1	Maj (Shiras)	AS	T	Inter-state dispute
Knowlton v. Moore	1900	1	Maj (Douglas White)	AV	NT	Taxation
Maxwell v. Dow	1900	1	Maj (Peckham)	AS	T	Privileges and Immunities (general)
Louisiana v. Texas	1900	1	Maj (Fuller)	AS	T	Inter-state dispute
Blake v. McClung	1898	1	Maj (Harlan-I)	AS	T	Privileges and Immunities (general)

Case	Year	Number of opinions with reference	Type(s) of opinion (author)	Aversive (AV) / aspirational (AS)	Textual (T) / non-textual (NT)	Substantive theme for reference
New York State v. Roberts	1898	1	Diss (Harlan-I)	AV	NT	Commerce Clause (dormant cc)
Hilton v. Guyot	1895	1	Maj (Gray)	AS	T	Full Faith and Credit Clause (general)
Pollock v. Farmers II	1895	2	Diss (Harlan-I); Diss (Howell Jackson)	AV; AV	NT; T	Taxation
Pollock v. Farmers I	1895	2	Maj (Fuller); Diss (Douglas White)	AV; AV	NT; NT	Taxation
Wharton v. Wise	1894	1	Maj (Field)	AS	T	Inter-state disputes (Interstate compacts)
Manuel v. Wulff	1894	1	Maj (Fuller)	AS	NT	Citizenship
Huntington v. Attrill	1892	1	Maj (Gray)	AS	NT	Full Faith and Credit Clause (general)
McPherson v. Blacker	1892	1	Una (Fuller)	AS	T	Elections (electoral college votes)
United States v. Texas	1892	1	Maj (Harlan-I)	AS	T	Inter-state dispute (boundary)
Hans v. Louisiana	1890	1	Maj (Bradley)	AS	NT	State sovereignty (immunity)
Wisconsin v. Pelicans Ins. Co.	1888	1	Una (Gray)	AS	NT	Inter-state dispute
Coffee v. Groover	1887	1	Una (Bradley)	AS	T	Inter-state dispute (boundary)
Robbins v. Shelby County Taxing District	1887	1	Maj (Bradley)	AV	NT	Commerce Clause (dormant cc)

TABLE 5.9 Supreme Court cases invoking the Articles (*cont.*)

Case	Year	Number of opinions with reference	Type(s) of opinion (author)	Aversive (AV) / aspirational (AS)	Textual (T) / non-textual (NT)	Substantive theme for reference
Van Brocklin v. Tennessee	1886	1	Una (Bradley)	AS	T	Taxation (states cannot tax fed gov)
Poindexter v. Greenhow	1885	1	Maj (Matthews)	AV	NT	Contracts Clause
Legal Tender Cases	1884	1	Maj (Gray)	AV	T	Paper money
Springer v. United States	1881	1	Una (Swayne)	AV	NT	Taxation
Hauenstein v. Lynham	1880	1	Una (Swayne)	AS	NT	Foreign relations (treaty power) (supremacy clause)
Ex parte Virginia	1880	1	Diss (Field)	AV	NT	State sovereignty (black jurors)
United States v. Forty-Three Gallons of Whiskey	1876	1	Una (Davis)	AV	NT	Indians
United States v. Cruikshank	1876	1	Maj (Waite)	AV	NT	State sovereignty (bill of rights)
Minor v. Happersett	1875	1	Una (Waite)	AS	T	Citizenship
Slaughter-House Cases	1873	1	Maj (Miller)	AS	T	Privileges and Immunities (general)
Hepburn v. Griswold	1870	1	Maj (Salmon Chase)	AS	NT	Paper money
Woodruff v. Parham	1869	2	Maj (Miller); Diss (Nelson)	AV; AV	T; T	Import-Export (tax)
Texas v. White	1869	1	Maj (Salmon Chase)	AV	T	State sovereignty
Lane County v. Oregon	1869	1	Una (Salmon Chase)	AV	NT	Taxation
Kentucky v. Dennison	1861	1	Una (Taney)	AS	T	Inter-state dispute (extradition)

Case	Year	Number of opinions with reference	Type(s) of opinion (author)	Aversive (AV) / aspirational (AS)	Textual (T) / non-textual (NT)	Substantive theme for reference
Jackson v. S. B. Magnolia	1858	1	Diss (Campbell)	AS	NT	Admiralty
Dred Scott v. Sandford	1857	4	Maj (Taney); Con (Campbell); Con (Catron); Diss (Curtis)	AS; AS; AS; AS	T; NT; NT; T	Citizenship
Dodge v Woolsey	1856	1	Maj (Wayne)	AV	NT	Contracts Clause
Florida v. Georgia	1855	1	Diss (Campbell)	AS	T	Inter-state dispute (boundary)
Howard v. Ingersoll	1852	1	Maj (Wayne)	AS	T	Inter-state dispute (boundary)
Oldfield v. Marriott	1851	1	Una (Wayne)	AV	NT	Commerce Clause (general)
Passenger Cases: Smith v. Turner and Norris v. Boston	1849	3	OP (McLean); OP (Wayne); Diss (Woodbury)	AV; AV; AS	T; NT; NT	Commerce Clause (general)
Luther v. Borden	1849	1	Diss (Woodbury)	AS	T	War power
Thurlow v. Massachusetts	1847	1	Diss (McLean)	AV	NT	Commerce Clause (general)
Waring v. Clarke	1847	1	Maj (Wayne)	AV	NT	Admiralty
Prigg v. Pennsylvania	1842	1	Diss (McLean)	AV	NT	Inter-state dispute (extradition)
Rhode Island v. Massachusetts	1840	1	Diss (McLean)	AS	NT	Inter-state dispute (boundary)
McElmoyle v. Cohen	1839	1	Una (Wayne)	AV	T	Full Faith and Credit Clause (general)

TABLE 5.9 Supreme Court cases invoking the Articles (*cont.*)

Case	Year	Number of opinions with reference	Type(s) of opinion (author)	Aversive (AV) / aspirational (AS)	Textual (T) / non-textual (NT)	Substantive theme for reference
Rhode Island v. Massachusetts	1838	1	Maj (Baldwin)	AV	T	Inter-state dispute (boundary)
Briscoe v. President and Directors of Bank of Kentucky	1837	1	Maj (McLean)	AV	NT	Paper money
Poole v. Fleeger's Lessee	1837	1	OP (Baldwin)	AS	T	Inter-state disputes (Interstate compacts)
Worcester v. Georgia	1832	1	Con (McLean)	AS	T	Indians
Cherokee Nation v. Georgia	1831	3	Maj (John Marshall); Diss (Baldwin); Diss (Thompson)	AV; AS; AS	T; T; NT	Indians
Doe ex dem. Governeur's Heirs v. Robertson	1826	1	Una (William Johnson)	AS	NT	Citizenship
Green v. Biddle	1823	1	Maj (Story)	AS	NT	Inter-state disputes (Interstate compacts)
McCulloch v. Maryland	1819	1	Una (John Marshall)	AV	T	Taxation
Martin v. Hunter's Lessee	1816	1	Una (Story)	AS	T	State sovereignty
Hylton v. United States	1796	1	OP (Iredell)	AS	NT	Taxation
Ware v. Hylton	1796	3	OP (Chase); OP (Iredell); OP (Wilson)	AS; AS; AS	T; NT; NT	Foreign relations (foreign grievances) (treaty power)
Penhallow v. Doane's Adm'rs	1795	2	OP (Paterson); OP (Iredell)	AS; AS	T; NT	Admiralty
Chisholm v. Georgia	1793	2	OP (Iredell); OP (Wilson)	AS; AV	NT; NT	State sovereignty (immunity)

PART 3

A Matter of Narratives

CHAPTER 6

Janus' Third Face?

The Spanish Constitutional Court at the Crossroads of History

Ángel Aday Jiménez Alemán

1 Introduction

History has weighed heavily in the Spanish Constitutional Court (CC) since its origin, because of the Court's own use of history and the issues it has had to face as the supreme interpreter of the Constitution.[1] In its break from the immediate authoritarian past, in 1978 the Spanish Constituent Assembly decided to include constitutional justice as an authentic, foundational pillar of our constitutional democracy. Constitutional justice is a rarity in Spanish constitutional history: only two of the nine Spanish constitutions have provided institutions for constitutional justice and the first, the Court of Constitutional Guarantees established in 1931, was ill-suited for its task. Without doubt, the transformative potential of the 1978 Constitution – a rational-regulatory constitution, as opposed to an historic-traditional one – owes much to the inclusion of constitutional justice, though it inevitably incorporates also pre-existing institutions.[2]

During its first decade (1981–1991), the Constitutional Court protected the nascent democracy by acting as a bastion against Franco-era legacies, declaring incompatible holdover legislation to be unconstitutional and setting an example for the ordinary courts. This established the regulatory nature of a constitution that has overcome the inertia of a history dominated by weak constitutions. However, jurists groomed under the dictatorship still filled the

1 This work has been carried out in the framework of the project funded by the Ministry of Science and Innovation (Spain) 'La Constitución como instrumento de integración de la sociedad y el sistema político' (Ref. PID2020-117503GB-I00), directed by Xabier Arzoz Santisteban. The author would like to express his deep gratitude to the editors of the volume, Justin Orlando Frosini, Jason Mazzone and Francesco Biagi, for their comments and help.

2 A constitution understood as a system of rules established at a single time, which fully establishes and regulates the functions and bodies of the State, as opposed to the historic traditional concept of constitution, which results from a slow historical transformation. Manuel García Pelayo, 'Constitución y Derecho constitucional. Evolución y crisis de ambos conceptos' (1948) 37–38 Revista de estudios políticos 53.

 | DOI:10.1163/9789004523739_008

benches of ordinary courts, including the Supreme Court. This complicated the task of the Constitutional Court as it reviewed the constitutionality of essential elements of Spain's transition to democracy, such as the Amnesty Law (CCJ 147/1986).

Prominent historical elements appear in the text of the Spanish Constitution (SC) of 1978, from the Preamble onwards, which are intended to protect the traditions of Spanish towns. In Article 1.1, the formula "Spain is hereby established as a social and democratic State, subject to the rule of law," constitutes a particularly intense expression of the desire to abandon the authoritarian form of state that persisted under the Franco dictatorship[3] in exchange for liberal democracy. Similarly, Article 46 offers a guiding principle in its provision for the protection of historic heritage. Recognition of the monarchy – featured in all prior constitutions except that of the First Republic and of 1931 – in Article 57.2, along with other traditional institutions, attests to the importance of history in the 1978 Constitution.[4] Other examples include constitutional recognition for customary and traditional courts (Art. 125 SC), the prohibition of Honour Courts (Art. 26 SC), and recognition of the historic rights of regional laws in the First Additional Provision.

While the 1978 Constituent Parliament prioritised the continuity of Spanish constitutional history in some areas, it pursued a fresh start in others, such as by adopting constitutional justice.[5] The Spanish Constitutional Court is a specialist court that only exercises constitutional review.[6] It is unique in its order, exerts national jurisdiction, and is separate from the ordinary judicial system. The Court is based largely on the Kelsenian centralised model, although ordinary courts collaborate in constitutional review by raising questions of unconstitutionality. This dual nature is common among constitutional courts created

3 1936 – 1975, and early reform under President Adolfo Suárez.

4 "2. The Crown Prince, from his birth or from the time the summons is originated, will have the dignity of Prince of Asturias and all other titles traditionally linked to the heir of the Crown of Spain."

5 The following description of the functions of the Spanish Constitutional Court can also be found in Ángel Aday Jiménez Alemán, 'The Spanish Constitutional Court and Foreign and Comparative Law: Theory and Practice of a Marriage of Convenience', in Giuseppe Franco Ferrari (ed.), *Judicial Cosmopolitanism. The Use of Foreign Law in Contemporary Constitutional Systems* (Brill 2019).

6 Departing from other previous functions, including criminal jurisdiction over the highest public authorities. See Martín Bassols Coma, *El Tribunal de Garantías Constitucionales de la II República: La primera experiencia de la justicia constitucional en España* (Boletín Oficial del Estado 2010).

after the Second World War.[7] Hence, the Spanish Constitutional Court is an *ad-hoc* constitutional body with organisational and budgetary autonomy, performing judicial functions outside the judicial system. According to Rubio Llorente, only the German *Bundesverfassungsgericht* asserts broader jurisdiction than that of the Spanish Constitutional Court.[8] It is hard to disagree, especially after the strengthening of the Spanish Constitutional Court's enforcement powers in 2015.[9] In light of the diversity of the powers granted, therefore, the form of constitutional justice established by the Spanish Constitution of 1978 is not pure in terms of its design. Title IX of the Spanish Constitution (Articles 159–165) and Organic Law 2/1979 CC empower the Spanish Constitutional Court to exercise constitutional review, resolve conflicts between constitutional and territorial bodies, and ensure the protection of fundamental rights.[10]

In order to perform its natural and primary function of constitutional review of legislative acts, the Spanish Constitutional Court has five instruments at its disposal.[11] First, the unconstitutionality objection (*recurso de inconstitucionalidad*) allows the Prime Minister, 50 members of the Cortes Generales, 50 members of the Senate, the Ombudsman, as well as the regional executive and legislative bodies to challenge any piece of legislation. Secondly, all ordinary judges and courts are required to cooperate in constitutional review by raising questions of unconstitutionality (*cuestión de inconstitucionalidad*). All ordinary judges and courts are interpreters of the Constitution, as are other public powers (Article 9.2 SC); however, the Constitutional Court is the supreme interpreter (Article 1 of the Organic Law on the Constitutional Court), and it alone has power to resolve any constitutional review proceedings. In addition to any piece of legislation, the Constitutional Court can exercise constitutional

7 See Mauro Cappelletti, 'Judicial Review in Comparative perspective' (1970) 58 California Law Review 1017; and Victor Ferreres Comella, 'The European Model of Constitutional Review of Legislation: Toward Decentralization?' (2004) 2:3 International Journal of Constitutional Law 461.

8 Francisco Rubio Llorente, 'Seis tesis sobre la jurisdicción constitucional en Europa' (1992) 35 Revista Española de Derecho Constitucional 9.

9 Ángel Aday Jiménez Alemán, '¿De poder neutro a poder activo? Sobre el eficaz pero inconveniente refuerzo de los poderes de ejecución del Tribunal Constitucional' (2019) 23(2) Anuario Iberoamericano de Justicia Constitucional 401.

10 Victor Ferreres Comella, *Una defensa del modelo europeo de control de constitucionalidad* (Marcial Pons, 2009).

11 For a detailed analysis (in English) of the Spanish Constitutional Court, see Victor Ferreres Comella, 'The Spanish Constitutional Court: Time for Reforms', in Andrew Harding (ed.), *Constitutional Courts: A Comparative Study* (JCL Studies in Comparative Law, Wildy, Simmonds & Hill Publishing 2010); and Victor Ferreres Comella, *The Constitution of Spain: A Contextual Analysis* (Hart 2013).

review *ex ante* of international treaties and self-government statutes (*Estatutos de Autonomía*),[12] and *ex post* review of regional fiscal regulations.[13]

The second function of the Spanish Constitutional Court is to resolve disputes concerning the jurisdiction of State bodies, constitutional bodies and regional bodies. In other words, in addition to resolving conflicts between constitutional bodies (the Government, the Parliament and the General Council of the Judiciary), owing to the current Spanish decentralised structure, the CC also settles disputes between territorial bodies (executive bodies at state, regional or local levels).

Finally, the most "unconventional" function (although the one that has played the leading role in case law) is the protection of fundamental rights through an *amparo* action (*recurso de amparo*). Any natural or legal person, as well as the Ombudsman and the Public Prosecutor, may challenge any act or omission by a public body that violates a fundamental right protected by the Constitution, by lodging an appeal with the Constitutional Court, after previously exhausting all available ordinary judicial remedies.

When exercising these three functions,[14] especially in relation to the protection of fundamental rights, the Spanish Constitutional Court has relied

---

12 Although there was a procedure for the *ex ante* review of the constitutionality of legislation, including in particular organic laws and self-government statutes, the abuse of this function and the consequent delays in the entry into force of legislation led to its abolition in 1985. The most recent reform of the Organic Law on the Constitutional Court revived this instrument in 2015, but limited it to the review of self-government statutes.

13 The Basque Country is subject to a different tax regime, separate from the ordinary Spanish tax regime. The Historical Territories of the Basque Country (Álava, Guipúzcoa and Vizcaya) regulate and collect almost every tax falling under their jurisdiction. The Autonomous Community of the Basque Country pays a contribution to the Spanish State for services provided, which is negotiated between the Basque Country and the Spanish State and approved by a legal instrument on regional tax regulations. The *normas fiscales forales* are the general provisions that regulate this matter. Despite their regional nature, the Spanish Constitutional Court has reviewed them since 2010. See Luis María Díez-Picazo, 'Notas sobre el blindaje de las normas forales fiscales' (2010) 3 InDret, Revista para el análisis del Derecho.

14 According to Article 161. D) of the Spanish Constitution, the powers vested in the Constitutional Court depend partially on the legislator. Hence, the jurisdiction of the Constitutional Court has been amended on several occasions, by the ten amendments thus far made to the Organic Law. As regards the changes in the procedure for the *ex ante* review of the constitutionality of legislation (see note 8), the *amparo* action seeking protection for constitutional rights has been repeatedly reformed. In terms of the allocation of new powers, it is sufficient to note Organic Law 7/1999 of April 21, which incorporated the disputes concerning the autonomy of local administrations, as well as the most recent reform in 2015, which granted significant enforcement powers.

extensively on foreign and comparative law as well as precedents from the constitutional or supreme courts of other countries, as discussed further below.

References to history abound in the judgments of the Spanish Constitutional Court. These judgments generally lack the brevity that was a virtue during the Court's early years of activity and are structured with three main parts. The first sets out the facts pertinent to the relevant case (*antecedentes*); the second establishes the legal grounds (LG) on which the Court bases its decision (*fundamentos jurídicos*); and the third contains the ruling (traditionally known as *decisum*) and its effects. The Court must give reasons for its decisions, and these must be guided by the principles of congruence.[15] If the parties have relied on history in developing their arguments, the corresponding historical references will be summarised in the first part of the judgment (*antecedentes*).

The resolutions contain the decision of the majority of the Court's judges. The President of the Court breaks any tied votes. The Court can sit in plenary session (*Pleno*) or can be divided into two Chambers (*Salas*) of 6 judges each, or into four Sections (*Secciones*) of 3 judges each. Judges may state their position in favour of a ruling while disagreeing with the legal grounds (concurring opinion) or they may object to the ruling itself (dissenting opinion).[16] Thus, it is not uncommon to find individual opinions in the resolutions. These have brought clarity to elements of constitutional debates while also providing insightful references to the constitutional and legal history that underpinned the positions of the judges.

This short introduction to the model of constitutional justice in Spain would be incomplete without mentioning the important academics who have engaged with the history of law as magistrates and legal counsel before the Constitutional Court, in particular the late professor Francisco Tomás y Valiente (1980–1992).

This chapter analyses how the Spanish Constitutional Court has made use of history and how the Court has responded when confronted with historical arguments. We will see, paradoxically, that the CC does not hesitate to use history to support its interpretations of the Constitution, but fights to maintain complete neutrality when ruling on historical events. The chapter briefly reviews legal and constitutional interpretation in Spain in Section II, before analysing, in Section III, the two sides of the historic method used by the Constitutional Court to interpret the Constitution: namely, the figure of

---

15 Ángel Garrorena Morales, 'La sentencia constitucional' (1981) 11 Revista de Derecho Político 7.

16 José Luis Cascajo Castro, 'La figura del voto particular en la jurisdicción constitucional española' (1986) 17 Revista Española de Derecho Constitucional 171.

the historical legislator and recourse to the constituent process. Section IV is dedicated to the study of cases in which the Court has been called upon to prosecute historical events related to the Spanish Civil War and the Holocaust. Section V sets out some conclusions.

2 Legal and Constitutional Interpretation in Spain

Early on, legal scholars warned of the consequences of incorporating constitutional justice, with its capacity to change the legal order and create law, into the Spanish legal system. Doing so implied a departure from the ruling model and an alteration of the legal order.[17] The problem of constitutional interpretation emerged essentially from the Constitution of 1978 – the authentic legal standard of mandatory application for judicial bodies and the Constitutional Court – although there were signs of constitutional interpretation by judicial bodies under previous constitutions.[18]

As a result of Spain's long, intense tradition of upholding the principle of freedom of interpretation, the Spanish legal order had no rules governing the interpretation of law until the reform of the Civil Code in 1974. Doctrine had drawn on Savigny's rules set out in the Spanish translation of his work *System des heutigen römischen Rechts* (1840–1849) in 1878. Those rules were accepted without controversy and were regarded as general guidelines for interpreting bodies, implying no restriction on freedom to choose the sources to be used in interpretation. Although never recognised as imperative, the rules were also used by authorities such as the General Directorate of Registers in the Resolution of 23 August 1894 and the Supreme Court.[19]

Currently, Chapter II (on the application of legal rules) of the Preliminary Title of the Civil Code, Article 3.1, provides guidance for interpreting bodies,[20] referring to the historical and legislative context, along with other interpretative methods from Savigny that have been internalised within doctrine: "Rules

17 Francisco Rubio Llorente, 'La jurisdicción constitucional como forma de creación de Derecho' (1988) 22 Revista Española de Derecho Constitucional 9–52.

18 Manuel José Terol Becerra, 'Sobre la interpretación de la Constitución y de la Ley en España (1812–1978)' (1993) 15 Revista del Centro de Estudios Constitucionales 183.

19 Federico de Castro y Bravo, 'Naturaleza de las reglas para la interpretación de la Ley (Consideraciones en torno al artículo 3º, apartado 1, del Código Civil)' (1978) Anuario de Derecho Civil 809, 829–830.

20 The Civil Code also includes specific rules on the interpretation of wills (Art. 675) and contracts (Arts. 1281 to 1289). Article 12 of the General Tax Law complements Article 3.1 of the Civil Code as regards this legal scope.

shall be construed according to the proper meaning of their wording and in connection with the context, with their historical and legislative background and with the social reality of the time in which they are to be applied, mainly attending to their spirit and purpose". Accordingly, the starting point for all interpretation lies in the sense of the words themselves, taking into consideration the demands for contextual or systematic interpretation, which affords priority to the area of the law to which the relevant rule belongs, although without ignoring the law as a whole. The provision distinguishes between "historical background", or the regulatory evolution of an area, and "legislative background", or the process of creating law. It also mentions the "social reality", in order to correct the effects of a rigid application of rules, opening up interpretation to values and experiences. Finally, teleological criteria and the purpose of the standards are mentioned in the text itself or can be inferred from the law as a whole.

Besides Article 3.1 of the Civil Code, other provisions regulate interpretation under Spanish law, starting with Article 9.1, which links public authorities and citizens to the Constitution and the rest of the legal order. The Constitution includes clauses on openness to extra-systemic factors, such as Article 10.2, which stands out as one of the most emblematic clauses within the text. It provides that the rules on fundamental rights and public freedoms must be interpreted in accordance with the relevant international treaties ratified by Spain. Article 120 establishes the principles for incorporating judicial decisions. Along with publicity and orality, reasons must be provided as a precondition for validity, indicating the grounds that led the judicial authorities to reach their decision, along with the relevant jurisprudence and legislation that required the relevant standard to be applied. Looking beyond the Constitution, Article 5.1 of the Organic Law of the Judiciary of 1985 requires judges and courts to interpret laws and regulations in accordance with constitutional principles and precepts as well as Constitutional Court doctrine. The Spanish Legal System imposes an obligation on jurisdictional and administrative bodies to issue a ruling even if the law is silent, opaque or insufficient (Art. 1.7 of the Civil Code, 88.5 of Law 39/2015, of 1 October, on Common Administrative Procedure of Public Administration; Art. 11.3 of Organic Law 6/1985, of 1 July, on the Judiciary), and sanctions non-compliance with disqualification from public office or employment for between six months and four years under Article 448 of the Criminal Code. Finally, Article 7.2 of the Civil Code prohibits any abusive interpretation of the rules.[21]

21 Pablo Lucas Murillo de la Cueva, 'Artículo 120' in Pablo Pérez Tremps and Alejandro Sáiz Arnáiz (eds.), *Comentario a la Constitución Española. 40 aniversario (1978–2018)*.

Constitutional doctrine has also provided basic criteria for interpretation. Constitutional Court Judgement (CCJ) 11/1981, Legal Grounds (LG) 7, stated that "The Constitution is a set of common points sufficiently broad to cover very different political-ideological choices. The task of interpreting the Constitution is not necessarily to block certain options or variants by imposing one of them in an authoritarian way. To this effect, it should only occur when the unambiguous nature of the interpretation is imposed by hermeneutical criteria". This provision vested the State with exclusive competence to establish requirements for interpreting the rules (CCJ 83/1986, 26 June, LG 3). According to the hierarchy of hermeneutic principles, (CCJ 149/1991), lawmakers cannot enact legislation for the sole purpose of interpreting the Constitution, thereby establishing a unique meaning for its provisions (CCJ 76/1983). The Constitutional Court is the organ responsible for clarifying the constitutionally appropriate meaning of a law (CCJ 5/1981, LG 6).

The specificity of constitutional interpretation cannot be denied under Spanish constitutional theory, given a Constitution that is binding (all of its regulations, whether rules or principles, are mandatory), open (political action is defined but not predetermined), positive (it is a positive standard established by the Constituent Parliament) and historical. The Constitution was adopted within a pre-existing legal order, a specific legal culture that must be taken into consideration by interpreters.[22] The Constitutional Court prevails among these and is responsible as the supreme interpreter of the Constitution (Art. 1.1 of the Organic Law on the Constitutional Parliament). In Kelsenian terms, interpretation is authentic and general:[23] it does not seek to identify true meaning but rather meanings that are not constitutionally incorrect.

Spanish legal doctrine is based on general definitions of interpretation, such as that provided by Francisco Javier Díaz Revorio: "the process through which a regulatory text is provided (without addressing whether it is 'discovered' or 'attributed') with meaning or content,[24]" in order to then consider constitutional interpretation. This is understood as a type of interpretation, given that

Libro-homenaje a Luis López Guerra (Tirant lo Blanch 2018), 1701–1702; Tomás Javier Aliste Santos, *La motivación de las resoluciones judiciales* (Marcial Pons, 2011). Juan Igartua Salaverría, *La motivación de las sentencias, imperativo constitucional* (Centro de Estudios Políticos y Constitucionales, 2003).

22 Javier Jiménez Campo, 'Interpretación Constitucional' in *Enciclopedia Jurídica Básica* (Civitas, 1995), 3685–3690.

23 Hans Kelsen, *The Law of the United Nations. A critical analysis of its fundamentals problems. With a supplement* (The Lawbook Exchange 2000).

24 Francisco Javier Díaz Revorio, *Valores superiores e interpretación constitucional* (Centro de Estudios Políticos y Constitucionales 1997), 39.

the subject – the Constitution – determines that hermeneutic operation by providing its own elements and criteria for accomplishing it.[25] Along these lines, Manuel Aragón, following the tenets of Smend and K. Larenz, insists that the specificity of constitutional interpretation lies in the "very specific status of the constitutional rule" and not in interpretation by a constitutional or ordinary court. Therefore, the criteria for interpreting traditional law cannot be transferred without alteration. Constitutional interpretation is necessarily evaluative, given that the Constitution contains values and principles in addition to regulations.[26] G. Zagrebelsky clarifies the point further, stating that theories of legal and contractual interpretation are insufficient to account for the constitutional reality. Contemporary pluralist constitutions do not consider the intentions of the original lawmakers or any consensus established among individuals, but rather universal principles for which a balancing point must be found.[27] Although purpose is the strongest determining factor in constitutional interpretation, we must not overlook the differences between an ordinary judge and a Constitutional Court justice. The former searches for the correct interpretation, while the latter seeks to point out unacceptable interpretations.[28]

Along with the systematic method of interpretation and some others, the Constitutional Court looks to the four methods of classical constitutional interpretation, which are understood as principles rather than rules. As suggested by Haberle,[29] this approach seeks to turn uncertainty into a virtue and make the most of the pluralism and openness of the Constitution. In spite of the fact that the general consensus in Spain endorses subjective theories – which focus on discovering the intent of those persons who issued the rule – over objective theories – which search for the meaning within the rule itself[30] – the Constitutional Court refers to all of them,[31] including what Peter Haberle

25 Ibid., 40.

26 Manuel Aragón Reyes, 'La interpretación de la Constitución y el carácter objetivado del control jurisdiccional' (1986) 17 Revista Española de Derecho Constitucional 85.

27 Gustavo Zagrebelsky, *Historia y constitución* (Traducción y prólogo de Migeul Carbonell) (Trotta, 2005), p. 86.

28 Luis Prieto Sanchís, 'Notas sobre la interpretación constitucional' (1991) 9 Revista del Centro de Estudios Constitucionales 175, 177.

29 Peter Haberle, 'Métodos y principios de la interpretación constitucional. Un catálogo de problemas' (2010) 13 Revista de derecho constitucional europeo 379.

30 Fernando Sáinz Moreno, 'Interpretación jurídica' in *Enciclopedia Jurídica Básica* (Civitas, 1995), 3700–3713.

31 See Mariam Ahumada Ruiz, 'The Spanish Constitutional Court' in Andras Jakab, Arthur Dyevre and Giulio Itzcovich, *Comparative Constitutional Reasoning* (CUP 2017), 604.

calls the fifth method of interpretation: comparative law.[32] The principles of constitutional interpretation have been accepted in Spain and have gained significance thanks to the translation of Konrad Hesse's work. These principles include the unity of the Constitution (contradictions between constitutional rules must be avoided), practical consistency (optimising constitutionally protected values through consideration), functional correction (constitutional bodies must remain within the functional framework established by the Constitution), integrating efficiency (the proposals upheld by political bodies take preference if they are upheld in the constitutional framework) and the regulatory efficiency of the Constitution (preference for interpretations that help to update the efficiency of constitutional rules).[33]

Accordingly, Ezquiaga Ganuzas has identified 12 arguments within the doctrine of the supreme interpreter of the Spanish Constitution: the analogical argument, the principle-based argument, the systematic argument, the argument *a fortiori*, the counter argument, the psychological argument, the argument of no redundancy, the apagogical argument, the pragmatic argument, the authority argument, the teleological argument and finally, the historical argument, to which this study is dedicated. Although historical interpretation is certainly not the most frequently used method (except early on, as a result of proximity with the constituent process), examples of it abound in party submissions, in individual votes and in the legal reasons provided for resolutions.[34] Occasionally, it has been decisive in the interpretative option chosen by the Court.

3 The Use of the Historical Method by the Spanish Constitutional Court: The Constituent Process and Appeals to the Historical Legislator

On many occasions, the Constitutional Court has turned to phylogenetic history, knowledge of the origin and evolution of the institutions of the Spanish

32 Ángel Aday Jiménez Alemán, 'The Spanish Constitutional Court and Foreign and Comparative Law: Theory and Practice of a Marriage of Convenience', in Giuseppe Franco Ferrari (ed.), *Judicial Cosmopolitanism. The Use of Foreign Law in Contemporary Constitutional Systems* (Brill, 2019).

33 Konrad Hesse, *Escritos de Derecho Constitucional* (Centro de Estudios Constitucionales 1983), 45–48.

34 The Spanish Constitutional Court issues four types of resolutions: judicial rulings, court orders, judgments and declarations. These are structured into the background, the legal grounds (LG) and the decision. In addition, justices can cast individual votes.

legal order, when engaging in constitutional analysis. Enrique Alonso García was one of the first to analyse the early years (1981–1984) of constitutional interpretation, including the historical method.[35] Given the lack of constitutional justice in Spain from 1939 until the establishment of the Constitutional Court by the Spanish Constitution of 1978, Alonso García referred to foreign doctrine. Aside from references to Forsthoff and the Austrian Constitutional Court as an example of petrified originalism, Alonso García cites North American literature, particularly the writings of C. Miller, Berger, Lusky, Brest and Perry. Starting with Miller, Alonso García built up his analysis on originalism as an "interpretative trend that grants special relevance to the constituent moment",[36] to the point of rejecting any movement away from the intention of the framers or the mandate given by the people or social elites. Petrification is an inherent risk that arises when constitutional interpretation is restricted to what was feasible for the framers, in a way that prevents courts from going beyond the implementation of the fundamental decision of the people, and hence not allowing them to deal with new situations. This trend contrasts with moderate originalism, which always considers the spirit of the framers when drafting the constitutional text, or even reflects on what they might have said were they able to give their opinion today.[37] Alonso García rejects originalism as a false link in legitimising the Court's decisions.[38] María Luisa Balaguer Callejón also studied originalism and its branches (literalism, which contemplates no interpretative matter beyond the norm, and intentionalism, which interprets by reconstructing the framers' intent) as a subjective theory of interpretation that seeks to limit judicial creativity.[39]

However, Ezquiaga Ganuzas[40] focuses on Spanish civil doctrine (particularly that of Hernández Gil and Castán Tobeñas), identifying two currents of legal thought in relation to the use of history within interpretation. The first is static conception, a 'historic school' current in which tradition serves as a criterion for interpreting tradition. This conservative instrument prioritises legal certainty and respect for legislative intention. The second, more dynamic

35 Enrique Alonso García, *La interpretación de la Constitución* (Centro de Estudios Constitucionales, 1984), 137–163.

36 Ibid.,138.

37 Ibid.,144.

38 Ibid.,147.

39 Nevertheless, she did not dedicate a full section of her work on constitutional interpretation to the historical method. See *Interpretación de la constitución y ordenamiento jurídico* (Tecnos, 1987), 80–83.

40 Francisco Javier Ezquiaga Ganuzas, *La argumentación en la justicia constitucional española* (Instituto Vasco de Administración Pública, 1987), 443–476.

concept is defended by the historical-evolutionary method. It requires that the social reality at the time the legislation was applied be included as a criterion, thereby turning history into an instrument for adapting legislation to changes in social life.[41] Ezquiaga Ganuzas also calls for separate treatment of the preparatory studies from the historic argument per se. This focus aims to "grant a document with interpretative doubts the meaning that reflects how the various legislators throughout history have regulated the legal institution regulated by the current document".[42] On the other hand, he considers the preparatory studies to form part of the psychological argument, which aims to discover the intent of those who prepared the regulatory text. That approach invokes a fictional, personified legislator and the principle of continuity in the legal order.[43]

Finally, Raúl Canosa acknowledges the usefulness of a historic method, although he argues in favour of the predominance of the systematic method. This allows for evolution from formalist postures by introducing historical and social elements from the time the Constitution was enacted, which feature in the preparatory studies. These would never determine an interpretation, although they might validate the suitability of a decision previously made. Canosa also mentions the potential paradox inherent within this method of interpretation: if constitutional interpretation is understood as a process of updating the text and the intention of the constituent body, then to seek solutions in the past would be contradictory.[44]

3.1 *The Historical Legislator*

The Constitutional Court has limited the value of the historical method on several occasions, for instance in its Judgment 102/1995. First, in LG 2, it held that "the pursuit of the constitutionality of the law has no historical sense, but rather a nomophylactic purpose". Later, in LG 5, it stated that "the solution will be guided, at least partially, by the pre-constitutional rules applicable in this regard, without affording any binding interpretative value to a judgement of constitutionality, even though it may be useful in providing objective orientation". Finally, in LG 21, it asserted that, "the past, the historic perspective, is always useful for understanding the present".

41 Ibid., 435–436.

42 Ibid., 439.

43 Ibid., 470–472.

44 Raúl Canosa Usera, *Interpretación constitucional y fórmula política* (Centro de Estudios Constitucionales, 1988), 101–103.

This guiding value of the historical method had been clarified earlier, for instance in CCJ 37/1988 of 3 March. After analysing the constitutionality of a provision of the law on criminal procedure regarding a guarantee provided to public defenders representing convicted persons appealing against their sentences (Art. 876 of the Civil Procedure Act of 1882, cited in the draft Law of 16 July 1949), the Court stated in LG 4 that "although the history of a precept helps to interpret it, clearly we must not judge the constitutionality of a rule by its history".

Despite its limited value, appeals to the historical legislator within constitutional doctrine are very common. The Constitutional Court cannot deny that its decisions are at least partially based on this source. In CCJ 45/1983 of 25 May, ruling on an appeal from a judgment holding that a Provincial Director of the National Institute of Social Welfare was not eligible to serve as a senator due to the constitutional prohibition on choosing senior State officials (Art. 70.1 SC), the Constitutional Court declared that the judgement adopted under ordinary jurisdiction was mistaken, based on the history, nature and regulations governing this Institute (LG 3). On the same subject, in CCJ 72/1984 of 14 June, a prior unconstitutionality objection regarding the constitutionality of a law on incompatibilities and ineligibilities for deputies and senators referred to the history of Spanish constitutionalism (as well as comparative law) in concluding that the grounds for the incompatibility and ineligibility of members of the legislative chambers are established by the Constitution or by electoral law, and that the framers had opted for an intermediate solution. It also considered the constituent process in order to clarify that this issue can only be regulated by electoral law.

Along with Spanish constitutional history, the Constitutional Court also refers to contemporary history when reviewing the general electoral system. In CCJ 75/1985 of 21 January on the constitutionality of the 3% electoral threshold, the Court mentioned that contemporary Spanish history and other parliamentary systems serve as a warning against the risks of excessive political atomisation. Therefore, the legislator may legitimately choose these instruments for rationalising political participation. The precedent was followed in CCJ 225/1998, 25 November, LG 5. Moreover, when ruling on any element of electoral law, the Court will uphold the legitimacy of its decisions based on their "relationship of continuity with other electoral laws in our history" (CCJ 24/1990, 15 February, LG 2).

Constitutional Court decisions make frequent reference to historical context. In CCJ 141/1986 of 12 November, the Court identified the criminal investigation process as pertaining to other historical times and held that it was incompatible with the current system of guarantees (LG 1). CCJ 89/1989 of 11

May, LG 5, mentioned the innovation implicit within Spanish constitutional history following the introduction of an article dedicated to professional associations (Art. 36 SC). CCJ 234/1992 of 14 December held that "periculum in mora", was a "long-standing tradition in our legal system", that protects the rights recognised in the proceedings (this precedent was followed in CCJ 104/1994, 11 April and CCJ 191/2000 of 13 June, LG 4). Judgment 174/2011 of 7 November affirmed that: "indeed, in our legal tradition the natural way of refuting incriminatory declarations made against an accused person is by personal questioning of the witness, which occurs within an oral trial". In CCJ, 123/2012 of 5 June, concerning a positive jurisdictional dispute with the Government of Andalusia regarding reintroduction of horse betting by the State, the Court drew on many arguments in support of the constitutionality of this action. It cited the precedent established in Constitutional Court Judgment (CCS) 49/1995 of 16 February in order to defend a broad concept of playing the lottery, which has had different manifestations throughout history and is used by the Spanish State Treasury as a non-taxable resource.

History provides background, but also serves as a pedagogical tool, as in CCJ 102/1995 of 26 June. In that case, the Constitutional Court recounted that the concept of the environment first appeared in Spanish law under Decree 2.414/1961 of 30 November, although there had been previous regulations on air pollution, noise pollution, vibrations, gas emissions and sanitation. Another turning point in this area came with Spain's accession to the European Community. The Constitutional Court referred to the environment as "a concept as old as humankind" (LG 6) and insisted on traditional care for the environment. The text recalled that Spain had established National Parks in 1916 and introduced the concept of ecology into the legal system. It concluded that "although it was another age, separated by half a century and different terminology, the objective and teleological core were the same, as was the concern" (LG 21).

Such contextualising also allows for processes of distinction, as in CCJ 124/2018 of 14 December, LG 2, which resolved a conflict between constitutional bodies. The dispute had been filed by the Congress of Deputies, as a result of the government's unwillingness to submit to the control mechanisms of the legislative chamber. The Congress of Deputies had requested an urgent statement by the acting Minister of Defence in order to report on the issues addressed at a NATO meeting. The events took place during the 11th Legislature, when the Congress of Deputies had not been able to appoint a Prime Minister (*Presidente del Gobierno*). The Government maintained that there was no relationship of trust between the acting Government and the Congress of Deputies. The Constitutional Court rejected this argument, ruling that the control function forms part of parliamentary government established by Article 1.3 and that there can be no governmental activity outside of parliamentary control (LG 9).

In that judgment, the Court rejected the argument of the State Attorney concerning the alleged existence of consolidated parliamentary practice that excluded acting governments from scrutiny by the parliamentary body. After recognising the "traditional" relevance of parliamentary practices as a regulatory instrument for the organisation and operation of legislative chambers, the judicial authority ruled that the exceptional circumstances of the 11th Legislature "lacked any precedent in recent Spanish constitutional history" and placed its ability to appoint a Prime Minister in doubt. Therefore, this practice would have no effect under different circumstances (CCJ 124/2018, LG 2).

History can also be decisive in situations in which the Constitutional Court, when interpreting the Constitution, alters the evolution of an institution in order to identify and assimilate its primary characteristics. CCJ 132/1989 of 18 July provided an account of the evolution of the Chamber of Agriculture, noting its public status and the mandatory inclusion of agricultural professionals. At that time, the Court recognised the establishment and regulation of certain groups for achieving a public goal. Again, in CCJ 74/1994 of 14 March, when considering when it should be compulsory to join an association for the professional administration of estates (which could result in the issue of fines for fraud), the Court turned to the origin of the "National Association for Estate Administration" and considered its evolution ("Let's make history, then, in this retrospective journey ... " LG 3). In CCJ 108/2005 of 30 June, concerning the regulation of taxes on alcoholic drinks in the Canary Islands, the Court looked to history to ascertain the most important characteristics of the Canarian tax regime (LG 5 and 6). Again, in CCJ 113/2004 of July 12th, the Court reviewed the constitutionality of the decision taken by the "Council of Wise Men" (*Consejo de hombres buenos*), a traditional institution in Murcia, in order to resolve conflicts concerning irrigation. The Court analysed the problematic implications of the resolutions provided under this institution in terms of the guarantees required for effective legal protection, as laid down in Article 24.1. In LG 2, the Court referred to the history of the "Water Courts and Judges, or Irrigation Juries", an institution that has traditionally performed judicial and police functions in relation to water and resolved conflicts between parties in dispute in the regions of Valencia (said to be the oldest), Aragon and Murcia. The Court recalled the heated debate surrounding this institution at the time of the 1812 Constitution; although it violated the constitutional principal of jurisdictional unity, it was not eliminated. The Court pointed to the medieval origins of the Council of Wise Men and the jurisdiction it had exercised since 1849, when it became subject to regulation, the limitation of its authority strictly to irrigation issues and the lack of any right to appeal from its resolutions to the ordinary courts.

Those involved in constitutional procedures are aware of how relevant historical methodology can be and do not hesitate to use it, as the State Attorney did in CCJ 196/2015 of 24 September. The Supreme Court had nullified a decree issued by the Autonomous Community of Andalusia after the Constitutional Court had declared invalid the statutory provision providing coverage. The judgement emphasised that this was the first time that the State Administration had regulated human and material resources previously transferred to the Autonomous Communities, which justified the use of the Decree Law to guarantee legal certainty. History was invoked by the national government in CCJ 112/2013 of 9 May in defence of the duration of the legal framework providing public protection for homes. The Constitutional Court endorsed this appeal against the argument of the historical legislator as its own. The government argued that the legal figure of protected housing has always stipulated a minimum period of time before resale is permitted in order to avoid speculation in assets that society has funded using public resources and budgets, so as to facilitate access by citizens at risk of social exclusion.

Finally, if there is one area where this method is consubstantial, it is in relation to legislation on historical territories. In CCJ 179/1989 of 2 November, LG 9, the Court considered whether an economic agreement constituted a legal rule in the Autonomous Community of Navarre. History was taken into account when resolving the case. In addition, CCJ 121/1992 of 28 September authorised the Autonomous Community of Valencia to regulate "historic leases" (LG 3) based on the "pre-established practices of legal use developed over time". Another example may be found in CCJ 118/2016 of 23 June, where the Court required historical context for a legal institution, in that case the Economic Agreement. The judgment resolved an unconstitutionality objection brought against a rule vesting jurisdiction over the provincial tax laws of historic territories in the Constitutional Court.[45] Before addressing the arguments raised

45 The historic or "*foral*" territories (the Basque provinces of Álava, Guipúzcoa and Vizcaya, as well as Navarra) are parts of the Spanish Monarchy that, during the 18th century and most of the 19th century, retained their own arrangements for organising public authorities and legal regimes in other areas (known as jurisdictions) after the unification of public law, which occurred in Spain through the Nueva Planta Decrees. The regime applicable to economic agreements constitutes one of the "historic rights" recognised to these provincial areas. Having their own tax regime, with exclusive powers, allows these territories to establish, regulate and manage their own tax system in conjunction with the State. Particular characteristics include the fact that it is the general councils (provincial representation and participatory bodies) and not the Basque Parliament that regulate the

by the parties, and ultimately rejecting them, the Court carried out an extensive historical analysis of this institution. As will be shown below, an apparent technicality of constitutional procedural law, according to which the organic legislator decided to expand the jurisdiction of the Constitution, called for this type of argument from the Constitutional Court. This is due to the complexity of the Spanish system of sources, which is largely caused by the progressive overlaying of unresolved issues of the past.

3.2 *Psychological Aspects* (*Parliamentary Debates When Drafting the Constitution*)

For the Constitutional Court, the parliamentary work involved in drafting the Constitution itself also assists and informs interpretation. The Constitutional Court has asserted that parliamentary debates during the constituent process provide information that is relevant for consideration. CCJ 5/1981, LG 9, specifically mentioned the interpretative task cited in Article 27: "parliamentary debates are an important, though not decisive, element of interpretation". More recently, CCS 8/2013 of 17 January, LG 8, quoted CCJ 68/1996 of 21 May, LG 10, which stated that "parliamentary debates can assist in discerning the scope and meaning of the constitutional provisions and those that form part of the 'constitutionality block'". This idea is repeated in CCJ 15/2003 of 30 January: "Time and again we have highlighted the relevance of the parliamentary process of drafting the Constitution when interpreting it, because it offers a relevant but not decisive hermeneutical criterion". In the more recent CCJ 31/2018, the relevance and importance of interpretation according to international human rights law (criteria mentioned in Article 10.2 SC) is evident with regard to the right to education recognised by Article 27 of the Spanish Constitution. Debates within the Constituent Parliament indicate that the hermeneutic provision on interpretation in accordance with international human rights law was vested in the Senate, specifically in the debate concerning what would later become the definitive version of Article 27 of the Constitution and the rights embodied in it. The content of Article 27 is closely linked to the intention of the framers that the Constitution be interpreted in light of the international texts signed by the Kingdom of Spain (LG 4), among other criteria. The Court has recognised the particular relevance of this element when

tax system for each provincial territory according to rules with regulatory status, as they do not have any legislative authority (exclusive power of the legislative bodies in Spain, *Cortes Generales* or self-governing legislative assemblies). Therefore, they represent a "unique type of regulatory standard".

combined with the literal and systematic methods of interpretation (CCJ 113/2004, 12 July, LG 6).

The Constituent Parliament also helped the Court in reaching a decision in fierce debates, as in CCJ 198/2012 of 6 November, which dismissed an unconstitutionality objection brought against legislation to legalise same-sex marriage. In LG 8, the Court accused the appellants of embracing an originalist interpretation of Article 32 and stated that, during the constituent process, the institutional guarantee of marriage was understood to be applicable between people of the opposite sex. Same-sex marriage was not a concern for the framers of the Constitution; their concern was to distinguish between marriage and family, to establish equality between man and wife and to address the issues of separation and undissolved marriages. The Constituent Parliament did not mention whether same-sex marriage was included or excluded.

In other cases, the psychological aspect has enabled the Court to correct ordinary judicial rulings. For instance, in CCJ 171/1990 of 12 November, the Court observed how the ordinary courts required an element that was not required under constitutional law in order to grant protection to the right to information: its objective nature. The Court recalled how an attempt was made to incorporate the element into the draft constitution, but that it was intentionally omitted from the final text (LG 9).

The psychological argument has also been useful in addressing institutional issues relating to the Constitutional Court itself, including the status of Constitutional Court justices. The Court has used this argument to object to the recusal of a justice who was a member of a political party. In Decision 180/2013 of 17 September, the Court held that the right of Constitutional Court justices to be members of political parties "differentiates them from members of the judiciary, which was intentionally established by the Constituent Parliament, as is apparent from the parliamentary works on the drafting of the constitutional text, and which reflects the special nature of the Constitutional Court, the temporary limitation of the mandate of its members, the political nature of their appointments by the three branches of the State and the effect of the Court's own resolutions, which may correct the decisions of those three branches" (LG 3). This is only one example. In CCJ 49/2008 of 9 April, LG 13, concerning the drafting of Article 159.1, the Court held that there was a clear intention within debates in the Constituent Parliament to ensure the participation of the Senate, as a chamber providing territorial representation, in the elections of members of the Constitutional Court (electing a similar number of justices to the Congress of Deputies), thus guaranteeing a principle of territorial participation in the election process that the legislative body could configure in a variety of ways. The Court also referred to debates in the

Constituent Parliament in order to uphold the constitutionality of extending the mandate of the President and Vice President of the Court until the Court's next renewal, stating that, during "the entire constituent process, the partial renewal of the Court was intended to occur at the same time as the expiration of the President's term in office, so much so that some of the amendments that sought to reduce the time interval between the various renewals also reduced the President's mandate by the same period" (LG 20).

Parliamentary debates on the constitutional drafting process have been useful in resolving fundamental rights and institutional issues, while also addressing questions relating to sources of law. Declaration 1/1992 of 1 July recalled that the possibility of an international treaty creating an exception to the constitutional precept was rejected during the constituent process; the Court concluded that a constitutional amendment was needed to allow European citizens to stand in elections. (LG 4). Another example is CCJ 76/1983 of 5 August, in which the Court justified its decision to reject the requirement of an Organic Law to regulate the overall devolution process, as the Constituent Assemblies had twice rejected a proposal to that effect (LG 2). The Court explained: "While there are some specific and certain reservations requiring the enactment of an organic law in the Constitution in relation to self-government processes, there is no explicit constitutional provision that reserves regulatory authority over this process to organic laws in general, nor can it be inferred that this was the intention of the Constituent Parliament; on the contrary, it was expressly stated by the Constituent Parliament during parliamentary debates that an organic law should not be enacted to develop Title VIII of the Constitution, when both the Committee and the Plenary Session of the Congress of Deputies rejected the motion to this effect tabled by a sole parliamentary group. The fact that the constituent legislator opted to make specific stipulations concerning reservations requiring the enactment of an organic law, and not a generalised requirement, makes it impossible to extend these reservations to other matters, as they are of similar importance in self-government matters." The Court can be very punctilious when using this sort of argument, as it was in Judgment 137/1989 of 20 July. In order to justify the exclusive "ius contrahendi" of the State, and its right to submit to obligations through international treaties, the Court noted the defeat during the constituent process of a constitutional amendment proposed by the Basque Nationalist Party, which would have granted the autonomous communities competence to make international agreements, with the consent of the State. (LG 4). In the same way, CCJ 126/1987 of July 16 clarified that the principle of legal certainty established by Article 9.3 does not include the non-retroactivity of tax regulations. This position had been maintained under the draft constitution until the Presentation Report, although it was eliminated by the Ruling of the Committee on Constitutional Issues (a precedent followed in CCJ 173/1996 of 31 October, LG 3).

Constitutional Court judgments also contain the arguments of the different parties and the justices concerning the constituent process. CCJ 48/2003 of 12 March involved a dispute between representatives of the Basque Government and the Senate. The former stated that the constituent authorities had expressly rejected any power of the Constitutional Court to conduct constitutional review in relation to political parties, by comparing them to other associations. The representative for the Senate disagreed with this argument, and the Court did too, on the basis that the express rejection did not mean that ordinary courts could not exercise legal control over political parties (LG 7).

4 The Neutrality of the Constitutional Court (and Its Limits) When History Becomes a Contentious Subject

4.1 *The Court's Resistance to Calls to Prosecute the "Harsh Reality of Spain's History"*

Early on, the Constitutional Court had to confront the recent past in Spain and the effects of rules adopted by the political regimes in power before the 1978 Constitution was adopted. In CCJ 28/1982 of 26 May, LG2, the Court coined the expression "the harsh reality of history" to refer to the fact that the Civil War had caused a breakdown of the republican legal order in rebel-dominated territories. The judgment was the outcome of an appeal seeking constitutional protection in which the plaintiff, a republican militant, had requested reinstatement to the Army, as provided for under a Decree from 1936. The Court stated that the republican rules had become mere facts without any binding effect, and were sometimes even criminalised. Thus, it fell to the legislature, and not to the courts, to pursue outcomes intended to achieve historical justice.

The judgments of the Constitutional Court and the ordinary courts are also very relevant to the scope of the Spanish Constitution, and for clearing up aspects of our authoritarian past that have become unconstitutional (CCJ 4/1981 of 2 February). The Court's judgments even gave rise to one of the legal instruments that represented the transition to democracy. Article 7 of the Amnesty Law of 15 October 1977 included compensation for civil servants and military personnel who had been punished under Franco (judgments 27/1984 of 24 February; 122/1984 of 14 December, 76/1986 of 9 June; 147/1986 of 25 November; 116/1987 of 7 July; 190/1988 of 17 October; and 215/1989 of 21 December).

We can find the presence of recent Spanish history, particularly of the Civil War, within constitutional doctrine beyond the foundational period, along with appeals to the Constitutional Court as a judge of historical facts. CCJ 43/2004 of 23 March considered whether the right to honour had been violated by the content of a television news report. The documentary was dedicated to the political figure Manuel Carrasco i Formiguera, founder of the political party Unió Democrática de Catalunya, and a member of the Constituent Parliament during the Second Republic. The party was subjected to a Council of War in 1937 and its members were convicted for adhering to the republican cause. Trias Bertrán had participated as a witness in this Council of War. Bertrán's children considered that his honour had been questioned by the assertions made in the documentary that individuals had been executed as a result of the statements made by Bertrán and other witnesses. In the documentary, Bertrán was accused of lacking compassion for having provided his statement voluntarily during the hearing.

The Constitutional Court upheld the historian's scientific freedom. The documentary narrated historical facts of public relevance concerning recent Spanish history that no longer directly affected present generations. The piece was directed by a journalist-historian, with the involvement of recognised historians, within a framework of freedom of production and scientific creation (Art. 20.1 (b) SC). The Court reasoned that the nature of this work inevitably invites judgements and assessments of historical facts, or "the scientific reconstruction of the past that we call 'historiography', recognisable knowledge with regard to its suitability for certain methods, and not by virtue of such purity, otherwise unenforceable, which overlooks any ideological or moral perspective in exposing the past" (LG 4). According to the Court: "The ability for contemporaries to form our own vision of the world based on the evaluation of unrelated experience depends on the existence of a free and methodologically-grounded historical science" (LG 4). The Court explained that it was not for it to assess the success of the documentary in the narration and staging of the events, and even less to judge responsibilities in relation to historical events. Instead, the Court observed, what it can do is balance scientific freedom with the right to honour. According to the Court, scientific freedom receives protection even stronger than freedom of expression, and it cannot be offset by the right to honour of those who participated in historical events. The Court explained: "it is only in this way that historical research is possible, which is always, by definition, controversial and debatable, as it is erected around assertions and value judgements where the objective truth is impossible to achieve with full certainty; this consubstantial uncertainty of historical debate is the aspect that is most valuable, respectable and worthy of protection because of the essential role it plays in forming a historical conscience suited to the free dignity of citizens in a free and democratic society" (LG 5). The Court also insisted on the need for courts to refrain from performing the historians' task: "Historical discussion is open to participation and replication in its own context and by its characteristic means, but it cannot be open to a legal solution, whose truth is not, by definition, pursued and constructed according to the historical method" (LG 8).[46]

This desire for neutrality in matters relating to the regulation of the legacy of history, even with respect to the most harrowing moments in recent Spanish history, is also apparent in the line of judgments on the establishment of a special regime for returning documents seized during the Civil War and regulating Spanish historical archives (CCS 20/2013, 38/2013, 67/2013, 68/2013, 136/2013). The State transmitted a set of documentary collections kept in the General Archive of the Civil War to the Generalitat de Catalunya, to be returned to the original owners or their heirs under Law 21/2005 of 17 November. In the Autonomous Community of Castile and Leon, more than fifty senators and more than fifty deputies of the Partido Popular filed unconstitutionality objections. The Court dismissed all of them in judgment 20/2013. The Court clarified that the legislative body had not provided for the removal of documentary heritage (prohibited under Art. 149.1.28 SC), since the information was protected by a requirement that documents be digitally copied prior to their return and by a specific protection and accessibility protocol. The Court ruled that there was no institutional guarantee protecting the scope of State-owned archives, and that there had been no violation of the allocation of powers, the prohibition on arbitrariness (Art. 9.3 SC), or the conservation of the historical, cultural and artistic heritage of Spain (Art. 46 SC).

In fairness to the Constitutional Court, it upheld again the recognition of an ample margin for decision-making for the legislator, as it had done so for nearly forty years since it was established, and not because these specific

46 The relationship between history and journalism has been addressed on other occasions. Most recently, the CC had the opportunity to address for the first time the "right to be forgotten" in relation to digital archives, in particular on the indexing of personal data by search engines operated by free-access media. In its judgment 58/2018 of 4 June, the Court resolved a new conflict that had arisen between the right to information and personality rights. It concluded that this powerful tool for researching the past, involving the indexing of the names and surnames of people without any public projection for use by the search engine in a digital archive of free-access communications media on the internet, violates the right to honour and privacy (Art. 18.1 SC) and the protection of personal data (Art. 18.4 SC), thus incorporating the doctrine laid down by the European Court of Justice in the Google Spain SL case (LG 7 and 8).

cases concerned Spain's recent past. Evidence can be found in all of the judgments declining to rule unconstitutional the traditional discrimination against women in the inheritance of nobility titles (CCS 27/1982 and 126/1997 of 3 July). It was necessary to correct this disparity through the enactment of legislation in Law 33/2006 of 30 October on the equality of men and women in the order of succession to nobility titles (CCS 159/2014 of 6 October, and 168/2014 of 22 October).

4.2 *A Limit to the Neutrality of the Spanish Constitutional Court: Protecting Holocaust Victims*

The Constitutional Court provided a revolutionary and brave interpretation of the law by granting protection to Violeta Friedman in Judgment 214/1991. In 1985, the magazine *Tiempo* published a report that included statements by Léon Degrelle, a former head of the Waffen SS. In the report, Degrelle denied the Holocaust and the existence of the gas chambers, accused Jews of proclaiming themselves victims, and called for a new Führer. The plaintiff, Ms Friedman, had suffered directly during the Holocaust. A Jewish resident of Marguita, Transylvania, during the German occupation, Friedman had been forced to wear the Star of David and she was ultimately sent to Auschwitz. Friedman's entire family, except for her sister, were killed in the gas chambers the first night after they arrived in Auschwitz. Friedman's lawsuit, asserting claims based on the right to honour (Article 18.1), presented a conflict with the fundamental individual right to freedom of expression, under Article 20.1 (a) of the Constitution. The three courts that took up the case dismissed it (Court of First Instance, Provincial Court of Madrid and Supreme Court), adopting a highly personal interpretation of the right to honour under which Friedman lacked standing to sue because Degrelle's statements did not refer to her personally and she could not raise a claim for the Jewish people as a whole.

The Constitutional Court rejected that approach. First, on the issue of the vesting of the right to honour, the Court held that that the personal nature of the right did not preclude recognition that the right could also protect groups. The Court found that Violeta Friedman, as a Jewish victim of the Holocaust, had a legitimate interest in protecting the right to honour of the Jewish community in Spain (LG 3 and 4), an interest that applied with respect to attacks directed at an entire social group.

Traditionally, the Court has held that freedom of information (Art. 20 SC) prevails when addressing the right to honour (Art. 18.1 SC) in matters of general interest and the formation of free public opinion. In this case, however, it had to strike a balance between freedom of expression (Art. 20.1 SC) and ideological freedom (Art. 16.1 SC). The Court recalled that the requirement of truthfulness, which is necessary to constitutional protection for information, does not extend to opinions and assessments of historical facts, even when they are "wrong or ill-intentioned". The Court therefore recognised that Léon Degrelle's statements would be protected under freedom of expression as regards the questioning of Nazi acts. While denying historical evidence constitutes a reprehensible misrepresentation, the Court was unable to assess subjective opinions concerning historical facts. However, the Court reasoned, that same freedom of expression could not extend to offensive, racist, xenophobic or anti-Semitic remarks, such as those suffered by the plaintiff and other members of the Jewish community, because they have no place in a political order based on the higher value of equality (Art. 1.1 SC) as a right (Art. 14 SC), along with human dignity (Art. 10.1 SC) (LG 8).

In judgment 176/1995 of 11 December, the Constitutional Court again insisted on its duty to refrain from assessing the value of demonstrations of freedom of expression in ruling on an appeal seeking constitutional protection against judgments that convicted the director and editor of a publishing company for having published an editorial with anti-Semitic content in a comic book. The comic book, which included depictions of humiliation of prisoners in extermination camps, amounted to a targeted attack on the Jewish people, via a graphic medium aimed at children and adolescents. The Court determined that the comic book sought to convert "a historical tragedy into a burlesque farce," with hate speech, gratuitous cruelty towards victims and glorification of the executioners, all directed at children and lacking any informative or cultural value. The Court ruled that the publication was not afforded protection under freedom of expression in a democratic system (LG 5) and the appeal was therefore dismissed.

One further case, CCJ 235/2007 of 7 November, deserves mention. The Court of First Instance convicted Varela Geis, the owner of a library in Barcelona, of glorifying genocide and of crimes involving the exercise of fundamental rights and public freedoms guaranteed by the Constitution (mainly, freedom of expression) to provoke discrimination, racial hatred and violence against groups or associations on racist and anti-Semitic grounds. On appeal, the court had referred a question of unconstitutionality regarding Article 607.2, which prohibited the dissemination of ideas or doctrines that justify or deny crimes of genocide, or that attempt to rehabilitate regimes or institutions that defend them, as incompatible with the protection for freedom of expression in Article 20.1 of the Constitution.

The Constitutional Court invoked the precedent of judgment 214/1991 of 11 November, for the proposition that freedom of expression encompasses subjective opinions concerning historical facts, even if they are erroneous and untrue, as long as those opinions do not infringe the dignity of persons or undermine the peaceful coexistence of citizens. The Court thus determined that prosecution for denial of genocide is unconstitutional, given that the dissemination of assessments as to whether or not events have taken place amounts to a form of scientific freedom and is protected under freedom of expression (Art. 20.1 b SC). Criminalisation thus encroached on a fundamental right guaranteed by the Constitution: the simple transmission of ideas. However, the Court distinguished between the denial of genocide and its "justification", which, the Court reasoned, indirectly incites a provocation to genocide.

The Court's judgment was accompanied by four individual votes. Subsequently, in the same case, the European Court of Human Rights ruled against Spain, in Varela Geis v. Spain (case no. 61005/09) of 5 March 2013.[47] That ruling did not, however, concern freedom of thought and expression, but rather a procedural issue: one of the crimes for which Varela Geis was found responsible both in the first instance and on appeal – dissemination of ideas or doctrines that justify acts of genocide – was not included in the indictment.

5 Conclusions

Every year, references to history can be found in the judgments of the Spanish Constitutional Court. Paradoxically, while uses of historical references as an instrument for strengthening the interpretation of the Constitution is not questioned, the Court struggles to remain neutral when it invokes historical references to judge past events.

Traditionally, the principle of freedom of interpretation has prevailed in the Spanish legal order, and still does. The Spanish Constitutional Court has used the four methods of the classical canon of constitutional interpretation, construing these interpretative methods as principles rather than fixed rules; the Court has also used other interpretive methods, particularly systematic interpretation. In Spain, subjective theories that prioritise the will of the body that

47 The Plenary of the Constitutional Court (composed of its twelve judges) decided the case without reaching a unanimous decision. The judges pointed out that Article 607.2 CC should have been declared constitutional (Judge Roberto García-Calvo y Montiel). They also recalled that in Europe the central fundamental right is the dignity of the human being, so the Court must be careful in the use of legal categories that do not belong to the European tradition (Magistrate Jorge Rodríguez-Zapata Pérez). And, finally, they warned of the dangers of falling into a "naïve democracy" in an attempt to avoid militant democracy (Magistrate Ramón Rodríguez Arribas).

laid down the legal rule are avoided. However, the Constitutional Court also reverts to subjective theories, including the historical method. The Court has recognised the guiding value of the historical method while clarifying that the constitutionality of a rule does not depend on its history. Another common historical source for the Court is the parliamentary debates during the constituent process, "a relevant but not decisive hermeneutical criterion" in the Court's own words (CCJ 15/2003).

In all the cases concerning the Spanish Civil War, the legislative body has had leeway to make decisions on issues concerning the regulation of historical heritage, including in relation to one of the most important events in recent Spanish history. The Constitutional Court has insisted on its duty to refrain from making value judgments about historical facts in its rulings. However, the Court adopted a revolutionary and brave interpretation in granting Holocaust victim Violeta Friedman and the Jewish people protection against anti-Semitic attacks on the ground that freedom of speech does not extend to offensive, racist, xenophobic or anti-Semitic statements. Despite criticism, the Court has also upheld scientific freedom and the existence of free historic science as our best instrument "for creating our own point of view about the world based on an assessment of other people's experiences" (CCJ 43/2004).

Appendix: Cases

CCJ 2/1981, 30 January.
CCJ 4/1981, 2 February.
CCJ 5/1981, 13 February.
CCJ 11/1981, 8 April.
CCJ 27/1981, 20 July.
CCJ 37/1981, 16 November.
CCJ 1/1982, 28 January.
CCJ 12/1982, 31 March.
CCJ 9/1982, 10 March.
CCJ 18/1982, 4 May.
CCJ 19/1982, 5 May.
CCJ 27/1982, 24 May.
CCJ 28/1982, 26 May.
CCJ 41/1982, 2 July.
CCJ 42/1982, 5 July.
CCJ 45/1983, 25 May
CCJ 51/1982, 19 July.

CCJ 58/1982, 27 July.
CCJ 67/1982, 15 November.
CCJ 72/1982, 14 June.
CCJ 75/1985, 21 June.
CCJ 3/1983, 25 January.
CCJ 38/1983, 20 May.
CCJ 42/1983, 20 May.
CCJ 52/1983, 17 June.
CCJ 67/1983, 22 July.
CCJ 77/1983, 3 October.
CCJ 81/1983, 10 October.
CCJ 11/1984, 2 February.
CCJ 35/1984, 13 March.
CCJ 91/1984, 9 October.
CCJ 100/1984, 8 November.
CCJ 110/1984, 26 November.
CCJ 141/1986, 12 November.
CCJ 147/1986, 25 November.
CCJ 126/1987, 16 July.
CCJ 128/1987, 16 July.
CCJ 37/1988, 3 March.
CCJ 76/1988, 26 April.
CCJ 89/1989, 11 May.
CCJ 132/1989, 18 July.
CCJ 137/1989, 20 July.
CCJ 179/1989, 2 November.
CCJ 8/1990, 18 January.
CCJ 24/1990, 15 February.
CCJ 130/1991, 6 June.
CCJ 214/1991, 11 November.
CCJ 121/1992, 28 September.
CCJ 234/1992, 14 December.
CCJ 159/1993, 6 May.
CCJ 74/1994, 14 March.
CCJ 89/1994, 17 March.
CCJ 104/1994, 11 April.
CCJ 49/1995, 16 February.
CCJ 76/1995, 22 May.
CCJ 102/1995, 26 June.
CCJ 173/1996, 31 October.

CCJ 126/1997, 3 July.
CCJ 132/1998, 18 June.
CCJ 225/1998, 25 November.
CCJ 191/2000, 13 July.
CCJ 16/2003, 30 January.
CCJ 43/2004, 23 March.
CCJ 108/2004, 30 June.
CCJ 113/2004, 12 July.
CCJ 67/2005, 17 March.
CCJ 123/2012, 5 June.
CCJ 198/2012, 6 November.
CCJ 20/2013, 31 January.
CCJ 38/2013, 14 February.
CCJ 67/2013, 14 March.
CCJ 68/2013, 14 March.
CCJ 136/2013, 6 June.
CCJ 159/2014, October 6.
CCJ 44/2015, 5 March.
CCJ 118/2016, 23 June.
CCJ 177/2016, 20 October.
CCJ 58/2018, 4 June.
CCJ 124/2018, 10 April.

Bibliography

Ahumada Ruiz M, 'The Spanish Constitutional Court' in Jakab A, Dyevre A and Itzcovich G, *Comparative Constitutional Reasoning* (CUP 2017).

Aliste Santos, TJ, *La motivación de las resoluciones judiciales* (Marcial Pons, 2011).

Alonso García E, *La interpretación de la Constitución* (Centro de Estudios Constitucionales 1984).

Aragón Reyes M, 'La interpretación de la Constitución y el carácter objetivado del control jurisdiccional' (1986) 17 Revista Española de Derecho Constitucional 85.

Balaguer Callejón ML, *Interpretación de la Constitución y Ordenamiento Jurídico* (Tecnos 1997).

Bassols Coma, M, *El Tribunal de Garantías Constitucionales de la II República: La primera experiencia de la justicia constitucional en España* (Boletín Oficial del Estado, 2010).

Canosa Usera R, *Interpretación constitucional y fórmula política* (Centro de Estudios Constitucionales 1988).

Cascajo Castro JL, 'La figura del voto particular en la jurisdicción constitucional española' (1986) 17 Revista Española de Derecho Constitucional 171.

Castro y Bravo F, 'Naturaleza de las reglas para la interpretación de la Ley (Consideraciones en torno al artículo 3º, apartado 1, del Código Civil)' (1978) Anuario de Derecho Civil 809, 829–830.

Cappelletti M, 'Judicial Review in Comparative perspective' (1970) 58 California Law Review 1017.

Díaz Revorio FJ, *Valores superiores e interpretación constitucional* (Centro de Estudios Políticos y Constitucionales 1997).

Díez-Picazo LM, 'Notas sobre el blindaje de las normas forales fiscales' (2010) 3 InDret, Revista para el análisis del Derecho.

Ezquiaga Ganuzas FJ, *La argumentación en la justicia constitucional española* (Instituto Vasco de Administración Pública 1987).

Ferreres Comella V, *The Constitution of Spain: A Contextual Analysis* (Hart, 2013).

Ferreres Comella V, 'The Spanish Constitutional Court: Time for Reforms', in Andrew Harding (ed.), *Constitutional Courts: A Comparative Study* (JCL Studies in Comparative Law, Wildy, Simmonds & Hill Publishing 2010).

Ferreres Comella V, *Una defensa del modelo europeo de control de constitucionalidad* (Marcial Pons, 2009).

Ferreres Comella V, 'The European Model of Constitutional Review of Legislation: Toward Decentralization?' (2004) 2:3 International Journal of Constitutional Law 461.

García Pelayo M, 'Constitución y Derecho constitucional. Evolución y crisis de ambos conceptos' (1948) 37–38 Revista de estudios políticos 53.

Garrorena Morales, Á, 'La sentencia constitucional' (1981) 11 Revista de Derecho Político 7.

Haberle P, 'Métodos y principios de la interpretación constitucional. Un catálogo de problemas' (2010) 13 Revista de derecho constitucional europeo 379.

Hesse K, *Escritos de Derecho Constitucional* (Centro de Estudios Constitucionales 1983).

Igartua Salaverría J, *La motivación de las sentencias, imperativo constitucional* (Centro de Estudios Políticos y Constitucionales 2003).

Jiménez Alemán AA, 'The Spanish Constitutional Court and Foreign and Comparative Law: Theory and Practice of a Marriage of Convenience', in Giuseppe Franco Ferrari (ed.), *Judicial Cosmopolitanism. The Use of Foreign Law in Contemporary Constitutional Systems* (Brill 2019).

Jiménez Alemán AA, '¿De poder neutro a poder activo? Sobre el eficaz pero inconveniente refuerzo de los poderes de ejecución del Tribunal Constitucional' (2019) 23(2) Anuario Iberoamericano de Justicia Constitucional 401.

Jiménez Campo J, 'Interpretación Constitucional' in *Enciclopedia Jurídica Básica* (Civitas, 1995), 3685–3690.

Kelsen H, *The Law of the United Nations. A critical analysis of its fundamentals problems. With a supplement* (The Lawbook Exchange 2000).

Moreno SF, "Interpretación jurídica" in *Enciclopedia Jurídica Básica* (Civitas, 1995) 3700–3713.

Moreno JJ, La indeterminación del Derecho y la interpretación de la Constitución (Centro de Estudios Constitucionales, 1997).

Murillo de la Cueva PL, 'Artículo 120' in Pablo Pérez Tremps and Alejandro Sáiz Arnáiz (eds.), *Comentario a la Constitución Española. 40 aniversario (1978–2018). Libro-homenaje a Luis López Guerra* (Tirant lo Blanch 2018), 1701–1702.

Prieto Sanchís, L, 'Notas sobre la interpretación constitucional' (1991) 9 Revista del Centro de Estudios Constitucionales 175, 177.

Requena López T, *Sobre la función, los medios y los límites de la interpretación de la Constitución* (Comares, 2001).

Rubio Llorente F, 'Seis tesis sobre la jurisdicción constitucional en Europa' (1992) 35 Revista Española de Derecho Constitucional 9.

Rubio Llorente F, 'La jurisdicción constitucional como forma de creación de Derecho' (1988) 22 Revista Española de Derecho Constitucional 9–52.

Terol Becerra MJ, 'Sobre la interpretación de la Constitución y de la Ley en España (1812–1978)' (1993) 15 Revista del Centro de Estudios Constitucionales 183.

Wolfe C, *La transformación de la interpretación constitucional* (Civitas 1986).

Wrobleski J, *Constitución y teoría general de la interpretación jurídica* (Civitas 1985).

Zagrebelsky, G, *Historia y constitución* (Traducción y prólogo de Migeul Carbonell) (Trotta, 2005).

CHAPTER 7

Competing Narratives

The Use of Historical Arguments in Constitutional Interpretation in Brazil

Ana Beatriz Robalinho

1 Introduction

When Courts engage in constitutional history debates, the underlying issues are usually far broader than the subject matter at hand. These exercises are useful because general and broad conceptions concerning constitutional history can be turned into valuable tools in the process of building a *constitutional identity*.[1] Gary Jacobsohn has described constitutional identity as "*a mix of aspirations and commitments expressive of a nation's past*",[2] underlining the inescapable connection between constitutional identity and national history.

Given competing historical narratives regarding the foundations of the constitution, the Brazilian constitutional system is plagued by a lack of identity. While a variety of factors can be raised to explain the difficulty in forging constitutional self-understanding, there is a strong relationship between indeterminacy and the disputed history of Brazil's transition to democracy. Was it a transaction negotiated amongst elites, or did it mark a revolutionary new beginning brought about by popular mobilisation and struggle? Since there is little historical research to support either claim, neither is sufficiently persuasive to take on the status of a prevailing professional narrative. Similarly, neither narrative can be fully discredited on the grounds that it is inconsistent with historical facts. The consequences of this pervasive duality on the consolidation of the Brazilian constitutional system are profound, although rarely examined.

This dispute has been made more complex by the fact that none of the players expected to resolve it have joined the debate. Following Jacobson's argument on constitutional identity being acquired "through experience" and

1 Mark Tushnet describes constitutional identity as the question of who "the people" are who govern themselves in modern constitutionalist systems. Mark Tushnet, 'How Do Constitutions Constitute Constitutional Identity?' (2010) 8 International Journal of Constitutional Law 671, 672.

2 Gary Jeffrey Jacobsohn, 'Constitutional Identity' (2006) 68 The Review of Politics 361, 361.

 | DOI:10.1163/9789004523739_009

dialogue between members of a society, expected participants are likely to be the voices charged with commenting, studying, interpreting and applying the constitution, including academia and the courts.[3] On one hand, constitutional scholars may defend the adoption of one or another founding narrative for a myriad of reasons, but none seem eager to engage in analysis of the historical merits of either narrative, or to debate with one another. This is attributed, at least in part, to a generally negative attitude towards constitutional history among contemporary constitutional scholars in Brazil. Deeming previous constitutional experiences in the country elitist and ineffectual, they sought to deny them by refusing to study or acknowledge them. This ban on history affected, in turn, the study of the current constitutional experience.[4]

On the other hand, the Supreme Court, which might have been expected to take a stance in the conflict, has instead alternated – seemingly at random – between adopting one narrative or the other without proper justification or historical support. The reasons for the Court's behaviour are certainly in part due to the way arguments are frame before it. But as it will be explored, that alone does not, nor should it, justify the confusion and, at times, the silence.

In this chapter, I explore this stance by analysing precedents in which the Supreme Court has attempted to deal with the legacy of the constitutional system's founding. Part 1 will introduce the two prevailing narratives concerning the nature of the Brazilian transition to democracy. Part 2 will explore precedents in which the Supreme Court has dealt with the legacy of the founding of the constitutional system. Part 3 will present a theoretical framework for analysing the contradicting narratives. Finally, Part 4 will suggest what stance the Supreme Court should adopt in the conflict. My goal is to assist in easing

3 'I argue ... that a constitution acquires an identity through experience, that its identity neither exists as a discrete object of invention nor as a heavily encrusted essence embedded in a society's culture, requiring only to be discovered. Identity emerges dialogically and represents a mix of political aspirations and commitments that is expressive of a nation's past, as well as the determination of those within the society who seek, in some ways, to transcend that past. It is changeable but resistant to its own destruction, and it may manifest itself differently in different settings (...)' Ibid., 396.

4 Christian Lynch remarked that 'Authors committed to changing the legal mentality in the 1980s and 1990s did not limit themselves to pointing out the decadence that constitutionalism would have reached during the authoritarian regime; condemned, en bloc, the entire Brazilian constitutional history. Against a supposed previous constitutionalist tradition, reputed to be elitist or ineffective, the authors of the new Brazilian constitutionalism emphasized the need to break with the past in order to establish, not a new, but a true regime of constitutionality'. Christian Edward Cyril Lynch and José Vicente Santos de Mendonça, 'Por uma história constitucional brasileira: uma crítica pontual à doutrina da efetividade' (2017) 8 Revista Direito e Práxis 974.

the tension between narratives and to suggest how Brazil might come to terms with the paradoxical features of its 1988 Constitution and finally build an identity that can assist in the process of consolidating its constitutional system.

This analysis will focus on the *Supremo Tribunal Federal* (STF), Brazil's Supreme Court, as a primary interpreter of constitutional meaning. First, I shall offer a diagnosis: the Brazilian Supreme Court has shown itself to be unwilling and unable to resolve the tensions between the existing foundational narratives that abound within Brazilian constitutional theory and practice. I argue that this inability has undermined the legitimacy of the Court's decisions and its reputation as an institutional player charged with furthering the consolidation of the constitutional system. Ultimately, Brazil will need to reset the debate on constitutional narrative and identity. To do so, the Supreme Court will have to take a stance regarding the tension between existing constitutional narratives as a way of both moving the debate within civil society forward while performing the expected task of constitutional consolidation. In-depth historical analysis seems to be the only way to assess the merits of each opposing narrative of the founding of the constitutional system, and scholars and lawyers must carry out this analysis first, in the hope that it may be later adopted by the Court.

2 Dual Narratives of the Foundation of the Brazilian Constitution

> The compromise solution, the 'top-to-bottom' transition orchestrated by political elites presents itself as a constitutive element of our identity, as an authentic cultural conclusion. The tradition is worth more than the Constitution itself, it conditions and legitimises the constitutional experience.[5]
>
> The [legitimacy basis] rested on the will, present in Brazilian society, and evidenced in movements such as 'Diretas Já', to break with the authoritarian past and establish the Brazilian State and legal order on more democratic ground. It was an authentic manifestation of popular will … in the mid 1980s, the country was living a typical 'constitutional moment', illustrated by the political vibrancy and the genuine popular

5 Leonardo Augusto de Andrade Barbosa, *História Constitucional Brasileira: Mudança Constitucional, Autoritarismo e Democracia No Brasil Pós-1964* (Biblioteca Digital da Câmara dos Deputados 2012) 33.

> mobilisation towards a 'new beginning'. That was the true source of the Constituent Assembly's legitimacy (…).[6]

On 5 October 2018, Brazil celebrated the thirtieth anniversary of the promulgation of its Constitution, a landmark event in what has been the longest period of democratic stability in its history. These three decades of constitutional democracy followed a period of emergence from military dictatorship through a paradoxical process featuring unprecedented popular participation and many negotiations with elites in order to control the transition.[7] The record rates of popular mobilisation and democratic participation–both in the *Diretas Já* movement[8] and in the Constituent Assembly[9]–and the new Constitution's

6 Daniel Sarmento, '21 Anos Da Constituição de 1988: A Assembleia Constituinte de 1987/1988 e a Experiência Constitucional Brasileira Sob a Carta de 1988' (2009) 29 Dados 11–12 <http://www.integrawebsites.com.br/versao_1/arquivos/22be85992a1067f5906835bbf44c6405.pdf> accessed 9 November 2015.

7 Gargarella categorised this state of affairs as that of a 'Mixed Constitution', combining at least relative control by the regime over the transition and a renewed democratic project and some mobilisation against authoritarianism. Roberto Gargarella, *Latin American Constitutionalism,1810–2010: The Engine Room of the Constitution* (New Oxford University Press, USA 2013) 157–162.

8 The first attempts to overthrow the existing authoritarian regime started when, following the authorisation of legal opposition parties, the 1982 parliamentary elections provided the opposition with the opportunity to organise itself within existing institutions. Political leaders then articulated a movement for direct elections of the President around a proposed amendment to the authoritarian Constitution of 1967 abolishing the electoral college. Political negotiations surrounding the endorsement of the amendment began months before any degree of mobilised popular involvement took place, although the amendment gradually won over popular support: the famous *Diretas Já* demonstration saw millions take to the streets. However, the besieged military government was able to resist popular pressure and manipulated congress into rejecting the amendment by a slim margin. Domingos Leonelli and Dante De Oliveira, *Diretas Já: 15 Meses que Abalaram a Ditadura* (Record 2004) 10-25-70.

9 The Constituent Assembly elected in 1986 was officially dominated by the main opposition party – which held 52% of the seats. However, the real political situation of the democratically elected body was far more complex. A game of musical chairs before the election had severely distorted the ideological spectrum of the 'opposition', with large numbers of military government supporters switching to the new majoritarian party before the election. General political analysis of the Assembly's composition reveals that a majority of its members held conservative and elitist views, detached from the liberal views of the general public. A minority of progressive constituents, however, was successful in partially neutralising the effects of the conservative centre by emphasizing the work of smaller committees in the drafting of the Constitution, rather than the plenary Assembly. Popular participation was also increased through the smaller committees, which could hold public hearings and receive 'suggestions' sponsored by civil society. Over 9,000 suggestions for the drafting of specific constitutional provisions were presented to the Assembly, resulting in the addition of 122 popular amendments to the body of the

extensive focus on fundamental rights, social justice and democratic institutions, all suggest an extraordinary, and unparalleled, revolutionary moment. However, there are also indications that the "slow and gradual" transition envisioned by the outgoing military government, which had ruled the country for two decades, was also successful.[10] The autocratic regime had orchestrated its own demise on this basis, envisioning a particular kind of political development that was modest and undisruptive and would return power to the *right* civilian hands. This approach was successful both in stifling popular demands for direct presidential elections in 1984 and also in interfering with the work of the Constituent Assembly.[11]

These paradoxical qualities of the Brazilian process of democratisation resulted in the emergence of conflicting narratives concerning the history of the Constitution's adoption. This process is often depicted both as a revolutionary break with Brazil's colonial and dictatorial past, as well as a negotiated transaction between political elites resulting in the continuity of the existing legal order. Unsurprisingly, these disputes over the most basic meaning of the adoption of the Brazilian Constitution have impaired the process of building a constitutional identity for post-1988 Brazil. Insofar as constitution-making "requires a break with the polity's prevailing conceptions of collective identity",[12] the process, which is fundamental in the consolidation of the

text. Through these and other democracy-enhancing mechanisms, a staggering 12 million people are estimated to have participated in the process of constitution-making in Brazil between 1987 and 1988 – roughly 10% of the population. On this subject see Carlos Michiles, *Cidadão Constituinte: A Saga Das Emendas Populares* (Paz e Terra 1989).

10 On the political struggles that resulted in the military government's decision to launch the process for a return to civilian power, see Elio Gaspari, *O Sacerdote e O Feiticeiro: A Ditadura Encurralada* (Intrinseca 2014).

11 The military government sought to "minimise the damage" caused by the progressive minority by exerting pressure at strategic points in the debate within the Assembly, most famously by forcing through the approval of a presidential system of government, even though a clear majority favoured a parliamentary system. For an analysis on the full extent of this interference, see Juan J. Linz and Alfred Stepan, Problems of Democratic Transition and Consolidation: Southern Europe, South America, and Post-Communist Europe (Johns Hopkins University Press 1996) 170; For an exploration of this narrative, see also Cristiano Paixão, 'Direito, Política, Autoritarismo e Democracia No Brasil: Da Revolução de 30 à Promulgação Da Constituição Da República de 1988' [2011] Araucaria: Revista Iberoamericana de filosofía, política y humanidades 146.

12 Michel Rosenfeld, 'Constitutional Identity' [2012] The Oxford Handbook of Comparative Constitutional Law 203 <http://www.oxfordhandbooks.com/view/10.1093/oxfordhb/9780199578610.001.0001/oxfordhb-9780199578610-e-37> accessed 16 March 2019.

constitutional system, has been profoundly affected by the historical understanding of the foundational moment of the new Constitution.[13]

The lack of any self-understood constitutional identity has affected most aspects of Brazil's thirty-year struggle with democratic and constitutional consolidation; it has had a major impact on narratives regarding the Constitution's foundation that are entrenched into society, as well as how these narratives are used in constitutional interpretation. Due to the strategic role played by the courts in building a constitutional identity, the Brazilian Supreme Court offers a particularly illuminating example of the pernicious effects of this problem. Examining how the Court has absorbed and dealt with the new constitutional regime since 1988 can offer a powerful diagnostic tool to identify not only the struggles of Brazilian constitutionalism with its own identity, but also the larger role that the courts are expected to play when faced with such struggles.

3 The Supreme Court as an Interpreter of Constitutional Identity

3.1 *Historical Interpretation in the Early Days of the New Republic*

In the days following the democratic transition, the approach of the Supreme Court was rooted in its notoriously obstructionist stance to the adoption of the Constitution.[14] The justices, who had been appointed by the military but were set to retain their positions under the new regime, openly advocated against any increase in the Court's powers under the new Constitution, which could be used to consolidate the new constitutional order. Additionally, the Court willingly cooperated with the outgoing military government in an attempt to thwart the Assembly's exercise of unrestrained constituent power.

13 Reva Siegel notes that, '[b]y telling stories about a common past, a group can constitute itself as a group, a collective subject with certain experiences, expectations, entitlements, obligations, and commitments. The stories that help forge group identity also supply structures of ordinary understanding, frameworks within which members of a society interpret experience and make positive and normative judgments concerning it'. Reva B Siegel, 'Collective Memory and the Nineteenth Amendment: Reasoning about "the Woman Question" in the Discourse of Sex Discrimination', *History, Memory, and the Law* (University of Michigan Press 2002), 161.

14 Koerner and Freitas relied both on records of the Assembly's internal debates and on declarations by the justices of the Supreme Court that appeared in the country's most important newspapers in the period in order to describe the justices' own agenda and the way the government used the Court as leverage against the progressive minority within the Assembly. See Andrei Koerner and Lígia Barros de Freitas, 'O Supremo Na Constituinte E a Constituinte No Supremo' [2013] Lua Nova: Revista de Cultura e Política 141.

Specifically, the Court acted as a fundamental arbiter in the dispute between the President and the Assembly regarding the length of presidential terms. President José Sarney was to serve a six-year term. The Assembly wanted to reduce the term to four years. When it became clear that a majority was forming in favour of the four-year option, the President threatened the Assembly with Court action, maintaining it did not have the authority to shorten the length of his term in office. In the end, the Court did not issue any decision concerning this matter; instead, a compromise was reached to allow President Sarney to remain in office for five years, while future presidents would serve four-year terms. However, the possibility of referral to the Supreme Court to reverse or reform particular decisions made by the Assembly remained a serious threat in the government's arsenal. This threat was even more significant because the Court's members were more sympathetic to the government than to the Assembly, even though the justices chose to maintain a low profile on issues that might still be referred to them for judgment.[15]

The Court was more vocal concerning the issue of the expansion of its own powers. Justices were categorically opposed to the provision for direct applications to the Court, which would transform the Court into a proper constitutional court, alongside its appellate duties, which would charge it with responsibility for answering hard constitutional questions early on in the new regime. Their outspokenness on the subject was even more alarming as they would be the people charged with performing the Court's new duties.[16]

Much has been written about the consequences of asking justices appointed under the old regime to enforce the new regime's policies.[17] This paradox is further enhanced by the fact that the justices played such a vocal and antagonistic part in the transition to the new regime. It is therefore unsurprising that, when first asked to turn the history of the democratic transition into a constitutional argument, a majority on the Court favoured the path of legal continuity. Two cases were especially relevant during these early days of judicial review under the 1988 Constitution. Both concerned the part played by the Court in consolidating the new constitutional regime by using the innovative tools provided in the Constitution. Each was brought before the Court by individuals or groups that had hoped to see the consolidation of the ground-breaking promises

15 Ibid.., 153–156.

16 Koerner and Freitas (n 14).

17 For a full study on the topic using the STF as an example, see Diego Werneck Arguelhes, 'Poder Não é Querer: Preferências Restritivas e Redesenho Institucional No Supremo Tribunal Federal Pós-Democratização' (2014) 25 Universitas Jus <http://www.publicacoes.uniceub.br/index.php/jus/article/view/2885> accessed 10 March 2019.

written into the new constitutional text. In these cases, however, the Court responded by rejecting the narrative of a new beginning and reaffirming that of continuity.

In Direct Challenge of Unconstitutionality (*Ação Direta de Inconstitucionalidade*, or ADI) 2, referred to the Court only days after the enactment of the 1988 Constitution, the constitutional question at stake was fundamental for the consolidation of the new regime: whether the STF could strike down as unconstitutional any laws or statutes enacted before the promulgation of the Constitution that were found to be incompatible with it. To the disappointment of almost all sides of the political spectrum, the Court answered that it was not. The majority opinion asserted that analysing the compatibility of a law or statue enacted prior to the new Constitution with the Constitution itself was *not* a question of constitutionality. As such, it could not be answered through a direct constitutional challenge, but must go through the normal process in the lower courts and reach the Supreme Court through the appeals process.

There is considerable documentation concerning how this decision constituted a departure from the intentions of the Constituent Assembly. Even in the period preceding the Constituent Assembly, especially from the *Diretas Já* campaign in 1984 until the Assembly's inauguration in 1987, there was relative consensus amongst various political groups that judicial powers should be increased.[18] The focus of left and right-wing ideological groups was different, with the right being more active in advocating for expanding the Supreme Court's powers during the initial stages of debates,[19] while the left focused on the establishment of a parliamentary system and the expansion of congressional power. At the beginning of the Assembly's deliberations, leftist progressives pushed for the creation of a Constitutional Court according to the German model, with exclusive jurisdiction to rule on questions of constitutionality and limited terms for justices. It would thus completely transform the existing structure of the Court, which is tailored in most aspects to resemble the US Supreme Court.[20] Meanwhile, the conservative right advocated the maintenance of the existing model of an appellate court that also ruled on constitutional questions.[21] Both models, however, entailed the expansion of

18 Koerner and Freitas (n 14), 144.

19 Manoel Gonçalves Ferreira Filho, 'O Estado de Direito, o Judiciário e a Nova Constituição' (1985) 160 Revista de Direito Administrativo 61, 70–72.

20 Dalmo de Abreu Dallari, *Constituição e Constituinte* (Saraiva 1984).

21 Manoel Gonçalves Ferreira Filho, 'Nova Perspectiva Do Processo Constitucional' [1985] Revista Brasileira de Estudos Políticos 129.

so-called "direct challenges," or allowing the Court to examine constitutional questions directly.[22] The issue of the expansion of direct access to the Court was even the subject of one of the 122 "popular amendments" channelled into the Assembly through civil society.[23] Project A, which was the final result of the first phase of the work of the Assembly–largely dominated by its progressive minority[24]–provided for a Supreme Court that retained the powers and structure of the existing STF but with significantly enhanced scope for "direct" judicial review.[25] While maintaining the existing structure represented a victory for the conservative right, the expansion of direct challenges reflected a point of consensus between the two political groups.

The second phase of the Assembly was dominated by the uneasy 'Centrão' coalition,[26] which targeted many of the most progressive aspects of Project A and changed its very essence by reverting to a presidential system. Nonetheless, it barely touched on the provisions concerning the Supreme Court except to expand a little further the provision for direct challenges.[27] Once the Constitution had been enacted, conservative scholars turned their critical eyes on the Court's newly-expanded powers, arguing that they would both make the already-packed docket unmanageable and that the function

22 Koerner and Freitas (n 14), 165–166.

23 Ibid., 167; On the issue of the 'popular amendments' and their repercussions, see Michiles (n 7). It has been documented that over 9,000 'suggestions' for the drafting of specific constitutional provisions were presented in the Constituent Assembly, resulting in the addition of 122 popular amendments to the body of the text.

24 A series of interviews informed the analysis of how and why a progressive minority was able to exert dominance during the initial phase of the Assembly through an intricate series of political negotiations. They were conducted in 2013 in Brasilia and São Paulo by members of a study group funded by the Brazilian Institute of Public Law (IDP) in Brasilia, in which I took part. Interviewees included Nelson Jobim, Fernando Henrique Cardoso, and Jose Serra (Member of the Constituent Assembly and Senator of the Republic). The interviews focused on their recollections of the constituent process, as well as their reflections on its effects on the 25th anniversary of the Constitution's adoption. The author has a transcript of the interviews, which is currently being edited into a book.

25 The final version of Project A and all accompanying debates in the systematisation committee can be found at 'Anais Da Constituinte: Comissão de Sistematização' <https://www.senado.leg.br/publicacoes/anais/constituinte/sistema.pdf> accessed 11 March 2019.

26 On the formation and characteristics of 'Centrão', see Daniel Marcelino, Sérgio Braga and Luiz Domingos Costa, 'Parlamentares Na Constituinte de 1987/88: Uma Contribuição À Solução Do "enigma Do Centrão"' (2010) 18 Revista Política Hoje <http://www.revista.ufpe.br/politicahoje/index.php/politica/article/view/19> accessed 11 March 2019.

27 Koerner and Freitas (n 14) 171.; The final version of the text, approved by the plenary Assembly, and all accompanying debates can be found at 'Anais Da Constituinte: Plenário' <https://www.senado.leg.br/publicacoes/anais/constituinte/atas.pdf> accessed 11 March 2019.

now expected of the Court–reviewing previous legislation for compatibility with the new constitutional regime–would threaten the stability and continuity of the legal order. At the same time, progressives celebrated the Court's new status and had extremely high expectations concerning its ability to adapt the existing body of law to the new constitutional order. Both sides fully expected the Court to make use of its new-found powers.[28]

However, the Court itself had other ideas. Its majority in ADI 2 turned to pre-constitutional precedents and legal traditions to justify the restriction of its own ability to enforce constitutional supremacy, all the while sustaining a narrative of legal continuity during the democratic transition. While the preliminary injunction was issued two weeks after the Constitution's adoption, the actual proceedings did not take place until early 1992. By then, the 11-justice panel still included five judges who had been appointed by the military. The two dissenting justices had been appointed after democratisation. The majority/minority dynamic concerning the history of the transition to the new constitutional regime followed a pattern that would become familiar in Supreme Court debates. The majority's arguments, sustaining long-standing judicial precedent, implied that the Court's precedents under previous constitutions should stand because the need for an undisrupted transition to the new regime did not justify reviewing them. By focusing on how the Court had dealt with the issue of incompatibility with the Constitution of laws enacted before it was adopted, the majority purposely ignored the profound change that the Constituent Assembly had hoped to achieve by significantly expanding the scope for direct constitutional challenges.

The minority's votes raised these objections. Justices Sepúlveda Pertence and Marco Aurélio Mello argued that the new Constitution had reinforced the STF's role as its guardian and enforcer and, therefore, its provisions should be interpreted accordingly. They also argued that the Constituent Assembly's clear and self-declared intentions of making the Supreme Court responsible for reviewing compatibility between legislation enacted under the previous regime and the new regime's constitutional paradigm should guide their analysis. However, the 9–2 ruling stood and played its part in considerably diminishing the Supreme Court's contribution to consolidating the new constitutional regime during its initial stages.

28 See Fabiana Luci de Oliveira, 'O Supremo Tribunal Federal No Processo de Transição Democrática: Uma Análise de Conteúdo Dos Jornais Folha de S. Paulo E O Estado de S. Paulo' [2004] Revista de Sociologia e Política 109–110 The study analyses publications by two of Brazil's most influential newspapers on the subject of the Supreme Court during and after the constitution-making process; Koerner and Freitas (n 14) 175.

An earlier precedent provided a similar indication of the Court's intentions in restricting the new and sweeping powers it had been granted by the Constituent Assembly. In 1989, the STF analysed one of the first attempts to use a brand-new constitutional tool: a writ of injunction (*Mandado de Injunção*, or MI) designed to seek a judicial remedy where the absence of regulatory legislation impaired the exercise of constitutional rights and freedoms. Analysis of the National Constituent Assembly debates shows that it intended to empower the Court to enforce fundamental rights by adopting provisional regulations in the absence of formal laws that fulfilled the constitutional mandate.

The Court's majority in MI 107 once again relied on precedent and judicial practices established under previous constitutions in order to find that the judiciary did not have the power to issue provisional regulations. It held that such acts would violate the separation of powers; therefore, a writ of injunction would have no practical effect other than to acknowledge Congress' obligation to issue the regulatory legislation. However, there would be no tools to enforce such a ruling. The minority once again argued that the express will of the Assembly should override previous constitutional interpretations and precedents; it reinforced the new Constitution's self-declared intentions to depart from a long-standing, inefficient tradition of passing provisions on fundamental rights, and argued that the Assembly's intentions should constitute an authoritative reading of the Constitution. However, the majority ruling set MI 107 amongst the precedents that asserted the Court's refusal to embrace its new constitutional status.

It is important to note that these were still the early days of the Republic. Military-appointed justices dominated the Court, and the legal profession as a whole was only just beginning to grasp the Constitution's sweeping new provisions and the tools provided to enforce them. The Court would eventually come round to embracing its new powers: during the second decade of the new regime, as old justices retired and new appointments were made, the STF gradually took on a more active role in consolidating the new Constitution's provisions. However, its approach to the history of the founding of the constitutional system remained distinctively problematic.

3.2 *New Encounters with History in the Face of Democratic Consolidation*

The Constitution was in effect for two decades before the Supreme Court was finally forced to engage directly with the history of the democratic transition. This was due to its restrictive precedents and political authorities' insecurities about the new Constitution's sweeping provisions. Removing all previously enacted legislation from the scope of ADIs meant that the Court was momentarily excused from examining the most controversial surviving legislation from the military regime through direct challenges; regular cases could take decades to reach the Court's overcrowded docket, or might never make it at all.

The situation only began to change in 1999 as politics began to evolve in Brazil. President Fernando Henrique Cardoso was finishing his somewhat-controversial second term, in which his over-use of presidential powers decreased rapidly. The 2002 elections would mark the rise of a profoundly different ideological system with the victory of the Workers' Party. The abrupt change in the governing political ideology, combined with difficulties in securing congressional majorities, pushed political debates to the judiciary. Andrei Koerner clarifies that:

> The presidential elections of 2002 resulted in partisan realignment, with the alteration of the coalition in the government. The new government was in opposition to the existing government regime and its proposal was to modify it. It had weak support in Congress, the presence of elites committed to the defeated coalition in the State and ... risks of invasion of its prerogatives by opponents. Given its low capacity to alter the legal structure of the existing governmental regime through Congress, the new government invested in other fronts. To overcome its difficulties and reinforce support, the Lula government encouraged changes through the judicial process. With the support of progressive lawyers and bodies from the legal profession, it sought to approach legal elites and promoted the formation of consensus, symbolised by the two republican pacts for the reform of the judiciary.[29]

The shift in the Court's position was completed when, under the influence of progressive jurists, legislatures finally enacted provisions to regulate the use of yet another new kind of direct challenge created by the Constitution. The Allegation concerning a Breach of a Fundamental Precept (*Arguição de Descumprimento de Preceito Fundamental*, or ADPF) was designed so that legislation enacted before the 1988 Constitution came into force could be challenged before the Supreme Court through a direct application. This led to the Court's two leading precedents regarding the new Constitution's assimilation

29 Andrei Koerner, 'Ativismo Judicial?: Jurisprudência Constitucional e Política No STF Pós-88' [2013] Novos estudos CEBRAP 69, 82, free translation.

of the old regime resulting from legislation enacted under the military regime, which was challenged through ADPFs.

ADPF 130 and ADPF 153 are leading precedents for several reasons. First of all, they challenged two of the most controversial pieces of legislation enacted during the military dictatorship: the 1967 Press Law imposing provisions that severely restricted freedom of the press and endorsed censorship, and the 1979 Amnesty Law pardoning state officials for crimes committed during the period of military rule. They are also of major significance in terms of their results. These cases are respectively the most celebrated and criticised precedents in the history of the STF. In both cases, historical arguments were crucial to the Court's debates. In fact, these were the cases in which the Court engaged most closely with the history and the legacy of the foundation of the constitutional system. Although the cases were decided within a year of each other (April 2009 and April 2010, respectively), the same panel of 11 justices formed different majorities to arrive at radically different conclusions on the significance of the history of the adoption of the Brazilian Constitution and its consequences for constitutional interpretation. The fact that the same justices produced the opinions in both cases makes them particularly astounding when read together.

ADPF 130, on the compatibility of the Press Law of 1967 with the 1988 Constitution, was decided on 30 April 2009. No military-appointed justices remained on the Court, and a remarkable majority of eight justices had been appointed by President Luiz Inácio Lula da Silva's Workers' Party (PT). The majority opinion, written by Justice Ayres Britto, held that the Press Law was entirely incompatible with the 1988 Constitution due to the historical lessons of the democratic transition. He argued, as did most of the concurrent opinions, that the 1987–1988 Constituent Assembly had drafted a constitutional document designed to refute and overcome the previous regime.[30] The years of military rule had been particularly hard on freedom of speech, and consequently the Constituent Assembly had been particularly concerned with upholding it, writing sweeping provisions into the Constitution protecting freedom of the press and banning censorship. In Justice Britto's words, "it is the definitive lesson of history that, in matters relating to the press, there is no room for compromise." The majority overruled all arguments that the activities of the press could not be left unregulated, even temporarily; they declared that

30 Justice Britto writes: "The current Press Law was conceived and promulgated during an extended authoritarian period of our sovereign State history … It lays down an exceptional framework that is widely or evidently irreconcilable with the airy precepts of democracy, which were finally rescued and proudly proclaimed in the 1988 Constitution."

all fundamental constitutional rights, including freedom of the press, were self-applying, and that there was no need to regulate censorship because the Constitution prohibited it in all of its forms.

The dissenting opinions focused on the traditions established by former Brazilian constitutions, all of which had contained provisions limiting the exercise of freedom of the press. According to Justice Gilmar Mendes, "[g]uarantees in the constitutional texts of freedom of the press as a value immune to restrictions of all kinds did not, however, prevent the legislative and jurisprudential delineation of its effective content." The arguments were yet again tailored to the authority of the traditions embraced by the old regime, with overtones stressing the legal continuity that enabled these traditions to apply notwithstanding the provisions of the new Constitution.

The proceedings in ADPF 153 took place a year later on 29 April 2010. In this case, a different seven-justice majority was formed to rule the Amnesty Law compatible with the 1988 Constitution. The history surrounding its adoption played a central role within the Court's debates. The majority opinion, written by Justice Eros Grau, focused on the conciliatory nature of the transition to democracy, which was only made possible by the negotiations and agreements between the military regime and opposing members of civil society ("there are those who oppose the fact that the transition from the dictatorship to political democracy has been a smooth transition due to certain compromises … it just so happens that the subversives have obtained it, amnesty, at the expense of this breadth"). The Amnesty Law, they argued, constituted the single most important step in this negotiated transition ("the formidable struggle for amnesty is expressive of the most vibrant page of resistance and democratic activity in our history"); as it simultaneously pardoned the crimes committed by both enemies of the regime and by state officials, the law became regarded as a symbol of the agreement that made the new Constitution possible. Proof of this can be found in the amendment to the 1967 Constitution, adopted under the dictatorship, which was the instrument used by the outgoing military government to set up the new Constituent Assembly and reiterated the terms of the amnesty agreement, arguably bestowing them with constitutional authority ("hence it would not make sense to question whether amnesty … was or was not endorsed by the 1988 Constitution … Constitutional amendment number 26 of 1985 establishes, in this sense, the … revolution that gives it legitimacy").

The dissent argued vigorously against such a historical reading. The justices in the minority maintained that no conciliatory agreement was reached between the regime and civil society leaders that resulted in Brazil's "double-edged" Amnesty: "in fact the Amnesty Law, far from having been approved within a context of mutual concessions and fulfilling a kind of 'tacit agreement'

… was drawn up amid a climate of growing popular dissatisfaction with the authoritarian regime." The minority also held that the political system in 1979 did not permit conditions enabling free and unencumbered public debate. While Brazilian society as a whole fought for and claimed amnesty for the exiled and imprisoned enemies of the regime, granting pardons to state officials had been decided on unilaterally by the military regime. No act of the military government, including the amendment that called for the convocation of a Constituent Assembly, had any authority to grant this amnesty ("It is irrelevant whether the [the Amnesty Law] was partially reproduced in constitutional amendment number 26 … because the 1988 Constitution, although it could have done so, did not ratify such an amnesty").

The legal community received each decision with great attention. ADPF 130 remains to this day one of the Supreme Court's most celebrated precedents. It represents a milestone for those who advocate a narrative of revolutionary rupture by the 1988 Constitution and is regarded as a profound repudiation of the dictatorship as a whole, especially because censorship was such a perennial problem during the years of military rule.[31] It is also of landmark significance for defenders of fundamental rights, as it sets out the parameters that have governed the defence of freedom of speech ever since.[32] Subsequently, the Court ruling on ADPF 153 drew immense criticism from both the public at large and the judicial profession. The majority was accused of rewriting history and distorting constitutional theory. At a time when Brazilian society viewed favourably its own political evolution and democratic stability, ADPF 153 acted as a powerful reminder of the heritage of restrictions from the dictatorship that remained.[33] These contrasting responses from the legal community might have signified a clear response on the *legitimate* narrative of the Brazilian founding, and consequently determined once and for all the place of each of the two precedents set a decade ago by the Supreme Court in the constitutional canon. However, the Court's refusal to revisit the peremptory terms of

---

31 See Thales Morais da Costa, 'Conteúdo e Alcance Da Decisão Do STF Sobre a Lei de Imprensa Na ADPF 130' (2014) 10 Revista Direito GV, 119.

32 Natália Paes Leme Machado, 'A "Plena" Liberdade de Expressão e os Direitos Humanos: Análise da Jurisprudência da Corte Interamericana de Direitos Humanos e o Julgamento da ADPF 130' (2014) 10 Revista de Direito Internacional, 280.

33 See Fernando José Gonçalves Acunha and Juliano Zaiden Benvindo, 'Juiz e Historiador, Direito e História: uma análise crítico-hermenêutica da interpretação do STF sobre a Lei da Anista' (2012) 17 Novos Estudos Jurídicos 182. See also Vera Karam de Chueiri and Heloísa Fernandes Câmara, '(Des) Ordem Constitucional: Engrenagens Da Máquina Ditatorial No Brasil Pós-64' [2015] Lua Nova 259.

constitutional history adopted in either precedent during the last decade has arguably helped to defy expectations regarding the fate of the two precedents.

While generally regarded as a positive decision, ADPF 130 drew some low-key criticism in later years, especially within the Court.[34] The decision was radically progressive, even by 2019 standards. Brazil does not have anything similar to the historical approach to freedom of speech followed in the US, and contemporary jurists tend to regard the ruling as too broad, especially in banning all kinds of censorship. It has been challenged by the lower courts during times of extreme political polarisation in cases involving criminal charges against public officials as well as fake online news websites. These have often been upheld by the Supreme Court. The revolutionary narrative adopted by the majority in ADPF 130 has become more familiar in the last decade, but has rarely been used to support such a far-reaching precedent.

Meanwhile, although it has become unfashionable among progressive-dominated academic circles to praise the ruling on ADPF 153 in any way, the continuity narrative it supports has remained strong through the years. Most precedents do not engage with the nature of the constitutional transition quite as *directly,* but they do allow for the same logic to inform constitutional interpretation.[35] It is still quite common to interpret the 1988 Constitution through the "tradition" set out in Brazil's former Constitutions – two of which were adopted during dictatorships, and one when the country was still a monarchy. The effects of ADPF 153 also endure: in November 2010, only a month after the trial, Brazil was condemned by the Inter-American Court of Human Rights for granting amnesty to state officials who had committed torture and other crimes against humanity. The decision led to ADPF 320, which challenged the original judgment in light of the international court's decision. However, the STF has refused to re-examine the issue, striking down any attempts to prosecute state officials for crimes committed during the dictatorial period.

Critics and champions of both decisions have analysed every aspect of each particular precedent – in far greater detail than is normally attributed to the study of any precedents, let alone their historical readings – but no diagnosis

---

34 Ivar A Hartmann, 'CRISE DOS PRECEDENTES NO SUPREMO: O CASO DOS PRECEDENTES SOBRE LIBERDADE DE EXPRESSÃO' (2020) 6 REI – REVISTA ESTUDOS INSTITUCIONAIS 109.

35 Richard Primus argues that broader perceptions about history often shape the way specific issues are decided: 'Indeed, a constitutional interpreter with a broad sense of the meaning or values of American constitutional history is likely to have that historical sense shape his or her approach to adjudication across a wide range of issues'. Richard A Primus, 'Judicial Power and Mobilizable History' (2006) 65 Md. L. Rev. 171, 172.

has been offered for the *inherent contradictions* in the Court's interpretation of the history of the democratic transition. Studies have successfully identified fundamental factors in the change in the Court's opinions in 1989 and 2009 respectively, claiming that profound alterations – both to the Court's internal composition[36] as well as the external composition of the representative powers[37] –were pivotal in allowing for a shift from profound self-restraint to profound activism. Yet the contradictions inherent within the two precedents remain unsolved and rarely criticised.

4 A Theoretical Framework for Constitutional Narratives

Law uses history to establish its authority. The use to which lawyers put history defines the relationship between history and the law. Historical argument is commonplace before constitutional courts; it is one of the *modalities* of constitutional argument, following Philip Bobbitt's classic construction.[38] While Bobbitt's definition of historical argument embraces originalist theories of interpretation, stating that it "depends on a determination of the original understanding of the constitutional provision",[39] he later clarifies that "we do not have an original commitment to a particular form of historical argument", and that what the constitutional interpreter really wants is something that no form of historical argument can give him: "the authoritative reading in a particular context".[40]

By dismissing the ability of historical argument to provide *the* authoritative reading of the Constitution, Bobbitt is negating the very premise of originalism and all the intellectual debate surrounding it. Originalism promises to use history to remove the inherent indeterminacy of constitutional interpretation, supposedly because historical facts are neutral and predetermined parameters for interpreters to follow. As Richard Fallon has noted, the real authority of history depends not on empirical facts, but "on current agreement manifest in the judgments of officials, judges, lawyers, and others concerning the

36 Arguelhes (n 17).
37 Koerner (n 29).
38 Philip Bobbitt, *Constitutional Fate: Theory of the Constitution* (Oxford University Press 1984).
39 Ibid., 9.
40 Ibid., 13.

contemporary legal significance of past events",[41] a concept that is neither neutral nor predetermined.

Fallon's statement answers the question of *what* constitutes an authoritative historical argument, but not *how* to achieve it. Bobbitt's statement suggests that history alone is not sufficient to guarantee the authority of a decision. There must be a premise connected to the historical reading that makes it particularly persuasive. This premise is often related to the history of a specific moment in time; under constitutional law, this is most often the time of a new constitutional text's adoption. *Adoption history*, to use Jack Balkin's term,[42] relies on the authoritative premise that something, fixed at the time the Constitution was adopted, conditions its proper interpretation. That 'something', however, can vary depending upon the theories and forms of historical argument utilized to interpret it. It can be original meaning, original intention, original public understanding, or something quite different, such as the character of the national ethos or the definition of its political tradition.[43] These latter and more complex forms of historical argument detach history from its ordinary purpose and turn it into a tool for constructing other forms of constitutional arguments.[44] This is usually done through the use of narratives. A narrative provides not only a historical reading, but also a *story* which better allows for the legal use of history that makes "sense of current controversies and the proper direction of political/legal change"[45] and shapes "the meanings we are prepared to give to our country's present and future".[46] However, narrative history is shaped into coherence for the purpose of the law, and therefore one is profoundly different from the other.[47]

---

41 Richard Fallon, 'The Many and Varied Roles of History in Constitutional Adjudication' (2015) 90 Notre Dame Law Review 1753, 1758.

42 Jack M Balkin, 'The New Originalism and the Uses of History' (2013) 82 Fordham L. Rev. 641, 641.

43 Ibid., 672.

44 Ibid., 659–660.

45 Jack M Balkin, *Constitutional Redemption: Political Faith in an Unjust World* (Probable First edition, Harvard University Press 2011), 44.

46 Bruce Ackerman, *We the People, Volume 1: Foundations* (Belknap Press 1993), 37.

47 Reva Siegel defines the relationship between history and narrative by affirming that we turn history into a source of narrative understanding. While the role of history is to 'reveal the nature and scope of constrains that bind us', she states it is also through history that we 'forge the collective subject -"We the People"- that is realized through the practice of constitutional argument', and in order to do so we make constant use of narratives. Reva B Siegel, 'Text in Contest: Gender and the Constitution from a Social Movement Perspective' (2001) 150 University of Pennsylvania Law Review 297, 342–343.

From the standpoint of professional historians, history for the lawyer is inherently anachronistic and didactic.[48] Narratives put to use in constitutional argument engage in selective identification (and misidentification); they pick history's winners and losers, and point towards a particular path that must continue to be followed in order to ensure continuing progress (towards the national ethos and culture, or towards the established political tradition). Disputes over "ethical-historical" constitutional arguments are therefore disputes on the meaning and purpose of these traditions and cultures rather than the precise accuracy of historical facts. Nevertheless, because the main purpose of such narratives is to provide authority and *legitimacy* for particular readings of the Constitution,[49] they often run into two separate and equally alarming problems. The first lies in the difference between explained or even simplified history and 'plain bad' history. As much as we might be aware of the inherent distortions that feed into narrative-construction, a story that is incapable of surviving an encounter with the facts of history is unlikely to hold much persuasive power. Simplifying and explaining, adding determinacy or coherence, should not provide lawyers with an excuse to embrace anachronism or dispense with fact-checking. The better narratives must be "truer to historical facts"[50] and thus preceded by actual historical work.

The puzzling aspect of this reality is that often neither scholars nor judges are motivated to perform such necessary work. Most of the time, historical argument is produced without solid historical research to ground it. Lawyers are rarely disposed to put the work of historians to use, except in a deeply selective and often decontextualised manner, nor are they willing to do the work themselves.[51] In this respect, most of the legal profession is likely to

48 Balkin (n 42) 680, maintains that '[a]rguments from ethos and tradition explain the meaning and trajectory of history, not from the standpoint of the past, but from the standpoint of the present. That is why these arguments are inherently anachronistic'.

49 Legitimacy and authority are complex subjects in constitutional law, and each author will have views of their own about what it means to call constitutional meaning legitimate. Reva Siegel, for example, states that history matters because the Constitution's authority resides in forms of understanding, which can only be arrived at through the narrative materials it supplies. Siegel (n 47) 344.; Bruce Ackerman, in turn, suggests that there is more than one legitimising logic for constitutions, while stating that 'the presence or absence of a widespread belief in constitutional legitimacy can play an important – sometimes, all-important – role in shaping political and social life'., thus reinforcing the importance of narrative study. Bruce Ackerman, Revolutionary Constitutions: Charismatic Leadership and the Rule of Law (Harvard University Press 2019), 7.

50 Ackerman (n 65) 5.

51 Akhil Amar has noted that when interpreting the Constitution, judges tend to rely on the sources most readily accessible to them. This makes the lack of interest of lawyers in serious historical endeavours particularly problematic, as they fail either to present

embrace the persuasive power of bad history. This collective agreement to turn a blind eye to actual historical facts only works as long as the legal community as a whole continues to ignore historical sources. When a significant group of scholars decides to undertake the task of confronting existing narratives with real history, or of crafting new narratives from it, new layers are added to the language of constitutional argument. The perception of what is reasonable and expectable, or "on-the-wall" to use Balkin's phrase,[52] shifts. Similarly, Richard Primus states that it is the role of law professors to "nurture" new historical accounts, as opposed to those usually adopted by Courts and common within legal language.[53] These exercises mean that, when Courts are confronted with historically checked narratives, they are likely to find it more difficult to uphold legitimacy narratives that are unsupported by historical facts.

The second problem is the very use of the plural: because narratives are interpretations of history, it is always possible to construct more than one narrative from the same historical events. This is the nature of what Robert Cover called *jurisgenesis*, or the creation of law, which takes place inside the various communities of a pluralist society, each with its own reading of the Constitution.[54] Primus describes this as the fact that "it is not clear as a theoretical matter that any one theory of history's proper force in constitutional law is normatively correct in a way that should exclude all others", but rather that historical argument should make sense of the Constitution's *persistence.*[55] However, Primus also acknowledges that "some approaches to the methodological question should be rejected as intellectually implausible or incompatible with the basic values or commitments of ... constitutional law",[56] meaning that conflicting narratives on constitutional meaning cannot *all* be supported by history, especially history that appeals to ethos and tradition, if they make opposing claims. If historical argument becomes so malleable as to maintain radically incompatible constitutional views, it is likely to lose its persuasive authority.

to judges arguments drawn from historical facts or to produce scholarship capable of putting historical thinking to legal use. Akhil Reed Amar, 'Our Forgotten Constitution: A Bicentennial Comment' (1987) 97 Yale LJ 281, 287.

52 Balkin (n 45), 179–180.

53 Primus (n 37), 175.

54 Robert M Cover, 'Foreword: Nomos and Narrative' (1983) 97 Harvard Law Review 11 <http://heinonline.org/HOL/Page?handle=hein.journals/hlr97&id=22&div=13&collection=journals> accessed March 11 2019.

55 Primus (n 37), 181–182.

56 Ibid., 182.

This problem is usually challenged by the adoption of particular narratives by strategically-placed actors within constitutional systems, such as courts. Cover describes this as the *jurispathic* function of the courts. This arguably provides stability for the constitutional system, or under a more critical view, halts the creation of a diverse body of law by asserting one particular legal source to the exclusion of the rest.[57] These *adoptions* by courts undoubtedly play an important role in developing narratives, given that "the episodes that courts treat as relevant to constitutional adjudication gain a privileged status among the possible bases for historically based constitutional arguments, and the historical arguments that courts credit become established as sanctioned interpretations within constitutional discourse".[58] Bruce Ackerman refers to this as a *professional narrative*, constructed by lawyers and judges and described as having "the most direct impact upon the ordinary lives led by all of us".[59] He argued that lawyers and judges are deeply constrained by the patterns of argument built up by the legal community over time – even when they are unaware of it.[60] Ackerman's construction suggests that there can be a *reigning* or *prevailing* professional narrative, which in due course can constitute the basis for the proposal of a new professional narrative. In the present context, it may be concluded that the narrative adopted by constitutional courts can be especially persuasive, with consequences that reach well beyond the results of individual cases.

Given the power they wield and the tools they have at their disposal when engaging in constitutional interpretation, it makes sense for courts to adhere to a professional narrative, thus providing a constant source of authoritative argument for their decisions. They have a large pool from which to do so; opposing political parties, social movements and other branches of government will constantly offer competing claims about what the history of the Constitution means.[61] However, there are standards, in any legal community and at any given point in time, on what constitutes a plausible constitutional argument. A professional narrative requires a reliable and reasonably accepted

---

57 Cover (n 54).

58 Primus (n 35) 173.

59 Ackerman (n 46) 38.

60 Ackerman (n 46) 39.

61 Jack Balkin, 'The Framework Model and Constitutional Interpretation' in David Dyzenhaus and Malcolm Thorburn (eds), *Philosophical Foundations of Constitutional Law* (1 Edition, Oxford University Press 2016) 241–242.

reading of historical facts; those who wield it must "take greater steps to ensure that their stories are accurate and typical".[62]

5 A Prescription for Courts

Jack Balkin distinguishes between three ways of criticising historical arguments, drawing on ethos and tradition, which are usually presented through narrative. First, one could challenge the underlying theory justifying the authoritative use of historical arguments. For instance, it can be argued that an interpretation cannot be inconsistent with the meaning of the national ethos unless that meaning is relatively clear. Second, one could challenge the characterisation or application of the national ethos, the political tradition, or the nature of the transition to the new constitutional regime. This might be because the characterising arguments are premised on the wrong narrative, i.e., one that is not the most appropriate for interpreting the historical facts. Third, one could challenge the quality of the history that supports arguments about ethos or tradition: it may be mis-characterising, oversimplifying or anachronistic.[63]

These critiques can result in one of three outcomes: counter-narratives, counter-lessons and complications. Under an initial analysis, Brazil might benefit from all three. There can be no question that constitutional practice would benefit, if not from the offering of a counter-narrative, then from the introduction of a professional narrative. The very nature of narratives points to the existence of multiple historical accounts of constitutional meaning in any complex society. However, in these complex societies courts are expected to impose order and to make determinations on the meaning of law. This does not mean that the court's decision is the best one, or that it is final; that is hardly the point. Courts must make decisions precisely because they can make mistakes, and because they cannot and will not have the final say. As Robert Cover argued when explaining the *jurispathic* function of courts, the very worst a court can do is refuse to act.[64] By making a decision about the meaning of law, courts invite the ongoing debates with those who disagree, which are the essence of constitutional law.

62 Daniel Farber and Suzanna Sherry, 'Telling Stories out of School: An Essay on Legal Narratives' [1992] Stanford Law Review, 807, 809.

63 Balkin (n 42) 48–55.

64 Cover (n 54) 64–66.

The Brazilian Supreme Court cannot keep alternating between opposing narratives regarding the founding of the current constitutional system, which are in turn used to justify opposite readings of the Constitution. By doing so, it is making no choice at all. On the one hand, the practice strips historical argument of its authority, and consequently deprives the Court's decisions of legitimacy. On the other hand, and perhaps most importantly, the Court must take responsibility for the normative choice of using a narrative to provide legitimacy for constitutional decisions. As has been summarized by Primus, "when judges tell certain stories and not others, they affect not only how we will understand those particular stories but also the universe of stories of which we are aware, and can contest, in the first place".[65]

Primus seemingly takes a negative view of the role of the courts in determining a professional narrative, challenging Cover's more optimistic hope that *jurispathic* rulings will invite further constitutional debates.[66] However, Primus then goes on to offer a solution to his own proclaimed problem – the judiciary's (great) power to shape the resources of argument in constitutional history – by stating that *other* interpreters of the Constitution must make affirmative efforts to promote alternative narratives: "to balance the judicial influence over constitutional history, nonjudicial actors might be well served not to let courts drive their choices about what materials should be added to our collective constitutional memory".[67]

It therefore seems that the courts' opposition is essential in fomenting nonjudicial debate on the creation of a constitutional narrative. This point leads to Balkin's second suggestion, and the conclusion that drawing counter-lessons from history and complicating the translation of historical facts into a coherent story will be decisive for Brazilians to conclude which narrative is better suited to their constitutional reality, thus establishing a constitutional identity. However, defying Primus' advice, Brazilian legal doctrine has shown staggeringly little interest in analysing the actual historical facts of the constitutional system's founding. This is not a matter of simple academic disinterest: Brazilian jurists have arrived at the puzzling conclusion that the only way to definitively establish a constitutional narrative is to forgo historical study entirely.[68]

---

65 Primus (n 35) 191–192.

66 Cover (n 54) 67–68.

67 Primus (n 35) 194.

68 See Christian Edward Cyril Lynch and José Vicente Santos de Mendonça, 'Por uma história constitucional brasileira: uma crítica pontual à doutrina da efetividade / Defense of studies on the constitutional history of Brazil: a critique of the doctrine of the effectiveness of the Constitution' (2017) 8 Revista Direito e Práxis 942. The authors argue that this phenomenon is not a necessary consequence of the kind of redemptive constitutionalism

From democratisation onwards, a group of scholars have fiercely advocated the revolutionary narrative of constitutional foundation. They have argued the enactment of the 1988 Constitution represented a true "new beginning", a complete departure from the legal and political tradition preceding it, and the result of political mobilisation and struggle reflected in the work of the democratically elected Constituent Assembly.[69] This strand of scholarly reasoning has become increasingly influential among constitutional lawyers over the last decade, especially after Luís Roberto Barroso, the most prominent defender of the theory, became a justice of the Supreme Court. However, *Neoconstitutionalist* theorising has drawn significant criticism from legal historians due to its disregard for historical analysis in its diagnosis of the nature of the founding of Brazil's constitutional system. Prominent legal historians have argued that, by preaching a radical break with the past in 1988, constitutional theorists have covertly advocated the abandonment of any study that reaches back before the adoption of the new Constitution. This is done in the belief that all previous legal and political tradition was representative of Brazil's long era of political oppression and control by elites, which had finally been overcome under the current regime.[70] However, by rejecting a historical analysis of pre-constitutional conditions, these jurists have been unable to root their narrative diagnosis on firmer ground.

Promoters of the continuity narrative have not been more successful. Historical construction of a narrative of negotiated transition and legal continuity has often occurred through careful selection of the actions and perspectives of a few key individuals, usually members of the political elite. This exercise of selective identification has been repeatedly denounced as a misleading use of history within and outside the Supreme Court, rarely allowing the analysis to move beyond the confines of a single case.[71]

Brazil needs to ascertain an identity for its constitutional system, and the Supreme Court has a significant part to play in the process of its consolidation. No decision or ruling made by the Court will or should be final, but it will provide a firmer setting for debates regarding the Constitution's history. It is

that neoconstitutionalists pursue, as the rise of the same kind of thinking in Europe has the opposite effect – redemptive constitutionalism resulted in the rise of legal history, and constitutional history in particular, in the second half of the 20th century.

69 See Luís Roberto Barroso, 'Neoconstitucionalismo e Constitucionalização Do Direito (o Trinfo Tardio Do Direito Constitucional Do Brasil)' in Daniel Sarmento and Cláudio Pereira Souza Neto, *A Constitucionalização do Direito* (Lumen Juris 2007).

70 Lynch and Mendonça (n 71), 950.

71 See de Chueiri and Câmara (n 35); See also Acunha and Benvindo (n 33).

only by coming to terms with the paradoxical features of the historical process leading to Brazil's democratisation that constitutional lawyers will be able to reclaim the authority of historical argument and to reassess the legitimacy of the ongoing constitutional project. As long as the Supreme Court continues to alternate between narratives, Brazilian constitutional history will continue to be rejected as a legitimising tool.

These requirements are not intended to incite rash political behaviour by the courts, but rather to provide opportunities to ensure balance. In fact, a rash consideration of the previous claims can lead to even more problematic judicial behaviour. While this author believes it to be profoundly necessary for the Supreme Court to take a stand in the ongoing debate over the identity of the founding of the Brazilian constitutional system, she also considers that the Court must be aware of the risks of narrative selection, especially given the its enhanced authority. While "part of purpose of history ... is to provide us with models of virtue and in action whom we should aspire to emulate",[72] we must be wary of building up inexistent virtues into heroes that become too large and unattainable by the mere mortals of the current generation.[73] That is why a prescription of storytelling comes with a strong appeal to deep historical, critical analysis.[74]

It may also be argued that the Court's institutional behaviour should be tamed, given the concerns that it may become a "target of institutional capture".[75] Reducing tensions created by the active exercise of judicial review in new democracies is a major concern within comparative literature, born out of a anxiety for governments' tendencies to attempt to interfere when courts become too vocal.[76] Preventing this backlash is a necessary part of the strategic behaviour expected of the courts. For the sake of the constitutional system they are charged with defending, courts must be capable of looking clearly into the political spectrum of the regime, as well as at their own part in its operation, and adjust their behaviour accordingly.

72 Amar (n 54), 290.

73 Ibid.

74 One must also be careful not to fall prey to the originalist mistake of taking history for purity, which is meant to 'cleanse constitutional interpretation of politics, discretion and indeterminancy'. On a more critical view of historical analysis, see Stephen M Feldman, 'Constitutional Interpretation and History: New Originalism or Eclecticism' (2013) 28 BYU J. Pub. L. 283, 284.

75 Tom Ginsburg and Aziz Z Huq, *How to Save a Constitutional Democracy* (First edition, University of Chicago Press 2018), 97.

76 Stephen Gardbaum, 'Are Strong Constitutional Courts Always a Good Thing for New Democracies?' (2014) 53 Colum. J. Transnat'l L., 285, 315.

Times of political stability are therefore particularly appealing for Courts to take a firmer stance in the construction of constitutional narrative. This firmer stance might even prove crucial if, and when, the system is later confronted with crisis. The balance courts must seek lies in assessing the level of achieved stability of the system as well as its need for identity consolidation. A passive court in stable times can be just as damaging as an overly active court in unstable ones. The premise of this paper, thus, remains valid: the Court must take on an active role in–meaning it must take a stand within the story of–the consolidation of the Brazilian constitutional system if it is to survive into the future.

6 Conclusion

Historical argument is neither neutral nor predetermined. It is not a universal truth waiting to be discovered. Rather, it is a construction whose legitimacy must be connected to a higher cause, be it the definition of original meaning, national ethos, or political tradition. The logical conclusion is that more than one historical argument–or constitutional narrative–can be crafted from the same set of historical premises. The disputed history of Brazil's democratic transition has generated two competing constitutional narratives: one a narrative of legal continuity with prior authoritarian regimes, and the other, a narrative of revolution resulting in a complete break with the past. The inherent tension between these narratives impedes the country's ability to consolidate its constitutional identity.

Courts are meant to face such competing narratives head on. As authoritative arbiters of legitimate constitutional readings, they have the power to establish the meaning of the Constitution at a determinate moment, simultaneously creating stability and inviting new challenges to the existing paradigm. The Brazilian Supreme Court has neglected its most basic function in a constitutional democracy by refusing to promote a particular historical reading of the Constitution. The Court's willingness to embrace poorly founded historical arguments has discouraged serious historical study and further jeopardises the country's search for a foundational story upon which it can build a constitutional identity. This apathy is particularly hurtful in a scenario of political stability, as it represents a waisted opportunity to establish valuable tools for the preservation of the constitutional system in times of crisis.

Constitutional Courts do not have the final say on constitutional meaning. However, they are expected the have *a* say, establishing the provisional dominance of one particular historical reading, which will in turn provide a basis for future disputes to be proposed by non-judicial entities such as scholars and lawyers. For the purposes of constitutional identity-building, legal actors necessarily play different roles in a circular fashion: legal historians must theorise, lawyers must argue, and courts must decide.

Bibliography

Ackerman B, *We the People, Volume 1: Foundations* (Belknap Press 1993).

Acunha FJG and Benvindo JZ, 'Juiz e Historiador, Direito e História: uma análise crítico-hermenêutica da interpretação do STF sobre a Lei da Anista' (2012) 17 Novos Estudos Jurídicos 182.

Amar AR, 'Our Forgotten Constitution: A Bicentennial Comment' (1987) 97 Yale LJ 281.

'Anais Da Constituinte: Comissão de Sistematização' <https://www.senado.leg.br/publicacoes/anais/constituinte/sistema.pdf> accessed 11 March 2019.

Arguelhes DW, 'Poder Não é Querer: Preferências Restritivas e Redesenho Institucional No Supremo Tribunal Federal Pós-Democratização' (2014) 25 Universitas Jus <http://www.publicacoes.uniceub.br/index.php/jus/article/view/2885> accessed 10 March 2019.

Balkin J, 'The Framework Model and Constitutional Interpretation' in David Dyzenhaus and Malcolm Thorburn (eds), *Philosophical Foundations of Constitutional Law* (1 Edition, Oxford University Press 2016).

Balkin JM, *Constitutional Redemption: Political Faith in an Unjust World* (Probable First edition, Harvard University Press 2011).

Balkin JM, 'The New Originalism and the Uses of History' (2013) 82 Fordham L. Rev. 641.

Barbosa LA de A, *História Constitucional Brasileira: Mudança Constitucional, Autoritarismo e Democracia No Brasil Pós-1964* (Biblioteca Digital da Câmara dos Deputados 2012).

Barroso LR, 'Neoconstitucionalismo e Constitucionalização Do Direito (o Trinfo Tardio Do Direito Constitucional Do Brasil)' in Daniel Sarmento and Cláudio Pereira Souza Neto, *A Constitucionalização do Direito* (Lumen Juris 2007).

Bobbitt P, *Constitutional Fate: Theory of the Constitution* (Oxford University Press 1984).

Costa TM da, 'Conteúdo e Alcance Da Decisão Do STF Sobre a Lei de Imprensa Na ADPF 130' (2014) 10 Revista Direito GV 119.

Cover RM, 'Foreword: Nomos and Narrative' (1983) 97 Harvard Law Review <http://heinonline.org/HOL/Page?handle=hein.journals/hlr97&id=22&div=13&collection=journals>.

Dallari D de A, *Constituição e Constituinte* (Saraiva 1984).

de Chueiri VK and Câmara HF, '(Des) Ordem Constitucional: Engrenagens Da Máquina Ditatorial No Brasil Pós-64' [2015] Lua Nova 259.

Fallon R, 'The Many and Varied Roles of History in Constitutional Adjudication' (2015) 90 Notre Dame Law Review 1753.

Farber D and Sherry S, 'Telling Stories out of School: An Essay on Legal Narratives' [1992] Stanford Law Review 807.

Feldman SM, 'Constitutional Interpretation and History: New Originalism or Eclecticism' (2013) 28 BYU J. Pub. L. 283.

Ferreira Filho MG, 'Nova Perspectiva Do Processo Constitucional' [1985] Revista Brasileira de Estudos Políticos 129.

Ferreira Filho MG, 'O Estado de Direito, o Judiciário e a Nova Constituição' (1985) 160 Revista de Direito Administrativo 61.

Gardbaum S, 'Are Strong Constitutional Courts Always a Good Thing for New Democracies?' (2014) 53 Colum. J. Transnat'l L. 285.

Gargarella R, *Latin American Constitutionalism,1810–2010: The Engine Room of the Constitution* (New, Oxford University Press, USA 2013).

Gaspari E, *O Sacerdote e O Feiticeiro: A Ditadura Encurralada* (Intrinseca 2014).

Ginsburg T and Huq AZ, *How to Save a Constitutional Democracy* (First edition, University of Chicago Press 2018).

Hartmann IA, 'CRISE DOS PRECEDENTES NO SUPREMO: O CASO DOS PRECEDENTES SOBRE LIBERDADE DE EXPRESSÃO' (2020) 6 REI – REVISTA ESTUDOS INSTITUCIONAIS 109.

Jacobsohn GJ, 'Constitutional Identity' (2006) 68 The Review of Politics 361.

Koerner A, 'Ativismo Judicial?: Jurisprudência Constitucional e Política No STF Pós-88' [2013] Novos estudos CEBRAP 69.

Koerner A and Freitas LB de, 'O Supremo Na Constituinte e a Constituinte No Supremo' [2013] Lua Nova: Revista de Cultura e Política 141.

Leonelli D and Oliveira DD, *Diretas Já: 15 Meses que Abalaram a Ditadura* (Record 2004).

Lynch CEC and Mendonça JVS de, 'Por uma história constitucional brasileira: uma crítica pontual à doutrina da efetividade' (2017) 8 Revista Direito e Práxis 974.

Lynch CEC and Mendonça JVS de, 'Por uma história constitucional brasileira: uma crítica pontual à doutrina da efetividade / Defense of studies on the constitutional history of Brazil: a critique of the doctrine of the effectiveness of the Constitution' (2017) 8 Revista Direito e Práxis 942.

Machado NPL, 'A "Plena" Liberdade de Expressão e os Direitos Humanos: Análise da Jurisprudência da Corte Interamericana de Direitos Humanos e o Julgamento da ADPF 130' (2014) 10 Revista de Direito Internacional 280.

Marcelino D, Braga S and Costa LD, 'Parlamentares Na Constituinte de 1987/88: Uma Contribuição à Solução Do "Enigma Do Centrão"' (2010) 18 Revista Política Hoje <http://www.revista.ufpe.br/politicahoje/index.php/politica/article/view/19>.

Michiles C, *Cidadão Constituinte: A Saga Das Emendas Populares* (Paz e Terra 1989).

Paixão C, 'Direito, Política, Autoritarismo e Democracia No Brasil: Da Revolução de 30 à Promulgação Da Constituição Da República de 1988' [2011] Araucaria: Revista Iberoamericana de filosofía, política y humanidades 146.

Primus RA, 'Judicial Power and Mobilizable History' (2006) 65 Md. L. Rev. 171.

Rosenfeld M, 'Constitutional Identity' [2012] The Oxford Handbook of Comparative Constitutional Law <http://www.oxfordhandbooks.com/view/10.1093/oxfordhb/9780199578610.001.0001/oxfordhb-9780199578610-e-37> accessed 16 March 2019.

Sarmento D, '21 Anos Da Constituição de 1988: A Assembleia Constituinte de 1987/1988 e a Experiência Constitucional Brasileira Sob a Carta de 1988' (2009) 29 Dados <http://www.integrawebsites.com.br/versao_1/arquivos/22be85992a1067f5906835bbf44c6405.pdf> accessed 9 November 2015.

Siegel RB, 'Text in Contest: Gender and the Constitution from a Social Movement Perspective' (2001) 150 University of Pennsylvania Law Review 297.

Siegel RB, 'Collective Memory and the Nineteenth Amendment: Reasoning about "the Woman Question" in the Discourse of Sex Discrimination', *History, Memory, and the Law* (University of Michigan Press 2002).

Tushnet M, 'How Do Constitutions Constitute Constitutional Identity?' (2010) 8 International Journal of Constitutional Law 671.

CHAPTER 8

Manipulating Constitutional, Legislative and Judicial History

Incremental Judicial Activism in the Japanese Supreme Court

Keigo Obayashi

1 Introduction

The use of history for constitutional adjudication by courts varies internationally as well as within individual countries. In the United States, some judges take an originalist approach under which constitutional meaning is fixed at the time of ratification,[1] while other courts view the U.S. Constitution as a living document whose meaning evolves over time.[2] There is also interest in blending elements from both approaches under the rubric of "living originalism."[3] Outside of the United States, "originalism" is rarely the method of constitutional interpretation; "living constitutionalism" is far more prevalent. Regardless of the interpretive method used, history almost always plays some role in deciding constitutional cases. Even living constitutionalism refers to history because this approach considers constitutional meaning in light of a changing society and historical development. As Professor Richard Fallon observes: 'Appeals to history, and to the authority of decisions made in the past, occur nearly ubiquitously in constitutional law.'[4]

This chapter focuses on uses of history in constitutional adjudication by the Supreme Court of Japan. This Court seldom invokes constitutional history as conventionally understood: its decisions rarely mention the origins of the Japanese Constitution, the processes of its adoption, or the historical meaning of its provisions. At the same time, the Court is deeply interested in and regularly makes use of three other kinds of history. First, in reviewing the

1 Christopher J. Peters, 'What Lies Beneath: Interpretive Methodology, Constitutional Authority, and the Case of Originalism' (2013) 2013 B.Y.U.L. Rev. 1251, 1259.

2 David Strauss, *The Living Constitution* (OUP 2010).

3 Jack M. Balkin, *Living Originalism* (Belknap Press 2011). *See also* Kermit Roosevelt III, *The Myth of Judicial Activism: Making Sense of Supreme Court Decisions* (Yale University Press 2006).

4 Richard H. Fallon, Jr., 'The Many and Varied Roles of History in Constitutional Adjudication' (2015) 90 Notre Dame L. Rev. 1753.

 | DOI:10.1163/9789004523739_010

constitutionality of statutes, the Court considers legislative history to assess the reasonableness of the legislature's factual findings. Such assessments raise the question of the competency of the Court to review factual determination and the level of deference that the Court should give to the legislature. Strikingly, the Court may consider the reasonableness of legislation not only as of the time of enactment but also in the present day. In the *Giinteisufukinko* case of 1976 (involving issues of malapportionment), the Court explained that, 'when a statute enacted in conformity with the Constitution has fallen short of the requirements of constitutionality due to the subsequent change of circumstances, it should be considered to have come to bear the defect of the unconstitutionality.'[5] This case is widely understood as setting a rule that a statute, valid at the time of enactment, should be reviewed for its present-day validity on the grounds of continuing reasonableness.[6]

Some lower courts have also utilized this interpretation. In the *Gaiboshujo* case of 2010, regarding compensation for industrial accidents, the District Court of Kyoto resolved legal problems in light of *social change*.[7] The old compensation system entitled women to receive a higher amount of compensation for facial injury following industrial accidents than men, even if the extent of facial injury was the same. The court held that this system was unconstitutional on the grounds that it violated equal protection. In this ruling, the court reviewed *legislative facts* from the time of enactment to the present day. According to the court, the system became unconstitutional as a result of social change, although it had been reasonable at the outset.

Second, the Court makes use of history in its invocation of *judicial precedents*. Of particular note, the Court at times views precedent itself as part of a relevant trajectory of historical development. This chapter considers the *Hichakushutsushi* case[8] of 2013 in which the Court addressed the constitutionality of an inheritance statute under which children born out of wedlock received a smaller share of the parental estate. Although past precedents had deemed the statute constitutional, the Court held that the statute had become unreasonable in light of subsequent social changes. As one piece of evidence of social change, the Court referred to the fact that some Justices of the Supreme Court had written separately to question the constitutionality of the legislation in earlier judicial decisions. Those minority opinions, the

5 [1976] 30 MINSHU 223, 247 (G.B.).
6 Tomoaki Sakurai, 'Jijo no Henko niyoru Ikenhandan nitsuite' (2011) 51 *Konanhogaku* 795, 805.
7 [2010] 2093 HANJI 72 (Kyoto D.C.).
8 [2013] 67 MINSHU 1320 (G.B.).

Court in *Hichakushutsushi* reasoned, were themselves evidence of an evolving view that now justified invalidating the inheritance statute.

The third way in which the Supreme Court makes use of history is by assessing the constitutionality of statutes in light of *contemporary community values*, such that statutes that have become obsolete, as measured by those values, are rendered unconstitutional. For example, the Court's assessment of whether publications can be prohibited as obscene is based upon its understanding of contemporary community values. The Court also assesses the validity of criminal punishments in light of contemporary understandings of reasonableness and fairness.

In its reliance upon these three types of history, the Court's approach to constitutional adjudication is dynamic and reflects a commitment to a version of living constitutionalism. The Court views constitutional history as flowing from the past to the future rather than as fixed points in time. The Court also understands the Constitution itself to require judges to recognize and invoke this historical trajectory by responding to ongoing change rather than by seeking to preserve the past. Although *the dynamic model* invites criticism on the ground that it risks judicial activism, the Court has shown that a living approach to constitutional adjudication can occur with adherence to constitutional requirements and in ways consistent with an appropriately constrained role for judges.

2 The Origins and Nature of Judicial Review

2.1 *The Role of Constitutional History*

As noted, the Japanese Supreme Court seldom refers to the history of the Japanese Constitution in cases of constitutional adjudication. Although the Court has not explained its unwillingness to touch on constitutional history, several reasons might account for its reluctance.

First, the Court is likely wary of engaging in a controversy that exists over the limits of constitutional revision. The current Constitution of 1947 was adopted in accordance with the revision processes of the 1889 Meiji Constitution. Although the 1889 Meiji Constitution didn't stipulate the limits of constitutional revision, this revision brought about significant change because it concerned sovereignty. There is ongoing debate as to whether the revised Constitution of 1947 exceeded the limits to constitutional revision by transferring sovereignty from the Emperor to the people.[9] Arguably, if the revision

9 Hitoshi Serizawa, 'Kenpokaiseikoui no Genkai' in Makoto Oishi and Kenji Ishikawa (eds.), *Kenpo no Soten* (Yuhikaku 2008) 328.

indeed exceeded the limitations, the legitimacy of the current Constitution is in some doubt. The Court might well be disinclined to weigh in on such a controversial issue.

Second, the Court might wish to avoid the additional controversy over whether the current Constitution is properly understood to have been imposed upon Japan by a foreign power. This issue has generated debates both in the academic and political spheres.[10] 'Japanese conservatives frequently promote this version of historical events [involving an imposed Constitution] in the hopes of undermining the 1947 Constitution's governing legitimacy and the historically substantial public support for its Renunciation of War Clause, which operates in law—though perhaps not in practice—to limit Japan's military capabilities.'[11] If the Court were to use constitutional history as a means of resolving a constitutional case, it would risk becoming an arbiter of a divisive issue concerning the Constitution's legitimacy.

Third, the circumstances under which the Japanese Constitution was adopted make reliance upon an originalist approach to constitutional meaning difficult. The Constitution was adopted through a process jointly conducted by the Japanese government and the General Headquarters (GHQ) of the United States. It is difficult to determine from this process whether there was any shared meaning or shared intent that could inform constitutional interpretation and adjudication. There is also a particular risk in relying upon evidence generated by or associated with GHQ, as doing so would lend support to the idea that Constitution was created by a foreign country.

Fourth, while reliance on constitutional history can help legitimize a court's review of legislation, Article 81 of the Japanese Constitution specifically gives the Supreme Court the power of judicial review. Thus, the Court may perceive less of a need to deploy constitutional history to explain its decisions as compared to the courts of other countries.

All of this said, the Supreme Court has invoked constitutional history in rare cases. Most significantly, soon after the Constitution took effect in 1947, the Supreme Court referenced history to confirm the nature of the power of judicial review under Article 81.[12] The *Ikenshinsa no Seishitsu* case[13] held that

---

10 David S. Law, 'The Myth of the Imposed Constitution' in Denis Galligan and Mila Versteeg (eds.), *the Social and Political Foundation of Constitutions* (CUP 2013) 239.

11 Christopher M. Young, 'War, Peace, and National Security in the Pacific: U.S. and Japanese Geostrategic Constitutionalism, and the Creation of the Japanese Constitution of 1947' (2016) 11 U. Pa. Asian L. Rev. 439, 442.

12 Article 81 provides that 'The Supreme Court is the court of last resort with power to determine the constitutionality of any law, order, regulation or official act.'

13 [1948] 2 KEISHU 801 (G.B.).

a lower court's decision could be reviewed by the Supreme Court. In its ruling, the Court provided extensive discussion of the nature of judicial review including invocations of constitutional history.[14] The Court noted that Article 81 of the Constitution explicitly provided for judicial review of 'official acts.' This provision, the Court held, extended not only to legislative and administrative acts but also to the rulings of lower courts. Rejecting the argument that the Court's power of judicial review served only as a check on the political branches,[15] the Court insisted that because Article 81 made the Court the body of 'last resort,' it was empowered to review cases from the lower courts in its capacity as the ultimate judicial authority.

In reaching this conclusion, the Court referred to the process by which the Constitution was drafted and adopted. The Court explained that the draft proposed version of Article 81 initially contained two sections: section 1 established the Supreme Court as a court of last resort, while section 2 set out the objects of judicial review. The Council of the House of Representatives amended the draft to generate a single provision. As a result of that change, the Court reasoned, Article 81 must be understood, in its designation of the Supreme Court as the court of last resort, to subject lower court decisions to its review.

2.2 *The Ideal of the Current Constitution*

The Supreme Court also noted the ideal of the current Constitution when it started to give effect to that Constitution. On the same day as the *Ikenshinsa no Seishitsu* case, the Court upheld the criminal prohibition on gambling as constitutional in the *Tobaku* case [The Gambling case].[16] In this ruling, the Court noted that the ideal of tolerance for gambling crimes could not be identified in the new Constitution solely on the grounds that individual freedom and rights were protected under the Constitution.

In that year, the Court clarified the history of Article 25–1[17] in light of the development of the political philosophy of constitutionalism in the

---

14 Yoshiki Takeda, *'Ikenshinsanotaisho'* in Yasuo Hasebe, Kenji Ishikawa and George Shishido (eds.), *Kenpo Hanrei HyakusenII* (7th edn, Yuhikaku 2019) 410, 411. It has been argued that this case clarifies the principle of judicial review.

15 According to this argument, judicial review is intended to check the power of political branches, as Article 76 provides that the judicial branch must be independent from the political branches. Article 76 stipulates as follows: 'The whole judicial power is vested in a Supreme Court and in such inferior courts as are established by law.'

16 [1948] 2 KEISHU 822 (1st.P.B.).

17 Article 25–1 provides that 'All people shall have the right to maintain the minimum standards of wholesome and cultured living.'

Shokuryokanriho case [The Staple Food Control Act case].[18] The defendant, who had violated the Staple Food Control Act,[19] argued that the law violated the right to life under Article 25–1 of the Constitution since it constrained the purchase and transfer of black-market food.

Although the Court rejected the defendant's argument, it held that the political philosophy of constitutionalism had initially meant respect for individual freedom from intervention by the state. Even so, the gap between the wealthy and the poor that resulted from laissez-faire economics required the state to respond. As a result, the welfare state was created to deal with situations of social unfairness. The modern state had a duty to set up an institution to implement social and economic policy. According to the Court, Article 25–1 amounted to a declaration of the state's duty as reflected by the history of constitutionalism.

2.3 *The Validity of the Law under the Transitional Constitutional Provisions*

Although the Supreme Court seldom cites constitutional history, the Court does mention the Meiji Constitution in cases concerning the validity of laws enacted before or during the 1889 Meiji Constitution. In the *Dajokanfukoku* case [Old Order case][20] the defendant, who had been sentenced to death, claimed capital punishment pursuant to a declaration[21] of the Grand Council of State (*dajokan*) was invalid because it was not a statute but an executive order. The declaration had been issued in 1873 before the Meiji Constitution was enacted in 1889. The Supreme Court held that the declaration was valid as a kind of statute not only under the Meiji Constitution but also under the current Constitution.

In regards to the validity of laws enforced under the Meiji Constitution, the Court held that any criminal laws in violation of the current Constitution were invalid.[22] As the defendant had been charged with violating an order issued on the basis of the overall delegation statute under the Meiji Constitution, he argued that the order was invalid because it violated the doctrine of non-delegation under the current Constitution. On this issue, the Court confirmed the general principle that the overall delegating statute was invalid under the current Constitution. Even so, the Court held that the order was constitutional

18 [1948] 2 KEISHU 1235 (G.B.).
19 Act No. 40, 1942.
20 [1961] 15 KEISHU 1106 (G.B.).
21 The Dajokanfukoku No. 65, 1873.
22 [1952] 6 KEISHU 1346 (G.B.).

because it was regarded as a substantive statute, even if it was referred to as an order. In other words, this order could function as a statute. Although it is a complicated decision, this case suggests that laws enforced under the Meiji Constitution would remain valid as long as they did not violate the current Constitution.

3 Legislative History

3.1 *Legislative Facts at the Time of Enactment*

Although the Supreme Court rarely mentions constitutional history, it sometimes reviews legislative facts when considering legislative history. In particular, the Court has often reviewed legislative facts in relation to issues of economic freedom. As economic regulations are often adopted to reflect social circumstances, legislative facts tend to attract focus when the reasonableness of regulations is established.

The National Diet, Japan's bicameral legislature, has broad discretion over legislative facts because it is concerned with enacting laws. The principle of the separation of powers requires the Court to review legislative facts from the standpoint of "second judgment" because the original legislative judgment must be respected. Moreover, the double-standard theory[23] requires the Court to defer to the Diet in economic matters. This theory distinguishes between spiritual freedoms concerned with civil, political, and personal rights, and economic freedoms. On the basis of this distinction, the double-standard theory requires strict scrutiny to be applied to spiritual freedoms, as it is necessary to maintain proper political processes within a constitutional democracy. A less stringent standard of review, such as a rational basis review, could be applied to economic freedoms because it is more appropriate for the court to defer to the judgment of the political branches on issues of socio-economic policy that constitute the outcome to the political process. As a result, the Court reviews legislative facts by presuming that the law was based on reasonable facts at the time of enactment.

For example, in the *Shokugyoanteiho* case of 1950 [The Employment Security Act case],[24] the Court held that the Employment Security Act[25] was constitutional because it was deemed necessary for public welfare in light of current situations. According to the Court, the Act did not violate any

23 Nobuyoshi Ashibe, Kenpo, (7th.edn. Iwanamishoten 2019)104–105.
24 [1950] 4 KEISHU 1049 (G.B.).
25 Act No. 141, 1947.

constitutional rights such as individual or economic freedom because it was intended to remove certain harms from the employment placement business and to achieve security of employment. This judgment instructed the courts to decide whether the law was compatible with the public interest in light of legislative facts.

However, the Court does not always defer to legislative authority. Where strict regulations affecting the core of the relevant right have been adopted, the Court subjects legislative facts to close scrutiny. In the *Yakujihokyoriseigen* case of 1975 [The Restriction of Geographical Location under Pharmaceutical Affairs Law case][26] on the constitutionality of Article 6 of the Pharmaceutical Affairs Law[27] regulating the location of pharmacies, the Court held that Article 6 was unconstitutional by reviewing legislative facts.

The plaintiff had applied for a general pharmaceutical sales store license yet the application was denied because it did not comply with the law's standard for locating pharmacies. The plaintiff brought an action seeking the revocation of the order denying the license, arguing that Article 6 violated the economic rights protected by Article 22–1 of the Constitution.[28] The government argued that Article 6 did not violate citizens' economic rights because geographical restrictions were necessary to ensure the quality and safety of medications. According to the government, the uncontrolled establishment of pharmacies caused by excessive competition could lead to the creation of subpar manufacturing facilities, and therefore to the distribution of substandard drugs.

The Court held that Article 6 was unconstitutional because no reasonable relevance of the means for the purpose could be identified. Despite the law's purpose being consistent with public welfare considerations, the Court reasoned that the means used under Article 6 were unnecessary and unreasonable for achieving this purpose.

Having examined the need for and reasonableness of regulations issued under the provision, the Court reviewed the legislative facts. First, the Court confirmed that the purpose of Article 6 was to prevent any danger of dispensing substandard drugs due to defective facilities caused by excessive competition resulting from the uncontrolled establishment of pharmacies. The Court held that setting standards for the location of pharmacies as a precondition for issuing pharmaceutical licenses did indeed serve the public interest.

---

26 [1975] 29 KEISHU 572 (G.B.).

27 Act No. 145, 1960.

28 Article 22 provides that 'every person shall have freedom to choose and change his residence and to choose his occupation to the extent that it does not interfere with the public welfare.'

Second, the Court inquired into the legislative facts to examine the reasonableness and necessity of the means. Reviewing the government's arguments, the Court accepted the presumption that the regulations were necessary. The Court held that 'in the event that some sort of geographical restriction with respect to places where pharmacies may be established were not instituted, as the defendant points out, it may be easily imagined that there is a possibility of inviting a situation such that pharmacies are unevenly distributed in urban areas and together with this there will be excessive competition among dealers, in some areas, with the result that the business operations of some dealers will become unstable.'[29]

Furthermore, the Court reviewed whether it was necessary and rational to apply the geographical regulation to prevent this situation from arising. Examining the provisions of other legal systems enacted to prevent the dispensing of drugs that are harmful to human health, the Court concluded that the geographical restriction was not unnecessary. However, the Court required the government to show that the hazard to human health without the restriction outweighed the impairment of economic freedom.

Considering the necessity and reasonableness of the regulations, the Court concluded that no legislative facts supported the relationship of cause and effect between pharmacy location and substandard drug manufacturing. The Court held that 'when we view the question in this way, to suppose the danger would arise to any significant degree of dispensing substandard drugs built upon a causal relation of intensification of competition, instability of operation, violation of laws and regulations at the stage of pharmacy is nothing more than a conceptual hypothesis, and it would be difficult to acknowledge this as a reasonable conclusion based upon a reliable foundation.'[30]

3.2 *Legislative Facts at the Present Time*

3.2.1 Still Reasonable Cases

In some cases, the Court's inquiries have extended further. The Court has reviewed the reasonableness of legislative facts not only at the time of enactment but also at the present moment. In short, the Court checks whether the law is still based on reasonable facts today.

The *Shuruihanbaimenkyosei* case of 1992 [The Liquor License case][31] offers an example of this. The plaintiff, who had been refused a liquor license, claimed

29 *Yakujihokyoriseigen* (n.26) 582.

30 ibid 583.

31 [1992] 46 MINSHU 2829 (3rd P.B.).

that the liquor license system under the Liquor Tax Act[32] violated economic freedoms protected by Article 22 of the Constitution. First, the Court explained that the law adapted the licensing system to ensure the collection of liquor taxes and to facilitate the transfer of the tax burden to consumers. Second, considering that the liquor tax accounted for a large share of total national taxes, the Court held that 'it must be said that it was necessary and reasonable for the Liquor Tax Act to adopt such system, via the amendment by Act No. 48 of 1938, for ensuring the national fiscal purpose, that is, realizing proper and secure assessment and collection of liquor tax, when said Act initially introduced this system.'[33] The Court held that the Act was necessary and reasonable at the time of its enactment.

Furthermore, the Court considered whether the Act was *still* reasonable at the time of the administrative refusal disputed in this case. Although the Court recognized that 'the share of liquor tax in the total national taxes, etc., was relatively in decline, in line with the subsequent changes in the situation in society and changes in the tax law system,'[34] the Court held that 'even at that time, the abovementioned mechanism relating to assessment and collection of liquor tax presumably cannot yet be considered to have become unreasonable ... taking these aspects into consideration, it is difficult to go so far as to declare that the legislative body's decision to maintain the licensing system for the liquor sales business at that time is beyond the bounds of its discretion for policy and technical matters as mentioned above and is therefore extremely unreasonable.'[35] In this ruling, the Court reviewed the reasonableness of inquiring into legislative facts at the time the case was being adjudicated.

Although the majority opinion upheld the licensing system based on the Liquor Tax Act, even considering recent social change, a dissenting opinion by Justice Toshio Sakaue argued that the licensing system was not reasonable and necessary because the facts underlying the system had already changed significantly.[36] Justice Sakaue found that the share of liquor taxes as a proportion of total national taxes had declined and that socio-economic circumstances had changed. Under these new circumstances, the law was no longer reasonable or necessary, but rather unconstitutional on the grounds that it violated economic freedom.

32 Act No. 6, 1953.
33 *Shuruihanbaimenkyosei* (n.31)2833.
34 ibid.
35 ibid 2833–2834.
36 ibid 2840 (Sakaue, J., dissenting).

In the *Nochiho* case of 2002 [Cropland case],[37] the Court also reviewed the present reasonableness of the law by considering the legislative facts. Articles 4(1) and 5(1) of the Cropland Act[38] required citizens to obtain permission from the prefectural governor to transform agricultural land into non-agricultural land and to establish or transfer certain rights with respect to agricultural land, thereby converting it into non-agricultural land. The defendant argued that the law violated his right to private property protected by Article 29 of the Constitution. The Court upheld the legislation as constitutional because the purpose of the restrictions was legitimate and the means were reasonable. In its ruling, the Court stated that the purpose of the Act was still valid, even after taking into consideration 'all the changes in the social situation surrounding agricultural land that 〔had〕 taken place after the enactment of the Agricultural Land Law 〔 … 〕 and none of the restrictions specified in the provisions mentioned above are unreasonable for the fulfilment of said purpose.'[39]

The Court has also reviewed legislative facts from the perspective of social change within the context of equal protection under Article 14[40] of the Constitution. The *Izokuhoshonenkin* case of 2017 [Accident Compensation case][41] involved a different requirement based on sex as a prerequisite for receiving a survivor's pension under the Local Public Officers Accident Compensation Act,[42] which was upheld as constitutional. The law imposed an age requirement for the widower to be eligible to receive a pension, whereas widows qualified for a pension regardless of age. The district court held that this violated the principle of equal protection, taking into account changing social norms. Although the age requirement had been reasonable when the legislation was enacted, as most married women were homemakers and needed a pension immediately following the death of their husbands, the district court reasoned that it was now common for married couples to have two incomes. Under such circumstances, the age requirement had turned into unreasonable discrimination. The district court therefore held that the law was unconstitutional.[43] By contrast, the Supreme Court upheld the distinction

37 [2002] 56 KEISHU 95 (2nd P.B.).

38 Act No. 249, 1952, §§ 4(1) and 5(1).

39 *Nochiho* (n.37) 98.

40 Article 14 provides 'All of the people are equal under the law and there shall be no discrimination in political, economic or social relations because of race, creed, sex, social status or family origin.'

41 [2017] 1672 SAIJI 89 (3rd P.B.).

42 Act No. 121, 1967.

43 [2013] 2216 HANREIJIHO 122 (Osaka Dist. C.).

drawn by the law. The Court examined recent social situations, focusing on the differences between men and women in terms of employment status and salary. Considering these differences, the Court decided that the system was still reasonable.

3.2.2 Unconstitutional Cases

In the 2005 *Zaigaihojin* case [Voting Rights of Japanese Residing Abroad case],[44] the Court held that the denial of voting rights to Japanese citizens residing abroad under the Public Offices Election Act[45] was unconstitutional. The plaintiffs, who were Japanese citizens living abroad, argued that the Act violated their voting rights. According to the Court, since voting rights are very important, the government may only restrict them if unavoidable reasons exist for doing so. The Court examined the constitutionality of the law by reviewing its development and social circumstances.

First, the Court focused on the law before the 1998 amendment. Before the amendment, Japanese citizens residing abroad were not included in the electoral register and could not vote in any elections. Considering that the Cabinet had already tabled an amendment bill to the 101st session of the Diet seeking to establish an overseas voting system in 1984, the Court took the view that it was possible to resolve election problems for Japanese citizens residing abroad. The Court held that there were no unavoidable reasons for the Diet to take action to establish an overseas voting system. Therefore, the legislation was unconstitutional. In its ruling, the Court noted the legislative recognition of the need to overhaul the electoral system.

Second, the Court reviewed how the law had been amended. Following the 1998 amendment of the law, Japanese citizens residing abroad were able to vote in elections for the House of Representatives and the House of Councillors under the proportional representation system. Nevertheless, they were not allowed to vote in elections to the House of Representatives under the single-member constituency system, nor in elections to the House of Councillors under the constituency system. At that time, it was asserted that it would have been practically difficult to provide Japanese citizens residing abroad with correct information concerning individual candidates. However, the Court reviewed the reasonableness of the legislative facts in light of social circumstances. According to the Court, 'considering the repeated use of the overseas voting system and remarkable progress in communication technology on a

44 [2005] 59 MINSHU 2087 (G.B.).

45 The Act No. 100, 1950.

global scale since the Amendment, it is no longer extremely difficult to provide Japanese citizens resident abroad with correct information on individual candidates.'[46] Therefore, the Court held that the law violated voting rights. In its ruling, the Court examined the possibility of enforcing the election given current social circumstances when reaching a decision concerning unavoidable reasons.

In the 2008 *Kokusekiho* case [Nationality Act case],[47] the Court held that Article 3(1) of the Nationality Act[48] was unconstitutional due to contemporary circumstances. According to that provision, a child born out of wedlock to a Japanese father and a non-Japanese mother who was acknowledged by the father after birth could not acquire Japanese nationality unless the child acquired the status of a child born within wedlock. In other words, an illegitimate child could not acquire Japanese nationality. The plaintiffs, who were unable to acquire Japanese nationality due to the provision, brought an action seeking a declaration that they had Japanese nationality.

First, the Court reviewed the legislative facts at the time the provision in question was ratified. The Court held that, 'according to the socially accepted views and under the social circumstances at the time when the provision of Article 3(1) of the Nationality Act was established, there may have been adequate reasons to consider that in the case of a child born to a Japanese father and a non-Japanese mother, the fact of the legal marriage of the parents would show the existence of the child's close tie with Japan developed through his/her family life with the Japanese father.'[49] Furthermore, the Court took the view that the 'trends in the nationality law systems enforced in foreign states at the time'[50] supported the position that the means adopted by the provision were reasonably relevant to the legislative purpose of requiring a link between the child and Japan. Therefore, the Court held that the reason for the provision had been reasonable at that time.

The Court then went on to review the reasonableness of the provision in light of current circumstances and social norms, writing as follows:

> Since then, along with the changes in social and economic circumstances in Japan, the views regarding family lifestyles, including the desirable way of living together for husband and wife, as well as those regarding

46 *Zaigaihojin* (n.44) 2098.
47 [2008] 62 MINSHU 1367 (G.B.).
48 Act No. 147, 1950, § 3 (1).
49 *Kokusekiho* (n.47) 1373.
50 ibid.

> parent-child relationships have also varied, and today, the realities of family life and parent-child relationships have changed and become diverse, as seen by the fact that the percentage of children born out of wedlock in the total number of new-born children has been increasing. In combination with these changes in the socially accepted views and social circumstances, as Japan has recently become more international 〔 ... 〕 the number of children born to Japanese fathers and non-Japanese mothers has been increasing. In the case of children whose parents are couples of Japanese citizens and foreign citizens, the realities of their family lifestyles (e.g., whether or not the child lives with a Japanese parent) as well as the views regarding a legal marriage and the ideal form of parent-child relationship based thereon are more complicated and diverse than in the case of children whose parents are both Japanese citizens, and in the former case, it is impossible to measure the degree of closeness of the tie between children and Japan just by examining whether or not their parents are legally married. Taking all of these points into consideration, it does not always match up to the realities of family life of today to determine that a child born to a Japanese father and a non-Japanese mother has a close tie with Japan to a sufficient extent for granting him/her Japanese nationality only after the Japanese father became legally married to the non-Japanese mother.[51]

In addition to these current domestic circumstances, the Court referenced how foreign states were moving toward the abolition of legal discrimination against children born out of wedlock, noting many countries had revised their laws to grant nationality if the relationship between a father who was a national and his child was established by virtue of his recognition. Given these facts, the Court stated that the requirement was not reasonably relevant for the legislative purpose. As a result, the Court held that the provision was unconstitutional on the grounds that it violated the principle of equal protection under Article 14 of the Constitution.

The *Saikonkinshikikan* case of 2015 [Prohibited Term for Remarriage case],[52] was also ruled unconstitutional by the Court. Article 733(1) of the Civil Code subjected women to a six-month prohibition on remarriage.[53] The plaintiff, who was unable to remarry at the desired time due to the provision, argued

51 ibid 1373–1374.

52 [2015] 69 MINSHU 2427 (G.B.).

53 Act No. 89, 1896, §733(1). Art. 733 provided that '(1) A woman may not remarry unless six months have passed since the day of dissolution or rescission of her previous marriage.'

that the rule violated Article 14 and Article 24–2[54] of the Constitution because it discriminated against women without reasonable grounds. The Court inquired into legislative facts occurring between Article 733's enactment and the present day. Considering this legislative background, the Court held that the legislative purpose of the provision was reasonable, as it was intended to avoid confusion over the paternity of a child who was born after the mother's remarriage, thus preventing paternity disputes from arising.

However, the Court decided that a six-month prohibition of remarriage was unreasonable because the time of the prohibition could not be justified on the grounds that the duration was scientifically necessary in order to avoid confusion over paternity. In its examination of the reasonableness of the prohibition's duration, the Court concluded a six-month period did not exist outside the scope of the reasonable legislative discretion granted to the Diet at the time of enactment. Nevertheless, the six-month duration had become unreasonable as the development of new medical techniques and scientific technology enabled the period to be shortened. Specifically, the Court stated that 'with the current progress in medical techniques and scientific technology, it must be said that it is now difficult to justify, from the abovementioned perspectives, the measure that does not limit the period of prohibition of remarriage to strictly correspond to an interval by which it is possible to avoid confusion over paternity, but rather sets a somewhat longer period of prohibition.'[55]

In addition, the Court explicitly referenced recent social changes in its finding. According to the Court, 'the realities involving marriage and the family have changed in Japan along with the changes in the social and economic environments, and, since the beginning of the Heisei period (from 1989) in particular, while more people tend to marry later, the numbers of divorces and remarriages have increased, and against such backdrop, there seems to be a growing call for reducing restrictions on remarriage to the greatest possible extent.'[56] Moreover, 'among other countries that previously prescribed the period of prohibition of remarriage, there is a tendency to legislate to abolish such prohibition.'[57]

54 Article 24–2 provides 'With regard to choice of spouse, property rights, inheritance, choice of domicile, divorce and other matters pertaining to marriage and the family, laws shall be enacted from the standpoint of individual dignity and the essential equality of the sexes.'

55 *Saikonkinshikikan* (n.52) 2436–2437.

56 ibid 2437.

57 ibid.

Taking all of these aspects into consideration, the Court held that the provision laying down a prohibition of remarriage for a period exceeding 100 days imposed an unreasonable and excessive restriction on women. As a result, the period referred to in the provision was found to be unconstitutional—nevertheless, restricting remarriage for 99 days or fewer remans constitutional.

3.3 *Impact*

In its aforementioned reviews of legislative facts, the Supreme Court of Japan has not interpreted the Constitution creatively, nor has it provided a new meaning to its text.[58] The Court may thus be able to avoid coming into conflict with political branches concerning the meaning of the Constitution, or override constitutional interpretations embraced by political bodies. Its legislative fact finding is equivalent to a timeless approach in that the Court examines the reasonableness of the law diachronically. In terms of history, this methodology reviews history to the present day.

Although this "timeless" review can render obsolete laws invalid by reflecting on contemporary values, it also involves encroachment by the Court on the legislative sphere through its review of the reasonableness of the law. This raises constitutional issues in terms of the legitimacy and the role of judiciary. It has been argued that the Court should defer to the Diet in its legislative fact finding; the judiciary lacks the legitimacy to review legislative history, which is within the legislative authority.[59] Even if the Court has this legitimacy, there is some question over whether the judiciary is qualified to do so because the legislative branch is better at fact-finding than the judiciary.

4 Judicial History

4.1 *Making History by the Judiciary*

The Supreme Court has sometimes brought about a desirable situation by accumulating judicial precedents. In other words, the Court construes *judicial history* in such a way as to bring about a situation that reflects contemporary values in its fact-finding. Obergefell v. Hodges[60] in the United States is well known example of this. In this case, the U.S. Supreme Court held that the

---

58 Keigo Obayashi, *Ikeru Kenpo to Kenpososho: Gokenseishinsa toshiteno Rippojijitsu* (2018) 91 *Hogakukenkyu* 395, 414.

59 Nobuyoshi Ashibe, 'Gokenseisuitei no Gensoku to Rippojijitsu no Shihoshinsa: America no Riron/Jittai to sonoigi' in Kenpo Sosho no Riron (Yuhikaku 1973) 117.

60 *Obergefell v. Hodges* [2015] 135 S. Ct. 2584.

prohibition on same-sex marriage was unconstitutional, taking account of the factual situation of most states that had recently approved same-sex marriage. The Court reached this decision due to an accumulation of unconstitutional decisions by lower courts, which resulted in the spread of same-sex marriage in many states.

The Japanese Supreme Court has also drawn on judicial history. The Illegitimate Child case[61] concerned the constitutionality of legislation that discriminated against illegitimate children in relation to the statutory share of an inheritance. Although the legislation was constitutional under the relevant precedents, the Court held that the statute had become unreasonable as a result of social change. As evidence of this change, the Court touched on minority opinions in precedents that had questioned the constitutionality of the legislation. Therefore, the minority opinions themselves essentially functioned as a factor of social change. Bringing about a desirable situation by using judicial history may incrementally advance judicial activism.

4.2 *Examining the Illegitimate Child Case*

Article 900 of the Civil Code provides that illegitimate children, legally defined as children born out of wedlock, are entitled to only half of the inheritance due to legitimate children. This provision is intended to maintain a family system based on legal marriage by drawing a distinction between the shares of an inheritance due to children born within and out of wedlock, and has been previously upheld under the relevant precedents.

In the 1995 case,[62] the Court held that the provision was constitutional because the rule providing for different inheritance shares was reasonably relevant for the purpose of maintaining the family system. In addition to the issue of relevance, the Supreme Court noted that the provision was only applicable if the deceased had died intestate. If the deceased chose to specify the respective shares in a will, the estate would not necessarily have to be divided in accordance with the provision. Considering the overall system, the Court held that the provision did not violate the principle of equal protection under Article 14 of the Constitution and thus upheld the provision by a majority of ten to five.

The concurring opinions of four Justices argued that, although the constitutionality of the provision had become questionable, it was still constitutional for the time being. Justice Katsuya Onishi stated that, 'while it may be

61 *Hichakushutsushi* (n.8).
62 [1995] 49 MINSHU 1789 (G.B.).

appropriate to discuss the possibility of reform as a matter of legislative policy, at this moment, it cannot be concluded that the provision is excessively unreasonable in relation to the reason of enactment.'[63] Justices Hideo Chikusa and Shinichi Kawai released similar statements. According to their interpretation, if the reasonableness of a law becomes questionable with the passage of time, it was desirable for the legislature to revise it, and if the law had clearly become unreasonable, the Court should rule it unconstitutional without waiting for the law to be amended. As far as Article 900 was concerned, they stated that 'it cannot be said that it has reached such a stage.'[64] These Justices took the view that Article 900 would become unconstitutional if the legislature did not eventually amend the rule. In short, it was already possible that the provision might be ruled unconstitutional within the space of only a couple of years after this case.

In fact, the Court struck down the provision in 2013.[65] In this ruling, the Court considered legislative facts, focusing on changes in social norms and governmental responses to these changes. First, it clarified domestic and foreign circumstances. Compared to the time when the provision was enacted in 1947, the current state of marriage and the family has changed: the number of children born out of wedlock had increased and many foreign countries had enacted laws to abolish any distinction between inheritance shares. Second, the Court considered the legislative response to these societal changes. Political branches had attempted to revise the provision on several occasions, first with a draft outline of the revision of the Civil Code concerning the law of inheritance, which was released by the Councillor's Office of the Civil Affairs Bureau of the Ministry of Justice in 1979; then with a draft bill for the partial revision of the Civil Code including a provision for an equitable inheritance distribution in 1996 which reported to the Minister of Justice; and finally with a bill to revise shares in inheritance prepared by the government in 2010.

However, the Court stated that these factors could not directly answer the legal question because they were merely facts. It was necessary to decide whether the provision violated the principle of equal protection in light of individual dignity and equality before the law. In its ruling, the Court remarked that the precedents concerning this matter suggested that the provision was unconstitutional. Although the precedents had upheld the provision as constitutional, in the 1995 case this occurred by a narrow margin. Furthermore, the concurring opinions expected the provision to be amended within a few

63 ibid 1803 (Onishi, J., concurring, joined by Sonobe J.).

64 ibid 1804 (Chikusa J., and Kawai, j., joint concurring).

65 *Hichakushutsushi* (n.8).

years. Considering this situation, the Court held that 'the abovementioned concurring opinions cannot be understood as suggesting that it is impossible to declare unconstitutionality of the provision by way of a judicial decision. In this respect, even if the provision is declared unconstitutional by way of the judicial decision, it is still possible to achieve balance with the assurance of legal stability, as explained in detail in Section 4 below.'[66] In short, the Court suggested that it would be possible to rule the provision unconstitutional with reference to judicial history.

Considering all of these changes, the Court held that:

> Even if the legal marriage system itself is entrenched in Japan, it is now impermissible, as a result of such change in the recognition, to cause prejudice to children by reason of the fact that their mother and father were not in a legal marriage when they were born a matter that the children themselves had no choice or chance to correct. Rather, it can be said that a notion that all children must be given respect as individuals and that their rights must be protected has been established.[67]

The Court therefore concluded that the provision was unconstitutional on the grounds that it violated the principle of equal protection under Article 14 of the Constitution.

In this ruling, judicial history based on case law and separate opinions played a critical role. The Court took the view that facts alone could not direct its conclusion. In order to rule on the issue of constitutionality as a legal question, the Court applied the test of whether the law violates individual dignity and equality before the law. In other words, if the principle of equal treatment for all children has been established, the provision will violate Article 14. It is at this point that the facts accumulated and established by the judiciary play a decisive role. Judicial history determines whether social change has occurred, such that all children must be regarded as being equal as a question of law.

4.3 *Changing Legislative Facts*

In general, a law is found to be unconstitutional if there is no reasonable legislative basis for it as evidenced by legislative fact finding. As noted in Part II.B. 2., the Supreme Court has held laws to be unconstitutional when there was no reasonable basis for them given current legislative facts, even if the factual

---

66 ibid 1329–1930.

67 ibid 1330–1331.

basis for the law at the time of its enactment was reasonable. In short, the law is presumptively unconstitutional if it is not supported by any reasonable legislative facts in light of contemporary circumstances.

In some cases, the Court has upheld the law by *adapting* the legislative facts to social change. A chain of *Koshuyokujo* cases [Public Bath House cases] followed this approach. In these cases, the Court upheld the same law restricting the geographical location of the public bath houses to uphold the public interest at different times.

In the *Koshuyokujo* case from 1955,[68] the defendant, who carried on the business of a public bath house without permission due to restrictions on geographical location, was charged with a violation of the Public Bath House Act of 1948.[69] According to the Court, a public bath house was necessary for local residents. If there were no regulations concerning geographical location, the resulting disarray would cause disruption for residents and harm public health. Against this backdrop, the Court decided that the law was constitutional since it maintained public health and prevented disarray which would be against the public interest.

After 34 years, the Court also upheld the law by adding another reasonable fact. In the *Koshuyokujo* case from 1989,[70] the Court confirmed that the public bath house was still necessary for residents, and had been so since the time of enactment. The Court then added that geographical regulation had been more required to protect owners of public bath houses from the recent financial difficulty of public bath caused by popularization of home bath. Therefore, the Court concluded that the law was suited to the public interest because it protected the business of public bath houses.

Two months later, the Court discerned a further legislative purpose in the law. In the *Koshuyokujo* case from 1989,[71] the Court held that the purpose of the law was not only to maintain public health but also to maintain the public bath houses themselves through stable management.

The line of *Koshuyokujo* cases did not take account of judicial history in the sense of accumulating prior judicial opinions such as the *Hichakushutsushi* case. Rather the Court took account of judicial history in that it tailored the law's purpose to the social circumstances at each moment in time of its review. Therefore, the Court altered legislative facts in light of the passage of time, which is another a form of judicial history making.

68 [1955] 9 KEISHU 89 (G.B.).
69 The Act No. 139, 1948.
70 [1989] 43 KEISHU 1 (2nd. P.B.).
71 [1989] 1301 HANJI 111 (3rd. P.B.).

5 Constitutional Tests Reflecting Contemporary Values

When a court takes the view that a law is unreasonable because it has become obsolete, some tests exist for deciding whether the law is too antiquated. Using a constitutional test, the court decides on the constitutionality of the law with reference to contemporary values. Constitutional tests for establishing whether material is obscene and whether punishment is cruel are two such examples.

Constitutional tests for these matters in the United States have become famous around the world. Judgments relating to obscenity in the U.S. raise issues concerning freedom of expression under the First Amendment[72] because the material determined to be obscene is excluded from constitutional protection. The U.S. Supreme Court has applied the "contemporary community standard" in obscenity cases. This test is used to determine whether material is obscene in light of contemporary community values, and has been applied since the 1957 case *Roth v. United States*.[73]

In the context of the Eighth Amendment,[74] the Court has applied the "evolving standard of decency" test to determine whether methods of punishment are cruel and unusual. Although the Justices who are proponents of originalism have disagreed with it, the test has been applied since *Weems v. United States* in 1910.[75] According to this test, the Court decides whether the method of punishment is objectively accepted in contemporary society.

5.1 *Contemporary Community Standard*

The Supreme Court of Japan has also applied constitutional tests in obscenity cases and death penalty cases. The leading case for obscenity is the *Chatareifujinnokoibito* case of 1957 [Lady Chatterley's Lover case].[76] The Court first followed the definition of obscenity mentioned in the relevant precedents, noting: 'It refers to that which unnecessarily excites or stimulates sexual desire, injures the normal sense of embarrassment commonly present in a normal ordinary person, and runs counter to the good moral concept pertaining to

72 The First Amendment of the United States Constitution provides that 'Congress shall make no law respecting an establishment of religion, or prohibiting the free exercise thereof; or abridging the freedom of speech, or of the press; or the right of the people peaceably to assemble, and to petition the Government for a redress of grievances.'

73 *Roth v. United States* [1957] 354 U.S. 476.

74 The Eighth Amendment provides that 'Excessive bail shall not be required, nor excessive fines imposed, nor cruel and unusual punishments inflicted.'

75 *Weems v. United States* [1901] 217 U.S. 349.

76 [1957] 11 KEISHU 997.

sexual matters (Decided by the First Petty Bench; page 1026, No. 6. Volume 5, Collection of Decisions.).'[77]

Applying this definition, the Court examined the criteria in order to determine whether the material was obscene. The Court stated that 'the criteria for the court in making adjudication is its conscience, that is the social concept generally accepted by society.'[78] Moreover, 'it should further be noted at this time that the social concept regarding sex is not the same depending *on time and place*; and even in the same society, it changes from time to time.'[79] This criterion is based on a social understanding rooted in time and place, although the non-public nature of sex acts under it has not been subject to evolution.[80] When the Court determines the obscenity of material, it examines the contemporary public understanding of obscenity. In that judgment, the historical development of social concepts is also considered as it is necessary to decide whether the current concept differs from the historical concept.

The Court followed a similar approach for determining obscenity in terms of general consideration of contemporary community standards in the *Yojohanfusumanoshitabari* case of 1980.[81] In this ruling, the Court noted that obscenity was determined in light of social concepts prevailing at the time. It explicitly held that contemporary social concepts are a critical factor in determining obscenity.

5.2 *Evolving Standard of Decency Test*

The constitutionality of the death penalty is also reviewed by applying a similar evolving standard of decency test. In the *Shikeihaishi* case of 1948 [Death Penalty case],[82] the Court held that the constitutionality of the death penalty should be reviewed in light of evolving contemporary standards. According to the Court, if it was generally accepted that the method was cruel based on humanitarian considerations prevailing during that era, it would be unconstitutional under Article 36.[83] In its ruling, the Court upheld the death penalty

77 ibid 1003.

78 ibid 1005–1006.

79 ibid 1006.

80 ibid 1006–1007. The Court held that, 'in spite of the fact that the social concept concerning sex is undergoing changes, it cannot be denied that there still exists in any society a demarcation which cannot be overstepped and that the demarcation is still being honored by the general public. This limitation is the nonpublic nature of sex acts referred to hereinbefore.'

81 [1980] 34 KEISHU 433 (2nd P.B.).

82 [1948] 2 KEISHU 191 (G.B.).

83 Article 36 provides that 'the infliction of torture by any public officer and cruel punishments are absolutely forbidden.'

because it was still accepted by society: contemporary public understanding of cruelty was thus the decisive factor in reaching its decision.

Even if the death penalty is constitutional, the constitutionality of execution methods still remains an issue. The Court decided that death by hanging as used in Japan was constitutional in the *Koshukei* case of 1955 [Death by Hanging case].[84] The Court accepted the constitutionality of execution by hanging, referring to other methods used in foreign countries. According to the Court, although various methods of execution were used in foreign countries, death by hanging as adopted in Japan at this time was not cruel compared to other methods. It should be noted that the Court mentioned 'the current' method of execution compared to other methods. This implies that the decision applied a test that reflected the contemporary situation.

6 Dynamic Model

As illustrated throughout this chapter, judicial references to history differ depending on the relevant area of law. The Japanese Supreme Court has seldom referred to constitutional history, although the Court has sometimes inquired into legislative history. If the situation calls for it, the Court itself has made history in some cases. The Court has also examined the historical development of law within the context of constitutional tests. The current methods used to review the reasonableness of the law amount to a kind of historical review; examining the history of the law from the past to the present in order to review the constitutionality of the law is equivalent to checking history. As G. Edward White notes, a historicist theory of history presupposes a clear understanding of the present so that a contrast between the present, the past, and the historical process of change can easily be drawn.[85]

6.1 *Dynamic Model and Practical Reason*

The Japanese Supreme Court uses history as the developing story within constitutional judicial review, while the Court rarely mentions constitutional history at a given moment in time, such as the time of constitutional enactment. This diachronic approach regards history as unconstrained by current popular

84 [1955] 9 KEISHU 663 (G.B.).

85 G. Edward White, 'The Arrival of History in Constitutional Scholarship' (2002) 88 Va. L. Rev. 485, 492.

will, or dead hand[86] control, and offers us an opportunity to respond to the current situation and historical change. I refer to this as a dynamic model because it considers history as continuously developing. However, the reason why the Court uses this model has not yet been determined. Are there any constitutional reasons to make use of this model?

I posit there are three key reasons for this judicial approach. First, this approach is influenced by the background of the Justices on the Supreme Court. Constitutional history is necessary to study and research certain historical materials and to engage in constitutional interpretation. As this is a form of academic work, constitutional scholars are well-suited to dealing with it. Notwithstanding, a constitutional scholar has never been a Justice on the Supreme Court of Japan.[87]

As enumerated upon in section I. A., there are several reasons as to why the Court is unwilling to cite constitutional history. Aside from these reasons, the authority of the Meiji Constitution still has some influence on the Justices. Although the current Constitution entirely revised the Meiji Constitution, it was revised following the revisional procedure detailed within it. Additionally, the Meiji Constitution was "sacred" in that it confirmed the sacred position of the Emperor. All people, including Justices, were subjects of the Emperor at that time. Justices could not refer to the ground and history of the Constitution because it was sacred and untouchable. Although the current Constitution has transferred sovereignty from the Emperor to the people, the Emperor still has the status as a symbol of the country. If the Meiji Constitution still wields influence, the Justices could not touch on constitutional history.

However, these are only practical reasons. Some provisions of the Constitution itself call for it to be viewed through a dynamic historical lens.

6.2 *The Constitutional Grounds of the Dynamic Model*

Originalism requires that constitutional interpretations be based on the public meaning at the time of constitutional ratification. Therefore, originalism regards history as being static in nature, fixed at the moment of a past event. On the other hand, the living constitutionalism approach takes the view that constitutional meaning, and in particular constitutional principles, develops over time. This approach regards history as dynamic.

---

86 Adam M. Samaha, 'Dead Hand Arguments and Constitutional Interpretation' (2008) 108 Colum. L. Rev. 606. Dead hand means that the dead hand of past binds the current popular will.

87 Some Justices who majored in Administrative Law or Anglo-American Law have sufficient knowledge of constitutional law, although they are exceptions.

The Japanese Supreme Court tends to take a dynamic view of history. There are some constitutional reasons as to why the Court should embrace a dynamic historical interpretation. The preamble to the Constitution declares a future-oriented ideal, stating: 'We, the Japanese people, acting through our duly elected representatives in the National Diet, determined that *we shall secure for ourselves and our posterity* the fruits of peaceful cooperation with all nations and the blessings of liberty throughout this land.' This phrasing instructs Japanese citizens to look to the future.

Other provisions on individual rights support this future-oriented ideal. Article 11 states that 'these fundamental human rights guaranteed to the people by this Constitution shall be conferred upon the people of *this and future generations* as eternal and inviolate rights.' Article 12 stipulates 'the freedoms and rights guaranteed to the people by this Constitution shall be maintained by the *constant endeavour of the people.*' The words 'constant endeavour' imply all generations. Finally, Article 97 provides 'the fundamental human rights by this Constitution guaranteed to the people of Japan are fruits of the age-old struggle of man to be free; they have survived the many exacting tests for durability and are *conferred upon this and future generations* in trust, to be held for all time inviolate.'

It should be noted that these provisions also exemplify the dynamic model of interpretation. According to Article 11, human rights are granted to present and future generations, meaning human rights extend from the present into the future. Article 12 mentions the 'constant endeavour of the people.' This phrase also implies continuity from the past into the future. Article 97 refers not only to present and future generations but also to past generations. It states that human rights are the successes of the past generation and that they would be granted to present and future generations. In short, these Articles stipulate a dynamic model by portraying human rights in Japan as a developing project.

In addition to these provisions on individual rights, the national review system also aims to use a dynamic model. The current Constitution provides for the national review system for Justices of the Supreme Court. Article 79 provides that 'the appointment of the judges of the Supreme Court shall be reviewed by the people at the first general election of members of the House of Representatives following their appointment, and shall be reviewed again at the first general election of members of the House of Representatives after a lapse of ten years, and in the same manner thereafter.' This embodies democratic control over the judiciary. Additionally, national review checks whether the Justices have worked well, whether they are responsive to the current popular will, and whether they will be suitable in future. The people review the Justices' work over time. In short, the Justices need to be responsive to the current popular will and to a changing society.

Considering these constitutional systems and provisions, the current Constitution adopts a dynamic model.

6.3 *Dynamic Model and Practical Cases*

The Court has embraced a developing history approach in relation to individual rights. In particular, constitutional judgments in voting rights and equal protection cases illustrate how the Supreme Court's approach is close to the dynamic model. Provisions governing the dynamic model presume that voting rights and equal protection lie at the heart of the model. This is due to the importance of voting rights in ensuring that each generation's rights are respected, and to maintain rights over time, each generation of Japanese citizens must be treated equally.

Considering constitutional cases on voting rights and equal protection, the Court responds to recent developments and social change. In the *Zaigaihojin* case, the Court reviewed the reasonableness of an election system that denied voting rights to Japanese citizens residing abroad and, in doing so, considered recent technological developments. After taking into account prevailing circumstances, the Court struck down the election system and thus approved and protected the voting rights of Japanese citizens residing abroad.

There are also some equal protection cases from the perspective of the dynamic model such as the *Illegitimate Child* case. The Court held that discrimination against illegitimate children in terms of their inheritance entitlement violated the principle of equal protection in light of changing social norms. In both of these rulings, the Court protected voting rights and the principle of equal protection in light of social change. This indicates that it is indispensable for a dynamic model to protect voting rights and equal protection.

The *Malapportionment cases* also reflect a dynamic model as they concern both voting rights and equal protection. The 1976 *Malapportionment* case held that the inequitable distribution of representatives was unconstitutional as equal voting rights have been sought throughout the history of democracy. Although the Court did not invalidate the election itself, it held that the Diet had not redistricted seats within reasonable bounds. At this stage, the Court reviewed the legislative responses to the redistricting of seats in those terms. This ruling focused on the developing situation, having regard to the legislative response. After this case, the Court repeatedly held that malapportionment was unconstitutional.[88]

As described in section II.A. and II.B., the Court has also reviewed legislative history in the economic domain. However, the Court almost always decided to uphold the law in this regard. It is assumed that economic rights are not as suited to maintaining liberty and equality across generations as voting rights and equal protection are.

7 Toward Incremental Judicial Activism with Integrity

7.1 *Toward Incremental Judicial Activism*

The dynamic model creates a problem of judicial activism because the Court uses history within constitutional adjudication to aggressively review the constitutionality of the law rather than to confirm the historical meaning of constitutional texts or to creatively interpret the Constitution. While 'there is little consensus on the meaning of the term "judicial activism,"'[89] and its definition differs depending on the context of academic field, in general, 'scholars often label the overturning of democratically enacted statutes as "judicial activism."'[90] However, this is a narrow conception: some cases that embrace the avoidance doctrine[91] and interpret the Constitution creatively without legislation being ruled unconstitutional also seem to involve a kind of judicial activism, even if the courts do not strike down the law.

In this article, judicial activism is classified into three types: strong, interpretive, and incremental. First, the approach in which the courts are willing to invalidate a political decision is called "strong judicial activism." It is the most far-reaching form of activism because it strikes down a democratic decision. Second, interpreting the Constitution creatively regardless of whether it is constitutional or unconstitutional is called "interpretive judicial activism." Although this approach does not have the same impact as strong judicial activism, it helps to establish constitutional order through constitutional interpretation. Third, the approach that aggressively employs judicial review without

---

88 [1985] 39 MINSHU 1100 (G.B.).

89 Caprice L. Roberts, 'In Search of Judicial Activism: Dangers in Quantifying the Qualitative' (2007) 74 Tenn. L. Rev. 567, 574.

90 Keenan D. Kmiec, 'The Origin and Current Meanings of "Judicial Activism"' (2004) 92 Calif. L. Rev. 1441, 1450–1451.

91 Neal Kumar Katyal and Thomas P. Schmidt 'Active Avoidance: The Modern Supreme Court and Legal Change' (2015) 128 Harv. L. Rev. 2109.

creative constitutional interpretation, regardless of whether it is constitutional or unconstitutional, is called "incremental judicial activism." At first glance, the impact on political branches seems to be low because political decisions are not always invalidated, leading to the creation of new constitutional meaning. However, this approach gradually expands judicial power as the courts step into the political domain.

The approach taken by the Japanese Supreme Court to legislative and judicial history is best described as incremental judicial activism. As far as legislative history is concerned, the review of legislative facts may encroach on the terrain of the legislature. The Court reviews the reasonableness of the law from enactment to the present day by reviewing legislative facts. This enables the Court to keep the reasonableness of the law under continuous review. Furthermore, when the Court reviews fact-finding, legislative materials such as legislative records are checked. As a result, the Court encroaches far into the legislative realm. As regards judicial history, the Court creates history by itself to provide evidence of social change. In the *Illegitimate Child* case, a situation reflecting contemporary values was created by referring to previous separate opinions. This method encourages the courts to act as independent policy makers on behalf of society. As held in the line of *Public Bath House* cases, the Court sometimes changes legislative facts in its own judgments, which *de facto* vests the Court with legislative authority.

These cases show that the Court engages in incremental judicial activism, yet the impact of this approach on political branches is neither stronger than strong judicial activism nor interpretive judicial activism. On the contrary, in instances such as the series of *Public Bath House* cases, it is used in support of constitutionality rulings. In terms of the separation of powers, the Court's approach might be regarded as an unjustified intrusion. Even if it does not violate the principle of separation of powers, incremental judicial activism may turn into a more powerful method depending on the particular Justices involved.

As far as judicial discretion is concerned, the tendency of the Supreme Court of Japan is to exercise judicial restraint rather than to engage in judicial activism.[92] There are some reasons for the judicial passivity of the Japanese Supreme Court. Professor Shigenori Matsui points to the lack of understanding of the power of judicial review among Justices. They sometimes reject defendants' appeals as poorly drafted and entirely ridiculous.[93] Moreover, since

92 Herbert F. Bolz, 'Judicial Review in Japan: The Strategy of Restraint' (1980) 4 Hasting Int'l & Comp. L. Rev. 87, 103–133.

93 Shigenori Matsui, 'Why Is the Japanese Supreme Court So Conservative?' (2011) 88 Wash. U. L. Rev. 1375, 1400–1402.

most Justices were appointed by the same political party, only eleven cases have resulted in a statute being ruled unconstitutional as of 2022. As this situation has been ongoing for a long time, this approach is set to be maintained.

7.2 *Toward Integrity*

Even though the approach taken by the Japanese Supreme Court represents a soft form of judicial activism, there is still another problem concerning the issue of *integrity*. The integrity of the Court's approach is questioned on the grounds that it lacks consistency and governing standards. As this paper illustrates, the Court has rarely mentioned constitutional history and has occasionally referred to legislative history. In determining whether the Court's approach truly lacks consistency and governing standards, it is necessary to examine the Court's justification when referring to legislative history and making judicial history. If there is no justified reason, the Court's approach evidently lacks integrity.

The concept of a living constitution is useful in explaining the Court's reasoning. In viewing the Constitution as a living document, both legislative fact-finding and the creation of judicial history in light of social change will result in the invalidation of earlier laws. This method adjusts the law in line with contemporary values. In other words, constitutional principles evolve in light of social change. This is similar to the concept of a living constitution.

Constitutional rules and tests focusing on contemporary values are also close to the concept of a living constitution. The Japanese Supreme Court uses constitutional tests, such as the contemporary community standard and the evolving standard of decency test, which are similar to those applied by the Supreme Court of the United States. These methods are regarded as indicative of a living constitution in the United States. Justice William Brennan and Justice Anthony Kennedy, who are regarded as living constitutionalists,[94] supported these tests.[95] As noted in section V.B., although the Japanese Supreme Court has never used the phrase "living constitution", the Court has adopted this concept, and the idea of a living constitution is embedded in several constitutional provisions.

94 Lisa K. Parshall, 'Embracing the Living Constitution: Justice Anthony M. Kennedy's Move away from a Conservative Methodology of Constitutional Interpretation' (2007) 30 N.C. Cent. L. Rev. 25.

95 Justice Brennan delivered the opinion of the Court in Roth v. United States, using the contemporary community standard. Justice Kennedy delivered the opinion of the Court in Roper v. Simmons, 543 U.S. 551 (2005), using the evolving standard of decency test.

Considering these points, the Japanese Supreme Court's approach to using history other than constitutional history is consistent with the perspective of the living constitution.

8 Conclusion

The Supreme Court of Japan manipulates history in constitutional cases. The Court seldom mentions constitutional history, possibly due to the difficulty in identifying the Constitution's original meaning and the lack of any need to refer to original intent in order to establish the legitimacy of judicial review. In contrast, legislative history is used occasionally. As illustrated throughout this chapter, the Court reviews the constitutionality of the law by focusing on social change and historical development. This approach regards history as being dynamic rather than static. Rather than using history to interpret the Constitution at the past moment of constitutional enactment, as originalism dictates, the Court instead uses history to review the constitutionality of law in light of historical development.

This dynamic model might suggest that the Court manipulates history in a capricious manner. Nevertheless, this model does not conflict with the current Constitution. Upon closer examination of the constitutional ideal and several key constitutional provisions, the Japanese Constitution *requires* a dynamic model. The preamble and Articles 11, 12, and 97 provide that individual rights must be protected for all generations, thus informing the judicial approach to consider recent circumstances. The national review system also supports this stance as Justices are reviewed by the people, under Article 79. This means that Justices must respond to social change in order to avoid dismissal.

The dynamic model closely resembles the model of living constitutionalism. In this model, the Court reviews the constitutionality of the law while adjusting old laws in line with present circumstances. Furthermore, the Court is not bound by any original public meaning in the past. This model might appear to further judicial activism as it leads the Court to review the constitutionality of the law aggressively. However, considering the existing judicial stance and current political situation, there is no need for the Court to change its approach. As the Court has continuously embraced judicial passivity in constitutional cases and practically the same governmental party has controlled judicial appointments, it is necessary for the Court to lean towards activism in order to redress this power imbalance.

Bibliography

Bolz, Herbert F., 'Judicial Review in Japan: The Strategy of Restraint' (1980) 4 Hasting Int'l & Comp. L. Rev. 87.

Law, David S., 'The Myth of the Imposed Constitution' in Denis Galligan and Mila Versteeg (eds.), the Social and Political Foundation of Constitutions (CUP 2013).

Matsui, Shigenori, 'Why Is the Japanese Supreme Court So Conservative?' (2011) 88 Wash. U. L. Rev. 1375.

Obayashi, Keigo, Ikeru Kenpo to Kenpososho: Gokenseishinsa toshiteno Rippojijitsu (2018) 91 Hogakukenkyu 395.

Parshall, Lisa K., 'Embracing the Living Constitution: Justice Anthony M. Kennedy's Move away from a Conservative Methodology of Constitutional Interpretation' (2007) 30 N.C. Cent. L. Rev. 25.

Sakurai, Tomoaki 'Jijo no Henko niyoru Ikenhandan nitsuite' (2011) 51 Konanhogaku 795.

Solum, Lawrence B., 'Intellectual History as Constitutional Theory' (2015) 101 Va. L. Rev. 1111.

Young, Christopher M., 'War, Peace, and National Security in the Pacific: U.S. and Japanese Geostrategic Constitutionalism, and the Creation of the Japanese Constitution of 1947' (2016) 11 U. Pa. Asian L. Rev. 439.

White, G. Edward, 'The Arrival of History in Constitutional Scholarship' (2002) 88 Va. L. Rev. 485.

PART 4

New Democracies and Illiberal Regimes

CHAPTER 9

How Not to Use History in Constitutional Interpretation

The Aborted Resurrection of the Historical Constitution in Hungary

Zoltán Szente

1 Introduction*

Legal history can influence the application of law and jurisprudence in a number of ways. One of these is the use of the historical method in constitutional interpretation, which relies on the legal facts, concepts, and institutions of the past in order to help resolve contemporary legal disputes. Within the various legal cultures, there are a number of traditional and well-embedded approaches to the historical interpretation of constitutional texts, which are well-known in the academic literature and form part of constitutional discourse. In the last decade, however, a new and unprecedented form of historical method has emerged, which is little-known in international constitutional scholarship.

Since 2010, profound changes have taken place in the political and constitutional system of Hungary, involving also the adoption of a new constitution. Within this framework, it was intended to resurrect the ancient, unwritten constitution of Hungary, which had previously been in force before the Second World War. In this way, a new kind of claim has emerged regarding the use of history within constitutional jurisprudence, which is worth exploring more closely, precisely due to its novelty and the fact that it is unknown.

2 Historical Interpretation from a Comparative Perspective

In Europe, the main classic categorisation of methods of legal interpretation is linked to the German jurist Carl Friedrich von Savigny, who distinguished between grammatical, logical, historical (referring to original intent of the

* The research was supported by the National Research, Development and Innovation Office's 129018 projects on the Responsiveness of the Hungarian Legal System 2010–2018.

 | DOI:10.1163/9789004523739_011

law-maker), and systematic methods of interpretation.[1] Laws have obviously been interpreted since the very outset (in Hungary, for example, since as early as István Werbőczy's *Tripartitum*, a collection of medieval customary law published in 1517, which contained references to the methods of legal interpretation). Savigny's significance lies primarily in his having systematised and theorised about possible interpretive methods. According to conventional wisdom, the essence of the historical method is to draw conclusions from the development of and changes in the law (or potentially the application of law) in terms of the content of the rule as interpreted.[2]

In the United States, before Savigny wrote, the American lawyer Joseph Story had already addressed the issue of correct constitutional interpretation when, in his voluminous commentary on the American Constitution, the first edition of which was published in 1833, he stated that: "[t]he first and fundamental rule in the interpretation of all instruments is, to construe them according to the sense of the terms, and the intention of the parties."[3] A scientific systematisation of interpretative methods appeared in American legal literature as early as 1837.[4]

Ever since, the historical method has become a more or less recognised method of legal interpretation in constitutional democracies, albeit in different ways. While in the United States, for example, this method arises mainly as an instrument of originalist interpretation, in some other countries, whose constitutions were drafted decades or even centuries ago (such as in Norway), it is used in order to clarify ancient concepts and institutions or (such as in the United Kingdom, where the constitution is still unwritten and historical in nature) in order to ensure that continuity remains at the heart of historical interpretation.

All of this makes sense because the historical method has various justifications and problems within different social, political and cultural contexts. For example, according to the classical form of originalism, the main purpose of constitutional interpretation is to give effect to the original intention of the

1 Friedrich Carl von Savigny, *Vorlesungen über juristische Methodologie: 1802–1842* (Vittorio Klostermann Verlag 2004) 91–95, 215–246.; Friedrich Carl von Savigny, *Das System des heutigen Römischen Rechts: Erster Band* (Veit und Camp 1840) 213–214. Although Savigny applied these methods of interpretation to private law, his classification is generally considered to be valid also in relation to constitutional law.

2 Helmut Coing, *Grundzüge der Rechtsphilosophie* (4th edn, de Gruyter 2011) 268.

3 Joseph Story, *Commentaries on the Constitution of the United States: Vol. I.* (Hilliard, Gray, and Company 1833) 383.

4 Francis Lieber, *Legal and Political Hermeneutics* (F. H. Thomas 1837). On Lieber's legal and political hermeneutics see also the special issue of 16 Cardozo Law Review (1995).

framers of the constitution, which is based on the consideration that only the authority that adopted the constitution was empowered to establish constitutional rules. Thus, identifying the original intention of the Founding Fathers is regarded as an absolute requirement stemming from the authority of the constitution, and the sole purpose of constitutional interpretation is to reveal this intention.[5] This interpretative method is often justified as the most effective way of limiting judicial discretion, since the law-maker's intention provides an objective measure for determining the meaning of the constitution, as against the interpreting bodies' own judgments.[6] In the absence of such an objective standard, so the argument goes, everyone would be able to interpret the text of the constitution as they pleased, which would undermine the supremacy of the constitution by blurring the distinction between truly constitutional and extra-constitutional norms, and thus the authority of the constitution.[7] It is to be noted, however, that for many years the dominant conception of originalism in the US has been that constitutional text should be given the meaning it had to the public at the time the text was adopted.[8]

In the United Kingdom, a number of conceptions of the unwritten constitution have developed over time, such as an emphasis on the antiquity and venerability of the constitution embedded in the ancient common law, harking back to the legal and political fabric of special periods in the past, or considering it as a guarantor of continuity between the past and the present with change or reform being an inherent feature of the ancient constitutional arrangements.[9] Some of these approaches are mutually exclusive, depending on which historical period's constitutional achievements are preferred, or whether they emphasise continuity or change.

5 Paul Brest, 'The Misconceived Quest for the Original Understanding' (1980) 60 Boston University Law Review 204.; Dennis J. Goldford, 'The Political Character of Constitutional Interpretation' (1990) 23 Polity 268.; Keith E. Whittington, *Constitutional Interpretation: Textual Meaning, Original Intent, and Judicial Review* (University Press of Kansas 1999) 46.; Clifford W. Taylor, 'Construing the Text of Constitutions and Statutes' (2004) 8 Texas Review of Law and Politics 367–368.

6 E.g. Antonin Scalia, 'Originalism: The Lesser Evil' (1989) 57 University of Cincinnati Law Review 863–864.

7 Goldford, (n 5) 268.

8 See e.g. Robert H. Bork, *The Tempting of America. The Political Seduction of the Law* (The Free Press, Collier Macmillan Publishers 1990) 145.; Richard S. Kay, 'Original Intention and Public Meaning in Constitutional Interpretation' (2009) 103 Northwestern University Law Review, 703–725.

9 J.W.F. Allison, *The English Historical Constitution: Continuity, Change and European Effects* (Cambridge University Press 2007) 15–16.

The doctrine of original intent has never played a prominent role in European civil law systems. Nonetheless, it is sometimes relevant in deciding on certain cases, and the courts do explore the legislative history in the course of constitutional review. For example, in the famous Flick case,[10] the German Federal Constitutional Court studied the circumstances surrounding the adoption of the German *Grundgesetz* (Basic Law) of 1949, and read from the minutes of the Parliamentary Council (the body that adopted the text of the Constitution) that parliamentary committees of inquiry had the power to access all executive documents relevant to an investigation. Moreover, when this Court asserted the State's obligation to protect the foetus when interpreting the concept of human dignity and the right to life, it also sought to show that the members of the Parliamentary Council had taken the view that protection for the right to life also covered the life of the foetus.[11]

My starting point is that the historical method of constitutional interpretation arises in a different context in Hungary than it does in other countries. In Hungary, this method is not one of the possible and legitimate methods of constitutional interpretation that could have its own doctrinal foundations, but is regarded as a tool for defining the 'achievements' of the unwritten, so-called 'one-thousand-year-old' historical constitution valid before the Second World War. In this country, historical interpretation has not played the modest role that it has had elsewhere in continental Europe following the collapse of the Communist regimes. This is mainly because Hungary was the only post-communist country in Central and Eastern Europe not to have adopted a new constitution during the democratic transition. On the contrary, most important principles and rules of the emerging constitutional democracy were institutionalised by a general revision of the 1949 (Stalinist) Constitution, which was adjusted to circumstances radically different from those prevailing at the time of its birth. However, later on, the historical context of the 1989 constitutional revision was not examined either because after the system changed nobody wanted to go back to the circumstances of the birth of the 1949 (Stalinist) Constitution. The reason for this was that the constitution-making process gave effect to the political agreement reached between the former Communist Party and opposition movements within the text of the constitution in the last 'Communist' National Assembly in power before the regime change. Moreover, neither the 'National Roundtable', as the framework

10 67 BVerfGE 100, 130–131 (1984).

11 See 39 BVERFGE 1, 38–42 (1975), and Donald P. Kommers, Germany: Balancing Rights and Duties, in Jeffrey Goldsworthy (ed), *Interpreting Constitutions: A Comparative Study* (OUP 2007) 197.

for informal negotiations between the Communist party and the democratic movements, nor the Parliament of the day, which approved the constitutional revision, had sufficient political legitimacy.

As a consequence of all of this, problems relating to the historical method of constitutional interpretation arise differently in Hungary than they do elsewhere. For example, one of the most common objections to originalist interpretation is that the original intention or understanding often cannot be identified, or at least interpreting bodies (especially courts) are unable to identify it. In Hungary, however, the social and political conditions prevailing at the time the 1949 Constitution was adopted were always considered to be irrelevant. Another well-known problem associated with historical interpretation is the indeterminacy of historical sources, which obstructs the authentic reproduction of the original intent, purpose, public meaning or circumstances.[12] As we shall see, this difficulty also arises in Hungary, albeit in a special way, as not only the interpretation of credible sources but also the selection of authentic sources is controversial. The application of historical methods of interpretation can also be problematic because, even if the meaning or significance of certain sources is clarified, this knowledge would have to be applied to quite different socio-political contexts from those in which they were created. Thus, many contemporary legal problems cannot be resolved by establishing historical facts in relation to the constitution-making process.

While the problem of interpreting historical sources is usually exacerbated by the fact that judges are not historians, and are simply not equipped to reveal and interpret historical facts,[13] so far, no such concerns have been raised in Hungary, where constitutional judges unscrupulously refer to certain institutions from the historical constitution without any evidence or justification.[14]

The usefulness of historical interpretation may also be called into question by changes in social conditions over time. For example, when the Norwegian Constitution was adopted in 1814, the position of Lutheranism as the state religion was still taken seriously, whereas today it is incompatible with the principle of state neutrality. Moreover, whereas the early application of the Equal

---

12 See e.g. Brest (n 5), in particular 211–220, Laurence H. Tribe & Michael Dorf, *On Reading the Constitution* (Harvard University Press 1991) 98–101.; Suzanna Sherry, 'The Indeterminacy of Historical Evidence' (1996) 19 Harvard Journal of Law & Public Policy, 437–442.

13 See e.g. Helen Irving, Outsourcing the Law: History and the Disciplinary Limits of Constitutional Reasoning, (2015) 84 Fordham Law Review 957–967.

14 Such as, e.g. the concept of 'acquired rights', defined as an achievement of the historical constitution. See Schanda Balázs, 'Alkotmányos értékek – alkotmányos identitás' in (Chronowski Nóra. Pozsár-Szentmiklósy Zoltán, Smuk Péter, Szabó Zsolt eds), *A szabadságszerető embernek. Liber Amicorum István Kukorelli* (Gondolat Kiadó 2017) 94.

Protection Clause contained in the 14th Amendment to the US Constitution adopted in 1868 originally focused on the prohibition of racial discrimination, it was only later extended to other types of discrimination. When the German Federal Constitutional Court declared the sentence of life imprisonment unconstitutional in 1977, it argued that the original intent of the framers of the Constitution was not decisive in interpreting the provisions of the Constitution, because the content, functions and impact of fundamental rights had become deeper and broader since then.[15] Although a similar question about changes in social conditions over time may also arise when interpreting the Hungarian historical constitution, as we shall see, the Constitutional Court does not consider the issue important, even for understanding institutions of medieval origin.

However, the most significant challenge to the historical method, especially when it is used to reveal original intent, is probably the 'dead hand problem'. The essence of this argument is that approaches of an earlier era cannot bind current and future generations, because democratic self-government entails the right of each generation to govern itself.[16] Interestingly, this argument has not appeared at all in Hungarian political and academic discourse. This can probably be accounted for by the fact that the Constitutional Court enjoys virtually unlimited freedom to choose which constitutional traditions should be followed and what they mean today.

3 The Constitutional Endeavour of Resurrecting the Historical Constitution in the Fundamental Law of 2011

During the course of the fairly recent constitution-making process in Hungary, which resulted in the adoption of the Fundamental Law of 2011, considerable efforts were made by the framers of the new constitution to link it to the so-called 'one-thousand-year old' historical constitution, which had been in effect in Hungary before World War II. Leading aside the issue of its feasibility, this enterprise was not in and of itself unreasonable. Since the opposition did not participate in the drafting and adoption of the Fundamental Law in

15 1 BvL 14/76.

16 See e.g. Michael W. Mc Connell, 'Textualism and the Dead Hand of the Past' (1998) 66 The George Washington Law Review, 1127.; Haig Patapan, 'The Dead Hand of the Founders? Original Intent and the Constitutional Protection of Rights and Freedoms in Australia' (1997) 25 Federal Law Review, 233–234.

2010–2011,[17] the entire text of the constitution was drafted and approved by the governing parties (which came to power in 2010 and gained a two-thirds (constitution-making) majority in Parliament). The Fundamental Law suffered from the lack of political compromise and, for this reason, has been unable from the very outset to perform one of its basic functions that is its identity-building role. Under these circumstances, it may have seemed particularly important to look for something to strengthen the ideological foundation of the new constitution.

This ideological basis was found by the governing parties in the relationship between the Fundamental Law and the historical constitution. This was not entirely surprising given that both the Holy Crown and the historical constitution[18] have been important parts of the political ideology of the domestic conservative right (and the far right) since the collapse of the Communist regime and the transition to democracy in 1989–1990.

The Hungarian Fundamental Law of 2011, which is the youngest constitution of Europe, introduced real innovation into European constitutionalism by reviving Hungary's ancient, 'one-thousand-year old' historical constitution, which had been in force before the Second World War. The preamble of the Constitution declares that '[w]*e honour the achievements of our historical constitution and we honour the Holy Crown, which embodies the constitutional continuity of Hungary's statehood and the unity of the nation*'. It is not simply the desire to create continuity between a modern, written constitution and an uncodified one, rooted in medieval times, that is relevant but also the way in which this goal is pursued. The Constitution provides that '[*t*]*he provisions of the Fundamental Law shall be interpreted in accordance with* (…) *the National Avowal* [the preamble] *and the achievements of our historical constitution*'.

Thus, constitutional history (or historical interpretation) is no longer merely a tool for constitutional interpretation. On the contrary, the courts are expressly required by the Constitution to give consideration to constitutional history.

17 Most opposition parties raised these objections to backsliding on the rule of law by the rightist conservative Government led by Viktor Orbán.

18 For a detailed analysis of the Hungarian historical constitution and the doctrine of the Holy Crown, see Szente Zoltán, 'The Doctrine of the Holy Crown in the Hungarian Historical Constitution' (2013) 4 Journal on European History of Law 109–115.

4 Attempting to Reconcile the Fundamental Law with the Unwritten Historical Constitution

One of the most bizarre tasks of the 2011 constitution-making process was to seek to reconcile the political will to revive the unwritten, historical constitution with the newly-created unified, written Fundamental Law. The politicians involved in the drafting of the new constitution, and the constitutional lawyers who supported their aspirations, made considerable efforts to identify a theoretical basis for this claim.

4.1 *Restoring Continuity with the Historical Constitution*

According to a pro-government politician who played a key role in the drafting of the new Constitution, 'When we created the Fundamental Law (...) one of our most important tasks was to rebuild the interrupted continuity', and the historical foundations of the constitutional system, to revive the 'millennial Hungarian constitutional tradition', and to 'restore continuity'.[19] Thus, the clear original intention was to create legal continuity between the Fundamental Law and the historical constitution.

The most ambitious approach was formulated by Attila Horváth, a legal historian and member of the Constitutional Court, who believed that 'the Constitution consisted in the Fundamental Law and the historical constitution', and who claimed that 'our historical constitution is also a source of law!'.[20] This view is akin to that taken by those who stress legal continuity without elaborating what it means. It is worth noting that some scholars who were sceptical about the historical constitution *per se* viewed the attempt to revive the historical constitution as an experiment designed to restore legal continuity with the ancient constitution.[21]

4.2 *Rehabilitating the Ancient Concept of 'Constitution'*

Another approach involved an attempt to fuse the old, unwritten constitution with the new Fundamental Law in a very special way, by referring also to the

---

19 Szájer József, *Szabad Magyarország, szabad Európa. Újabb tizenöt év. Beszédek, írások, dokumentumok 1998–2013* (Self-published 2014) 825, 845.

20 Bakó Beáta: *A történeti alkotmányunk is jogforrás! – Horváth Attila a Mandinernek.* <http://jog.mandiner.hu/cikk/20161214_a_torteneti_alkotmanyunk_is_jogforras_horvath_attila_a_mandinernek>.

21 'The obvious purpose of the Fundamental Law is to restore legal continuity with the pre-1949 situation'. Csink Lóránt, Fröhlich Johanna, *Egy alkotmány margójára: Alkotmányelméleti és értelmezési kérdések az Alaptörvényről* (Gondolat Kiadó 2012) 129.

importance of respect for the historical past. 'Today's Fundamental Law (...) is part of a larger whole, part of a newly created historical continuity', which is also expressed by its name. 'We wanted to preserve the phrase of »constitution«, or to give it back to a living legal body with a thousand-year history, which is to be revived'.[22] On this view, the concept of the 'constitution' covers an entire constitutional system, denoting the overall body of constitutional rules and traditions. Restoration of the name was necessary because the communist constitution[23] 'expropriated the term constitution, depriving it of its original historical meaning'.[24] In any case, the Fundamental Law is only one part of the Constitution, and the revived constitutional concept incorporates the Fundamental Law.[25]

4.3 *The Historical Constitution as an Interpretative Aid*

Some other scholars have recognised that the historical constitution is no longer applicable 'because its scope cannot be precisely defined, and a significant part of it has no effect or is contrary to the law in force'.[26] In fact, the Fundamental Law does not give any legal effect to the historical constitution, but defines its 'achievements' as an 'interpretative framework'.[27] This implies a conception of the historical constitution's achievements which, like the *acquis communautaire* of the European Union law, is 'the result of the common European system of values laid down in concrete legal rules and in the practice of the state'.[28] It should not be forgotten, so this line of argument continues, that the Fundamental Law refers only to the 'achievements' of the historical constitution and, when its content is defined, 'a qualitative selection criterion is applied. The old rules that no longer correspond to today's values do not form part of this living constitutional law; they fall outside of tradition and are not achievements'.[29] Thus, only those rules that 'have stood the test of time and are still guiding force today' should be taken to be valid. In other words, only those elements of the constitutional tradition should be classified as 'achievements' that are in harmony with the principles and values of modern European constitutionalism. If the achievements of the historical constitution

22 Szájer (n 19) 840–841.
23 Act XX of 1949.
24 Szájer (n 19) 840.
25 Szájer (n 19) 840–841.
26 Varga Zs. András, 'Történeti alkotmányunk vívmányai az Alaptörvény kógens rendelkezésében', (2016) 12 Iustum Aequum Salutare 87.
27 Ibid.
28 Ibid.
29 Szájer (n 19) 825, 840.

are used as an 'interpretative framework' or a 'guiding principle', the precise definition of their content will primarily fall to the Constitutional Court and the ordinary courts.[30] Another constitutional judge also regards the achievements of the historical constitution as interpretative aids, and proposes criteria for identifying those rules and principles of the ancient constitution that can still be interpreted today.[31]

4.4 *The Reconceptualisation of the Historical Constitution*

Some commentators have tried to facilitate the acceptance of the relationship between the Fundamental Law and the historical constitution by incorporating certain elements of post-1944 constitutional development into the concept of the latter. However, this approach would appear to be overly ambitious in the light of the fact that the Preamble to the Fundamental Law, i.e. the National Avowal, states that 'we do not recognise the suspension of our historical constitution due to alien invasions', specifying 19 March 1944 (the date of the German occupation of Hungary) as the time when Hungary lost its sovereignty (and, indirectly, the end of the historical constitution).

László Sólyom, the President of the first Constitutional Court (1990–1999) has argued that the achievements of the historical constitution should be understood as those constitutional standards that have been established after 1990, primarily within the jurisprudence of the Constitutional Court.[32] His position has been endorsed by some other authors.[33] Moreover, the time when the historical constitution ceased to have effect is also identified differently. While some scholars regard Act I of 1946 as forming part of the historical constitution,[34] others argue that it was only replaced by the adoption of the communist (written) constitution in 1949.[35] However, all these views are barely defensible; the meaning of the historical constitution is bounded by the sense in which this concept was used to refer to the unwritten constitution before the Second World War (this notion was especially popular during the inter-war period). Act I of 1946 (often referred to as the 'little constitution')

30 Szájer (n 19) 841.; Ablonczy Bálint, *Az Alkotmány nyomában: Beszélgetések Szájer Józseffel és Gulyás Gergellyel* (Elektromédia 2011).

31 Schanda (n 14) 94.

32 See Sólyom László, Alkotmány és alkotmányos kultúra Magyarországon. Előadás a Történelemtanárok 21. Országos Konferenciáján, 2011. október 8.

33 See e.g. Smuk Péter, 'Nemzeti értékek az Alaptörvényben' in Szoboszlai-Kiss Katalin, Deli Gergely (eds), *Tanulmányok a 70 éves Bihari Mihály tiszteletére* (Universitas-Győr Nonprofit Kft. 2013) 455.; Csink and Fröhlich (n 18) 133.

34 Bakó (n 20).

35 See e.g. Csink and Fröhlich (n 21) 129.

introduced the republican form of government, and its real intention was to break with the pre-war constitutional system. Thus, when the Stalinist constitution was passed in 1949, no institutions from the historical constitution existed any longer.

5 The Historical Constitution in the Constitutional Court's Jurisprudence

In spite of all of the theoretical difficulties, there is a constitutional requirement to respect the achievements of the historical constitution within constitutional interpretation, which requires the Constitutional Court to take account of the ancient constitution when identifying the meaning of the Fundamental Law. Within the Hungarian academic literature, there is a consensus that the Court has not yet developed a doctrinally sound method or theory of how to take into account the achievements of the historical constitution.[36] Nevertheless, on some occasions the Court has desperately tried to prove that its practice meets with the requirement laid down by Article R (3) of the Fundamental Law, even though the Constitutional Court does not have a uniform conception of the nature of the achievements of the historical constitution. Its interpretative practice is consistent only in the sense that a legal norm may not be invalidated solely on the basis of Article R (3). In actual fact however, references to the historical constitution are little more than embellishments of the reasoning in support of the Court's rulings.[37] Thus, in one of its decisions, the Constitutional Court explained the importance of historical arguments on the grounds that, without this knowledge, 'our present-day public law and our legal culture in general would be rootless'.[38] It should be noted here that the institution of the Constitutional Court itself – like, for example, the President of the Republic or the unicameral Parliament – was not recognised and would even have been anachronistic under the historical constitution. Since there was no written basic law in a formal sense before World War II, the issue as to which body had the power to resolve contradictions between ordinary legislation and the Constitution was never even raised.[39] Finally, it is really strange to

36 Vörös Imre, 'A történeti alkotmány az Alkotmánybíróság gyakorlatában' (2016) 9 Közjogi Szemle 46.

37 See Szente Zoltán, 'A historizáló alkotmányozás problémái – A történeti alkotmány és a Szent Korona az új Alaptörvényben' (2011) 4 Közjogi Szemle 10.

38 Decision 33/2012. (VII. 17.) of the Constitutional Court.

39 Egyed István, *A mi alkotmányunk* (Magyar Szemle Társaság 1943) 56.

hear this statement being made by a body that did not even exist before 1990. Moreover, the constitutionality of a legal institution or rule does not depend on how old it is.

As regards the relevant case-law, the Constitutional Court has often made merely formal statements, stressing that the body 'took it into account' the fact that freedom of the press was an achievement under the historical constitution established by Act XVIII of 1848.[40] However, it does not make any sense today to trace back freedom of the press to the revolutionary laws of 1848,[41] since it is rooted in the Fundamental Law of 2011 and regulated in greater detail by the media laws adopted in 2010.[42] The Court has referred several times to guarantees of judicial independence as an achievement of the historical constitution, as if the legal source of these guarantees – such as the principle of the immovability of judges – were Act IV of 1869 on the exercise of judicial power, rather than the current Constitution and the Cardinal Act CLXII of 2011 involving the legal status and remuneration of judges. In any case, the reference to this 'exemplary achievement of the historical constitution' has not provided any added force or any real legal protection against the removal from office of more than 250 judges (approximately eight per cent of all judges) under a law that dramatically lowered the compulsory retirement age for judges within the space of one year in 2012.[43]

Some references to the historical constitution have revealed an ignorance of as well as disregard for (or perhaps more confusion concerning) its real content and context. For example, Constitutional Court ruling 16/2016 (X. 20.) refers to the Preamble to Act I of 1946 as an achievement of the historical constitution, despite the fact that this law deliberately interrupted the chain of continuity with the ancient constitution in all of its essential elements, such as the form of government, the issue of sovereignty, and the structure of legislative power. Another of the Court's rulings has held that the old constitution also contained the inherent rule that, when the prosecutor loses a lawsuit, the costs of the judicial proceedings are charged to the state treasury.[44] The only basis for this statement, which would probably have come as a great surprise to all public

40 Decisions 28/2014. (IX. 29.) and 3002/2018. (I. 10.) of the Constitutional Court.

41 This law, for example, protected communication by lithograph, and imposed fines against anyone who 'ridiculed' 'decent morals' or disobliged the King.

42 See Laws CIV and CLXXXV of 2010.

43 This law was declared unconstitutional by the Constitutional Court, as it also violated EU law. See Decision 33/2012. (VII. 17.) of the Constitutional Court and *Commission v Hungary*, Case C-286/12, Judgment 6 November 2012.

44 Decision 3089/2016. (V. 12.) of the Constitutional Court.

lawyers before 1945, was that this provision was incorporated into Act I of 1911 concerning the Civil Procedure Law. The reasons provided in support of Decision 17/2015 (VI. 5.) of the Constitutional Court state that the 'commonage assembly', which was established by an Act of 1894, was also an achievement of the historical constitution, and was specifically followed by the enactment of new legislation on land transactions at the time when land committees were set up. According to the dissenting opinion of one of the Constitutional Court judges, Barnabás Lenkovics, social benefits provided by the state to parents and children should be regarded as an achievement of the historical constitution, because after 1919 such state assistance was always provided.[45] There are a number of further examples of the misuse of the historical constitution. However, in reality, not all legislation enacted before 1944 was incorporated into the conceptual framework of the historical constitution, but rather only those 'fundamental' or 'cardinal' laws concerning the exercise of public powers or laying down individual rights and freedoms.

Another frequently used legal method is to establish a perverse or erroneous link between present-day ideas and claims on the one hand and ancient concepts on the other. For example, in one of his concurring opinions Constitutional Court judge András Varga Zs. traced the concept of human rights and the limitation of public powers back to the Golden Bull (*Aranybulla*) of 1222; respect for 'public law autonomies' to the so-called *Tripartitum* of 1517; freedom of religion to the 1568 Edict of Torda; the requirement of the lawful exercise of public power to the so-called *Pragmatica Sanctio* of 1723; parliamentary government and equality before the law to the revolutionary laws of 1848; and the principle of power-sharing, the recognition of judicial independence and the protection of national minorities to the laws of 1867 on the Austro-Hungarian Compromise.[46] In fact, almost all of these references are incorrect. The Golden Bull did not recognise any 'human rights' (the concept was only 'discovered' centuries later), but was rather a medieval charter that guaranteed the privileges of the nobility and restrained royal power. Moreover, it is rather bizarre today to refer to the Golden Bull as a source of civil rights, when this charter stated that Jews could not hold any official positions and could not pursue certain occupations in the country. The purpose of the *Pragmatica Sanctio* was not to ensure the 'lawful exercise of power', but to extend the hereditary rights of the Habsburg dynasty to its sister branch, and it prescribed 'the indivisible and inseparable co-existence of Hungary and its associate countries

---

45 Decision 3023/2016. (II. 23.) of the Constitutional Court.

46 See the concurring opinion of András Varga Zs. in the Decision 22/2016. (XII. 5.) of the Constitutional Court.

with the kingdoms and countries represented in the former Austrian Imperial Assembly'. The laws of the Revolution of 1848 (apparently, Act III of that year) did not introduce parliamentary government, but rather established a constitutional monarchy in Hungary. The 'Edict of Torda' in Transylvania guaranteed freedom and equality to the four accepted Christian denominations (*recepta religio*), but not freedom of religion in its current sense. Similarly, to derive protection for nationality from the laws on the Great Compromise is a genuine – albeit worthless – innovation.

This kind of approach truly demonstrates how freely the historical constitution can be used for present-day purposes. Although the ancient constitution embraced certain standard values and institutions (such as the monarchical form government or the so-called Holy Crown doctrine), its actual content changed over time.[47]

6 The Problems and Risks Associated with the Resurrection of the Historical Constitution

6.1 *Theoretical Misconceptions and Doctrinal Gaps*

Among the attempts to identify theoretical links between the Fundamental Law and the historical constitution, the weakest refer to continuity between the ancient and the present-day constitutions. Legal continuity does not have any plausible conceptualisation that could support such claims, either before 1944 or within contemporary constitutional theory. According to the traditional Hungarian approach to public law, legal continuity had two forms. So-called 'formal continuity' referred to the requirement that amendments to the constitution could only be adopted in a lawful manner, i.e. in accordance with the procedure laid down in, and in a manner consistent with, the historical constitution.[48] By contrast, the conception of 'material legal continuity' insisted on the ancient institutions and values of the historical constitution, i.e. the unbroken preservation of the cornerstones of the constitutional past,

47 As the legal historian Ferenc Eckhart wrote, many articles of the Golden Bull were already invalid a hundred years after its adoption. Eckhart Ferenc, 'Jog és alkotmánytörténet' in Hóman Bálint (ed), *A magyar történetírás új útjai* (Magyar Szemle Társaság 1932) 316. The famous Article 31 of the Bull, which provided for the *ius resistendi* of the nobility, was abolished in 1687.

48 Bölöny József, *A magyar közjog időszerű kérdései* (self-published 1941) 17.; Egyed (n 39) 46–48.

such as the monarchical form of state, the bicameral Parliament and the theory of sovereignty based on the doctrine of the Holy Crown.[49]

However, the Fundamental Law of 2011 was adopted pursuant to Article 19(3)(a) and Article 24(3) of the former Constitution of 1949, rather than in accordance with the unwritten procedural rules of the historical constitution.[50] The Fundamental Law was passed by the members of the unicameral National Assembly, which was elected on 25 April 2010 as the 'constituent power'. However, this procedure was a far cry from what the historical constitution required in its own time. According to the ancient constitution, Parliament itself did not have any constitution-making power. 'Fundamental' or 'cardinal' laws could only be adopted by the bicameral National Assembly with the consent of the King. Moreover, the notion of a unified and written constitution was itself an anachronism under ancient Hungarian constitutional theory.

As far as 'material legal continuity' is concerned, the most important institutions of the Fundamental Law – such as the republican form of state, the President of the Republic, the neutrality of the state, the institution and powers of the Constitutional Court, and the transfer of sovereignty in relation to European Union membership – are fully incompatible with the values embraced as well as the system of public powers and fundamental rights under the historical constitution.

The conclusion that the historical constitution is in no way a source of the law today follows from the lack of legal continuity with it. Moreover, neither the Fundamental Law nor any other legal norm contains any provision that could conceivably have reintroduced the historical constitution or any part of it. Today, the Fundamental Law is the exclusive source of legitimacy for all public law institutions, as the Fundamental Law declares itself to be the basis of the entire legal system[51] and the supreme law of the land, such that no law can make any provision that is contrary to it.[52] The Fundamental Law quite simply cannot be rivalled by any other legal source.

The enterprise of postulating the achievements of the historical constitution as an aid for constitutional interpretation was *ab ovo* a hopeless idea, which has been proved within the practice of the Constitutional Court in recent years. The framers of Article R (3) of the Fundamental Law were probably in a difficult situation, consequently the Fundamental Law does not define the scope or meaning of the achievements of the historical constitution. Under these

49 Egyed (n 39) 49–50.

50 Closing and Miscellaneous Provisions, point 2, Fundamental Law.

51 Article R (1) of the Fundamental Law.

52 Article T (3) of the Fundamental Law.

circumstances, the inventive advocates of the Fundamental Law have used the "thick-and-thin" formula: the content of achievements will be specified and elaborated on both by the Constitutional Court and by the ordinary courts by way of legal interpretation. However, revealing the past meaning of previously non-existent legal concepts, such as the 'achievements of the historical constitution', is pointless. It is also not clear how this category could offer any help within interpretation by the Constitutional Court or by other courts if its content must be determined by these bodies themselves.

The interpretive tool proposed for defining the achievements of the historical constitution is also unreasonable: if the achievements are only those parts of the historical constitution that correspond to contemporary constitutional values, what use is there in referring to the historical constitution at all? What is the function and the benefit of the tenets and principles of the historical constitution, if the only criterion for their recognition is whether they are in keeping with the existing legal values and the normative content of the Fundamental Law?[53] What is the point of referring to the historical constitution if we can pick and choose among its values and institutions, embracing some and ignoring others, depending on whether they coincide with the provisions of the existing Constitution? As soon as a constitutional value can be inferred directly from the Fundamental Law, it seems, it is unnecessary to seek out any other source of legitimacy.

Some of those who have emphasised the obscurity of the content of the historical constitution have probably only been seeking to pave the way towards freedom to choose from the results of hundreds of years of constitutional development in line with prevailing political considerations. The purpose of such operations is frequently to serve contemporary expectations, rather than to discern the meaning of the historical constitution. For example, Balázs Schanda (currently a member of the Constitutional Court) has referred to the alleged historical principles of 'the extension of rights' or 'the protection of acquired rights', 'whether in relation to property rights or even the right to vote', concluding that 'any provision contrary to the extension of rights cannot constitute an achievement of the historical constitution'.[54] However, he failed to prove the existence of such principles within the historical constitution, and his arguments were probably written in defence of the controversial extension of voting rights to Hungarians living in the neighbouring countries.

53 For this reason, the reference of Article R (3) to the historical constitution is a tautology. Jakab András, *Az új Alaptörvény keletkezése és gyakorlati következményei* (HVG-ORAC 2011) 185.

54 Schanda (n 14) 94.

Such arbitrary and undertheorised conceptualisations of the achievements of the historical constitution are, however, meaningless because they do not have any real function or effect in practice. Nevertheless, Article R (3) may actually result in an increase in legal indeterminacy, and there is a risk of a more activist approach to the interpretation of this constitutional provision. As Imre Vörös, a former Constitutional Court judge has pointed out, the search for the achievements has become a brainstorming exercise that undermines legal certainty. Moreover, it can be misused and the incorporation of this clause into the text of the Constitution can be traced back to political goals.[55]

6.2 *The Evils of This Ill-Founded Judicial Practice on the Historical Constitution*

As noted above, the Constitutional Court has not elaborated any well-established doctrine on how to use the achievements of the historical constitution within constitutional interpretation. In addition, legal scholarship has not produced any coherent theory or explanation either. As a matter of fact, most scholars are sceptical about whether the historical constitution is applicable at all. To date, only a few apologetic attempts have been made to defend the relevant constitutional provisions. However, these efforts have failed to eliminate the problem of arbitrariness in using the historical constitution in constitutional jurisprudence. Since the wording of the Constitution does not provide any objective criteria for identifying the achievements of the historical constitution, any theory of interpretation must appeal to extra-constitutional presumptions.

The most imaginative scholars trace the roots of the historical constitution back to the foundation of the Hungarian State in 1000, or even earlier, before the conquest in the late 9th century (this was a dominant view among Hungarian legal historians before WWII). However, even if we disregard such romantic views, the historical constitution did indeed undergo development over the centuries. Until now, the Constitutional Court has not sought to determine which period(s) should be considered when seeking to identify the most glorious results of ancient constitutionalism. The Court refers to the historical constitution sporadically and unpredictably, and it is not possible to discern any inherent logic in the use of history in its practice.

Although the Constitutional Court has not yet repealed any legislative act exclusively on the grounds that it violates Article R (3) of the Fundamental Law, i.e. because of a violation of the achievements of the historical constitution,

55 Vörös (n 36) 47, 55.

there is a serious risk that this constitutional provision may be abused. The danger can be illustrated by referring to Decision 22/2016. (XII. 5.) of the Constitutional Court, which held that Hungary's constitutional identity is based on the historical constitution. The reasoning contained in this ruling states that Court itself will elaborate on the precise content of constitutional identity 'in accordance with the historical constitution, from case to case'. In doing so, the Court established its own power to examine also whether the joint exercise of competences with EU institutions violates Hungary's constitutional identity as rooted in the historical constitution. This ruling reversed the previous practice of the Court and its compatibility with EU law is questionable.[56] The risk of the historical constitution being abused as a standard for constitutional interpretation is even greater if we take account of the broader constitutional context. Exploiting their constitution-making parliamentary majority, governing parties have successfully packed the Court since 2010, and also passed a constitutional amendment depriving all Constitutional Court rulings issued prior to the entry into force of the new Fundamental Law of any effect.[57] In particular, in 2018 the Seventh Amendment to the Fundamental Law declared that constitutional identity is 'rooted in our historic(al) constitution' and that it 'is a fundamental obligation of the State' to protect it,[58] thereby providing a textual basis for the Constitutional Court's claim to strengthen its relevant jurisprudence.

The risk of arbitrary interpretation also stems from the fact that the Fundamental Law seeks to return to a tradition that never existed: aside from certain principles and institutions, the content of the historical constitution changed constantly over time; for example, the Golden Bull and the *Pragmatica Sanctio* were never fully in force in Hungary at the same time, while the revolutionary laws of 1848 radically changed the substantial content of the former feudal law. All in all, most elements of the historical constitution were never simultaneously applicable in Hungary. Today however, all elements of the historical constitution that were developed under the thousand-year history of Hungarian statehood are considered as a unified whole. This means that, in principle, even the laws and conventions created under the rule of the first

56 Zoltán Szente and Fruzsina Gárdos-Orosz, 'Judicial deference or political loyalty? The Hungarian Constitutional Court's role in tackling crisis situations' in Zoltán Szente and Fruzsina Gárdos-Orosz (eds), *New Challenges to Constitutional Adjudication in Europe: A Comparative Perspective* (Routledge 2018) 99.

57 Zoltán Szente, 'The Political Orientation of the Members of the Hungarian Constitutional Court Between 2010 and 2014' (2016) 1 Constitutional Studies 123–149.

58 Preamble to the Fundamental Law.

Hungarian King St. Stephen (1000–1038), Louis I the Great (died 639 years ago) or Matthew I (who ascended to the throne 563 years ago) can potentially be raised today within constitutional discourse. There is no need to point out how difficult it is to determine the precise meaning of the laws of long-distant ages and their present-day relevance.

Finally, the use of the achievements of the historical constitution within constitutional review of legislation has other dangers besides that of arbitrary interpretation. First and foremost, the historical constitution, and in particular its substantive tradition, the doctrine of the Holy Crown, have many elements and postulates that are not at all compatible with the principles and values of modern European constitutionalism (which are also acknowledged and stressed by the Fundamental Law). For example, the sovereignty of the Holy Crown, which embodies the state's supreme power, does not coincide with the principle of popular sovereignty, as its monarchical nature is incompatible with the present-day republican form of government. In addition, the historical constitution was inextricably linked to the Catholic religion and church for a thousand years. However, a state religion and state church are irreconcilable with the constitutional principles of the separation between church and state, as well as the neutrality of the state, even against the backdrop of the Fundamental Law. Moreover, the inalienable claim of the Holy Crown to ownership of the state territory that once belonged to the Kingdom of Hungary is incompatible with the principles of public international law and a number of international treaties to which Hungary is a signatory.

7 Conclusions

Although historical interpretation does not have the same strong tradition and influence in Europe as it does through the school of originalism in the United States, this form of constitutional interpretation is also legitimate on the European continent. Nevertheless, the Hungarian Fundamental Law of 2011 and the constitutional development of Hungary over the last decade have produced a new, hitherto unknown, historical method of constitutional interpretation. This recent development formally seeks to link Europe's youngest constitution with an ancient, unwritten, historical constitution of medieval origin. The ambition reflects not only a political intention to preserve traditions, which attaches only symbolic significance to the constitutional past, but also the goal of giving real constitutional significance to the revival of the historical constitution, in that the requirement to interpret the text of the Constitution in line with the achievements of the historical constitution is prescribed by the Fundamental Law.

All of this poses a serious challenge both for the Constitutional Court, which is primarily responsible for enforcing the requirement, as well as for constitutional scholars who wish to provide a theoretical basis for the claim. Reconciling the historical constitution with the Fundamental Law has been a futile undertaking from the outset, as these sources differ in terms of form and content: whereas the former was an ancient, unwritten constitution rooted in medieval times, the content of which was based on a consensus concerning certain cardinal laws, international treaties, conventions and customs developed over the centuries, the latter is a fully-fledged, modern written constitution. Many of the core institutions and values of the historical constitution are not only different from those of the Fundamental Law, but are absolute antitheses to them, including the doctrine of sovereignty, the form of state and government, the organisation of legislative power, and the recognition of a state religion and state church.

Nevertheless, a number of attempts have been made to justify continuity, including the conception of the historical constitution as a source of law and the reconceptualisation of otherwise commonly used concepts. Thus far, these attempts have proven arbitrary or unfounded. The only plausible effort to justify the revival of the historical constitution, which is also the one most closely linked to the text of the Constitution, sees it as an aid to constitutional interpretation. However, due to the inherent contradictions within this approach, it cannot serve as a basis for the construction of a new theory either. Its main flaw is that the content of the 'acquis' of the constitutional past should be developed by the Constitutional Court and the ordinary courts, the same institutions that are supposed to be guided by it. The weakness within this view is also shown by the judicial practice of using the historical constitution as a framework for interpretation. The jurisprudence of the Constitutional Court concerning the issue has so far been incidental and arbitrary, referring to the historical constitution only as embellishment within the reasoning for individual decisions.

In addition, the application of the historical method not only renders constitutional interpretation unpredictable and contradictory, and devoid of any sound theoretical basis, but is also potentially risky and dangerous. The concept of the 'achievements' of the historical constitution is undeveloped and can be used as justification for any kind of decision. When the broader context is taken into account, especially the packing of the Constitutional Court and the unilateral enactment of a new constitution by a political majority, these risks become even more apparent. Some of the key institutions and values of the historical constitution, such as the rejection of the idea of popular sovereignty, the official nature of the dominant religion and church, and the territorial integrity of the historical Kingdom of Hungary, appear to be in stark contrast with the principles of modern European constitutionalism. Nevertheless, the study of the special Hungarian form of the historical method of constitutional interpretation itself remains instructive by showing a path that is not worth following.

Bibliography

Allison, J.W.F., *The English Historical Constitution: Continuity, Change and European Effects* (Cambridge University Press 2007).

Irving, Helen, 'Outsourcing the Law: History and the Disciplinary Limits of Constitutional Reasoning' (2015) 84 Fordham Law Review.

Sherry, Suzanna, 'The Indeterminacy of Historical Evidence' (1996) 19 Harvard Journal of Law & Public Policy.

Szente, Zoltán, 'The Doctrine of the Holy Crown in the Hungarian Historical Constitution' (2013) 4 Journal on European History of Law.

Szente, Zoltán and Gárdos-Orosz, Fruzsina (eds), *New Challenges to Constitutional Adjudication in Europe: A Comparative Perspective* (Routledge 2018).

Tribe, Laurence H. & Dorf, Michael, *On Reading the Constitution* (Harvard University Press 1991).

CHAPTER 10

Using the Authoritarian Past for Constitutional Interpretation in New Democracies

The Example of the Taiwan Constitutional Court

Shih-An Wang

> Only by looking at our history … can we hope to gain a sense of what values must be credited in striking the balance of ordered liberty for our own times.
>
> REBECCA BROWN[1]

1 Introduction

What role does history play in law? For decades, legal scholars have been interested in the normative guidance that a particular understanding of history in legal interpretation can offer for the future.[2] For countries that democratised during the late twentieth century, this issue is strikingly important, especially in the field of constitutional interpretation. Having emerged from authoritarian rule, these new democracies face two challenges to their post-authoritarian constitutional development.[3] First, these countries are in urgent need of establishing constitutional democratic values such as fair and open elections, the separation of powers and fundamental rights protections.[4] At the same time, the impact of the historical illiberal rule is still pervasive and

1 Rebecca L. Brown, 'History for the Non-Originalist' (2003) 26 Harv J L & Pub Pol'y 69, 77.

2 See Matthew J. Festa, 'Applying a Usable Past: The Use of History in Law'(2008) 38 SHLR 479, 479–480. Gerald J. Postema, 'On the Moral Presence of Our Past' (1991) 36 McGill LJ 1153, 1156–1157. Daphne Barak-Erez, 'History and Memory in Constitutional Adjudication'(2017) 45 FL Rev 1, 1–2. Helen Irving, 'Constitutional Interpretation, the High Court, and the Discipline of History' (2013) 41 FL Rev 95.

3 See Samuel P. Huntington 'Democracy's Third Wave' (1991) 2 J Democracy 12.

4 Chien-Chih Lin, 'The Judicialization of Politics in New Democracies' (JSD thesis, University of Chicago 2015) 1–4.

 | DOI:10.1163/9789004523739_012

may be detrimental to the implementation of these values. Therefore, a key issue in new democracies is how to address their authoritarian past through constitutional interpretation in a way that can bring about substantive consolidation of constitutional democratic values.

Many scholars and human rights activists have engaged in rigorous debates over the issues mentioned above. Their discussions are useful for critically analysing whether and to what extent history should be addressed in constitutional interpretation. The scholarship of transitional justice, for example, provides a strong view in this respect. Its proponents suggest that an ultimate break from the authoritarian past is necessary to forge human rights norms by genuinely recognising and redressing the suffering of victims under authoritarian rule.[5] The opposite view posits that transitional justice can be harmful to democratic consolidation. In newly born democracies, transitional justice measures aimed at reforming authoritarian powers may be politicised and manipulated to stoke antagonism inside an already fragile, unstable society. This is unhealthy for social cohesion, which is integral to the implementation and enforcement of democratic practices.[6]

Apart from transitional justice, treating history as a mere background reference in constitutional interpretation may imply a reluctance on the part of courts to attach any normative salience to their own past practices or those of other actors. However, referencing historical events within constitutional decisions does not necessarily indicate that the opposite is the case: these events can be discussed by the courts either as canons to be followed or as nightmares to be abandoned. In fact, the selection of these models reflects different assessments of the endurance of historical legacy in the contemporary world, and accordingly, of the need for and value in a country placing greater weight on a certain type of constitutional interpretation.

Any usage of history in constitutional interpretation should also take into consideration post-authoritarian contexts in which old powers can remain resilient within the political structure. Moreover, the delicate role performed by constitutional courts adds complexity to the understanding of their interpretative activities. The empowerment of an independent, apolitical constitutional court is widely regarded as a key guarantee for new constitutional

5 Ruti Teitel, 'Transitional Jurisprudence: The Role of Law in Political Transformation' (1997) 106 Yale LJ 2009, 2032.

6 Priscilla Hayner, *Unspeakable Truths: Confronting State Terror and Atrocity* (Routledge 2001) 185–186. Bruce Ackerman, *The Future of Liberal Resolution* (Yale University Press 1994) 71–90. Claus Offe, *Varieties of Transition: The East European and East German Experience* (MIT Press 1996) 82–88.

norms.[7] However, as an institution lacking substantive powers, it would appear to be politically infeasible to build a system based on newly adopted constitutional values, especially in situations in which the old powers are still to be reckoned with. As such, can constitutional courts really play a role in reforming post-authoritarian constitutional structures through the constitutional interpretation of the authoritarian past?

The Taiwan Constitutional Court (TCC) can provide instructive insight for the study of these issues. After the promulgation of the Constitution of the Republic of China (ROC) in 1947, the TCC was established in 1948 and it interpreted the Constitution for the first time in 1949. Under the authoritarian rule of the *Kuomintang* (Chinese Nationalist Party, KMT) from 1948 to 1991, the TCC did not play an active role in overseeing governmental action.[8] However, from the late 1970s onwards, social and political forces calling for democratisation strengthened, gradually leading to a political transition from the authoritarian rule of the KMT. The government eventually revoked martial law in 1987 (which had been in force since 1949) and ended the national mobilisation in 1991 (which had been in force since 1948).[9]

This political transformation led to a dramatic shift in the interpretational model of the TCC.[10] Through a number of judicial interpretations, the TCC interpreted the authoritarian history as "exceptional". In so doing, the TCC successfully departed from its past support for authoritarian rule and established a new system based upon the liberal democratic constitutional order without being bound by its past decisions. At the same time, the TCC left scope for political actors to assert the legitimacy of governmental actions from the past. The TCC was also reluctant to critically recognise or mend the wounds of the victims of authoritarian rule.[11] Through its actions, the TCC not only maintained political stability as the prerequisite for democratic development but also perpetuated historical injustice, regarding it as a necessary compromise with the past legality of the legal rule, the cost of redress, and the old powers.

Treating Taiwan's authoritarian history as an exception to the full application of constitutional norms is an interpretational approach that was recently

---

7 See Section III.

8 Cheng-Yi Huang, 'The 70th Anniversary of the Taiwan Constitutional Court–The Second Life of a Constitutional Court: Taiwan Constitutional Court and its Struggling with the Past' *I-Connect Blog*, (13 December 2018), <https://rb.gy/usfm2d> accessed 16 August 2022.

9 ibid. Jiunn-Rong Yeh and Wen-Chen Chang, 'The Emergence of East Asian Constitutionalism: Features in Comparison'(2011), 59(3) Am J Comp L 805, 812–814.

10 Huang (n8).

11 See Section V.

altered in Judicial Yuan (J. Y.) Interpretation No. 793 (given on 28 August 2020). In the case, the TCC reviewed the Act Governing the Settlement of Ill-gotten Properties by Political Parties and Their Affiliate Organisations, which required state assets unduly owned by KMT-affiliated organisations to be returned to the government. In its ruling, the TCC recognised governmental interests to review and remedy unjustifiable appropriation of property by the past regime. That is to say, the TCC looked back to the historical wrongdoings of the prior regime and evaluated whether they could be tolerated in the present time, in sharp contrast to the TCC's previous historical approach.

The following chapter will examine how this "belated" decision was reached by analysing the different roles authoritarian history has played in the development of constitutional interpretation in Taiwan. Section 2 will analyse the normative values that different constitutional interpretations of history can entail, focusing particularly on the static, dynamic, critical, and radical models. Then we will consider the distinguishing features of constitutional politics and the delicate roles played by constitutional courts in Section 3 by examining the post-authoritarian Taiwan context in which the TCC was created, has operated and has transformed itself. Section 4 will analyse different interpretations of the authoritarian past in cases involving the separation of powers and human rights protection. Section 5 will emphasise long-term democratic development, addressing the normative construction of a constitutional order and engagement with the authoritarian legacy to evaluate the interpretative strategies pursued by the TCC. Finally, Section VI will set out concluding remarks.

2 The Use of Past in Legal Interpretation: Models and Normative Implications

In order to study the different uses of history in legal interpretation, this chapter will borrow from the work of Professor Robert Gordon in 1996 to derive an analytical framework.[12] Professor Gordon's purpose in writing was to examine how American lawyers creatively selected historical practices for legal advocacy to challenge the seemingly canonical idea of "legal tradition" in a politically-divided context.[13] While the progressive and conservative camps have differed in their views as to whether and to what extent the government should intervene in the private sphere, Gordon argues that both camps have

12 Robert W. Gordon, 'The Struggle over the Past'(1996) 44 Clev St L Rev 123.

13 ibid 140–143.

sought to justify their political inclinations through the law.[14] This understanding of litigation activities as a process of reasoning involving the application of norms to facts with the aim of furthering certain values and interests has been argued to be a core characteristic of judicial interpretation as well.[15] Given this similarity, Professor Gordon's observation of litigation practices is suitable for understanding how the past is used in judicial interpretation.

According to Professor Gordon, American lawyers have shown a tendency to refer to specific historical events in their legal arguments. Their use of history can be categorised into three major models: static, dynamic, and critical.[16]

2.1 *Static Model: Continuity with the Past*

The static model understands history as remnant wisdom that has been established, developed, and crystallised by past generations. It remains fixed within written records because it has withstood the challenges of its time.[17] The static model affords special normative authority to the past use of the law, including rules and legal practices. These legal sources entail a crucial future-binding effect on judicial decision-making.[18] Courts must therefore discover the original, and thus the real, purposes or intentions of those who created these legal sources and ground their legal reasoning faithfully in them.[19] The use of this historical approach means that authentic forms and meanings cannot be distorted. Any manual alteration of the meanings and implications of historical materials may be considered "disloyal" to tradition and therefore an incorrect interpretation of the law. Given this endorsement of the past, the static model can be perceived as the most conventional attitude towards the role of history in legal interpretation. It is also depicted by Professor Daphne Barak-Erez as aiming to promote uninterrupted "continuity with the past".[20]

One may be curious as to the rationale for adopting a static model. One reason, as mentioned above, is that history is regarded as the "wisdom of the ages", which has undergone numerous tests over time. To abandon these practices whilst adopting an untested method would therefore appear to be

14 ibid 123–124.

15 See Robert M. Cover, 'Nomos and Narrative'(1983) 97 Harv L Rev 4, 7–8. Shannon Stewart, 'The Art of Constitutional Interpretation' (1991) 17 JCL 91, 99. Larry A. DiMatteo, 'Reason and Context': A Dual Track Theory of Interpretation'(2004) 109 Penn St L Rev 397, 483.

16 Gordon (n12) 124.

17 ibid 125.

18 ibid. Postema (n2) 1157.

19 Gordon (n12) 125. Barak-Erez (n2) 10.

20 Barak-Erez (n2) 9–10.

impractically risky.[21] Another reason is that reliance on the past yields stability and predictability. It sends a message that similar subjects can be treated alike, helping people to act accordingly based on expectations grounded in past practices.[22] This consistency also ensures that rules satisfying these legitimate expectations can provide a fair and just application of the law among people whose circumstances are similar.[23]

2.2 *Dynamic Model: Continuity through Change*

While the static model treats history as something unchangeable that has a binding effect on interpretation by future generations, the dynamic model emphasises the dimension of change throughout history.[24] In this model, history is not static but rather an evolving process into which new human decisions, practices, and thoughts will be gradually added.[25] Changes are potentially driven by two forces. First, new activities cannot be explained or interpreted based upon the existing understanding of history. In addition, old views about history may need to be changed in response to political or social transformations.[26] Over time, these efforts accumulate into an "evolutionary path" in which the meanings of previous materials are linked to their future counterparts, transforming into something new.[27] To borrow the metaphor of Ronald Dworkin, these coexisting changes and continuities can be regarded as a collaborative "chain novel" that is written by cross-age authors to further certain public or private goals.[28]

In order to meet contemporary needs arising out of continuously changing situations, legal interpreters are eligible or even required to give new meanings to legal texts, rules, and principles developed during the course of history. Under the dynamic model, history has legal authority, although not in the sense that the future is strictly controlled by a dead hand. History is binding because the past is "continuously connected with the present" through *incremental* changes.[29] Therefore, any change of legal interpretation or other

---

21 Postema (n2) 1165–1166.

22 ibid 1168–1169.

23 ibid 1166–1168.

24 Barak-Erez (n2) 13.

25 ibid. See also Benjamin Cardozo, *The Nature of the Judicial Process* (Yale University Press 1921) 52–53.

26 Barak-Erez (n2) 13. Gordon (n12) 125. Benjamin Cardozo also notes that "[L]ogic and history, and custom, and utility, and the accepted standards of right conduct, are the forces which singly or in combination shape the progress of the law". See Cardozo (n25) 112.

27 ibid.

28 Ronald Dworkin, *Law's Empire* (Hart Publishing 1986) 228–229.

29 Barak-Erez (n2) 13.

legal activities does not amount to a detour from the past; on the contrary, it amounts to the most faithful response to the true meaning of history as an evolutionary path.[30]

There are conflicting views on the nature of history as an evolutionary path. Professor Barak-Erez holds a somewhat linear view, seeing history as "an incremental advance in the historical development of the past".[31] In this interpretation, human activities can lead to social improvements. While this journey is not without obstacles, human beings can overcome these challenges and eventually achieve the desired positive outcome.[32] In a similar vein, lawyers and judges should hold legal values such as freedom, equality, and the rule of law as a guide for their legal activities and fulfil these goals by re-understanding and interpreting the meanings of historical precedents or practices in the contemporary world.[33] Interestingly, Professor Gordon argues that the so-called "development" engineering by progressives was actually regarded by conservatives as a loss of the American liberal tradition.[34] This reveals how the understanding of history is multidimensional and cannot be simply recognised as a journey towards a specific end.

2.3 *Critical Model: Disconnecting from the Past*

Unlike the above two models, the critical model rejects the authority of the past. Professor Gordon notes that this model asserts a clean break between the present and past.[35] Under this model, history is evaluated not as an acclaimed norm on which the courts should rely but rather as something illegitimate. When past governmental practices are no longer acceptable from the perspective of contemporary legal principles, history is often treated as a background reference, yet lacks critical legal authority. It is "the man who cannot be named"—its existence is recognised, but no one is allowed to mention or adopt it in resolving current disputes.[36] Under this model, when interpreting the law and applying it to facts, courts are reluctant to rely on past practices or legislative history. They resort to other legal authorities, such as the principles of jurisprudence or philosophical argument.[37] Professor Barak-Erez refers

30 ibid. Gordon (n12) 125.
31 Barak-Erez (n2) 13.
32 ibid. Gordon (n12) 127, 130.
33 Barak-Erez (n2) 13.
34 Gordon (n12) 131.
35 ibid 125–126.
36 ibid. Barak-Erez (n2) 11–12.
37 Barak-Erez (n2) 11–12.

to this treatment as a demand for "contemporary justice".[38] In order to avoid using history in the law, the courts purposefully deter the new system from repeating past mistakes. In the cases she mentions, the history of authoritarian or totalitarian rule has been treated by courts as a dark, undesirable abyss that should be left behind. No one should let it happen again.[39]

These three classic models do not exhaust all kinds of constitutional interpretation of the past. As Professor Barak-Erez notes, some countries, such as Germany, have not stopped at isolating the present from the past, but have adopted proactive measures to deal with human rights violations under Nazi rule.[40] Therefore, from a theoretical point of view, it is necessary to explain the rationale behind the type of constitutional interpretation that can support a stronger position when dealing with the enduring effects of historical events.

2.4 *Radical Model: Identifying and Redressing Historical Wrongdoing*

Rather than endorsing the approach of pure isolation from history, some theories of constitutional interpretation suggest that the truth of historical wrongdoings may be discovered through measures such as compensating victims. Scholarship on transitional justice emphasises the need for and legitimacy of dealing with past large-scale governmental injustices after a political transition.[41] It recognises that history is always rooted in the contemporary era and requires redress. By critically identifying and remedying historical injustices, transitional justice aims to facilitate the implementation of a new norm encompassing justice, the rule of law, and reconciliation, among other normative goals.[42]

The ideas of justice, the rule of law, and reconciliation are understood in a number of ways. In terms of justice, it is generally believed that criminal justice, i.e., the prosecution of high-ranking offenders, can provide an institutional opportunity for the offenders to obtain redemption from the state and

38 ibid 11.

39 ibid.

40 ibid 12.

41 See Ruti Teitel, *Transitional Justice* (OUP 2000) 3. John Elster, *Closing the Books: Transitional Justice in Historical Perspective* (CUP 2004) 1. Ruti Teitel, 'The Law and Politics of Contemporary Transitional Justice' (2005) 38 Cornell Int'l LJ 837, 845–847. Harry Hobbs, 'Locating the Logic of Transitional Justice in Liberal Democracies' (2016) 39 UNSWLJ 512, 516–517.

42 Teitel (2000) (n41) 6. Ruti Teitel, 'The Role of Law in Political Transformation' (1997) 106 Yale LJ 2009, 2014–2015, 2078. Festa (n2) 499, 500. On the role of constitutions in achieving transitional justice, Cheng-Yi Huang (ed) *Constitutionalizing Transitional Justice: How Constitutions and Constitutional Courts Deal with Past Autrocity* (Routledge 2022).

the public if they are willing to make efforts to apologise or compensate for their wrongdoings. As to restorative justice, it requires an acknowledgement of and redress for the damages suffered by victims, such that their pre-damage statuses, can be restored.[43] The rule of law, as understood by some transitional justice scholars, stresses that the authority of the law is superior to personal beliefs and rationales for the behaviours of individuals. As Professor Padrig McAuliffe points out, by prosecuting perpetrators and compensating victims, transitional justice improves legal accountability in the sense that violations of legal norms will not be tolerated.[44] Finally, a reconciliation project is especially meaningful within deeply divided societies. As a strong sense of community is lacking, social antagonism in these countries often aggravates distrust in the government, which creates obstacles to democratic consolidation. By discovering different individual experiences hidden in the past, transitional justice can provide contentious social groups with an opportunity to understand and recognise victims' grievances.[45] Through re-examining and interpreting history, citizens may be able to build a collective historical narrative shared by all members, which is believed by Professor Alexander L. Boraine to be the foundation for national development.[46]

However, not all scholars agree with the adoption of transitional justice. One reason for this hesitancy is that transitional justice retroactively views past behaviours through the prism of new constitutional values. It may also contradict with the procedural maxim of "no punishment without law" (*nulla poena sine lege*) "after the fact" (*ex post facto*).[47] This principle, as Professors Eric Posner and Adrian Vermeule note, is often conceived of as being a key element of the rule of law. As such, examining the behaviour of officials during the authoritarian period with "new" values creates an unreasonable moral burden for them.[48]

43 Teitel (2000) (n41) 8, 27. Alexander L. Boraine, 'Transitional Justice: A Holistic Interpretation' (2006) 60 J Int'l Aff 17, 24–25. Jemima Garcia-Godos, 'Reparations' in Olivera Simic (ed), *An Introduction to Transitional Justice* 178–179 (Routledge 2017).

44 Padraig McAuliffe, 'Transitional Justice's Impact on Rule of Law: Symbol or Substance?' in Cheryl Lawther (ed), *Research Handbook on Transitional Justice* (Edward Elgar Publishing 2017) 79–80.

45 Boraine (n43) 22–23.

46 ibid. Pius Langa, 'Transformative Constitutionalism' (2006) 17 Stellenbosch L Rev 351, 351, 358–359.

47 Eric A. Posner and Adrian Vermeule 'Transitional Justice as Ordinary Justice' (2004) 117 Harv L Rev 761, 792.

48 ibid 792–793.

Other scholars, while not denying the existence of historical wrongdoings, are concerned that redressing history may be detrimental to the fulfilment and consolidation of democracy.[49] The discovery of history is largely based on available resources, and limited or disordered archival files can make this extremely difficult. Even if relevant resources are sufficient for historical writings, there are scarce objective criteria for appreciating them. Therefore, the neutrality and reliability of these writings are often challenged in politically divided societies. Professor Bruce Ackerman argues that a retrospective review of history in young, fragile democracies can be easily exploited to attack the political opposition. In the name of identifying historical wrongs, the criminal prosecution or public criticism of past political actors may lead to abuse of power. It further intensifies the hostility between new and old political rivals to the detriment of enhancing mutual respect and acknowledgement, foundational elements for a multi-power democratic structure.[50] This implied notion of power balance is also reflected in Professor Claus Offe's concerns about transitional justice measures: the resilient, old power-structure remaining in a new regime can entail "continuity with the past," with the result that the redress of historical wrongs may never be fully accomplished.[51] Given these deficiencies, Professors Ackerman and Offe believe that looking to history is too costly for a new democracy. More emphasis should be placed on building the infrastructure to establish standards for liberal democracy, the rule of law, and the separation of powers as soon as possible.

3 Constitutional Characteristics in a Post-authoritarian Context

3.1 *Constitutional Law within Transformative Constitutional Politics*

Constitutional paradigms are not established in a vacuum. Instead, they are highly contingent on social contexts.[52] Former Chief Justice of South Africa Pius Langa has stated that constitutional law must be altered in response to social changes.[53] In particular, the establishment of long-term constitutional norms should factor in constitutional interpretation. Unlike established democracies, transformative countries generally lack a common consensus on how to interpret constitutional texts, doctrines, precedents, and principles.[54]

---

49 Hayner (n6).
50 Ackerman (n6).
51 Offe (n6) 82, 88.
52 Langa (n46) 351, 358. Teitel (n5) 2076.
53 ibid.
54 Langa (n46) 354.

In terms of the long-term development of constitutional democracy, constitutional interpretation should not only refer to the implementation of fundamental constitutional values, but should also ensure that the understandings of constitutional meanings are relatively fixed and stable.[55]

However, judicial elaboration on the meanings and scopes of constitutional values is not enough. The social and political foundations on which these norms are built may have an impact on the efficacy of such a constitutional project.[56] For example, the old legacy of an illiberal rule may still remain resilient in post-transition structures. Special consideration must be given to this legacy when establishing a democratic constitutional system.[57] While social forces may support a robust constitutional infrastructure,[58] overly-antagonistic gestures toward authoritarian successor parties and elites may incite their resentment towards the new government, which in turn may be pernicious for the long-term development of constitutional democracy.[59] As such, democratic development seems impossible without at least the acquiescence, if not support, of old elites in terms of implementing and enforcing constitutional values within new democracies.

3.2 *Fragile Constitutional Courts*

Due to its relative neutrality and independence from political tensions, a constitutional court is often believed to be capable of performing the above tasks.[60] Through constitutional adjudication, constitutional courts can develop consistent and predictable understandings of constitutional texts, doctrines and principles.[61] Professor Ruti Teitel identifies how such tasks are carried out.[62] First, having been established as a part of the centralised national power

---

55 ibid. 352. Teitel (n5) 2015.

56 Jiunn-Rong Yeh and Wen-Chen Chang, 'The Changing Landscape of Modern Constitutionalism: Transitional Perspective' (2009) 4 NTU L Rev 145, 158.

57 Langa (n46) 354.

58 Thomas Weishing Huang, 'Judicial Activism in the Transitional Polity: The Council of Grand Justices in Taiwan' (2005) 19 Temp Int'l & Comp LJ 1, 3–4.

59 Ackerman (n6) 87–90.

60 Teitel (n5) 2033–2035.

61 Alexander Tsesis, 'Footholds of Constitutional Interpretation' (2013) 91 Tex L Rev 1593, 1594. Langa (n46) 357. Teitel (n5) 2032. Jiunn-Rong Yeh, 'The Role of Transitional Court: On the Interactions between Constitutional Interpretations and Constitutional Revisions'(轉型法院的自我定位：論憲法解釋對修憲機制的影響) (2003), 32 NTU LJ 29, 29. Yung-Chin Su, 'Constitutional Interpretations and Social Changes in Taiwan' (大法官解釋與台灣的社會變遷) in Su, *The Theories and Practices of Constitutionality Control* (合憲性控制的理論與實際) (Angle Publishing Co. 1994) 271–314.

62 Teitel (n5) 2032.

during the political transition, constitutional courts often highlight the new power configurations in post-authoritarian states. Second, by enlarging popular access to justice, courts can increase the volume of their input through constitutional interpretation.[63] In addition, by infusing foreign doctrines and international standards into their constitutional interpretation, constitutional courts can gradually create more powerful norms supporting the rule of law, limited government, and individual rights, which are beneficial for strengthening a liberal, democratic, and constitutional culture.[64]

Nevertheless, the judiciary is conceivably the weakest branch compared to the executive and legislative branches. Without any tax or police powers, the courts do not have a strong apparatus for preserving their institutional independence from political intervention. Therefore, courts usually need a certain level of public trust in order to ensure that they have a degree of popular legitimacy, allowing them to defend themselves against falling under the control of political authorities. Scholars have found that constitutional courts thus develop a "reactive and cautious" approach to interpreting the constitution.[65] They are said to be reactive because courts usually provide solutions to political disputes passively and do not take the initiative to promote social or political reforms. Moreover, when interpreting new constitutions, courts are well-aware of and respond cautiously to the complex issues concerning the delicate post-transition structure.[66] As the following sections will show, the usage of history provides clear evidence of these distinctive interpretative approaches.

3.3 *Contextualising the TCC in the above Settings*

The TCC was established in 1948 as the "Council of Grand Justices" in charge of judicial review.[67] Contrary to requirements under the Constitution of the ROC at that time, the TCC did not play a role in safeguarding constitutional values throughout almost the entire period of authoritarian rule by the KMT government.[68] In 1948, the KMT government enacted the Temporary Provision for National Mobilisation, which substantially suspended the principles of the separation of powers under the Constitution.[69] The KMT implemented a

63 ibid.

64 ibid 2030, 2032, 2076.

65 Yeh and Chang (n9) 823–824.

66 ibid.

67 Chien-Chih Lin, 'Autocracy, Democracy, and Juristocracy: The Wax and Wane of Judicial Power in the Four Asian Tigers' (2017) 48 Georgetown J Int'l L 1063, 1118.

68 ibid 1119.

69 Huang (n8). In 1960, the KMT government abolished the term limit for presidents, enabling presidents to be re-elected without any limitation. This significantly expanded

one-party system and took control of the central legislative body. Despite these actions, the TCC served as a rubber stamp for the executive branch, playing no role in checking its use of power.[70]

By refraining from challenging political decisions, the TCC was a participant in the authoritarian structure of Taiwan. For example, in J. Y. Interpretation No. 31 given on 29 January 1954, the TCC addressed whether representatives of the Legislative Yuan and Control Yuan who had been elected in and emigrated from Mainland China before 1949 should remain in office after their term had expired. The Executive Yuan justified its decision by holding that new elections were not possible at that time. The TCC later upheld the constitutionality of this executive decision, arguing that the country was in a state of extreme political upheaval, which made another election "practically infeasible". In this sense, the TCC affirmed that those members from Mainland China in the above branches could legitimately assume power, taking no account of how the population of Mainlanders in Taiwan they represented were small compared to that of Islanders.[71] This case illustrates how the judiciary was strikingly exposed to external pressure whilst also being sensitive to the domestic political structure. Therefore, the TCC failed to check the encroachment on constitutional principles by the KMT.

This rubber-stamp image of the TCC started to change in parallel with Taiwan's political transition. Due to external and internal challenges to its legitimacy, the KMT government—led by Chiang Kai-Shek's son Chiang King-Kuo—implemented political reforms in the 1970s and abolished martial law in 1987.[72] In 1990, Chiang King-Kuo's successor President Lee Teng-Hui abolished the Temporary Provision for National Mobilisation and embarked upon a series of constitutional reforms, including the direct election of the President and constitutional amendments.[73] During the 1990s, the political structure became more comfortable with the ideas of limited government and popular participation in governmental affairs. Constitutional values once sealed and hidden

---

presidential powers. Wen-Chen Chang, *Constitutionalism in Asia: Cases and Materials* (Hart Publishing 2014) 20.

70 Huang (n8). Lin (n67) 1119.

71 Judicial Interpretation No. 31 (decision rendered 29 Jan 1954) < https://cons.judicial.gov.tw/en/docdata.aspx?fid=100&id=310212> accessed 16 August 2022. Lin (n67) 1121–1122. Chien-Chih Lin, 'Constitutions and Courts in Chinese Authoritarian Regimes: China and Pre-democratic Taiwan in Comparison' (2016) 14 I-CON 351, 364–365.

72 Wakabayashi Masahiro, *The "Republic of China" and the Politics of Taiwanization: The Changing Identity of Taiwan in Postwar East Asia* (National Taiwan University Press 2014) 137–138, 158–165.

73 Huang (n58) 3–4. Lin (n67) 1119–1120.

from view were now being discussed in a way that supported stronger control and supervision of the government. In 2000, the Democratic Progressive Party (DPP) won the presidential election, leading to the first-ever change in political power in Taiwan. Eight years later, the KMT returned to executive power by defeating the DPP at the ballot box.[74] Amid this rapid political transformation, the issue of how to make the TCC a guardian of constitutional commitments, as Justice Langa describes, turned into a crucial question: would the use of history in constitutional interpretation support this new constitutional infrastructure?

4 The TCC's Constitutional Interpretation of Authoritarian History

4.1 *Separation of Powers*

4.1.1 J. Y. Interpretation No. 261[75]

As noted above, J. Y. Interpretation No. 31 consolidated the suspension of regular elections. However, regular elections became a rigorously debated issue when the tidal wave of democratic transition arrived in Taiwan. In March 1990, members of the National Assembly attempted to extend their terms from six to nine years. Like those in the Legislative Yuan and Control Yuan, members of the National Assembly were also national representatives. They had remained in office for more than thirty years due to the alleged impossibility of holding regular elections. In an era marked by strong calls for democratic reforms, the National Assembly's attempt to entrench its power elicited strong social criticism. This prompted the first large-scale student movement in Taiwan to challenge the legitimacy of these national representatives. In June 1990, the TCC issued J. Y. Interpretation No. 261, ruling that all national representatives should leave office by 31 December 1991, and the government should schedule the next election of national representatives. In doing so, the TCC for the first time recognised the importance and legitimacy of elections in Taiwan.

It should be noted that J. Y. Interpretation No. 31 was not abolished at the time when J. Y. Interpretation No. 261 was issued. From the perspective of a static or dynamic model, it should have had a binding effect on subsequent decisions. Therefore, it is interesting to study how the TCC understood the role of J. Y. Interpretation No. 31 and how it based its current decision on this historical interpretation. In fact, in J. Y. Interpretation No. 261, the TCC did not

74 Lin (n67) 1120.

75 J. Y. Interpretation No. 261 (decision given on 21 June 2000) <https://cons.judicial.gov.tw/en/docdata.aspx?fid=100&id=310442> accessed 16 August 2022.

invalidate J. Y. Interpretation No. 31 but held that the suspension of elections was not unconstitutional: it was legitimately made and necessary in order to maintain constitutional order during the authoritarian period.[76] Instead, the TCC emphasised that this decision was an *exception* from the ordinary constitutional requirement of term limits. An exception was legitimate given the supposed de facto impossibility of holding elections due to severe calamities and extreme upheaval. Maintaining the legitimacy of such an exception was constitutional, even though it was not in keeping with contemporary constitutional principles.[77] This interpretation of exceptionality also shows that the TCC concluded that the political foundations of J. Y. Interpretation No. 31 no longer existed, revealing a detachment from the authoritarian past.[78]

Does this approach indicate that history does not have any weight in constitutional interpretation? The answer of the TCC was not necessarily: specifically, the TCC did not otherwise abandon all reliance on history when engaging in interpretation. For example, given the growing number of seats in the national legislature since 1969, the TCC considered it necessary for first-session national representatives to retire and thus ensure democratic constitutional order through regular elections—in keeping with citizens' modern preference for popular elections. Furthermore, it is noted that J. Y. Interpretation No. 31 did not imply that the first-session representatives of the Legislative Yuan and Control Yuan could exercise their power permanently or alter their constitutionally required term limits. Accordingly, successive elections incrementally turned into one normative source of maintaining regular elections under a constitutional norm. The TCC's decision shows that historical events also had a binding effect on constitutional interpretation.

Although the TCC took account of historical events, the legal authority for suspending elections could not outweigh the new constitutional norm. This constitutional norm is derived from the provisions of the ROC Constitution on term limits, the ambiguity of J. Y. Interpretation No. 31 as to whether national

---

76 Ming-Sung Kuo 'Judicial Review as a Solution to Political Gridlocks? A Study of Taiwan's Grand Justices Council Interpretations Regarding the Jurisdictional Disputes within the Political Branch' (2001) 30 NTU LJ 251, 251 <https://ssrn.com/abstract=1428995> accessed 16 August 2022.

77 ibid. See Jiunn-Rong Yeh, 'From Transitional Court to Normal Court: A Comparative Analysis on Ruling Characteristics and Transitional Context between Interpretations No.261 and No.499' (從「轉型法院」到「常態法院」：論大法官釋字第二六一號與第四九九號解釋的解釋風格與轉型脈絡) (2002) 31 NTU LJ 59–96.

78 Huang (n58) 51. Chien-Yuan Tseng, 'The Twenty-Year Constitutional Development After the Abolishment of Martial Law' (解嚴二十年來的憲政發展) (2008) 12 Taiwan Bar J 4, 4–16.

elections could be restrained in normal situations, and electoral practices over time. More importantly, the TCC emphatically recognised the regular election of representatives as being sine qua non for reflecting the popular will, which was necessary for giving effect to constitutional democracy. Since regular elections were prescribed in the ROC Constitution, the TCC's approach could be considered a way to resort to the Constitution's "original intent". However, this interpretation would inevitably encounter a fundamental conundrum regarding the discrepancy between the current territorial and population base of the ROC and the one considered by founders when drafting the ROC Constitution—which encompassed mainland China.[79] Resorting to "original intent" would possibly trigger more controversial issues about the sovereignty of the ROC, issues which are hardly solvable by the TCC. As a result, it seems safer for the TCC to dissociate authoritarian history, without addressing the issue of sovereignty by mentioning the drafting history of the Constitution, to ensure this history is not adhered to in future judicial interpretation.[80]

4.1.2 J. Y. Interpretation No. 419[81]

This decision concerns whether the Vice President can hold a concurrent position of the Premier at the same time, which was partly a result of the distinct governmental system in Taiwan. The governmental system originally adopted in the ROC Constitution was closer to a parliamentary system, requiring the executive to be responsible to the legislature. Therefore, the Premier, serving as the head of the executive, must take charge of public affairs, and the appointment of the Premier by the President as the head of the state was subject to the approval of the legislature. This institutional design remained intact until the constitutional amendment of 1997, which transformed the governmental system into a semi-presidential system. Ever since then, even though the executive should attend legislative interpellation, the President has been granted the authority to appoint his Premier at will without a legislative approval.

The issue of J. Y. Interpretation No. 419 happened exactly around the transition period as the presence of new political players challenged the utility of the existing institution. Following the elections of the Legislative Yuan in 1995, the first presidential election was held on 23 March 1996, granting popular legitimacy to the president. After the election, the newly-elected President intended to appoint the Vice President as his Premier, which was not explicitly

79 ibid.

80 ibid.

81 J. Y. Interpretation No. 419 (decision given on 31 December 1996) <https://cons.judicial.gov.tw/en/docdata.aspx?fid=100&id=310600> accessed 16 August 2022.

prohibited in the Constitution and had happened twice before in Taiwan's history. Nevertheless, viewing its constitutional authority as being questioned, the Legislative Yuan filed several petitions with the TCC seeking a constitutional interpretation.[82] Arguing in favour of the constitutionality of dual mandates, one petition stated that these two historical incidents did not create barriers to the operation of the government and should be considered as binding precedents for the TCC.

The TCC did not accept this argument. In support of its judicial reasoning, it pointed to how the Premier had resigned immediately after being elected as Vice President in the two prior cases. Accordingly, history could not offer any lessons as to whether concurrent service was constitutional. Instead, the TCC sought authority in the text of the Constitution and accepted that it contained ambiguities in terms of the compatibility of the offices of the Vice President and Premier. The TCC then considered the functional reason that the Vice President should be in a "standby position" in order to ensure that the nation could also have a head of state, as required under the Constitution, when the President is unable to discharge his responsibilities. If the same person were to be serving as both Vice President and Premier, this function would be diminished and even undermine the objectives pursued by the Constitution of having separate individuals discharging the duties of Vice President and Premier.[83]

Compared to J. Y. Interpretation No. 216, J. Y. Interpretation No. 419 adopted an even more passive stance towards the normative position of history in constitutional interpretation. It emphasised the conflicting nature of history, which made the use of historical resources less plausible. Nevertheless, this conflicting nature did not necessarily lead to a rejection of the use of historical information. In J. Y. Interpretation No. 261, at the same time that elections to national legislatures were suspended, elections were being held for other legislatures during the authoritarian period; here, the Court held that the latter model should be sustained and followed. However, the TCC declined to give any normative salience to *both* historical precedents.[84] It could be said that the TCC recognised the need to avoid dual mandates as outweighing the authority of prior cases that had allowed dual mandates. Even so, the TCC did not state any legal authority for the practice of avoiding dual mandates. In this sense, it rejected the force of history in constitutional interpretation.

---

82 ibid.

83 ibid.

84 In-Jaw Lai, 'The Compulsory and Distanced Historical Interpretation' (歷史解釋法的強制與疏離) (2017) 21 Taiwan Prosecutor Rev 158, 171.

4.1.3 J. Y. Interpretation No. 499[85]

J.Y. Interpretation No. 499 can be regarded as the most ground-breaking and influential interpretation in the history of the TCC. As mentioned above, during Taiwan's democratic transition period, the old representatives in the national legislative branches were criticised as "old thieves", squatting in office and refusing to leave. Faced with such challenges to their legitimacy, on 4 September 1999 the National Assembly passed a constitutional amendment to extend the terms of national legislators and thus entrench their legitimacy in the Constitution. This amendment also planned to require the seats of the National Assembly to be determined by the proportion of votes received from each political party and independent candidate in elections to the Legislative Yuan.[86]

The TCC ruled that this amendment was unconstitutional. In terms of the extended term limit, the TCC cited J. Y. Interpretation No. 261 and held that there was no legal authority for the suspension of elections. In a forward-looking manner, the TCC reiterated that the circumstances on which J. Y. Interpretation No. 31 was based were extraordinary and no longer applied. Accordingly, historical practices of extended terms should no longer be considered as "constitutional precedents under normal circumstances".[87] Based on a constitutional commitment to regular elections, the TCC held that the adoption of such an amendment violated the constitutional order of liberal democracy. As regards the adoption of proportionate representation, the TCC held that it violated the spirit of representative democracy: the National Assembly would have the power to implement or amend the Constitution without any direct authorisation.[88]

This case led to extensive discussions on the rise of constitutionalism, the legitimacy of judicial review of constitutional amendments, notions of representation, the purpose of regular elections, and voting procedures.[89] However, very few studies have approached the case from the perspective of historical sources within constitutional interpretation. Drawing on J. Y. Interpretation

---

85 J. Y. Interpretation No. 499 (decision given on 24 March 2000) <https://cons.judicial.gov.tw/en/docdata.aspx?fid=100&id=310680> accessed 16 August 2022.

86 ibid.

87 J. Y. Interpretation No. 499 (decision given on 24 March 2000) <https://cons.judicial.gov.tw/en/docdata.aspx?fid=100&id=310680> accessed 16 August 2022.

88 ibid.

89 See Tzong-Li Hsu, 'An Unconstitutional Constitution?' (憲法違憲乎？) (2000), 60 Taiwan L Rev 141. Tzu-Yi Lin, Jiunn-Rong Yeh, Jau-Yuan Hwang and Wen-Chen Chang, *Constitutional Law—Separation of Powers* (憲法—權力分立) (2nd supp, 2nd ed, New Sharing Publishing Co. 2009) 2–3, 128–129.

No. 261, the TCC seemed to endorse an understanding of suspended elections as "a past that should be abandoned". It again referred to the idea of exception in order to describe the role of this notorious authoritarian practice within the constitutional development of Taiwan. There were two elements to this exception: 1) severe calamities experienced by the state leading to 2) the practical impossibility of holding elections. What constituted a severe calamity and who had the power to decide if one was occurring remained unclear. The failure to make such a determination may or may not have been an intentional act of the TCC. Regardless, by recognising the evidently abnormal nature of the authoritarian rule, the TCC did not need to directly challenge the constitutionality of these past practices. Instead, viewing the law as "no longer appropriate" or "factually operable" could justify the change in a constitutional norm. As such, the TCC drew a line between the norm and the exception, between urgent measures and regularity, and between the past and the present.

4.1.4 J. Y. Interpretation No. 793[90]

Following the above decisions, there is no clear evidence to suggest that the TCC intended to further develop its interpretative approach to the use of history. This situation changed in 2020. In 2016, the DPP regained power in both the presidential and congressional elections. Having displayed a sharply different attitude to transitional justice compared to the KMT government when it was in power from 2000 to 2008, the DPP government firmly declared that it would take action to implement transitional justice in Taiwan.[91] In 2016, the Legislative Yuan passed the Act Governing the Settlement of Ill-gotten Properties by Political Parties and Their Affiliate Organisations (Ill-gotten Properties Act) with the aim of obtaining the return to the State of governmental assets still held by the KMT and its affiliate organisations.[92] In 2018, the Legislative Yuan also passed the Promotion of Transitional Justice Act, which authorised the Committee for Promoting Transitional Justice to enforce transitional justice policies.[93] This was the first time that the government had decided to engage honestly with the authoritarian past instead of merely compensating victims without finding out who the perpetrators were.

---

90 J. Y. Interpretation No. 793 (decision given on 28 August 2020) <https://cons.judicial.gov.tw/docdata.aspx?fid=100&id=310974> accessed on 16 August 2022. There is no English translation of this Interpretation (at the time this Chapter went to press).

91 See Ernest Caldwell, 'Transitional Justice Legislation in Taiwan Before and During the Tsai Administration' (2018) 27 Wash Intl LJ 450, 472–473.

92 ibid 475–477.

93 ibid 477–480.

With the enactment of the Ill-gotten Properties Act, a number of private entities were classified by the Ill-gotten Party Assets Settlement Committee (Committee) as "affiliated organisations" whose personnel, finances, or operations were once substantially controlled by the KMT and had acquired their separate status and assets without having paid a fair price. They were therefore required to transfer the assets they had unjustifiably received back to the State, local governments, or original owners.[94] These entities were two LTD companies, which previously provided financial assistance to the KMT government in order to implement related policies, and the National Women's League of the ROC, which was established by Chiang Kai-Shek's wife Soon May-Ling to strengthen female patriotism and promote social and women's welfare. These organisations launched litigation against a number of provisions of the Ill-gotten Properties Act on which the above decisions were based, arguing that the powers conferred on the Committee violated constitutional principles of equal treatment, non-retroactivity, proportionality and the separation of powers, as well as the constitutional requirements applicable to party regulations.[95]

The TCC upheld the relevant provisions of the Ill-gotten Properties Act as constitutional. In order to arrive at this decision, the Court held that its legislative objectives were legitimate and that it was necessary to reassess and remedy the unlawful and inappropriate measures infringing upon the liberal democratic constitutional order, which severely violated basic constitutional rights. It strongly took the view that the KMT government had accumulated its party properties in a manner at odds not only with the formal rule of law, but also with the substantive rule of law, and had acquired a disproportionately superior status compared to other political parties. Although the KMT can currently be regarded as a political party in Taiwanese politics, the properties it received previously created a distorted political environment which was detrimental to the promotion of political competition.

In reasoning this way, the TCC connected the goals of transitional justice with the ideals of fair party competition. These ideals are considered important elements of liberal democratic rule, and they increase the normative salience of historical review in several senses. First, as an empirical matter, the idea that history is "past" is nothing more than an illusion—historical measures and decisions have an impact on today's world. Second, based on this understanding, it is necessary for subsequent generations to consciously decide whether to accept the continuation of historical legacy. This attitude was also apparent

94 Article 4.2 of the Ill-gotten Properties Act.

95 J. Y. Interpretation No. 793 (n90).

within the judicial process: the Committee provided substantial factual and historical evidence to support its decisions, and several expert witnesses suggested that the case in question called for a normative evaluation of the past.[96] Echoing their calls for the review of historical events, the TCC provided a new normative perspective to inquire into history. Remedying history represents one step towards achieving a competitive political environment, and for this reason, the evaluation of history is an integral part of democratic consolidation. Historical review therefore does not stand in opposition to democratic governance, as some scholars who reject transitional justice might suggest. It is instead integrated into and consolidated within the aspirations of liberal democracy in a forward-looking way.

4.1.5 Transforming from a Critical Model to a Fourth Model

While it may be difficult to study the reasons behind the TCC's choice of interpretative methods, it is worth noting that J. Y. Interpretations No. 261 and No. 499 indicate an inclination towards the critical model. These two cases both concerned regular elections as the prerequisite for democratically reflecting the popular will.[97] In the early stages of democratisation, the TCC was required to deal with the sensitive and delicate issue of democratic legitimacy.[98] Although social and political forces were desperately calling for reforms, the TCC needed to strike a balance between social expectations and the existing power structure; otherwise it would have risked serious political turbulence, which could undermine the stability of the fragile, new-born system. In J. Y. Interpretations No. 261 and No. 499, the relics of authoritarian history were put before the TCC to deal with these political issues, and the TCC endeavoured to detach the historical legacy of authoritarian rule from the present. The TCC focused on the implementation of constitutional principles of a democratic rule while rejecting continuity in the historical use of the law, regardless of whether such use was stably established or conflicting in nature.[99]

While this critical model was not reflected in J. Y. Interpretation No. 419, it transformed into a more radical model in J. Y. Interpretation No. 793. Compared to previous cases which regarded the past as an exception to the modern norms of constitutional democracy, J. Y. Interpretation No. 793 clearly addressed the role of history in constitutional interpretation and required the adjustment

96 ibid.

97 Lin, Yeh, Huang, and Chang (n89) 261–262.

98 Tzong-Li Hsu, 'How does the Judicial Activism of Taiwan's Constitutional Court shape the Liberal Democratic Constitutional Order in Taiwan?' (2018) 1923 Judicial Weekly 16, 38.

99 ibid 43–44.

of any unlawful or unjustifiable historical legacy. One may wonder how this transformation was brought about. One intuitively plausible explanation is that J. Y. Interpretation No. 793 was made under the rule of the DPP, and many of the sitting Justices in this case had been appointed by the DPP President. Additionally, the DPP government was more open to the idea of transitional justice. However, a mere political explanation could risk a dangerous jump to the conclusion that transitional justice was targeted specifically at the KMT. This over-simplifies and distorts efforts to normalise the goals of transitional justice within Taiwan's liberal democracy. A more comprehensive explanation should include the shifting attitudes of the Court's Justices: the Justices sitting on the case were more liberal-minded and inclined to the idea of constitutional democracy. For this reason, the TCC may have played a more proactive role in reviewing wrongdoing from the authoritarian period compared to other TCC decisions, which could enhance protection for citizens' individual rights and freedoms as well as the maintenance of the rule of law and limited government.[100]

4.2 *Human Rights Protection*

Since martial law was abolished in 1987, the TCC has struck down a number of authoritarian laws in order to deter them from having an impact in the democratic era. This reflects a notion that a new era had dawned in which the government should rule in accordance with constitutional democratic norms. For example, in J. Y. Interpretation No. 384, the TCC struck down several provisions of the "Act for the Prevention of Gangsters".[101] This Act granted the police powers to register and arrest gangsters without judicial authorisation. These provisions violated purported gangsters' rights to an open and fair trial and required them to be subject to correctional measures even after they had served their sentences. Therefore, the TCC deemed the measures to have unconstitutionally delegated excessive power to the executive branch and to have overly encroached on personal liberties.[102] Furthermore, in J. Y. Interpretation No. 445 (decision given on 23 January 1998), the TCC invalidated several provisions of the old Assembly and Parade Act on the grounds that they imposed a requirement of prior restraint on outdoor assemblies and parades and forbade any advocacy of communism or the secession of territory during such activities.[103]

---

100 Hsu (n98). Caldwell (n91) 467–472.

101 J. Y. Interpretation No. 384 (decision given on 28 July 1995) <https://cons.judicial.gov.tw/en/docdata.aspx?fid=100&id=310565> accessed 16 August 2022.

102 Hsu (n98) 52–53.

103 J. Y. Interpretation No. 445 (decision given on 23 January 1998) <https://cons.judicial.gov.tw/en/docdata.aspx?fid=100&id=310626> accessed 16 August 2022.

The TCC held that these regulations constituted a seriously disproportionate encroachment on the constitutional protection for free speech and freedom of assembly. In a similar manner to separation of powers issues, the TCC rejected the view that the past legal order should have any influence on today's constitutional interpretation.[104]

Nonetheless, the TCC was not a firm supporter of the third classical model. As was reflected in subsequent cases, the TCC struggled with the question of whether it should adopt the radical model—that is, whether past practices should be reviewed under the lens of contemporary constitutional principles. Recently, it seems to have answered this question in the affirmative, after all the struggles of the judiciary in looking for a new path.

4.2.1 J. Y. Interpretation No. 272[105]

J. Y. Interpretation No. 272 was the first case in which the attitude of the TCC to reviewing authoritarian history was clearly stated. After martial law was abolished, the KMT was well aware of the fact that it could no longer sustain its monolithic power in the politics of Taiwan; however, it also worried that rotation in and out of power would force it to debase politically. It therefore passed the "National Security Act during the Period of National Mobilisation for Suppression of the Communist Rebellion" ("National Security Act") on 23 June 1987, which was later amended as the "National Security Act" on 7 July 1992 after the Temporary Provision for National Mobilisation was abolished. According to Article 9, paragraph 2 of the National Security Act, criminal defendants who had been convicted and sentenced in military trials during the martial law period, except soldiers in active military service, could not appeal their final decisions to the ordinary courts following the abolishment of martial law.[106]

The TCC upheld this provision for the following four reasons, all of which illustrate its attitude towards history. First, echoing its previous decisions, the TCC held that martial law should have been the last resort to uphold national security and maintain social stability during the authoritarian period, as martial law restricted a number of constitutionally protected individual rights. However, during times of emergency, it was necessary and legitimate to limit protection for individual rights in order to address exceptional circumstances. Second, the TCC noted that the fact that martial law had been in place for more

104 Huang (n58) 22–26. Hsu (n98) 39–40.

105 J. Y. Interpretation No. 272 (decision given on 18 January 1991) <https://cons.judicial.gov.tw/en/docdata.aspx?fid=100&id=310453> accessed 16 August 2022.

106 Tseng (n78).

than 30 years had established a stable legal norm through judicial adjudication and that, based on this norm, society had developed into a similarly stable social order. It would not be practical for the country to invalidate the law at the cost of legal stability. Third, this conclusion was even more compelling in light of the difficulty in collecting and investigating evidence during the previous authoritarian period. Fourth, while an appeal to ordinary courts was not available, there was still scope for extraordinary litigation and applications for remedies, where applicable. Therefore, the right to justice or to remedies of the criminal defendants had not been impaired.[107]

Again, the TCC recognised the exceptional nature of authoritarian rule and maintained a clear distinction between the past and the present. The TCC was clearly aware that the infringement of personal rights was inappropriate when viewed through the lens of contemporary constitutional principles. Even so, the TCC believed that the principles of constitutional democracy could not be adopted when the nation was in an extreme state of emergency. It thus rejected any review of the authoritarian past in a backwards-looking manner.[108] In support of this major holding, other holdings offered intriguing insights into the theory of transitional justice. Echoing the concerns of Professors Ackerman and Offe, the cost of the investigations was raised as an issue.[109] Additionally, the holding concerning potential turbulence undermining legal stability illustrates the TCC's internal dilemma within the transitional rule of law. On the one hand, the bases for the rule of law, including consistency, clarity, and stability, may be undermined if the law's forms, content, and understandings cannot be maintained as they were before. This may be perplexing for individuals subject to the law who may be unaware of how they should act in the absence of a clear and consistent rule. Such a situation could trigger concerns over fairness, as it would appear to run contrary to our moral intuition that similar situations should be treated in a similar manner. On the other hand, the demands for a new norm providing a new sense of fairness and guidance are also important. Especially in the context of a democratic transition, these voices can assist in rejecting the old regime's legitimacy and promote the rise of a democratic constitutional regime that can truly take individual rights seriously, among other fundamental principles. Balancing these two sets of aspirations thus becomes difficult. Accordingly, the TCC refrained from taking a more radical approach

107 J. Y. Interpretation No. 272 (decision given on 18 January 1991) <https://cons.judicial.gov.tw/en/docdata.aspx?fid=100&id=310453> accessed 16 August 2022.

108 ibid.

109 ibid.

to addressing the potential inadequacy of current judicial safeguards against arbitrary measures.[110]

4.2.2 J. Y. Interpretation No. 477[111]

J. Y. Interpretation No. 272 closed down the option of judicial redress for historical injustice. This tendency was to some extent adjusted in J. Y. Interpretation No. 477. In the 1990s, the KMT government started to implement transitional justice policies. In 1995, the Legislative Yuan passed the "Act Governing the Recovery of Damage of Individual Rights during the Period of Martial Law Rule" (戒嚴時期人民受損權利回復條例, Recovery Act), with the aim of compensating victims who had been convicted in military procedures under authoritarian rule. The Act excluded victims who had not been convicted of offences against internal or external security, and therefore triggered the question of equal protection.[112] It was challenged, and ended up before the TCC.

Recognising the inadequacy of judicial remedies for criminal cases ruled on by military trials during the period of martial law, the TCC held that the government had a legitimate purpose in compensating these victims. In this sense, the TCC seemed to be starting to adjust its views concerning the authoritarian period. Nevertheless, the TCC adopted a deferential attitude towards the legislature's assessment of the scope of the remedy, provided that such decisions complied with constitutional requirements. The TCC again refrained from overturning political decisions and reviewed history to a quite limited extent.

4.2.3 J. Y. Interpretation No. 567[113]

Changes began to occur. In 2003, the TCC issued J. Y. Interpretation No. 567 concerning the constitutionality of Article 2, paragraph 1 of the Recovery Act. This provision was intended to provide national compensation to those falling under Article 2 of the "Disciplinary Measures for the Prevention of Repeat

---

110 Huang (n8). Tseng (n78).

111 J. Y. Interpretation No. 477 (decision given on 12 February 1999) <https://cons.judicial.gov.tw/en/docdata.aspx?fid=100&id=310658> accessed 16 August 2022.

112 J. Y. Interpretation No. 624 also adopted a similar rationale when striking down Article 1 of the Act of Compensation for Wrongful Detentions and Executions, which required compensation to be paid criminal defendants convicted according to ordinary judicial procedures, other than those subject to military trials. J. Y. Interpretation No. 624 (decision given on 27 April 2007) <https://cons.judicial.gov.tw/en/docdata.aspx?fid=100&id=310805> accessed 16 August 2022.

113 J. Y. Interpretation No. 567 (decision given on 24 October 2003) <https://cons.judicial.gov.tw/en/docdata.aspx?fid=100&id=310748> accessed 16 August 2022.

Offences by Communist Espionage Criminals during the Period of National Mobilisation for the Suppression of the Communist Rebellion". (戡亂時期預防匪諜再犯管教辦法, Communist Espionage Act). According to this provision, after finishing their sentences or re-education, criminals convicted of communist espionage or treason should be subject to an indefinite period of rehabilitation involving compulsory work and strict disciplines, if they were deemed to be at risk of re-offending. The powers to decide on this extensive restriction of personal freedom were conferred on the security organs, but not the courts.

For the first time, the TCC held that authoritarian rules should be subject to judicial review. The court was empowered to examine and determine whether the government had violated the "minimum extent of human rights protections" required in times of crisis. Since personal freedom is one of the most fundamental rights, the restriction of which should be subject to judicial approval and other constitutionally required procedural safeguards, the TCC invalidated Article 2 of the Communist Espionage Act due to its substantial interference with personal freedom. In addition, this provision allowed the government to pursue ideological reforms by ordering works for the purpose of rehabilitation in the name of preventing potential re-offending. Thus, it unconstitutionally interfered with freedom of expression as the foundational element of freedom of speech, human dignity, and the liberal democratic constitutional norm. For the above reasons, the TCC also ordered that those persons who had been subject to these indefinite programs be compensated in accordance with Article 2, paragraph 1, of the Recovery Act.

In this case, the TCC adopted a new interpretative approach in order to recognise that the exceptional nature of authoritarian rule could not be exempted from judicial examination. Indeed, during the authoritarian period, the nation was under extraordinary danger, and the protection afforded to individual rights could not have been identical to that guaranteed under normative circumstances. However, the Constitution required, as interpreted by the TCC, that the restrictions on individual freedoms should be explicitly regulated by law and that the right to justice should not be interfered with. In this sense, the TCC established a principle that the exercise of governmental power and the protection of individual rights, even in times of emergency, must nevertheless comply with constitutional requirements.[114] As such, the TCC's attitude can be regarded as a transformation from the third model to a fourth model, under which history was not only disconnected from the present but also had to be examined from the standpoint of contemporary constitutional law.

114 Huang (n8).

4.2.4 Transforming to a Fourth Model

Compared to cases concerning separation of powers, the TCC has consistently shown a stronger tendency to review authoritarian wrongdoing and its impact on the current democratic regime in cases involving human rights. By maintaining the legality of historical measures and their compatibility with current constitutional principles, the TCC has gradually shown its inclination to commit to transitional justice. This direction is both backward- and forward-looking: backwards-looking in that government regulations or actions previously covered by a set of potentially more lenient regulations are now examined based on the current understandings of constitutional principles; forward-looking insofar as its restoration of the past seeks to restore the present and to give guidance for the future.[115] Referring to J. Y. Interpretation No. 793, it is reasonable to assert that the TCC's support of historical review is even stronger.

Can we identify the reasons for the difference in interpretative models between J. Y. Interpretations No. 567 and others? This is not an easy task. Indeed, J. Y. Interpretations No. 272 and No. 477 show a deferential attitude to the decisions made by political authorities. As the nature of transitional justice is itself political, involving political tensions in a post-conflict context, fears over robust opposition by remnants of the old guard may account for the adoption of the third model—to hedge against tensions between different political actors, while at the same time, maintaining the principles of constitutional democratic order in the safest position. This political explanation may also be reflected by the supportive stance taken by the DPP in remedying the wrongs of the authoritarian government. For instance, in the old "February 28 Incident Disposition and Compensation Act" enacted in 1995, the KMT government insisted that its uses of military and police powers during the Incident of 28 February 1947 were legitimate. However, thanks to the DPP's efforts, the Act was amended in 2007 to deliver the message that violence had been used. Nevertheless, as illustrated above, the legal professionalism of the Justices must not be overlooked as well. These factors complicate the issue of discovering the reasons driving the transformation of the TCC's attitude towards history and its normativity. It requires more pieces of historical evidence to be discovered in order to conduct subsequent research.

115 Hsu (n98) 54.

5 Evaluation of Interpretative Model(s): A Post-authoritarian Perspective

5.1 *Separation of Powers*

In cases involving the separation of powers, it is apparent that, by stating that the circumstances have changed, the TCC has established a new norm by implementing constitutional principles such as deliberative democracy and the rule of law. In particular, the ideals of regular elections and representation have been incorporated into the judicial interpretation of the ROC Constitution. Although the TCC defended electoral practices during the period of authoritarian rule, opposition to the suspension of elections not only marked a break with the past but also signalled a clear preference for democracy over authoritarianism. In addition, by deploying the notions of exception, emergency, and crisis, the TCC recognised new constitutional values whilst respecting the legal authority of past practices. Indeed, the past might not match up with contemporary principles of regular elections. However, by stating that it was developed in response to the extraordinary circumstances under which dangers to national security were alleged to undermine the stability of the state, the TCC provided past justification for the lack of constitutional protection. In considering past practices to be necessary but exceptional, the TCC limited its ability to use past practices within contemporary constitutional interpretation. This cautious approach ensured that the legitimacy of its decisions would not be challenged by the KMT, which remained the largest political party even after the democratic transition. By using the third model, the TCC could establish a new set of constitutional principles without challenging the legal authority of authoritarian rule. The TCC's interpretative approach helped it to maintain a balance between new values and the old order.[116]

Nevertheless, by focusing on implementing regular elections, the TCC did not take a further step to examine whether the post-authoritarian infrastructure of political completion had been fair and robust enough. It was not until J. Y. Interpretation No. 793 that the TCC recognised and rectified this issue. Indeed, Taiwan has experienced two changes of government, in 2000 and 2008. Along with other checks and balances, Taiwan can be said to have successfully completed its political transition and joined the club of consolidated democracies. However, in a similar manner to other new democracies, relics of its authoritarian political structure remain even after its transition.[117] The

116 ibid.

117 Iong-sheng Lin, 'Legal Functions of Transitional Justice'(2016), 12 Taiwan Int'l Stud Q 177, 177. Yeh and Chang (n56)147.

authoritarian legacy, as is acknowledged by Professor Offe, is still scattered throughout the machinery of democratic governance. It was not until 2016 that the KMT lost its majority in the Legislative Yuan for the first time.[118] As legislators are considered to represent the interests of their constituents, the persistent role of the KMT in the legislative body signals its enduring influence on the management and allocation of public resources at the local level. Without casting a critical eye on the impact of authoritarian rule on the current political structure, it would appear to be difficult to drive the system towards a more competitive arrangement. It is for these reasons that the TCC changed its past indifferent attitude towards transitional justice in relation to the separation of powers, moving towards stronger support for the review of history.

Accordingly, this development suggests that the court's view of the history is extremely important in the sense that it reflects whether the court and the government accept the residual impact of an extremely large political organisation on other groups of people living in the political community.[119] In relation to this aspect, the TCC has started to show its inclination towards the fourth model of constitutional interpretation.

5.2 *Human Rights Protection*

In this context, the TCC again struggled when deciding what stance to adopt in regard to the role of history in constitutional interpretation. Considering the limitation imposed in J. Y. Interpretation No. 272, regardless of how salient the normative foundation is for critically reviewing the past in J. Y. Interpretation No. 567, it seems hard to imagine how the ideal of "minimum human rights protection" can be realised in the judicial system. Due to concerns regarding legal stability, the limitation of resources, and the so-called "sufficient judicial safeguards" confirmed in J. Y. Interpretation No. 272, the TCC and other ordinary courts have been prevented from directly examining human rights violations by the authoritarian government.[120] While Article 6 of the Promotion of Transitional Justice Act grants the power to the Committee for Promoting Transitional Justice to annul judicially unjust judgments, with the aim of addressing the restriction on appeals as instructed in J. Y. Interpretation No. 272, this legislation raised the further issue as to the basis on which the

---

118 Samuel Issacharoff, *Fragile Democracies: Contested Power in the Era of Constitutional Court* 134–136 (CUP 2015). James Loxton and Scott Mainwaring, *Life After Dictatorship: Authoritarian Successor Parties Worldwide* (CUP 2018) 88- 89.

119 Jiunn-Rong Yeh, *Democratic Transition and Constitutional Change* (Angle Publishing Co. 2003) 444–445.

120 Caldwell (n91) 462.

executive branch and the legislative branch that delegated this power could annul judicial decisions.

Nevertheless, J. Y. Interpretation No. 793 provided relatively clear constitutional guidance to the government for reviewing history within the constitutional framework. Indeed, there are no active judicial cases directly concerning the constitutionality of transitional justice measures associated with human rights protection, redress, or compensation. It is difficult to predict whether it will be possible to enforce the instructions of J. Y. Interpretations No. 793 or No. 567 sufficiently at lower levels. It must also be noted that these interpretations were adopted in a deferential manner. The TCC did not challenge the legislature's role in defining the scope of redress intended to remedy the victims of authoritarian abuses. However, one point is certain: the importance of authoritarian history in constitutional interpretation is being increasingly recognised, if one looks back at the evolution of the TCC's interpretations. This experience, which also forms part of the historical development, should be capable of shedding light on further judicial decision-making in relation to issues of transitional justice, political competition, as well as every aspect of liberal democratic rule.

6 Conclusion

This chapter has examined how the TCC's past engagement with authoritarian history in constitutional interpretation has transformed over time, becoming more capable of achieving constitutional norms of a robust political environment and human rights protection. In order to study this topic, the chapter first establishes a framework for analysing the normative implications arising out of the various uses of history in legal interpretation. Consistent continuity with the past aims to ensure predictability and fairness. An evolving continuity through changes aims to balance the pursuit of the above values as well as new social needs. Disconnection from the past outweighs the importance of establishing new norms ensuring predictability and fairness, as understood under the first model. The most radical type—redressing historical wrongs—believes that none of the above models can fulfil the commitment of justice, as the damage caused in the past is intolerably severe.

The interpretive models once adopted by the TCC focused on the future by disconnecting the present from the past, paying relatively little attention to historical wrongs or their impact on contemporary constitutional structures. The TCC held that the use of power during the authoritarian period was legitimate because of the need to maintain national security and social stability.

In addition, the Court showed a strong tendency to avoid investigating and challenging abuses of power committed during the authoritarian period. It precluded applying justifications for the measures made by the authoritarian regime to the contemporary era as Taiwan has fully transformed into a constitutional democracy. The TCC clearly distinguished between the democratic period and authoritarian rule, rejecting the legal authority of past practices during the democratic period. Admittedly, this method ensured liberal democratic norms could develop in a stable and incremental manner, without being overly challenged by the opposition. This approach also managed to strike a balance between the demand for democratic reforms and the need for the Court to shield itself from potential objections that it had abused its powers.[121] Moreover, in J. Y. Interpretation No. 261, the TCC recognised that local elections had been incrementally installed over time, a historical fact that enhanced the legitimacy of implementing elections to national legislative branches. Nonetheless, for decades the TCC only declared that the government's use of power should be in accordance with the Constitution as a general principle, regardless of whether such power was exerted during the authoritarian period. The TCC therefore did not place sufficient attention on nor deal with the legitimacy of authoritarian rule in a holistic way.

Over time, the TCC has shown an increasingly supportive attitude towards reviewing Taiwan's authoritarian history. At first, this attitude was only reflected in sporadic cases concerning compensation for the victims of military trials. In J. Y. Interpretations No. 477 and No. 567, the TCC started to come round to the idea that history should not be completely exempted from review in the spirit of constitutional democracy. The government's exercise of power, even under extraordinary circumstances, must conform with minimum constitutional requirements. Subsequently, this tendency transformed into a fourth model in J. Y. Interpretation No. 793, in which the TCC recognised the need to review history for the purpose of maintaining a liberal democratic constitutional order and preserving fundamental rights. Based on the perspective that redressing historical wrongs is a necessity for implementing constitutional norms, the TCC's current approach to disconnecting history from the contemporary world, as well as addressing Taiwan's authoritarian legacy, sets a foundational bedrock for the long-term development of its democracy, albeit belatedly.[122] The strength of this development should be subject to further observation, as

121 David Law and Hsiang-Yang Hsieh, 'Judicial Review of Constitutional Amendments: Taiwan' (2019) Washington University in St. Louis Legal Studies Research Paper No. 19-02-01, 50.

122 Lin (117) 195.

the TCC has so far rarely intervened to assert historical review where no prior political action was taken.

Since historical arrangements have always exercised some form of influence on current constitutional systems, for post-authoritarian countries, the issue of how to alleviate these impacts will remain relevant within the judicial community, governmental circles, and public discourse. Therefore, as the guardian of constitutional rule, the TCC and constitutional courts in other jurisdictions should constantly seek to identify and evaluate these impacts, in the pursuit of a more desirable form of collective governance. In this sense, the use of history in constitutional interpretation is not a matter of interpretative style, but rather a question of how to achieve ideal constitutional arrangements. A review of the road being taken can offer an answer to this question.

Bibliography

Ackerman B, *The Future of Liberal Resolution* (Yale University Press 1994).

Barak-Erez D, 'History and Memory in Constitutional Adjudication'(2017) 45 FL Rev 1.

Boraine A, 'Transitional Justice: A Holistic Interpretation' (2006) 60 J Int'l Aff 17.

Brown L, 'History for the Non-Originalist' (2003) 26 Harv J L & Pub Pol'y 69.

Caldwell E, 'Transitional Justice Legislation in Taiwan Before and During the Tsai Administration' (2018) 27 Wash Intl LJ 450.

Cardozo B, *The Nature of the Judicial Process* (Yale University Press 1921) 52–53.

Chang WC, *Constitutionalism in Asia: Cases and Materials* (Hart Publishing 2014).

Cover R, 'Nomos and Narrative'(1983) 97 Harv L Rev 4.

DiMatteo L, 'Reason and Context': A Dual Track Theory of Interpretation'(2004) 109 Penn St L Rev 397.

Dworkin R, *Law's Empire* (Hart Publishing 1986).

Elster J, *Closing the Books: Transitional Justice in Historical Perspective* (Cambridge University Press 2004).

Festa J, 'Applying a Usable Past: The Use of History in Law'(2008) 38 SHLR 479.

Garcia-Godos J, 'Reparations' in Olivera Simic (ed), *An Introduction to Transitional Justice* (Routledge 2017).

Gordon R, 'The Struggle over the Past'(1996) 44 Clev St L Rev 123.

Hayner P, *Unspeakable Truths: Confronting State Terror and Atrocity* (Routledge 2001).

Hobbs H, 'Locating the Logic of Transitional Justice in Liberal Democracies' (2016) 39 UNSWLJ 512.

Hsu TL, 'An Unconstitutional Constitution?' (憲法違憲乎？) (2000), 60 Taiwan L Rev 141.

Hsu TL, 'How does the Judicial Activism of Taiwan's Constitutional Court shape the Liberal Democratic Constitutional Order in Taiwan?' (2018) 1923 Judicial Weekly 16.

Huang CY (ed), *Constitutionalizing Transitional Justice: How Constitutions and Constitutional Courts Deal with Past Atrocity* (Routledge 2022).

Huang CY, 'The 70th Anniversary of the Taiwan Constitutional Court–The Second Life of a Constitutional Court: Taiwan Constitutional Court and its Struggling with the Past' *I-Connect Blog*, (13 December 2018), <https://rb.gy/usfm2d>.

Huang T, 'Judicial Activism in the Transitional Polity: The Council of Grand Justices in Taiwan' (2005) 19 Temp Int'l & Comp LJ 1.

Huntington S. 'Democracy's Third Wave' (1991) 2 J Democracy 12.

Irving H, 'Constitutional Interpretation, the High Court, and the Discipline of History' (2013) 41 FL Rev 95.

Issacharoff S, *Fragile Democracies: Contested Power in the Era of Constitutional Court* (Cambridge University Press 2015).

Kuo MS, 'Judicial Review as a Solution to Political Gridlocks? A Study of Taiwan's Grand Justices Council Interpretations Regarding the Jurisdictional Disputes within the Political Branch' (2001) 30 NTU LJ 251, 251 <https://ssrn.com/abstract=1428995> accessed 16 August 2022.

Lai IJ, 'The Compulsory and Distanced Historical Interpretation' (歷史解釋法的強制與疏離) (2017) 21 Taiwan Prosecutor Rev 158.

Langa P, 'Transformative Constitutionalism' (2006) 17 Stellenbosch L Rev 351.

Law D and Hsieh HY, 'Judicial Review of Constitutional Amendments: Taiwan' (2019) Washington University in St. Louis Legal Studies Research Paper No. 19-02-01.

Lin CC, 'The Judicialization of Politics in New Democracies' (JSD thesis, University of Chicago 2015).

Lin CC, 'Constitutions and Courts in Chinese Authoritarian Regimes: China and Pre-democratic Taiwan in Comparison' (2016) 14 I-CON 351.

Lin CC, 'Autocracy, Democracy, and Juristocracy: The Wax and Wane of Judicial Power in the Four Asian Tigers' (2017) 48 Georgetown J Int'l L 1063.

Lin IS, 'Legal Functions of Transitional Justice'(2016), 12 Taiwan Int'l Stud Q 177.

Lin TY, Yeh JR, Hwang JY and Chang WC, *Constitutional Law—Separation of Powers* (憲法—權力分立) (2nd supp, 2nd ed, New Sharing Publishing Co. 2009).

Loxton J and Mainwaring S, *Life After Dictatorship: Authoritarian Successor Parties Worldwide* (Cambridge University Press 2018).

Masahiro W, *The "Republic of China" and the Politics of Taiwanization: The Changing Identity of Taiwan in Postwar East Asia* (National Taiwan University Press 2014).

McAuliffe P, 'Transitional Justice's Impact on Rule of Law: Symbol or Substance?' in Cheryl Lawther(ed), *Research Handbook on Transitional Justice* (Edward Elgar Publishing 2017).

Offe C, *Varieties of Transition: The East European and East German Experience* (MIT Press 1996).

Posner E and Vermeule A, 'Transitional Justice as Ordinary Justice' (2004) 117 Harv L Rev 761.

Postema J, 'On the Moral Presence of Our Past' (1991) 36 McGill L. J. 1153.

Stewart S, 'The Art of Constitutional Interpretation' (1991) 17 JCL 91, 99.

Su YC, 'Constitutional Interpretations and Social Changes in Taiwan' (大法官解釋與台灣的社會變遷) in Su, *The Theories and Practices of Constitutionality Control* (合憲性控制的理論與實際) (Angle Publishing Co. 1994).

Teitel R, 'Transitional Jurisprudence: The Role of Law in Political Transformation' (1997) 106 Yale LJ 2009.

Teitel R, 'The Role of Law in Political Transformation' (1997) 106 Yale LJ 2009.

Teitel R, *Transitional Justice* (Oxford University Press 2000).

Teitel R, 'The Law and Politics of Contemporary Transitional Justice' (2005) 38 Cornell Int'l LJ 837.

Tseng CY, 'The Twenty-Year Constitutional Development After the Abolishment of Martial Law' (解嚴二十年來的憲政發展) (2008) 12 Taiwan Bar J 4, 4–16.

Tsesis A, 'Footholds of Constitutional Interpretation' (2013) 91 Tex L Rev 1593.

Yeh JR, 'From Transitional Court to Normal Court: A Comparative Analysis on Ruling Characteristics and Transitional Context between Interpretations No.261 and No.499' (從「轉型法院」到「常態法院」：論大法官釋字第二六一號與第四九九號解釋的解釋風格與轉型脈絡) (2002) 31 NTU LJ 59–96.

Yeh JR, 'The Role of Transitional Court: On the Interactions between Constitutional Interpretations and Constitutional Revisions'(轉型法院的自我定位：論憲法解釋對修憲機制的影響) (2003), 32 NTU LJ 29.

Yeh JR, *Democratic Transition and Constitutional Change* (Angle Publishing Co.2003).

Yeh JR and Chang WC, 'The Changing Landscape of Modern Constitutionalism: Transitional Perspective' (2009) 4 NTU L Rev 145.

Yeh JR and Chang WC, 'The Emergence of East Asian Constitutionalism: Features in Comparison', 59 Am J Comp L (2011).

Conclusion

Which History, Whose Past?

Diego Werneck Arguelhes

In 2010, the Brazilian Supreme Court (*Supremo Tribunal Federal,* or 'STF') declared that the amnesty law enacted by Congress in 1979, under the military dictatorship, was compatible with the 1988 Constitution.[1] The opinions relied on traditional tools of constitutional reasoning, including purposive interpretation and textual analysis, discussing, for example, the meaning of expressions such as 'political crimes' in international human rights and criminal law. These issues are inevitably about the past, as the editors of this volume point out in their introduction. Whether the question is one of transitional justice, federalism, or fundamental rights, constitutional judges routinely make decisions about the meaning of *past* decisions of other people and institutions. What did legislators or constitution-makers have in mind in drafting a particular clause? What did a previous court mean by its choice of words in a past ruling? What is the relationship between institutional decisions made in different points in time, by different institutions – for example, how to reconcile an older statute with a recent constitutional amendment or a human rights treaty?

In this sense, constitutional judges are looking back into the past whenever they engage in legal reasoning. But they sometimes also engage with the past in a different sense. In the amnesty law ruling, the STF judges debated the nature of the political transition and of the act of constitution-making itself. What are the legal implications of understanding the Brazilian transition and the constitutional convention of 1987–88 as the outcome of a 'negotiation' with the outgoing regime? What is the new constitution's and the amnesty law's place in those negotiations?[2] Answering those sorts of questions means engaging with the past not as a set of official decisions, but as history, memory, and narrative. It means (re)telling stories about a community's past – the roads taken, and the ones not taken, in building the existing constitutional order as something new and different from previous regimes.

In terms of constitutional interpretation, judicial engagement with the past includes (but is not limited to) debates on the merits of 'originalism' as an

1 STF ADPF 153 (Judge Rapporteur Eros Grau), decided in 29.04.2010.

2 See Ana Beatriz Robalinho's ch. in this volume.

 | DOI:10.1163/9789004523739_013

interpretive methodology. Such ideas are central to U.S. scholarship and judicial practice, and comparative law scholars have found similar debates and concerns in many other jurisdictions.[3] The debate about 'originalism' still largely encourages us to think of judicial engagement with the past in terms of using history to construct, interpret, and apply legal texts or provisions. However, this is only part of what courts do when they rely on history to decide cases.

For example, courts might engage with the past to construct and justify their role in constitutional adjudication, sometimes with little or no explicit grounding in legal provisions. When courts decide how much weight they should give to drafting history and enactment context in constitutional adjudication, they are also implicitly defining their role in a constitutional democracy. Sometimes, judges do this by means of a much broader dialogue with the past. They might argue, for example, that because our community has gone through certain experiences, judges have the responsibility to perform specific roles – protecting fundamental rights of vulnerable minorities, or making sure that elections are competitive, among other possibilities. In these contexts, judicial decision-making is explicitly fueled by narratives about past political events – something that requires more than investigating the meaning or intent behind a choice of words in a provision, to be glimpsed through its drafting history, the biographies and personal documents of the people who drafted the relevant provisions, or dictionary definitions.[4] Moreover, in engaging with history in this broader sense, courts can have an impact beyond the settlement of legal questions. The judicial voice might be added to historical debates themselves (even though it cannot settle them).

The essays collected in this volume discuss and illuminate these and other possibilities of judicial reliance on historical arguments and narratives, beyond interpreting the meaning of past decisions by public officials. From conceptual analysis and normative arguments to in-depth case studies of judicial practices, the contributing authors map, analyze, and compare how constitutional and supreme courts interrogate and reread the past in several contexts, for varied purposes, and with surprisingly different results.

The outcome of judicial engagement with history is multidirectional. Constitutional courts can engage with the past to draw *contrast*, emphasizing the scope and nature of the constitutional break with the previous order. But

3 See, e.g., Yvonne Tew, 'Originalism at Home and Abroad' (2014) 52 (3) Columbia Journal of Transnational Law 780.

4 For an expanded account on different varieties of 'originalist' arguments, including appeals to a particular *ethos* of the community, see Jack M. Balkin, 'The New Originalism and the Uses of History' (2013) 82 Fordham Law Review 64.

they can also resort to history to establish *continuity*, perhaps even across different political and constitutional regimes, of the law and the court's role in applying it.

When we use the current constitution as the point of departure for this conversation, the two possibilities – contrast and continuity – are as familiar as they are debatable. Should we emphasize what we still have in common with that past moment – the main values and concerns at stake when the constitution was enacted? This is the path taken by courts in Germany and South Africa, for example. Without adopting an originalist methodology, the two courts present themselves as 'guardians of a new order, preservers of collective memory and enforcers of common commitments'.[5] Or should we instead highlight how different things have become since the constitution was enacted, and how much the law must be adapted to current values and circumstances?[6] In the case of Japan, the Supreme Court has understood history in this 'dynamic' fashion. The constitution itself, the court claimed, encourages interpreters to look to the future and emphasize what the community is becoming or should become, not what it looked like in the past.[7]

The conversation looks different when judges are searching for answers *before* the current constitution, investigating the path (including previous constitutional regimes) the community has taken until that point. We are more used to constitutional courts finding contrast whenever they refer to what came *before* the current legal order. In this domain, continuity is in principle surprising, perhaps even suspect. Our perspective is influenced both by standard legal discourses and highly visible political experiences across the globe.

From the point of view of conventional constitutional theory, the enactment of a new constitution replaces the foundations of the previous regime, so that (a) the previous constitutional norms are made void by the enactment of a new constitution, and (b) the previous non-constitutional norms remain in place only if they can be reconciled with the substance of the constitutional principles and rules laid down in the new charter. Either way, whenever the new and the old principles and legal material are in tension, the new constitution trumps the past. Moreover, since WWII, waves of democratization have generally (though not always) implied the drafting of a new constitution, or at least the adoption of amendments to the existing document. This has been the general trend from the defeat of fascism in Western Europe to anti-colonial

5 See Justin Collings's ch. in this volume.

6 This is the general direction taken by the Supreme Court of Canada (see Jean-Christophe Bédard-Rubin's ch. in this volume).

7 See Keigo Obayashi's ch. in this volume.

struggles in Africa and Asia, from the fall of military dictatorships in Latin America to the collapse of communist regimes in Central and Eastern Europe.

In such scenarios of 'new constitutional beginnings', the political break with the past regime is matched by a constitutional one, and a new constitution 'emerges as a symbolic marker of a great transition in the life of a nation'.[8] From a legal perspective, the new constitution plays a double role in breaking with the past regime. First, it establishes a new foundation for authority and political decision-making, setting the previous one aside. Second, it enshrines new substance in the legal realm, translating the political values from the transition into legal principles and rules. The current constitution, therefore, because it was drafted to mark such drastic regime changes, is not only new, but also *different*. Indeed, because it is new, it *should* also be different. Regime transitions without at least a formal amendment to the existing constitution become almost like deviations, and, conversely, changed constitutional texts are taken as the legal manifestation of clear, drastic political ruptures. The lifespan of constitutions is seen as coextensive with the lifespan of the regimes whose fundamental principles of governance they purport to institutionalize.[9]

But how do these bright lines and clear-cut expectations fare in practice? The task of translating ideas into concrete legal outcomes ultimately lies in judicial hands. Whenever the new constitution does not unequivocally set aside some aspect of the previous regime's legal order, judges will have significant room to decide what remains from the legal past. It is up to them to compare the new constitution with previous documents and decisions and define what exactly has changed. However, as several of this volume's chapters show, judges are not necessarily harbingers of change. In the U.S., for example, the Articles of Confederation – the very document that the U.S. Constitution replaced – were employed by judges to decide cases after 1787, sometimes with results that converged with pre-1787 practices and understandings.[10] In the case of Hungary, the constitutional court has juggled conflicting ideas: the commitment to the new constitution, and the preservation of the 'achievements' of the unwritten, historical constitution.[11] When the constitutional text and the reconstructed memory of the historical constitution conflict, attempting to reconcile both

8 Bruce Ackerman, 'The Rise of World Constitutionalism' (1997) 83 (4) Virginia Law Review 771.

9 See Zachary Elkins, Tom Ginsburg and James Melton, *The Endurance of National Constitutions* (Cambridge University Press, 2009). The authors' observe that, although 'closely related', constitutional change and regime change are 'not synonymous' as 'regime change (…) is not a sufficient condition for constitutional change, nor is it a necessary one' (at 59–62).

10 See Cem Tecimer's ch. in this volume.

11 See Zoltán Szente's ch. in this volume.

may result in interpreting the new constitution with old lenses, perhaps reshaping its substance towards the court's vision of the past.

In Brazil, when the STF decided separation of powers cases after the enactment of the 1988 Constitution, it often read the new document with old lenses. That generation of judges resorted to legal ideas from the authoritarian period to interpret constitutional clauses related to the relationship between branches of government.[12]

Consider one aspect of the pre-88 constitutional order that members of the National Constitutional Assembly deliberately attempted to transform in the new constitutional text. In the preceding decades, Brazilian authoritarian regimes typically endowed presidents with vast law-making powers. Congressional and judicial oversight over these powers, when they existed, was ineffective at best. The 1969 Constitution, imposed by the military dictatorship, empowered the president to issue decree-laws (*decretos-lei*) that became immediately binding. In direct response to this problem, the 1988 Constitution created a more constrained form of presidential law-making. According to the original wording of Article 62, in cases of 'urgency and relevant public interest' the president could immediately adopt 'provisional measures' (*medidas provisórias*) with 'the force of law'. Such measures are immediately subjected to congressional scrutiny and approval, but they become legally binding as soon as enacted.[13] But, unlike the *decretos-lei*, the *medidas provisórias* have an expiration date. If, after thirty days, Congress has not decided on the merits of a provisional measure, it expires and ceases to have further effects.

However, in a series of decisions taken a couple of years after the 1988 Constitution was enacted, the STF eroded the constitution-makers' attempt to break with the old arrangements of presidential law-making. The court's

12 I have explored different manifestations and implications of this phenomenon in the STF's case law and patterns of decision-making in the 90s. See, e.g., Diego W. Arguelhes and Mariana Mota Prado, 'Resistance by Interpretation: Supreme Court Justices as Counter-reformers to Constitutional Changes in Brazil in the 90s' in Richard Albert, Carlos Bernal Pulido, and Juliano Zaiden Benvindo (eds), *Constitutional Change in Latin America* (Hart Publishing 2019); Diego W. Arguelhes, 'La moderación judicial como legado autoritario: el Supremo Tribunal Federal brasilero y las facultades legislativas presidenciales' (2020) 24 (1) Discusiones 143; Diego W. Arguelhes, 'Transformative Constitutionalism: a view from Brazil' in Philipp Dann, Michael Riegner, and Maxim Bönnemann (eds) *The Global South and Comparative Constitutional Law* (Oxford University Press 2020).

13 Executive decrees that have the same legal force as regular laws are a feature of several presidential countries (see José Antonio Cheibub, Zachary Elkins, and Tom Ginsburg, 'Latin American Presidentialism in Comparative and Historical Perspective' (2011) 89 Texas Law Review 1707). They should not be confused with measures taken by the Executive to detail, implement, and/or execute statutes that have already been enacted.

reading of the *medidas provisórias* turned them into something very similar to the *decretos-lei*.[14] First, the court restricted the scope of judicial review of the constitutional requirements of 'urgency and relevant public interest'; to do so, the majority opinion invoked caselaw from the authoritarian period. Second, the court ruled that the *medidas provisórias* could be indefinitely re-issued by the president, as long as this was done within the expiration period. However, Article 62's expiration period had been drafted as an explicit rejection of the previous system, in which Congress had the burden of directly engaging with and repealing a presidential *decreto-lei*. Article 62 reversed the effect of congressional inaction – from solidification to nullification of presidential legislation. The new constitution attempted to create a system in which both branches would inevitably have to decide together on every single *medida provisória*. The president could take initiative, but congress would share responsibility for confirming the resulting legislation. The STF's understanding, however, made this institutional dialogue optional.

In sum, instead of redeeming the promise of transformation in these new provisions, the court turned them into something much closer, in substance, to the previous constitutional order. A new constitution, then, may be the announcement of a new era, but judges might not hear the full message – or, even if they do, they can politely disagree, and adopt their own view of the scope of the break with the past.

Collings writes in his contribution to this volume that 'the self-understanding of courts is informed by memory'.[15] After the Brazilian transition to democracy, however, the STF's self-understanding was shaped not simply by national history, but by the specific memory of the institution itself: an old court, which had survived drastic regime transitions and the enactment of several constitutions since the 19th century. In the early 1990s, when the military-appointed judges still formed a court majority, many key decisions expressed a very restrictive conception of the judicial role – one that arguably helped the court safely navigate the difficult political environment of the dictatorship, but that had been deliberately set aside by the constitution-makers.[16] Reliance on institutional memory – caselaw and ideas taken from the repertoire the court developed during the dictatorship – shaped a judicial role at odds with the constitutional break with the past.

14 For further elaboration of this argument, see Arguelhes, La moderación judicial como legado autoritário, n 12.

15 See n 5.

16 Arguelhes and Prado, 'Resistance by Interpretation' (n 12).

This takes us to a further point. Why would the relevant history, as expressed in constitutional adjudication, be necessarily national? Why would judges limit themselves to their own country's past, instead of engaging with regional or global narratives? Historians often look at judicial records by connecting them and placing them in the context of broader, global movements that cut across national boundaries and narratives.[17] In a similar way, judges engaging with the past can position themselves, their constitution, and their institution in transnational narratives, just as they can focus on their institution's memory or on the community's larger picture, or on either continuity or change.

We are used to constitutional courts that, in 'new constitutional beginnings', enhance their legitimacy and power by presenting themselves as the enforcers of regime change, or as the guardians of commitments that, if followed, will prevent past injustices from happening again. In Brazil, the first generation of post-transition STF judges seemed more comfortable in emphasizing instead what they had in common with the previous order. Most of the judges in that old institution did not immediately embrace the rhetoric of the break with the past in justifying their role in the new order.

The court's rhetoric about its role in Brazilian democracy, however, looks very different today. Consider the *Ellwanger* case, decided in 2003, in which the STF upheld the conviction of a publisher of anti-Semitic books for 'practicing racism' – conduct the 1988 Constitution itself makes a serious crime and that the court majority deemed to include anti-Semitism.[18] *Ellwanger* is relevant here not so much for its outcome, but for the justifications provided for the decision. Some of the judges articulated a new and broader vision of the court's role to justify their reading of the constitution. They retraced global developments on fundamental protections since the atrocities of WWII, inserting the STF's mission within this narrative. More than a traditional institution in the Brazilian polity, the STF was presented in that case as a constitutional court whose main role is protecting fundamental rights, especially regarding vulnerable minorities.

While the court was ultimately interpreting the national constitution, these judges framed their institution's task within a global story – the narrative of how constitutional courts were created to ensure that the rights of vulnerable minorities would never again be violated by democratic majorities. This

17 See, e.g., Peter Haliday, *Habeas Corpus: from England to Empire* (Harvard University Press 2010) (observing that 'Law – its concepts, usages, and personnel – had always moved easily from Westminster, across the empire, and back again', at 313).

18 STF HC 82424 RS Judge Rapporteur Moreira Alves, decided in 17/09/2003.

narrative is embraced by several constitutional courts across the globe, even in countries where the specific issue of Nazism is not a relevant part of the country's history. It is a shared story of the origins and role of constitutional courts in a democracy, regardless of the specific commitments of national constitutions and the political events that led to them.

By the early 2000s, scholars had noticed many national high courts increasingly engaging in global dialogues.[19] In 2003, commenting on the preceding decade, Kahn observed that 'constitutional-court judges around the world often seem to believe that they are engaged in a single, transnational conversation with their counterparts'.[20] In contrast, until 2003, the STF had not explicitly spoken of itself as part of the global constellation of rights-protecting constitutional courts.

Throughout the 1990s, even as it decided cases involving rights, the STF's vocabulary would have sounded familiar to Brazilian lawyers and judges from much earlier eras. It included such ideas as limiting arbitrary uses of state power, protecting the rule of law and the supremacy of the constitution, and guaranteeing due process of law and basic civil liberties. Expressions such as 'human rights' and 'fundamental rights' (as opposed to references to the specific rights at stake, such as due process, freedom of expression, or the right to vote) were infrequently found in the court's decisions. From 2000 onwards, however, the court increasingly adopted a whole new set of global memories as its own.

In 2016, the court ruled that the constitution forbade treating adoptive and biological mothers differently. The opinions extensively discuss international human rights treaties, and the case reporter begins his opinion by tracing the origins of current children's rights to the aftermath of WWII. This is a stark contrast with a previous case, in 2000, when the court decided whether the constitution granted maternity leave to adoptive mothers.[21] Because the constitution used the term '*pregnant* [women]' [*gestante*], said that majority opinion, the right to a maternity leave had to be connected to the biological fact of pregnancy. There was no hint of the vision of the STF as the local representative of a global enterprise, connected to a broader struggle to protect vulnerable minorities in a democracy. The STF would only begin to adopt that narrative as its own in *Ellwanger*.

19 Anne-Marie Slaughter, 'A Global Community of Courts' (2003) 44 (1) Harvard International Law Journal 191.

20 Paul W. Kahn, 'Comparative constitutionalism in a new key' (2003) 101 Michigan Law Review 2677, 2679.

21 STF RE 197.807-RS (Judge Rapporteur Octávio Gallotti), decided in 30.05.2000.

Even when they present this narrative as a global memory that has been in place for decades, national judicial decisions engage with it in different points in time, in different countries. In Brazil, for a whole generation of judges after the end of the military dictatorship, the relevant history or memory was institutional (the STF's own continuity with the past) and primarily national. Constitutional judges might eventually make a global narrative their own, as they do so in Brazil today, but they do so over time – and in their own time.

The chapters in this volume focus primarily on national courts, relying on national history. Still, the fact that the horrors of Nazism are so often part of these courts' engagement with history should encourage further investigations on how national judges adopt (and adapt) global narratives. As they 'remember' the lessons of WWII, or other comparable narratives, courts might be implicitly facing the question of whether the relevant history is national, regional, or even global.

References

Ackerman B. 'The Rise of World Constitutionalism' (1997) 83 (4) Virginia Law Review 771.

Arguelhes DW. 'La moderación judicial como legado autoritario: el Supremo Tribunal Federal brasilero y las facultades legislativas presidenciales' (2020) 24 (1) Discusiones 143.

Arguelhes DW. 'Transformative Constitutionalism: a view from Brazil' in Philipp Dann, Michael Riegner, and Maxim Bönnemann (eds) *The Global South and Comparative Constitutional Law* (Oxford University Press 2020).

Arguelhes DW and Prado MM, 'Resistance by Interpretation: Supreme Court Justices as Counter- reformers to Constitutional Changes in Brazil in the 90s' in Richard Albert, Carlos Bernal Pulido, and Juliano Zaiden Benvindo (eds), *Constitutional Change in Latin America* (Hart Publishing 2019).

Balkin JM. 'The New Originalism and the Uses of History' (2013) 82 Fordham Law Review 64.

Cheibub JA, Elkins Z, and Ginsburg T. 'Latin American Presidentialism in Comparative and Historical Perspective' (2011) 89 Texas Law Review 1707.

Elkins Z, Ginsburg T and Melton J. *The Endurance of National Constitutions* (Cambridge University Press, 2009).

Haliday P. *Habeas Corpus: from England to Empire* (Harvard University Press 2010).

Kahn PW. 'Comparative constitutionalism in a new key' (2003) 101 Michigan Law Review 2677.

Slaughter AM. 'A Global Community of Courts' (2003) 44 (1) Harvard International Law Journal 191.

Tew Y. 'Originalism at Home and Abroad' (2014) 52 (3) Columbia Journal of Transnational Law 780.

Index

www.ingramcontent.com/pod-product-compliance
Lightning Source LLC
LaVergne TN
LVHW010639300926
849161LV00005B/987
9789004437050